What they are saying about **Last Guy Waltzing**

"I admire all that you've done to promote art and artists. They are noble efforts and you should be proud of your accomplishments."
— Frederica von Stade, International Opera Star.

" A lifetime's uncompromising devotion to the arts, threaded with personal insecurity, excess, rehab. And finally, acceptance of a kindly divaship. Courageous and inspiring."
— Valmai Howe Elins, Author of *The Dreams of Zoo Animals; The Loneliness of Angels;* and *The Rights of the Pregnant Parent.*

"Eric Gustafson's remarkable journey from the streets of the Bronx to the elegant haunts of the glittering and famous, an odyssey of self-image molded by the movies, theater, ballet and opera, is also a cautionary tale of giddy, alcohol-fueled excess, dawning self-awareness and redemption. His tale is both deliciously gossipy and spiritually enlightening. And what more could you ask?
— Jonathan Richards, Actor, cartoonist, movie critic, and co-author of *Nick and Jake.*

"If life is an opera, then Eric Gustafson hits all the high notes. He designs the sets and costumes, too, and assembles an all-star cast from across the panorama of modern life. He's offering readers one of the best seats in the house. A fascinating memoir by a fascinating man."
— Michael Redmond, Music Critic.

LAST GUY
WALTZING

A Tale of Reinvention

LAST GUY WALTZING

A Tale of Reinvention

R. Eric Gustafson

with Vincent Virga

Opposite: R. Eric Gustafson in the Octagonal Library, Lu Shan, New Jersey.

I have tried to be accurate in telling my story,
but names have been changed on a few occasions
to protect the closets of some participants.

Published by W A M Press
1000 Cordova Place, #230
Santa Fe, New Mexico 87505

ISBN 978-1-889921-53-2

Library of Congress : 2013953758

Cover design by Jim Mafchir, Western Edge Press
Book format by Carol O'Shea and Julian Hands

Printed by Image Ratio,
Santa Fe, NM, USA

All photographs from author's collection unless indicated otherwise below image.

Printed in the USA

Dedication

*For all the divas of both sexes and all occupations
who have illuminated my path
with magic and loving care.*

Acknowledgments

Sincerest gratitude to Vincent Virga, who stimulated me into examining the events along my twisting path. His persistent inquiries into the "why" and "wherefore" of my journey prodded me into a fuller, more accurate assessment of the meaning and value of my existence. It was sometimes painful, but necessary!

I feel deep gratitude to the memory of Dorothy Eweson and to her daughter Christine Allen for her ongoing encouragement and support. My eternal thanks are extended to the many personalities such as Lila Tyng and Ysabel Aya among others who helped catalyze events in my peregrinations and continual reinvention.

The efforts in the production of this tome include the generous participation of Porter Dunaway, Michael Redmond, Gisela Minke, Valmai Howe Elkins, Carol O'Shea and Julian Hands in editing, formatting and the helpful services in the birthing of this project. Bless all of you!

REG

Table of Contents

Preface...viii

Introduction...ix

1935..xi

1 Early Practice at Divadom 1

2 The Lord Won't Mind... 19

3 There's a Place for Us 43

4 Eluding La Dolce Vita 63

5 The Birth of the David Dynasty 79

6 Is the Sucker Paying for the Call? 99

7 The Seven-Year Itch Came Early... 115

8 Bon Voyage on Your Road to Oblivion... 121

9 Catching a Tiger by the Tail.. 131

10 1 + 1 Make More than 2 147

11 Following the Italian Army is Hell 167

12 They All Said My Idea Was Crazy... 179

13 You Don't Need a Taxi, You Need an Ambulance 203

14 Younger than Springtime—in ¾ Time.. 221

15 Have at It Sweetie, Nature Abhors a Vacuum! 241

16 Get Your Ass Over to Betty Ford 259

17 De-Lucing, Decimation through Death... 273

18 A Sage Who Somehow Strayed 293

Epilogue: Ushnisha with Tiara; the Making of a Diva.................................... 323

Appendix 1: La Marchesa, La Marchetta Chronicles..................................... 327

Appendix 2: Happiness is a House on a Hill in Kovalam.............................. 333

A Postscript 337

Index 338

Preface

I avoid most memoirs these days and am indulgent with people who tell me they really should be writing theirs or I should be writing a book about them. I'm a seasoned reader and the battered genre called memoir has been polluted by traumatized children with nothing but their desultory celebrity and their psychic wounds to write badly about for TV talk shows and sympathetic reviewers. So when the real deal occasionally enters my life, a friend with an extraordinary life to share and the skill to do the job with real panache, I sit up and pay attention, usually as a cheerleader and sounding board, knowing most people cannot sustain the discipline, i.e., the grind of writing a book and re-writing a book and then re-writing a book again to get it right.

I'm reminded of a friend at a New York Public Library's literary luncheon, seated between the wife of an award winner and the wife of a benefactor. "My husband can do what your husband does," said the rich latter.

"I'm sure he can," said the wife of the honored writer. "The only difference is my husband does it."

Well, readers, *Last Guy Waltzing* is done to a turn, and I am very pleased to have something to do with it, as a hand in the mix. (I asked lots of questions and offered a few phrasing options.)

To my mind, Eric has always been a stylist of both life and art. From his earliest days, he was a boy with a mission, a boy who wished upon a star only to discover the star was himself, if he played his cards right! And with the fierce determination of a dreamer in Technicolor, he taught himself how to become a master of the game, no matter what hand he was dealt, by utilizing his strengths — his intelligence, beauty, curiosity, and ambition — and when there was some card missing in his hand, he assiduously worked his butt off to acquire it. He was a work in progress not perfection, as they say, though he often achieved perfection in his life and in his work. If anyone could write a damn good book, he is the one and that's done.

Vincent Virga
2013

Introduction

Last Guy Waltzing recounts the recollections of a mature man in Santa, Fe New Mexico, as he reflects on his amazing journey from a babe born in the northeast corner of the Bronx, through a web of hyperactive international entanglements, to finally achieve, decades later, the peaceful introspection of a calm inner life, the best path to travel.

Re-invention with verve began for me by re-enacting glamorous roles in exotic locales provided by Technicolor films at the local Bronx movie houses. Further personal development was spurred on by the "feel good" films during World War II, which opened for me the grand world of beautifully garbed and jeweled society, so foreign to my neighborhood on East 222nd Street. The manner of speech was so refined and contrasted with the "dems" and "doze" I heard around me. My determination to change my Bronx accent for one akin to Mayfair began before I was twelve years old.

Divas on stage began to re-shape my life, with my active participation as an avid audience member at the Metropolitan Opera, then later the New York City Ballet at City Center, and finally the theater world on and off Broadway during my high school years. By college and post-graduate school, I began to have direct contact with many divas in the performing arts. My identity focused on the world of the theater. The grip my early Lutheranism had on me loosened, replaced by my serially embracing sexual partners. It was the Sexual Revolution, and I was a flamboyant participant in my defiant new skin, belying deep insecurities and anxieties.

When my dreams of a personal theater career were shelved, I resolved that I would always cherish in my life the healing power of the arts to nourish my soul. With my access to the very rich and illustrious personalities on the scene through my avid networking, I began to perceive my life as a work of art. It seemed I had been everywhere with everyone, drinking at the fountain of the muses and participating in life's banquet. This was a remarkable transformation, but rife with perils.

I strove to be a Renaissance man — cultivated, urbane, and an active contributor to the arts — through my curating of exhibitions, lecturing, and writing. Inwardly crippled with fear, covered by increasing alcohol consumption, my life spun out of control into a topsy-turvy world. Redemption through a growing spirituality and reliance on sober living was to be achieved thanks to the efforts of one of my divas, Elizabeth Taylor. "Get you ass over to Betty Ford," was her admonition to a mutual artist friend, R.C. Gorman, but I heeded it.

Diva traditionally means goddess or divine one. It is often a term used to refer to an opera star. My use is for both female and male subjects, often from the opera world but inclusive of all the performing arts, society, political figures, and good friends who have informed me along my path in life. They have provided curious vignettes worthy of creating mirth, joy, surprise, and even sadness.

Expecting the unexpected, counting on the *deus ex machina* in the form of a miracle, my optimism, enormous energy and creative imagination for reinvention have nurtured a remarkable life, worth sharing, in gratitude, with the world around me.

REG

1935

In 1935, Shirley Temple, the darling child star, was the highest paid-film personality in Hollywood. It was the year that Amelia Earhart became the first to fly solo from Hawaii to California, but humorist Will Rogers and aviator Wily Post were killed when their plane crashed in Alaska; and Howard Hughes set an air speed record of 357 miles per hour.

In 1935, during the depth of the Depression, America suffered an unemployment rate of 20.1%; the Social Security Act was put into effect; Alcoholics Anonymous was founded, and the board game Monopoly was released by Parker Brothers. It was the beginning of the Bruno Richard Hauptmann trial for kidnapping Charles Lindbergh, Jr.; the opening of *Porgy & Bess*; the birth of Swing by Benny Goodman; and the year Babe Ruth hit his final home run of his career, number 714.

In 1935, Adolf Hitler announced rearmament in violation of the Versailles Treaty, and enacted the Nuremburg laws to strip Jews of their civil rights. Benito Mussolini attacked Ethiopia.

In 1935, there were several births of personages who were to enhance the world through their talents: Luciano Pavarotti, Julie Andrews, Floyd Patterson, Elvis Presley, and Woody Allen among them.

In 1935, at 8:15 a.m. on October 7th, Robert Eric Gustafson was born in Westchester Square Hospital in the Bronx. It was an event unmarked by the world outside of his immediate family, but it lead to a most unusual life that was shaped and spent amidst this atmosphere particular to the times.

Chapter 1

EARLY PRACTICE AT DIVADOM

"Have you ever had a normal day?" my newest friend queried after I shared some of my experiences, which were only the tip of the iceberg of my life's adventures. Every morning when I awake, I embrace life, which I find a normal response—and then something happens . . .

Robert Eric Gustafson

The baby boy my mother brought from Westchester Square Hospital to the family home in the northeast corner of the Bronx that October day in 1935 was destined to pass through several life phases, many subtly orchestrated by her. She did not really desire another child after the birth of my sister, Florence Mae, six years earlier, when my brother, George Edward, was two years old. She would have much preferred a doll she could dress up as America's darling, Shirley Temple, who was all the rage in the movies. Yes, Robert Eric ("Bobby") had baloney curls and adorable outfits for a very long time!

Lying in her bed, I remember my mother playing with me and holding me next to her pendulous breasts. My father was often away supervising the building of schools or hospitals, leaving us alone for long periods of time. She took comfort in her cooking, baking, gardening, and knitting (all of which she taught me at an early age), while indulging me in cookies and sweets. Disillusioned with her married life and never feeling quite at home in the United States, she clung to old Swedish habits, just as her mother did, distrusting modernity and the American way of life.

Opposite page:
Top left to right: Dad in the Royal Swedish Cavalry, Young Ebba (mother).
Center: Mother's Doll at 11 months.
Bottom left: Young marrieds with dog, Buck, in canoe.

Although she loved Shirley Temple, Mother's Lutheran upbringing encouraged her to sniff with disapproval at the goings-on of film star "hussies." Mae West seemed to especially rile her up, which, or course, encouraged me to pay closer attention to this amazing film personality. Many years later, it occurred to me that my mother must have had some secret yearnings to experience the forbidden pleasures these film stars portrayed. Although she may not have been aware of this closet "diva-ness," she did discreetly encourage me in fulfilling my own pursuits, perhaps as a convoluted means of achieving her thwarted desires — maybe Freud was correct in this matter?

Often, I was taken to the movies, where I fell in love with the exotic, full-color adventure films taking place in thrilling locales somewhere in the Arabian Desert, long ago. They provided perfect material for me to dramatically perform in our garden, over and over again. My scenario was very simple: The Princess, in captivity, would writhe and strike poses of distress when the menacing Sheik approached. Though not even ten years old, I mustered the drama to act out those scenes I had so relished on the screen, with the likes of Yvonne De Carlo fending off the lascivious attentions of the evil villain.

Fetchingly draped in a sheet or a curtain, I stretched out on the canvas camp cot on the back lawn of our home. Though I could imagine myself in some gorgeous diaphanous gown, I did not quite believe my blond, blue-eyed younger sister Helen to be capable of being the malevolent rogue. However, I settled for the poor casting because I enjoyed playing those re-enactments, whether emulating Yvonne De Carlo, the flaming red-haired Maureen O'Hara or tempestuous Hedy Lamarr. This make-believe playing gave me a sense of having achieved grown-up glamor. I knew that, some day, I would be rescued by Turhan Bey or on other occasions Errol Flynn. There was no doubt in this boy's mind.

These exotic, romantic films appeared in Technicolor in either of our two neighborhood movie houses during World War II. Both were adjacent to the Hillside Housing, a few minutes walk from our house at 1211 East 222nd Street. When I was old enough to pose as a twelve-year old, I escorted my younger sister in for matinees several times a week. The feature films were accompanied by newsreels that portrayed the intense and brutal fighting against the Nazis and the Japanese. The audience booed and hissed vehemently.

Sometimes, we saw a "feel good" film that relieved the horrors and deep sorrows created by the war. These black-and-white films took place in beautiful country estates in England or on Long Island. Waiters, dressed in white ties and tails, elegantly carried in their white-gloved hands large silver trays covered with flutes of champagne; the society ladies were adorned in grand gowns and fabulous jewels. My imagination was expansive enough for me to be able to portray a young, beautiful heiress in my growing repertoire of roles.

I also noticed how wonderful everyone sounded. Their speech was so different from what I heard in the Bronx. These people had speech patterns that

I immediately wanted to imitate—what a difference from the nasal "dems" and "doze" and "yeahs" I heard around me in the neighborhood!

Of course, our house compared very unfavorably to the fancy manor houses in the film. We had a simple two-story home that we entered either from the front stoop by a short stairway (with bannisters painted red with white wooden supports) or from the back, either through a laundry room or above that, through a porch. A garage in front went under part of the first floor to the basement, but we did not usually go that way, since Helen and I were too little to manage that roll-up door. On one side and in the back were small gardens and tall trees. We used an empty lot on the right to walk to neighbors' single-family homes on the quiet street behind us. Certainly, no liveried men in service bore flutes of champagne on silver trays, and neither my mother nor her friends had any long dresses or glittering jewelry. And, of course, no one spoke as though they were bred in Hampshire or Mayfair…

However, never should one underestimate the power of young children to incorporate into their own lives aspects of a society far different from their own. As a result of the films I saw, I began to study European aristocracy. I found library books that listed the ranks of royalty and the comparison of these ranks between countries—I studied the relationship of a duke to a king and a count to a marquis—and how to address each one correctly. It was information that little Bobby was going to use in the not too distant future.

Meanwhile, when not dressing in drag or addressing a fantasy royal personage, I happily learned from my mother how to plant flowers in the garden beds around the tall maple and oak trees. We planted bulbs, such as iris and peonies, and seeds, such as zinnias and asters. My mother encouraged me to help her in the kitchen, too. Although this may have only been a device to keep me busy and within her sight, I learned skills that I later would use to great advantage. At a very early age, I had learned to wash, press and manage my own clothes. This grooming for self-sufficiency became an ongoing valuable tool in my life and helped give me a sense of individual style and taste.

My father hired a carpenter to build a playhouse, which often served as a theatrical venue for my sister Helen and me to act out whatever script we dreamed up. It sat under the tall trees in the back garden, and had doors and windows that opened. Helen and I would take tea there and gossip in imitation of my mother and her cronies. With much pleasure, we used empty miniature cups, saucers, and a teapot. The way we kept the floors swept and the windowpanes clean would have matched Joan Crawford's housekeeping in her portrayal of Harriet Craig. Ah, yet another role in my expanding repertoire.

My older sister Flo, later nicknamed "Red" by her soon-to-be husband, played both an active and passive role in my development. When she was not busily working at U.S. Plywood Corporation in Manhattan, she might take Helen and me to one of the two neighborhood movie houses. Flo liked to dance, and she

Playhouse for Helen and me.

encouraged me to develop my terpsichorean skills by instructing me in the fox trot and waltz. This was the beginning of my budding delight in dancing, which later grew to become a major absorption in my life.

From my young eyes, Flo was a lively young woman, with lovely red curly hair, who was courageous in standing up to my mother, who objected to her wearing lipstick and her accepting an invitation to go on a date to the Stork Club, a famous nightclub in the "sinful" city. While she was busy at work, surreptitiously, I would borrow some of her clothes and high-heeled shoes to act out with Helen in the garden some heroine from a recently viewed movie.

Sometimes, we went to the movies with my parents' friend, Olga Peterson. Her husband would drop her off for the day when he drove in from Lake Carmel. Best of all, each Christmas, Olga would take Helen and me to the glamorous Radio City Music Hall to see a film and the famous stage show. What a treat it was to see spectacular live performances as well as a big screen film in that palatial venue! I remember the magnificence of both the lobby and the enormous movie theater itself, as well as the crowds and the adventure of being in the midst of the bustle of New York City at holiday time.

In contrast to that opulence, we made occasional forays with our mother to the East 86th Street area. After her chiropractic treatment on Lexington Avenue, she would take us to a movie on 86th Street. In addition to the movie, we saw a live stage show with diverse entertainment — singers, dancers, jugglers, magicians, and comedians. The vaudeville program always included a strip tease act, which greatly distressed my mother. Clearly, we were to disregard it as disgraceful, or ignore it as is expected of a Lutheran. Usually, before driving back to the safety of our Bronx home, we proceeded to nearby Germantown, where our mother purchased sausages and other specialties.

One of my favorite childhood pastimes was having picnics, often behind our playhouse. Sometimes, with sandwiches made from soft, white Wonder bread smeared with jam, the two of us would prop ourselves up against an apple tree to observe the old Italian — who was probably in his forties — plow the adjacent field with his mule.

On one occasion, I decided to create a zoo to generate some small income. I affixed a metal shelf from the kitchen oven (to serve as a cage bars) to the open end of a large carton in which I placed our pet cat, Tabby. Another large box displayed our sweet tempered dog, Buck. Viewers of these "ferocious beasts" were expected to drop some coins into the wooden box I had painted a bright Chinese red and placed at the entrance to the garden area. It was not a success, partially because of the lack of traffic, but it began my entrepreneurial career.

The biggest attraction in our bucolic neighborhood was a perusal from the outside of the building just down the street where the infamous Bruno Hauptmann had lived before he was arrested and tried for the murder of Charles Lindberg's kidnapped baby. Other than that, the neighborhood was very low key, with entertainment only from the movie houses and the radio that kept us informed on latest developments in the soaps featuring Helen Trent, Stella Dallas and My Gal Sunday, or episodes of Fibber Magee and Molly or George Burns and Gracie Allen.

Sister Flo's confirmation:
George, Mom, Dad (rear)
and Bob, Helen, and Flo (front).

My second grade teacher, Jean Herman, casually asked our class one day if anyone knew of someone to help her at home as a housekeeper. As my mother seemed to thrive on doing things around the house, I volunteered her. This seemed a good way to earn brownie points with the teacher, but it was to have long-range repercussions.

My mother had developed a rivalry with my father. She learned to use tools to fix things as he did, and decided to expand her independence by earning her own money. My mother began working longer hours at the Hermans' house. They were thrilled to return from work not only to a clean house, but also to freshly baked goods or a prepared meal on the stove. Dr. and Mrs. Herman had two children who took kindly to the "Mrs. Santa Claus," who doted on them before returning to her own brood.

With our mother not at home, Helen and I were often left to our own devices after school. We depleted cookie jars and candy supplies that fueled our flights of fancy in the garden or playhouse or movies. There was much time to expand our make-believe worlds, and, in my case, develop my repertoire of roles. Radio soaps provided good material to try out my acting abilities by playing Helen Trent or Stella Dallas.

During the summer of 1942, my father transported the family to Elmira, New York, where he was working on supervising the building of a school. We were to enjoy the warm months there before returning to the Bronx to attend school at PS 78 in the fall. One fine day, we were invited for a visit to a nearby farm. Here we played with a few local children, romping about the barn, jumping from haylofts, and playing tag. At one point, I was "it" and had to chase everyone else. A tool chest had been placed to block a door so that I would have difficulty opening the door to tag my playmates. I pushed hard and fell over the tool chest. Between the jumping from haylofts and falling in the barn, I began to feel ill with stomach cramps.

Not to worry! My mother felt competent to handle the situation, as she did in most other matters. Thinking I had a flu coming on, she dispensed several doses daily of blackberry brandy. (This was an excellent introduction of alcohol into the young life of an alcoholic-in-the-making!) However, after a couple of days, my condition did not improve. It was only when I turned green and began urinating blood that my mother decided that her expertise perhaps needed to be augmented with the consultation of a doctor.

I remember the attractive young doctor arriving to examine me. In my young life, this was the first handsome man who came to my rescue. He quickly called the hospital, alerting them to prepare for an emergency operation. He wrapped me in a blanket as I swooned into his arms, while he informed my mother that she almost killed me. I could have been dead days earlier from the erupted appendix that had wrapped around my intestines! The doctor continued to angrily chastise my mother as we made our way to his small green coupe. As he placed me inside, I was surprised that anyone could speak to my mother in such angry tones. She followed us to the hospital in her car.

A tube, intended to go down my throat, was inserted into my nose. I vehemently fought this intrusive action using many expletives. Embarrassed, my mother protested she had no idea where I could have learned such language! Had she forgotten her arguments with my father, from which I culled a growing vocabulary?

The hospital recovery stage was a long one, but I was showered with gifts from my father's employees. I was taken to our Elmira home to rest for the balance of the summer, which I spent knitting in the garden in my wheelchair. On one memorable occasion, a dog wandered by. After a sniff, he raised a leg and peed on me! "Moth–er-r-r!" I cried out, detesting this gratuitous golden shower.

After returning to East 222nd Street, life resumed almost as before, except that I grew increasingly apart from the other children. Some classmates thought I was a sissy. My sister, although two years younger, would jump in to defend me. She was a bit of a tomboy, and would walk me back from school as my protector from the ruffians' sassy taunts. Helen was possibly emboldened by my having cast her as a male villain or hero savior in our earlier make-believes.

Before leaving for school one morning, I heard over the radio that President Roosevelt had died. I eagerly raised my hand at the beginning of class to share this valuable information with Mrs. Conti and the 3rd grade class. I was convinced I would be praised for bringing such important information. Instead, she was very abrupt with me, probably upset from having heard the dismal news herself earlier. I felt hurt when I was promptly silenced as though I had done something wrong. This was one of many lessons for me to learn: grownups can behave strangely, even a teacher.

With the approach of my last two years at elementary school, my parents decided to sell our house and move to Jarvis Avenue, located in the Pelham Bay Park area of the Bronx. Before moving, I had won a school competition by making the best maquette of a symphony orchestra with cutouts. It was painstaking but attractive when completed. I won a book about famous composers of classical music, which introduced me to the realm of classical music performed by large orchestras. It also provided an awareness of possible outlets for my creativity.

I had not paid much attention to music, but it gained a stronger emphasis in my life in my new school, PS 71. After I took up playing the fife and learned to read music, I joined the marching band at school and soon became a sergeant. I would have loved to be the leader of the band, swinging the large baton around and wearing the attractive cape and tall hat that came with that honored position. Alas, I could not muster the courage to display such confidence and leadership, so I quietly led the fife division of the band until graduation. Feeling a great insecurity about my identity as a growing boy, I was very shy with my peers.

Sex was a deep mystery to me that created growing confusion and concern. One night on Jarvis Avenue, my father came into the kitchen to get something from the refrigerator. He had on only a tee shirt and pair of boxer shorts. Standing next to him, I noticed his penis through the open fly when he bent into the refrigerator, and was intrigued. I had never seen a man's penis before. After he left, I took a banana and peeled it, making a replica of his penis and carving the head with my teeth. I proceeded to savor it in my mouth and throat. Then, I ate it with satisfaction. This was a significant incident that was etched deeply into my memory.

It stimulated me to try to discover what my brother's private parts looked like. When he showered in his bathroom on the ground floor, I would furtively wander by the window in the narrow walk space outside. I was never successful in seeing him, but I tried many times. Each time, I was afraid of being caught spying and was too hurried to catch any meaningful glance.

Television became an entertainment fixture in my budding life at this point. Across the street lived a plain-looking girl whose family had a coveted television set. Being a friendly neighbor, Paula would invite me in to see various programs like the *Sid Caesar Show*, with that inimitable Imogene Coca, and the *Hit Parade*. I also saw programs that introduced serious music with a light touch. The NBC Symphony with Arturo Toscanini and concerts from Lewisohn Stadium (affiliated with City College) gave me a taste of the wonder of classical music. It was a marvelous escape from the humdrum life on Jarvis Avenue. Sometimes, when bidding "goodnight" to Paula, we would exchange a tentative kiss on the lips — a first for me. This created more consternation within me than pleasure.

World War II had been over for a couple of years. My brother had returned from his stint in the Navy and was enrolled in New York University as an engineering student. My father willingly paid his tuition with the knowledge that George would continue his career in the building business. George had worked for my father first as a water boy and then doing minor jobs to earn pocket money during his high school summers. Engineering was a logical step further into his future, approved of by my father.

My older sister Flo had managed to free herself from my mother's Lutheran-tainted restraints by getting married. She and her Irish Catholic husband, Jack, took an apartment in Parkchester, down the IRT line a few stops from where we lived. Flo and I always had a warm rapport. She seemed sympathetic and supportive of my attempts at self-awareness. With money saved from my small weekly allowance, I could buy inexpensive seats to events. When I discovered classical concerts, she once came with me to Carnegie Hall for a program of Russian Romantic music. Like my mother, Flo quietly encouraged my exploration into life. Also, like my mother, she lived vicariously through my adventures, which were a distraction from her own disappointments. Both women struggled with alcoholic husbands who often left them lonely and in uncomfortable situations.

As time went on, war between my mother and father escalated into open physical abuse. Arguments—often precipitated by my mother's purposeful provocations—erupted into fisticuffs or pulling of knives. Wielding a knife always aroused immediate revulsion and fear within me, perhaps as a result of seeing horrible scenes of violence in the movies. Both Helen and I were frightened, and we resorted to hiding from the tumult. Sometimes, in tears, I fled through my bedroom window to escape the sounds from their fighting. I felt emotionally distraught and helpless. As a result, I developed a protective shield from situations threatening to my emotional wellbeing by shutting down or removing myself, while maintaining a cool exterior. This defense mechanism, formulated during this period of family strife, was to be perfected and effectively implemented when needed during later episodes in my life.

My father was an easygoing guy who worked hard but liked having a good time as a reward. Although he found alcohol to be a great release, it led him deeper into danger zones. When my mother seriously took on weight and shied away from his physical desires, he went elsewhere for ribald drinking, dancing, and carnal pleasures. Retribution was to follow from "the Field Marshall," as I later referred to my mother. Scorn from the wronged wife was humiliating to my father. He drank more and more, further rupturing their relationship.

Some of my father's energy was directed to building a brick three-story house at 3433 Bruckner Boulevard, across from Pelham Bay Park. It was only a few blocks from our house on Jarvis Avenue and would become not only a residence for the family, but also a source of added income from the rental apartment on the top

Opera star Risë Stevens and I bonded over Carmen.
(Photo: Alice Schumer Giovinco Collection)

floor. My brother and I had the ground floor apartment; my parents and Helen lived on the first floor; and the tenants, the Steinbergs, lived on the top floor.

The Steinbergs' daughter Emily and I became pals. She helped me write letters to Risë Stevens, an opera star I had heard on television's *Bell Telephone Hour*. Her voice was familiar to me from the Saturday afternoon radio broadcasts of "Live from the Met." Milton Cross gave wonderful program notes and introduced me to opera very effectively. Risë Stevens's *Carmen* was unforgettable. How much I imagined myself to be that wild gypsy woman who was in love but dramatically invited death rather than give up her freedom.

Risë and I bonded over *Carmen*. We were soul mates, sharing the same role! So, I began writing her fan letters, and Emily joined me in forming the Risë Stevens Fan Club of the Bronx. We requested free tickets to be in the audience for any radio or TV show that she was going to be on. After the airing, I went backstage and got her autograph on phonograph albums or on the programs. I never revealed myself as the writer of all that fan mail, and the recipient of her notes of thanks from either her secretary or herself. Risë Stevens was the first opera diva of note in my life that I saw face to face, not just on the silver screen or television.

What impressed me about this opera star was her warm, dignified demeanor. It was in contrast to her sexy, lusty, willful Carmen. The notion that the performer could have an identity quite different from the role she portrayed was an eye opener for this naïve nearly twelve-year-old. I was in love with Risë Stevens and the world of opera, which was constantly opening wider and more meaningful horizons for me.

When I was about to graduate from elementary school, I had my confirmation in the Lutheran Church. In my confirmation class was an attractive young woman named Nancy. She impressed me with her adult, sophisticated manner. Nancy and I would go on adventures together. She suggested we go to the opera at the Brooklyn Academy of Music to hear *Aïda*. Her mother let her use her fur coat, and off we went on the subway to Brooklyn. I put on my Sunday church-going suit, the best choice from my skimpy wardrobe.

How captivating it was for me to experience live opera! In the movies, Diana Durbin and Jane Powell would perform an occasional operatic selection. Also, I had seen excerpts from concerts on Paula's TV, but nothing compared to the live costumed cast in an exotic setting. The music was so beautiful. I could easily relate to that very dear Aïda dying in the arms of handsome Radames in the tomb! Yes, another role for me to adopt!

Shortly thereafter, Nancy and I experienced *Faust* at the Metropolitan Opera House. We managed to secure inexpensive seats in the balcony. I remembered that my great-great aunt Christine Nilsson had opened this opera house in 1883, singing the leading role of Marguerite in *Faust*. I also recalled my mother's disapproving remarks about how her distant aunt, whose destiny was to become a famous opera singer, fooled around in the haystacks in her youth. (I was later to discover she was the prototype for Christine in *Phantom at the Opera*.)

Gaining momentum in our opera going, we then saw *Carmen* at the New York City Opera. Heady with excitement, I was glued to every Saturday afternoon broadcast from the Met and would soon join the standees at that old opera house on West 39th Street in New York City, becoming the youngest standee and a mascot for some of the regulars.

Life for me on Bruckner Boulevard was about to take a dramatic change. My parents had decided to purchase, at a very low price, a large Victorian house in the Hudson Valley. It had belonged to an old friend's family. This curious, rundown

Great, great aunt, opera singer Christine Nilsson. (Photo: National Swedish Art Museums)

house on a hilltop had been added on to a pre-Revolutionary structure, with an entrance to an emery mine, long since defunct. Montrose, the name of the town, was evidently named after this once prepossessing edifice on a hill of roses.

My father was going to retire, and he brought my younger sister Helen, my mother, and our pets there to live. Helen would transfer to a local school in Montrose, but I was to stay within the New York City limits to qualify for attendance to the all-boys honor school, Stuyvesant High School, in lower Manhattan. I had passed the entrance examinations and was accepted. My brother George had gone there in preparation for university; I was to follow suit.

Having been instructed by my mother in the ways of self-sufficiency—food preparation, clothes management, and a strong Lutheran sense of good behavior—I was to live in the ground floor apartment under the supervision of my older brother. What my parents did not realize was that George had priorities of his own. He had a lively fraternity house in which to carouse, and he spent lots of time with his girlfriend at her place before they eventually married. In school when not at play, he was away from home most days, leaving me to ponder the many questions of pubescent life. I traveled to school and back by the elevated IRT to 14th Street in Manhattan. A few other boys took the same trip in the neighborhood, but they returned each day to a waiting family. I had only my books and classical music records for company. With poignant Chopin and heartbreaking strains of Tchaikovsky echoing in my head, I took long, soulful walks in the enormous Pelham Bay Park. A deep-rooted sense of loneliness settled into my innermost being.

Great comfort came from standing at the opera and assimilating the various grand moments imprinted on my imagination. I particularly enjoyed observing the beautifully dressed people sitting in the boxes comprising the Golden Horseshoe above. I imagined how someday I would be sitting with them in that exalted, glamorous location and mingling with these entrancing people in Sherry's during intermission, sipping champagne in elegant evening clothes. On occasion, someone close to me in standing room would begin to lean upon me or attempt a probing of my body. It frightened me and made me recoil into my Lutheran virginity, but not without confusion and some forbidden curiosity.

In spite of how bold I was in my mental play acting of operatic roles, I was increasingly shy and defensive in dealing with my peers at school and in the world I was passing through. My parents instilled in me the importance of the work ethic and encouraged me to take on a part-time job while attending Stuyvesant. A schoolmate of mine was the son of the manager of the Paramount Theater on Times Square, and my sister Florence now worked for the president of Paramount Pictures. Through her, I managed an interview at the theater to be an usher, and was promptly hired.

I was eager for more live entertainment on stage as well as movie escapism. The interior of the Paramount Theater was a grand and glamorous palace for the moviegoer. A magnificent marbled lobby and huge stairway leading to several tiers of balconies welcomed the awed visitor. However, this was only a prelude to the wondrous world within the house. Classical-styled statuary bathed in pink, dim lights in alcoves on either side of the stage, and a vaulted, starry blue heaven many stories overhead created an enchanting atmosphere. Here, yet another world was opened up to me!

Mother would have been shocked if she knew! The underbelly of city life turned up dressed as ushers. Their free-living life style startled me, but I tried not to show it. The young female usherettes often went to Times Square bars to pick up men. Usually, they just wanted to be plied with drinks and avoided putting out for them by climbing out of restroom windows in Holly Golightly fashion. Tales of lascivious living abounded, greatly embarrassing me. But, there was Robert, a fair haired, slim out-of-work actor who seemed more in my world. I got the impression he was gay, but we avoided ever discussing that taboo subject, while both of us carefully applied Clearasil to our faces before appearing on the floor to work long hours directing and assisting people in the huge theater. (Many years later, I ran into him in a coffee shop. He looked haggard and was desperate for me to go to his place. Now, I suspected he was hustling.)

The main attraction for me working at the Paramount Theater was the famous live stage shows in between film viewings. Stars like Johnny Ray, Frankie Laine,

Rosemary Clooney, and many others appeared there while I worked my shifts. Sarah Vaughn caused the audience to gasp at one performance when her strapless gown slipped down. She turned away from the audience to make a fast alteration and returned to "sing a song I feel like doing: *I feel like running back home!*" she announced with aplomb. I watched Ella Fitzgerald play cards with the band backstage in between shows, and French film star Denise Darcel gave me her dressing room key, still heavily scented from her recent drenching of Chanel No. 5.

I was able to meet Rosemary Clooney at the Paramount.

Sniffing her key intoxicated me during my duty running the back elevator, and I sang to myself her song, "Some girls need a penthouse to give them romance..." Cece Robinson taught me a Charleston step backstage. In general, when I was backstage, the personalities treated me warmly, which thrilled this teenager, but I was not allowed to be there often, unfortunately, as my chief duty was to usher in the theater.

Paramount days: Denise Darcel and Billy Eckstein.

The most outstanding event in my life as an usher happened on one busy Saturday night. The captain of the ushers needed someone to effectively direct the disbursement of the crowds to the five-tiered balcony. Due to some regulation, it usually was someone 18 years of age or older. That evening, he had no one available, so he asked me to do it even though I was underage.

The crowds were filling the enormous downstairs lobby. Lines were waiting to ascend in the elevators, but only one elevator at a time was permitted to leave the lobby, as the other one filled with excited movie goers anticipating the entertainment to follow. As the evening progressed, I became extremely exhausted. A friendly elevator operator was about to descend to pick up the next group of people when I pressed my gloved hands on the open elevator doors to talk with him, allowing the doors to close just enough for me to rest my head inside. I assumed I could push them open again when we finished our conversation. Unfortunately, the doors had closed too far. My head was inside the elevator, but my body was outside. The doors would not open as they were set up to open again only after the doors were completely closed. It would mean decapitating me! In desperation, I asked the elevator operator NOT to call the manager's office, as I did not want to be fired or get him into trouble. Billy Eckstein was crooning "Caravan" while the restive crowds were growing in numbers down below in the lobby. A woman on her way to the ladies room saw my body protruding from the elevator and started to scream, "Some man has his head caught in the elevator!"

The phone rang. It was located just above the operator's lever for moving the elevator car. I heard explanations stammered by the perturbed elevator operator, while a fireman arrived and inexplicably shoved a pole inside the elevator between my spread-apart feet. Crowds gathered. It became necessary for a rescue worker to take an elevator in the adjacent Paramount office building to ascend to a higher floor and proceed to the specific theater elevator shaft I was trapped in. He then had to descend down the ladders inside the shaft for a dozen floors to release the latch above the elevator so that the doors could be opened manually.

Relief at last! However, I was badly shaken and taken to the manager's office, where my story was nervously reported. The manager's main concern was that I was not injured. To my relief, he exonerated my elevator operator friend from blame. With my connections to Paramount, it was clear my being fired was out of the question; however, I was too insecure to realize that. I was sent home to recover, and a sign was placed in the locker room: "Employees are to keep all parts of their bodies away from closing elevator doors!"

By "acting as if," I bluffed a tenuous camaraderie with the other ushers. I did not want them to realize how innocent and virginal I was. In fact, I felt utterly adrift from any understanding of the mysteries of life. My co-workers lived in a world that contrasted sharply to my Lutheran values, which may have kept me safe but also kept me ignorant of vital information needed for my development as a young man. My peers at school did not share with me any intimacy that encouraged a free flow of worldly knowledge; my older brother was never around or available to talk with me; and my parents were away up the river and probably would never

Three generations: blood memory.

help solve the puzzlements confronting me. So much had to be repressed and stuffed away for another day.

In the meantime, I discovered the theater and the ballet. A Broadway theater was showing the film, *The Red Shoes*. This introduction to ballet thrilled me. Some blocks further north was the City Center, featuring the New York City Ballet. In the vicinity were other theaters inviting my attendance. Participating as a viewer in this cornucopia was a powerful temptation. Oh, joy! Not only could I feed my hungry soul with opera, but also now I had the magic of the stage, with plays and dance to entrance me! I forgot about the birds and the bees in favor of *pirouettes*, *grands jetés*, and larger than life gestures, tears of grief, and the ecstasy of passion-drenched words.

What extraordinary talented mentors to lead me along the glorious paths of future creativity: Moira Shearer and Robert Helpmann; André Eglevsky with Maria Tallchief and Tanaquil LeClerq; Eva Le Gallienne, Laurence Olivier, and the musical star Carol Channing, to name but a few of the influences in my burgeoning exposure to the performing arts. My heart was won over by the performers, the characters they portrayed, and the productions themselves. My lifeblood began to pump to the pulse of the stage now, as it had with the screen.

Clearly, this did not make a good basis for participation on a baseball or basketball team. Most summers, my mother would drive Helen and me to visit my ogre grandmother in Lynn, Massachusetts. When we were very little, my grandfather died, leaving my grandmother as sole occupant of a large Victorian house atop a hill. (My father's parents were unknown to us as he hadn't been in touch with them since he departed from Sweden on a ship bound for Argentina many years before.) Grim-faced Tilly Johnson would greet me upon arrival by taking one of my ears and twisting it. She always warned me against using too much toilet paper when availing myself of her toilet. Later, she would offer me a homemade root beer soda, which was a much more granny-style behavior.

For summer recreation, my cousin Ernie would always be playing out on the baseball diamond. I shied away from much contact with Ernie and his sporty friends, not feeling any rapport despite our closeness in age. His family lived at the foot of my grandmother's sloping property, just across a dirt road from the baseball diamond. Despite my inner conviction that it was a dangerous mistake, on one occasion I agreed to go join the boys in a game of baseball. I was to play first base.

Being distracted watching the fluttering of a colorful butterfly, I was shouted at to catch a fast oncoming ball. I turned and the ball smashed into my face. The blood and a broken nose quickly ended my very undistinguished career in baseball.

During the same week, my father finished the job of breaking my nose while visiting in Lynn. I said something sassy that incensed him. My father had been drinking, and he reacted incautiously by smacking me across the face. The nose got the brunt of it. He was immediately repentant, and deeply regretted his volatile action. To this day, people who have long known me will suddenly discover in certain lighting that my nose has an irregularity in contrast to my otherwise well-formed, perfectly-aligned Swedish-American visage.

Hence, I have never yearned to be a Joe DiMaggio, nor even yearned to have Joe DiMaggio. This cannot be said of the many comely dancers, singers and actors I have observed and known. How I admired Gene Kelly in *An American In Paris*, and I had a great surprise when finally seeing the choreography to Gershwin's music. I had listened to the music many times before experiencing the film. In my mind, I invented my own choreography. It was amazing how similar it turned out to be when I saw the film! I would have enjoyed taking Leslie Caron's place so as to dance with Gene Kelly to "our" routines.

Curiously, some years later, I saw Gene Kelly at the Hollywood Bowl after a performance of the New York City Ballet. There was no reason to introduce myself, but I did have conversations with Leslie Caron more recently in Paris. I did not mention wanting to take her place in the film . . . happily!

My musical career was a rosebud that withered on the stem. When my father would not permit my studying piano and refused to purchase one, I chose to learn to play the cello. It was an instrument that I could take home to practice on free-of-charge. Though I loved the mellow sound of the instrument, I could never quite manage each hand doing a different action. The bowing and the fingering did not mesh. With the fife, I could easily use both hands to finger. My nervousness attempting to play the cello showed by my perspiration running down the finger board, to the distress and impatience of Professor Stoffragen, heading the music department. He suggested I give up the cello and help him with administrative duties. That was a relief to me and would prove to be invaluable later on in my career when I created and produced a festival of the arts.

It had been rumored the Hollywood film actress June Allyson was born in my neighborhood of the Bronx. Now, another even more astonishing personage was to take center stage as a local celebrity. George William Jorgensen, Jr. lived close to our home, and after groundbreaking procedures in Denmark, he returned as Christine Jorgensen. The world was astonished!

During March of 1953, just before I graduated from Stuyvesant High School, came a very curious event in my life: the Woman of the Year Award was given by the Scandinavian Societies of Greater New York to the much publicized Christine Jorgensen. I attended the event with other members of the Swedish folk dance group to which I belonged. (Young people interested in performing Swedish folk dances met at Vasa Castle Hall on 149th Street to rehearse for native-costumed performances at special Scandinavian events. Anita Carlson, who influenced my going to Queens College, and some church members encouraged me to join and perform with the group. It was a great way to socialize, but I felt shy dancing at the performances.) Even my brother and his cronies were there, along with members of my Swedish Lutheran Church. I was too absorbed in my own confused awkwardness to remember the salacious remarks doubtlessly made.

Christine Jorgensen, Woman of the Year, with Bob looking on.

Newspapers and newsreels splashed images of a very glamorous blond woman who only months before had been a young man. It amazed and confounded me, as might be indicated by the photo of us taken at this dinner dance at the Manhattan Center on West 34th Street. Among the hundreds of people attending this first major appearance of Christine Jorgensen, who managed to be at her shoulder looking befuddled? Me! This increasingly became a pattern in my life: placing myself in the path of a celebrity.

The second and last time I saw this unusual personality was at the birthday party for Johnny Carson held at Toots Shor's, a gathering place for theater personalities. It was one of her final appearances. Looking sad with a cigarette and martini, sitting alone, Christine Jorgensen was not someone I wished to emulate. However, she inspired the idea of re-invention, albeit in the extreme. It is a notion that I have incorporated into the evolution of my life's journey.

Learning before age twelve that I had to get rid of the Bronx accent and investigations into European royalty were early forays into re-invention, as was the role playing of film heroines on the back lawn of the family house during this pre-teen period. As a teenager waiting in line to attend the Metropolitan Opera for standing room space, I actively reconstructed who I was and wanted to become.

Sal Mineo, June Allyson and Christine Jorgensen all having come from my Bronx environs held a green light up for me to achieve a similar success in reshaping my future. The absorption of stage and screen experiences fired my imagination for a re-birth of "Bobby," starting with baloney curls and headed towards a very colorful world of verve and artistic vitality.

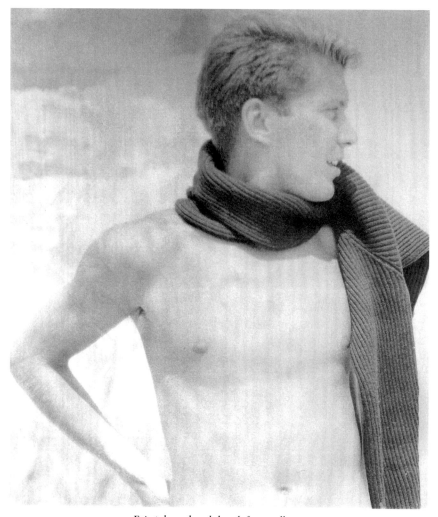

Eric takes a beach break from college.

Chapter 2

THE LORD WON'T MIND

Dad said "No!" I had made it clear that I would not be pursuing a future in the construction business as my older brother had done. Conforming to my father's wishes, George had his university expenses paid for by my father. My intentions were very different and alien to my father. So, if I were to pursue a life in the arts, I would have to manage a further education on my own, though a small living allowance would be forthcoming.

Anita Carlson, from my Swedish folk dance group, had shown me the attractive Spanish-Mediterranean styled Queens College campus in Flushing, which she attended. It was a part of the city-funded educational system. I thought it an attractive solution to achieving my higher education, especially as I qualified as a city resident and would pay only a nominal fee for admittance. I relished the open-air feeling of the campus, almost like the big name universities I had seen in photos and at the movies. I loved seeing the skyline of Manhattan beyond the soccer field, reminding me of the glamor and venues available there. Easy forays to Manhattan's cultural centers from the campus were an obvious advantage to attending Queens College.

My first few years at Queens were spent commuting from the Bronx over the Whitestone Bridge, passing the simple house where Sal Mineo had lived before going to Hollywood. (If this young man could make it in Hollywood coming from such a humble beginning, maybe I could make my mark in the arts, too?) The lengthy bus trip was sometimes avoided by my hitch hiking to school, for the adventure and economy of it. The ride on the highway that led over the Whitestone Bridge was a pleasant route. Being on the open road was something I enjoyed, and I intended to do more of it when opportunities presented themselves.

My early notion of college life included being a member of a fraternity. I thought rushing for the most prestigious fraternity on campus would help straighten me out, and earn me acceptance to what I thought was the most popular and attractive group of students. I had such sexual ambivalence that I believed exposure to the straight, swinging fraternity/sorority life would earn me stature on campus just by my association with them. Perhaps my ambivalence and confusion would go unnoticed? I was popular with the sorority girls because I would invite them to the many dances held off campus. As I was considered a good dancer and an attractive escort, they helped pave my way into acceptance by the fraternity of my choice. My older sister Flo had taught me how to waltz and do other social dances at home. As part of physical education, social dancing was a required class, and one I achieved top grades in. I enjoyed socializing with the girls, so dancing with them was an asset to my campus standing. The girls spoke highly of me to the guys in the fraternity. This helped ease their concerns about my eligibility in the straight fraternity life.

It was clear to me that I was leading a double life. One was as the avid fraternity member, playing out the activities of the college's extra-curricular life, whether it was joining in the social parties and dances or hanging out after class at a local bar, being one of the boys. The other life was the magnetic pull of the theatrical life in the Big Apple.

Often, after class, I would go into Manhattan by bus, changing to the subway in Flushing. Sometimes, my goal was to get a standing room ticket for the Metropolitan Opera. Otherwise, my new pursuit was attending the performances of the New York City Ballet at the City Center. I discovered that I could pry the balcony door open from the fire escape and gain furtive admission into the theater. By observing others doing this, I quickly caught on to the trick. An alternate ploy was called "second acting" — waiting until intermission and entering while closely investigating the program in my hand as though I were returning to my seat. The program was from a previous performance, but no one could tell the difference.

Ballet star André Eglevsky mightily impressed me with his vital manliness in partnering Maria Tallchief in *Swan Lake* or Tanaquil Le Clercq in *The Firebird*. Other highlights included Nora Kaye in *The Cage* and the attractive Jacques D'Amboise in *Afternoon of a Faun*. I swooned at the masculinity of Nicholas Magallanes and thrilled at *Symphony in C* and *Dancers at a Gathering*. The dancers' lovely movements and the romantic environment on the ballet stage completely riveted me. I participated emotionally with Diana Adams, Melissa Hayden and Allegra Kent, but I felt a general affection for everyone on stage as well.

Although I admired them from my seat in the theater, I sometimes made brief explorations back stage, nervously sneaking in after a performance, past the backstage doorman. I wanted to get glimpses of life backstage, with hopes that someone would start a conversation and discover me as a worthy friend. I had met the Balanchine ballerina Allegra Kent through her actress sister, and once sent

Queens College: Helen Athos and Bob with their Charleston flappers.

her a very modest bouquet of flowers. It was embarrassing for me to notice her receiving huge bouquets at curtain call, and then my paltry one was presented. I found her backstage and she thanked me for them. I had no idea then that many of these dancers and other stars to come would become moments and chapters in my personal life. Slowly, while continuing to attend classes at Queens College, I was beginning to be absorbed into the inner world of the performers.

It was during this period that I decided to limber myself up and take dance classes at a studio off Times Square. Seeing the advertisement in the trade publication *Back Stage*, I ventured self-consciously into the studio and signed up for a one evening class a week. Being a full-time student at Queens College, and careful with my pocket money, it was what financially and time-wise I could afford. Fortunately, I chose to take classes with Jean Erdman (who I later discovered was the wife of philosopher/writer/teacher Joseph Campbell). The class was made up of other young people such as myself, on a non-professional level but eager to dance. She gently informed me of what my body might be trained to do, and helped me to further appreciate what I was seeing on the ballet stage.

What budding gay man-in-the-making could resist the temptations of indulging in the golden age of Broadway musicals? They were great works of American art with inherent historic qualities, and they were available in abundance: *Oklahoma, South Pacific, The King and I, Bells Are Ringing,* a revival of the American opera *Porgy & Bess, Guys and Dolls, The Pajama Game,* and *Annie Get Your Gun,* to name a few. My first musical was the enchanting *Kismet,* which reminded me of my exotic acting out of MGM movies. It also had the thrilling ballet music of Borodin. The second one was *Gentlemen Prefer Blondes*, with the hilarious Carol Channing. "Diamonds are a girl's best friend" amused and enchanted me for years. I was on my way along the Great White Way in committed delirium. So long lasting was this soon-to-be engrained influence that, more than 50 years later when I played Mother Ginger in the New Jersey Ballet's *Nutcracker*, a critic described my performance as "Carol Channing on Acid." I am not certain if I am a quick learner, but I know I am not a quick forgetter.

Putting a coin into the imaginary jukebox in my head, I can vividly play any of my favorite golden moments from those unforgettable performances. With utter determination, "I'm on my way to find my Bess" gets me going, just as "Some Enchanted Evening," sung by Ezio Pinza to Mary Martin, continues to strike me through the heart. I could relish that romantic sentiment and carry it with me forever. "Shall We Dance?" always makes me want to fly around the room with some new romance, while "The Party's Over" has me in melancholy, self-pitying doldrums.

Recalling thrilling performances is not limited to the Broadway musicals. I also tap into great moments in the opera and ballet that I have nearly fainted over, such as Birgit Nilsson's Brünnhilde, as well as her Sieglinde with Siegmund in *Winterstürme* and "Du Bist der Lenz" in *Die Walküre*. Who can forget later in Act Three, when she is about to fly to the East, her vocalizing a brief passage guaranteed to create an involuntary sigh from the audience? Other examples of singers and arias are too numerous to mention. Ballet has its own treasured memories for me, as well. Are we all not fortunate that we can bank these treasures and recall them from the vaults of memory for continual enrichment?

To help pay for the forays into the New York theaters, I worked two part-time jobs at the college. One was helping out in the cafeteria, clearing tables of soiled dishes, glasses, and flatware on certain nights; the other was helping to give instruction in social dancing on Tuesday evenings in the adult education program. I loved to dance, thanks to early indulgence in lessons from my older sister. All thoughts of training in ballet were dismissed when I realized my legs were too short, with a very poor turn out that would not be changed at this age. However, being long-waisted and with good posture, I could do social dancing to great effect. Gene Kelly and Fred Astaire, watch out! (A few years later I actually did an impromptu floor show with Rita Hayworth at Hal Prince's wedding. I shudder at the memory, but will save it for later!)

During the summer months, my moneymaking activities were more diverse. In the summer of 1955, I ventured out towards the end of Cape Cod, Massachusetts. A lively girl from Queens College named Diane had mentioned how each summer she was a waitress in Wellfleet, and during her spare time rehearsed and acted in a summer stock theater production there. I traveled to the quaint and elegant, smallish colonial-style hotel where she was employed, but I could only manage to get a job as a dishwasher. Eulelia Price was the upright owner of the establishment who hired me. I slept alone in the large Chart Room, once a cocktail lounge for the hotel. My work was not difficult and the waitresses were pleasant and easy to get along with. I had minimum interchange with the cook, so the occasional appearance of the elderly, stern Eulelia and the college-girl waitresses comprised my only conversation at work. During free time, I could stroll down the road into town where a soda fountain was the meeting place for all the young people to hang out.

Wellfleet is an old whaling town with quaint gray weather-beaten clapboard houses on small streets. A harbor runs along one side of Wellfleet. Out beyond the horizon, far across the placid waters — which twinkle indiscriminately under sunshine or moonlight — lies Boston. The Cape curves like a bent finger in the area around Wellfleet. One side of land is exposed to the fickleness of the open ocean along Newcomb Hollow, while the other side enjoys a buffered zone created by pines and deciduous trees to protect the town along the harbor. Going away from the harbor, across cranberry patches and traversing the highway between Sandwich and Provincetown, one can reach the ocean and the attractive sand dunes. Scrub bushes bearing wild rose-like blossoms turn into beach plums as the summer season progresses. The crashing surf splashes the air with salt spray, while dolphins may decide to play off shore. There is a romantic urge to search for the presence of whales in the distance. Whether enduring a strong onshore wind while walking bundled up along the ranting ocean, or, at another capricious moment, basking under strong sunshine on a breathless, endless-seeming stretch of beach favored by nudists, people find this part of the Cape's seashore to be magnificent in its changeable moods. For those seeking a more conservative ambiance in nature, between ocean and town are a couple of pleasant ponds. These are ideal for summer swimmers who do not wish to brave the cold ocean or the climb around dunes, instead choosing to be safely protected from being blown about by the sudden whims of Mother Nature.

Painters and writers have been attracted to the quiet charm of this part of the Cape for ages. The enormous sea cliffs near Truro, between Wellfleet and Provincetown, inspire awe and inspiration for many of the visiting artists. I felt deep admiration for the diverse beauty of Cape Cod—and a furtive fascination for Provincetown, steeped in lurid tales of dissipation and gay perversions. Eugene O'Neill and Hans Hofmann were among the many artists who lived there, together with flaming drag queens and hordes of gays I had heard disparaging remarks about. Though intrigued, I felt trepidation about visiting Provincetown.

Wellfleet was such a sweet place for me to spend the summer. It had not yet attracted the mobs of tourists just over the horizon. I discovered the studio of artist Clare Leighton. Her woodcuts of men toiling at sea, whether fishing or hunting the great whales, were skillfully transferred onto sturdy plates. I managed to finally be able to buy eight of these artistic plates. My siblings agreed to go in with me to present them to our parents for an anniversary gift later that year. Painters and sculptors had studios in town, but I was drawn particularly to Clare's woodcuts, as something to take back to New York.

Diane and her friends were very amiable and good company. Some local boys, attracted by the young women, joined the group for various activities. The rumblings of my sexual volcano began to vibrate in their presence, but I was completely inactive. Our group would go to the ocean beach or a nearby pond for swimming. It was at one of these ponds that I met the daughter of Ingrid Bergman, who was trying to be incognito. Attempting politeness, we made believe we did not know who she was. Rumors of her true identity prevailed; I could see Jenny's strong resemblance to her mother. Jenny Lindstrom, later known professionally as Pia, was a quiet and lovely girl probably about sixteen. Her famous actress mother had just captured world headlines by her scandalous, adulterous affair with her legendary Italian director, Roberto Rossellini, while filming in Stromboli, Italy. Years later, when I reminded Pia of our Cape Cod time, she exclaimed that I was probably the one who gave her the first alcoholic drink. Her father had put her on the Cape to remove her from world attention; however, this was the start of a long, tormented journey for her, battling addictive behavior.

A group of us participated in preparing costumes for the annual Artists' and Writers' Ball, to be held in nearby Provincetown. Our costumes were to represent us as cannibals. We all decided to clean the discarded bones from the hotel kitchen and string them around our necks. The guys wore loincloths and the girls dressed like "Jane of the Jungle." Dark body makeup completed the presentation. This was a great adventure for most of us as Provincetown was the infamous meeting place of homosexuals and other "degenerates." The girls did not make much of the Provincetown anomaly, but the local guys made constant slurs about the gays. It was perhaps necessary for macho locals to do that, especially at their anxious age between puberty and manhood. I was eager to see what it was like.

Provincetown is on the tip of Cape Cod. Unlike quiet, sedate Wellfleet, Provincetown had many more shops, restaurants, bars, and places to stay. A large dock in the center of town accommodated the arrival of the fishing fleet each day. Beyond the dock and across the harbor, a white lighthouse flashed its beams round and round. A high memorial stone tower, also in the center of the town, could be seen from great distances.

The town hall was where the Artists' and Writers' Ball was held. This large clapboard building, near the monument and diagonally across from the dock, had a busy flow of outrageously garbed revelers by the time we arrived. Some wore skimpy attire; many featured feathers and flesh more than costumes. Our savage getups were naïve compared to the flamboyant, glamorous creations we saw at this event. We meekly appeared in the midst of the festivities, keeping closed ranks. If any one noticed me, I was not aware of it. I do not think we stayed very long once we entered into this other world. Our foray was short and superficial. I felt my local Wellfleet local boys were sexier than the made up fairies twirling about hysterically. I was not used to that over the top behavior, and preferred the masculine hicks to the painted queens.

Nathaniel Saltonstall, a noted Boston Brahmin architect, built a lovely complex of accommodations on the bay at Wellfleet. One of the Minnesota girls working at the hotel had parents visiting who rented a cottage at "The Colony." She and a few of her waitress colleagues decided it would be a great place to have a casual get together while the parents were off on a brief trip. They invited a few other recently met visitors to join them, and I was included, but none of the local boys we sometimes went to the beach with were asked to attend. This was a small gathering of "nice" young people wanting to share a summer's evening together, relaxing after work.

While strolling in town the next morning, I stopped to chat with one of the local boys whom I found very attractive, but presumably straight. I wanted to have the local boys who were not invited to think I was very worldly and risqué in my carryings on the night before at "The Colony." Hoping I would seem a manly participant in the summer events, I hinted that sexual interludes had occurred during the evening. Promoted by me, gossip of illicit activities spread around town. When I went to the service at the Presbyterian Church the next Sunday, the minister gave a sermon about the Prodigal Son. He and the congregation stared at me with disapproval. I was the only one in the church who had attended the party. The girls at the hotel did not go to church, or least not this one. They probably never were aware of my foolish gossip. I took the brunt of the blame. It was clear that it was time to leave town. Abashed, I returned to New York with my small earnings.

The next summer, 1956, I intended to take a summer school theater course at UCLA. My brother's fraternity had a chapter there, so I approached them about renting a room. Happily, I could share a room with another young man on a short-term basis. Tom was a quiet, friendly fellow who took the top bunk of our bunk beds. Each time we went nude swimming in the pool, I was made aware of his beautiful endowments. Though thrilled, I was too repressed to suggest any further investigation in the privacy of our room. I lacked the courage to follow through, and thought I might just be experiencing a passing fancy. My suppressed interest in men was aroused by some of the handsome fraternity brothers and by the Wellfleet guys the summer before. Now, I had a hunk of a nice guy within daily grasp in our bedroom. This was far more challenging and confounding to me. Inaction, as usual, was my mode of operation. I might have found some relief in masturbating. However, that was something I never had done or even thought about as a possibility. It was totally out of my ken. My naïveté was incredible, doubtlessly a result of the staunch, repressive Lutheranism drummed into me while growing up.

Near the fraternity house was the Alpha Delta Pi sorority house, sister chapter to the one at Queens College. Somehow, I got to know a young woman residing there, Terry Spadone, a teacher from Long Island who was in love with the theater. One day, we went to lunch on Hollywood Boulevard. At the next table was a handsome young man who engaged us in conversation. After we left him at the restaurant, I asked Terry if she realized that our conversational friend was the up-and-coming new sensation of the screen, Jimmy Dean. She thought he was, but we both avoided any reference to his identity during lunch conversation. This was part of the delight of spending time in the Hollywood area. Even in UCLA's Westwood area, one never knew who would be pushing the shopping cart at the supermarket.

For some reason, I cannot recall why my summer class at UCLA did not pan out, so I felt the necessity of gaining some coins of the realm for the upcoming year at QC. After scanning the want ads, I opted to try being a salesman of Catholic Bibles. Until then, I had not considered how hard it was to sell Catholic Bibles. I had not even given thoughts to the Catholic Bible, being exposed only to the King James version of the Bible.

Each morning, I was given a particular neighborhood to canvass for my sales. The few times I was successful in gaining the attention of a potential buyer, I would sometimes have a surprise. Scantily-dressed lonely housewives seemed more interested in having me talk to them than seriously committing to a sale. But I believed in my product and had some success. On rare occasions, an elderly woman would ask me to stay and partake of dinner with her, or visit her private chapel. I am not certain how many potential clients really believed that I was Catholic, but some sales were accomplished, earning me enough money to prepare for my return home.

A couple of girls at Terry's sorority house were going to be returning to college, driving east as far as Minnesota. It seemed a great idea to jump into the car with them, sharing the gas and getting east in an adventurous way. One of them had a boyfriend who was the manager of a gas station in Yellowstone National Park in Wyoming. We all were eager to see this natural wonder, which was on our way.

Once I got to the park, I yearned to spend more time with Mother Nature. It was utterly thrilling to walk along the edge of the canyon and view the magnificent waterfall and to stroll through the forest with the prospects of meeting bears and other wild life. I wanted to remain for a little longer. The manager kindly gave me the opportunity to be a gas station attendant for the few weeks before I needed to return to QC. The manager was a college student himself, as were all the other attendants. He knew that I was green to the endeavor but I would be given some basic instructions. Normal guys my age could easily maneuver around a gas pump and service station. That was the beginning of a series of disasters, warning me to learn my own limitations.

The first blunder took place around twilight, when I thought I would check whether a gas tank was full to the top. My first thought was to light a match to peer down the tank. Mercifully, common sense, the fast response from another attendant, and a NO SMOKING sign in clear sight negated any such foolhardy action. Although I began driving a car at age fifteen, I really did not know much about the working of cars. I momentarily forgot that gasoline was very explosive around a flame.

Noticing that some attendants made tips by changing oil, I drove a customer's car onto the lift and raised it up enough for me to go underneath to undo the oil screw for draining, just as I had noted the other attendants doing. Gorgeous golden oil flowed into the used oilcan, and I thought how foolish this man was to think he needed to change his oil. "That's not my oil you're draining!" the angry man shouted as he looked under his car. "That's the fluid drive!" Because this type of car used fluid drive, there was one screw for fluid drive and another for the oil. Mistakenly, I unscrewed the wrong one. I spent some time replacing the lost fluid drive with a fresh supply, using an eyedropper from the front of the floor on the passenger side. I paid for this embarrassing mistake!

One very cold morning, I was to open the gas station while the rest of the crew slept warmly in their beds. It had just been painted the afternoon before and was sticky to the touch. In came a man who requested that I fix his flat tire. In earlier days, I had fixed many leaks with patches on the inner tubes of my bike tires. This was the same procedure but incorporated a machine bolted into the cement floor that a tire could be affixed to. When the tire with the patched inner tube was repaired, I placed the air hose nozzle onto the tit of the tire. It inflated — and inflated — and inflated. I could not pry the nozzle free and saw the wrinkles growing more and more evident in the ballooning tire. I had heard from my brother-in-law, who was a chauffeur, of severe injuries inflicted by exploding tires. I strongly urged the man to back out of the gas station, and he did, while I retreated in horror a step or two as the tire exploded, pulling the machinery out of the cement floor and blowing out the windows! Dust from the floor caked on the not-quite-dry painted walls. Bells were ringing in my ears and continued throughout the day. The man told the manager, who was awakened from deep sleep in his bed, that it was not my fault. It turned out that the machinery was faulty. I did not have to pay for the tire, nor the destruction in the gas station, but I knew it was time to be on my way back to the safety of Manhattan.

At this time, Broadway was enjoying a very rich cornucopia of plays created by a world of genius: Williams, Inge, Miller, and O'Neill, as prime examples. The culmination of a great American art form, the musical theater was busy presenting those history-in-the-making productions such as *My Fair Lady* and *The Pajama Game*. College theater became my focus, with field trips to the city for theater. There certainly was a very heady conglomeration of productions available in the New York performing arts scene for this young man to indulge in. This is a world long-gone now, replaced by a tourist-based mega-hit corporate industry.

As an extension of my studies in theater arts, I made occasional appearances as a supernumerary, both at the Metropolitan Opera and the New York City Opera. It was not difficult to get an interview with the stage manager, requesting a supernumerary position. My physical appearance and age qualified me for such an undertaking.

My role at the City Opera was that of a torero in *Carmen*. During the first act, I would appear from stage right and accept an orange from a pretty red-haired vendor. She was soon to become world recognized as Beverly Sills. Later in the opera, I sat around pretending to have a drink at the Inn while Escamillo impressed Carmen. At the Met, I avoided any role that involved disrobing since

I felt uncomfortable in the dressing room atmosphere of gay flirting. I stuck to wearing a pull-on clerical robe in *Tosca*, but turned down appearing as a scantily clad slave in *Aïda*.

A friend from the music department came along with me to do extra work. He and I stayed close for rehearsals and performances, and we became known by some back stage workers as "the *Tosca* lovers," since we played each *Tosca* performance together. Though I felt a strong attachment to him, and I felt it was mutual, neither of us made any move to come out of the closet. During this period, I shared the stage with the legendary talents of Ljuba Welitsch (who sang the *Tosca* in the performances I played a cleric), Birgit Nilsson, Kirsten Flagstad, Lawrence Melchior, Franco Corelli, and Jussi Björling, to name a few on the sterling roster of stars. This attractive young man was being educated by masters. It was a time of highest achievements in the American theater, and I felt privileged as a recipient of this gift.

Though it was thrilling to be on the huge stage of the Met, my shyness and theater protocol discouraged any one-on-one with the stars. I would see them engaged in conversation with other people, but I kept my distance. A strongly enforced edict was that a supernumerary was not permitted to linger around backstage. We were put into costume, herded on stage, and then expected to retreat to the dressing room so as to keep the backstage uncluttered. Rehearsals were in a room away from the stage, and other than at dress rehearsal and performances, the extra was not in the stage area. Snatches of operatic moments were heard while backstage, but only bits and pieces. While on stage, I could examine lighting and technical aspects of productions. This was particularly true if I stayed on stage for a period of time, as I did in Second Act of *Carmen*, when I sat in the tavern before Escamillo's grand entrance.

Daydreaming about what I had seen on stage occupied much of my school hours. Slowly, I realized that I was not interested in my courses in Education, prerequisite for getting a teaching license. I had been very absorbed when I directed O'Neill's B*ound East for Cardiff* for the student-teaching class I was doing at Great Neck High School, but otherwise I did not care for my Education studies.

My fraternity life became an obstacle to my indulgence in the performing arts, so I disassociated myself from that prestigious group. I discovered the lure of the theater department's classes in acting and directing. The young, recently appointed instructor, Ray Gasper, inspired his students and immersed them into various stylistic concepts of theater. We learned about Presentational Theater used by Brecht in contrast to the Chekhovian realism of the 19th Century, and we examined the concepts of Max Reinhardt and other innovators in theater. Enthusiastically and with burning commitment to his instruction, we plunged ourselves into the thrilling world of the theater, greatly broadening our horizons.

It was stimulating to participate in any school production he directed. His patient exploration of the inner life of a play, his aid into internalizing a character, and his skill in plotting the most effective use of all the aspects of a theatrical production were brilliant instruction to those willing to pay attention. Shy of acting on stage, I often did a technical job involving sound effects or lighting. Dr. Gasper created a most moving *Glass Menagerie*. It featured as the lead character, Tom, a fellow to whom I would have greatly enjoyed giving up my virginity. There was not a hint or encouragement from him, so I stayed my repressed and tormented self.

For a couple of years, I had a good friend interested in becoming a writer. We spent many hours talking into the night about stuff guys our age pondered over, but never getting personal enough to help each other. Neither of us came out to each other, so I never knew for sure if he was gay or not. We were both fearful and reluctant to take a leap into exposing our inner selves. Yet, both of us clearly wanted each other's approbation and camaraderie. This was the *Blut-bruderschaft* of D.H. Lawrence that I had read about in contemporary literature class. Neither of us was able to admit the possibility of being gay. Charlie and I parted ways during my last year working in the theater department.

I read about theater history and undertook a project involving writing about the complete works of Eugene O'Neill. Ray considered it worthy of a Master's thesis and gave me highest marks for the engaging effort, an A plus. For this project, I described each and every play on filing cards, compiled a bibliography of books about O'Neill and his plays, and gathered quotes from these sources that were used in connection with my discussion of his individual plays, often drawing references from his life reflected in his work. During this time, I saw some of his plays staged on Broadway and elsewhere, together with films. I included biographical materials that appeared in his plays in my essay. It was a Herculean task.

This concentration on O'Neill took its toll on me. Being highly impressionable, I absorbed the sufferings and miseries of his protagonists into my system, twisting my outlook into a dramatic somberness. I began to confuse his plays with the reality of everyday living, causing me great inner turmoil. Perhaps the alcoholic drinking and violence resonated with memories of my earlier home life. Perhaps it was because of the vulnerability I felt at this time in my life that appreciated the sufferings some of his characters experienced.

It was in this state of mind that I completed my studies and departed for Europe immediately after graduating with my Bachelor of Fine Arts. I brought with me the many unanswered mysteries of life—the quest for the meaning of life, the nature of the existence of God, the elusive understanding of sex. It was a Pandora's box that I seemed reluctant or unable to open—yet.

My monies were just enough for some months of parsimonious exploration abroad. Upon my return, I planned to continue theater training in directing by going to graduate school in Pittsburgh at Carnegie Tech, soon to become Carnegie Mellon. During my final year at Queens College, I had taken an equivalent of Directing 101. I headed up the very successful production of the O'Neill play at Great Neck High School, as well as some directing projects with Ray Gasper, who claimed I had a directorial mind capable of understanding and handling the necessary details, as well as the big picture, with clarity and creativeness. I felt confident I had interacted as a perfect colleague, working with cast and crew in these school theatrical productions. Dr. Gasper's enthusiastic recommendation was a great factor in my being accepted to Carnegie Tech as one of the ten eligible in the country for a Master of Fine Arts from one of the finest schools in the country, ranking with Yale Drama School.

It was February of 1957. I did not have the money for graduate school next September, but would worry about funding closer to the time of admission. It was imperative that I get to Paris now to assuage my battered spirit. I managed the European sojourn by selling every possession I had for this precarious trip into the unknown. Monies from the sale of my very expensive tape recorder, camera and other items went into the travel fund that had some savings added to it, as well. Nurtured by films, plays and books about France, and in particular Paris, I made the City of Light my destination. I was frightened about being immersed in a strange land away from the security of home with little money at my disposal, and scantier knowledge of French. However, I felt it was my destiny to experience with bravura the mysteries and romance of Paris that had captivated Fitzgerald, Hemingway, and the other writers, painters, and performers in bygone years.

Proud to be granted a passport, I then booked a Eurail pass valid for three months of European train travel from date of activation. I would activate it in Paris when I was ready to travel south to Rome or wherever. Starting in a third-class inside cabin aboard the SS *United States*, I was off daring a mysterious impending future.

Despite the stabilizers the SS *United States* was proud of, the rough winter sea challenged the fast progress the ship was noted for. Unlike many of the passengers, I enjoyed the rolling and bouncing around on the ocean, especially when I ventured out on to the deck, often pelted with rain. The air in an inner cabin can be stale, and without a porthole it can become unpleasant. I had been told that to circumvent seasickness, one should concentrate on the horizon, so the inner ear avoided the confusion of up from down. Being above deck was the best place to be, especially on turbulent seas. This initial crossing was accomplished, and I gathered myself for the assault on Gay Paree!

A boat train from Le Havre into Paris brought me closer to my destination. I remember viewing the cathedral at Rheims with wonderment from the train window, recalling the Monet renditions of it. With some bold resoluteness, I took a metro from the center of Paris out to Cité Universitaire, where I applied for lodging at the American students' hostel. I had heard of it from other students, and felt it might suit my immediate needs. I convinced a sympathetic older woman, Mme. Prokovsky, who was in charge of admittance, that I was doing research on theater arts in Paris in advance of my graduate work in the USA. This dear woman gave me a room to share with a European student who was studying at the Sorbonne.

Soon, Mme. Prokovsky invited me for tea in her apartment there. I believe she sensed my tenseness and vulnerability from being away in a strange environment. I remember tasting a dessert cheese there for the first time, and hearing her speak of her son, André, who danced with the Roland Petit ballet company in Paris. I was later to meet André at his mother's small apartment, and when he came to New York with the group the next year, I entertained him a couple of times.

The Cité Universitaire was composed of several buildings, spread out with lawns, bushes, and trees creating a very agreeable campus. They welcomed students from all over the world. Being in the midst of other students my age enabled me to form warm friendships with people I could enjoy meals with in student restaurants, and with whom I could go around Paris. Sometimes, dignified French ladies had tea and refreshments in their homes, encouraging international students to experience Parisian hospitality. I ate many delicious finger food delicacies on these occasions, and felt gratitude to the women who made the visits possible.

It was very economical and fun to explore the fabulous city of Paris with student status. I could get tickets to the opera or ballet at the famous opera house, Salle Garnier, as well as the Opéra Comique and Comédie Française at the Salle Richelieu at reduced prices. My exposure to great theater and music was greatly enhanced, and I was ecstatic! Whenever possible, I would read the play before seeing it performed in French. Acquainting myself with the American Library provided a great source of books for easy reference. Fortuitously, the actors at the Comédie Française spoke French clearly and beautifully, enabling me to understand the language better.

Enjoying a student status, my getting to know the City of Light was attempted with gusto and pleasure. The ubiquitous *pissoir* (no longer in existence) surprised me, as I was not accustomed to men urinating in public, but I made good use of them while wandering about Paris. Despite the current conviction that the Parisians were rude and horrible to Americans, I found them agreeable and patient with my attempts to make myself understood. Perhaps it was because I tried sincerely to attempt their language. Daily mixing with the students and the citizens of Paris was a constant delight. The expansive boulevards were impressive, while the backstreets with an occasional pocket park enchanted me. The *gloire* of France, resplendently evident in the architecture and plan of the city, impressed this New Yorker enough to make him memorize the history and savor the artistic achievements of this dynamic civilization. One of the most sacred arts in France was food preparation. The gastronomy in even a simple restaurant was amazing; unlike today, at that time one could not get a bad meal in Paris.

With time on my hands and a desire to share something related to my having this wonderful experience, I turned to pen and paper (later to be typed out). It occurred to me that I could start a newsletter to my theater department friends at Queens College, describing the richness of the offerings on the Paris stages. I decided to interview a couple of notable performers. Very handsome Jean-Pierre

Aumont was starring in Giraudoux's *Amphitrion 38*, and he kindly invited me to visit him in his dressing room before the performance. This was in response to a note I had directed to him at the theater where he was performing. I admired him in films and looked forward to meeting him in person. Happily, Aumont spoke very good English. We had a warm rapport, and he arranged for me to have a choice seat in the theater. When he suggested I come backstage after the show to see him, I felt he had intentions. I was stuck in my Swedish Lutheran stance, frightened to step out of the closet. I did not accept his invitation, and often wondered how different my immediate future might have been had I acquiesced.

My invitation to visit with one of the most distinguished stars of the Comédie Française (who shall remain nameless) was another memorable experience. His kind response to my written request for an interview permitted my entry to his dressing room during a non-performance afternoon. This historic theater is beside the charming Palais Royal and near the Louvre. The Salle Richelieu backstage has a series of dressing rooms unlike anything I had ever seen before, or since. I had been backstage at the Met, City Center and a few Broadway theaters where cramped space and dinginess prevailed. At the Comédie Française, each star had a commodious dressing room, decorated to the performer's personal taste, replete with antiques, paintings, and luxurious trappings. It was a setting fit for a king, or in this instance, a queen. This veteran actor ushered me into his beautifully appointed lair, complete with a zebra skin rug and a Napoleonic mahogany chaise lounge upholstered in a rich brocade. It was very impressive, but the lechery of this star quickly encouraged me to make a retreat after a polite conversation. I escaped but was troubled by my prudish propriety.

On many occasions at the American hostel, I received propositions for sexual investigations, both by the young male students as well as some of the females staying on this large international campus. At one party, all the guys there quietly joked at my reticence. I had not realized I was attending a gay gathering. Shortly afterwards, I expressed surprise to another student acquaintance, "I think they are all homosexuals." He was amused for, unbeknownst to me, he was gay too! These were pre-Stonewall days, and it was Paris, where things seemed more relaxed than in the United States. There was more permissiveness, but life was not completely open.

The Hungarian revolution had just caused a flow of refugees to seek a haven in Paris. One lovely young Hungarian woman extended warm friendship to me and introduced me to various theater people in the Paris area with whom she was acquainted. It was clear that she would have liked a more intimate relationship, but I ignored every advance.

My shyness extended to resisting the opportunity to visit with Alice B. Toklas, who often entertained Americans visiting in Paris. Even though her life mate, Gertrude Stein, had died, she was still available for conversations over tea. I felt I did not have anything to say worth her while and was reluctant to take up her time entertaining a young man from the Bronx without any credentials. Even though I was a college graduate with acceptance to a great drama school, I did not feel worldly enough or sufficiently accomplished to offer this great woman anything of interest.

The big event during my stay at the Cité Universitaire was the arrival of young Queen Elizabeth II and her handsome consort, Prince Philip, to Paris. We students went in a crowd to the place in front of Notre Dame to view the royal barge, approaching down the Seine, with water displays from the fire boats lit by colored spotlights and lots of gorgeous fireworks. It was a long time since a British monarch had made a state visit to France, and this young couple was strikingly attractive. This was a moment in history to savor.

While in Paris, I visited the office on Rue du Pantheon affiliated with the unique St. Helena monasteries in Greece. To visit this special remote retreat, where only men were allowed, required a special permit. Though I had the application in hand, I never submitted it. Fear of being compromised by bearded, grizzled monks in such a distant location was too much for me to submit to, so I shelved that notion. It may have been over-dramatizing or even perverse wishful thinking, but my fear of getting into an awkward, unpleasant situation far removed from an easy escape kept me from going to what might have been a great spiritual adventure.

After a couple of months and with spring advancing, I decided to investigate Italy and Switzerland before returning to Paris and on to England, to complete my first European sojourn. With the Eurail pass validated for travel, I was prepared for the long train ride to Rome. Students had told me of an inexpensive pension on the Via Babuino, near the Spanish Steps in Rome. I took lodgings there.

What a joy to investigate the sunny, warm streets of the Eternal City, where countless fountains splashed amidst the clamor of traffic over cobblestoned streets. The Romans seemed to thrive on making everyday life operatic, with expansive hand gestures and dramatic vocal expressions of joy, anger, or salutations. Their temperament was amusing and befitting the climate. It was a perfect place to shelve immediate plans for returning to school in the fall. My priority was to absorb and enjoy the wonders of Europe while I was there. I had confidence that plans would work out for graduate school—later.

Pasta fagioli replaced the potato-leek soup; the sun over the Arno replaced the clouds of the Seine; robust interchanges replaced measured politeness. I was in magnificent Rome, not in splendid Paris. My knowledge of Spanish helped me formulate rudimentary Italian phrases and vocabulary, making communication easier. However, money, or lack of it, became a concern. Traveling had depleted much of my money budgeted for Italy, so I decided to try my hand at being an extra in a film being shot at Cinecittà, just outside Rome. Through the English-speaking grapevine, I understood I could make the equivalent of $20 US dollars per day doing extra work in a film. In the Fifties, this sum was considered handsome and bought several meals at local trattorias. Extra work would be an excellent solution to my finances, so I set out for the film studios.

At the entrance to Cinecittà was an official to check entry on to the lots. He was on the phone when I approached, so I bent down out of his line of vision and went past the open upper portion of the Dutch door arrangement, unnoticed. I found myself in a large area occupied by several buildings not unlike warehouses. I did not know where to go, so I entered the nearest one, where a movie was being filmed. I encountered Sir Michael Redgrave, made up for his part in a historical drama. Sizing me up with an intense gaze, he inquired if he could help me. When I expressed an interest in getting film extra work, he asked me to sit down and indicated a nearby chair. He said he would be right back, but had to go onto the set for a little while. A gruff stagehand found me there and ordered me off the premises. Obediently, I left, somewhat relieved that I would not have to fend off the intentions of the distinguished Redgrave. However, he had imparted a sense of validation, though mingled with oppressive fear.

Obviously, this great actor had found me attractive, which stroked my ego. But what price would I have to pay to accept the attentions of a man of this supreme stature? Things seemed to boil down to the bottom line: sex! This shook my deepest Lutheran beliefs of chastity, purity, and virtue. It was awkward and uncomfortable, so I went into my usual avoidance mode.

Meanwhile, I had heard that an American actor by the name of Tony Perkins was making a movie there. I asked someone on the street of the movie lots in my poor Italian where I might find him. He pointed to a group of people taking a break and standing up ahead, and he indicated which man was Perkins.

I nervously approached Tony Perkins. He broke from the group to talk to me. I explained I was an American theater student with some stage experience and needed an extra's job to ease my financial distress. He looked at me carefully, then asked me to remove my very dark glasses. He told me never to wear glasses hiding my eyes from the person I was talking to, and he called a man over. Perkins asked the man to arrange for me to get a job as an extra in his film, for which I was greatly relieved.

I was to report the next morning to an elegant hotel in the Parioli district of Rome to begin my work on *The Sea Wall* (renamed in America as *This Angry Age*). Within a short time, René Clément, the famous director of the film, decided he needed someone to be in the lobby when his star, Silvana Mangano, exited the elevator. I was spotted and told to make believe I was reading a letter to a young woman chosen to stand next to me. I was now a bit player who picked up the handbag dropped by the star as she passed me. This small scene needed several takes, as did every scene I watched in the filming. There was a general confusion as three languages were being used constantly—Italian, French, and English—to accommodate the director and actors from three countries. All dialogue would be dubbed later, so they did not have to stick closely to any script. The time spent on each take and in between takes was tedious. It contrasted to what I remembered from my visit to Paramount's shooting of *The Ten Commandments*, directed by

Cecil B. deMille, when I spent a summer in Los Angeles selling Catholic Bibles. The Hollywood takes were far more efficiently shot, with a quicker paced production.

Silvana Mangano acted with cool aplomb, doing exactly what was expected of her. She looked great and accepted her key importance in the scene. It was exciting to give the star her dropped purse, over and over again, using pantomime and a smile, without dialogue. Then, back to reading the love letter, after delivering the retrieved purse. The young woman to whom I read the letter had to respond with attentive affection, despite the impish utterances I inserted about her bad breath and knock knees, gratuitously added to lighten my boredom in repetition. At first, I was self-conscious when the camera was on me, but by the umpteenth shooting, I relaxed enough to enjoy it. I had no dealings with Perkins during shooting, but he did join us once during a break. At the hotel location, a woman asked him how she could get into Cinecittà for a visit. Perkins suggested that she ask me, as I was an expert at that!

Perkins lived in the Hotel de Ville at the top of the Spanish Steps; I lived in a pensione at the foot of the Spanish Steps. Consequently, on occasion, we would be on the same street at the same time. He made me very nervous. Seemingly, I had the same effect on him, as he stammered whenever we met. To avoid discomfort, I would elect to cross the street or change direction. We had minimum further contact both on the set and off, but many years later, I had the chance to thank him for keeping hunger at bay by getting me that job.

My chance came during the '80s. Mia Farrow was giving a Valentine's Day dinner dance at a New York hotel. When I arrived, the producer of her Broadway show, whom I had known over the years, asked me to do a Viennese waltz with her for the television cameras. He knew my waltzing capability and thought it a good ploy for TV viewers' consumption. We accomplished our impromptu terpsichorean stint, and I was introduced to Marisa Berenson's sister, Berry, who was now the wife of Tony Perkins. (I wondered what did Rudolf Nureyev and other men in Perkins's life think of that?). After a brief conversation, I asked her to request Tony to come over to my table at his convenience, as I had a message for him. When he came to the table, I finally expressed my gratitude for his kind act in Rome years earlier. Neither of us reacted with any of the previous nervousness, perhaps because we were in a safe social atmosphere and had more confidence that came with being some years older.

In Rome, I hooked up with other American students touring around Europe. I joined them on a motor trip through Switzerland, getting back to France to cross by ferry over to England. It was pleasant to speak English all the time, without struggling with either French or Italian. London still had telltale signs of World War II—empty lots where houses had once stood and damaged portions of buildings. I was stunned by the sights of ravaged London. It brought the newsreels from World War II back to life. As Londoners were still burning coal or peat, the air was heavy with polluting fog. The sunny, carefree atmosphere of Rome was only in my memory. As in Paris, the skies were often leaden. London needed much repairing and rebuilding, but scenes of historic London—the Houses of Parliament, St. Paul's Cathedral, and the Pall Mall leading to Buckingham Palace—were in the distance. However, it was a shock to see how the war had diminished London in contrast to the magnificence of Paris and Rome.

The rooming house that I stayed in off the Bayswater Road was near an English couple I met in Rome. They introduced me to pub life, which was very merry. As in earlier times, one place still had a piano player at an upright, encouraging everyone to sing along to popular, vintage songs. Also performers would, on occasion, sing on a small stage. This colorful scene has long since disappeared from London pub life.

I, too, was to disappear, by thumbing my way to explore Scotland. St. Andrews was my destination, as I had heard about a small theater there run by Americans. The day before getting to St. Andrews, I was marooned on the road with darkness settling around me. I entered a pub and inquired about cheap lodgings. The near-by hotel was out of my financial range, but I was advised to catch some sleep in the haystacks just near the pub. It seemed the most expedient solution, so I settled into a haystack of my choice and was admiring the stars, when I noticed someone from the pub approaching, smoking a cigarette. He was whistling as though to gain my attention. I could follow him by the lit end of the cigarette, and it became clear he was searching me out by his meanderings about. I did not want to be caught in what might become an awkward situation, so I tucked myself out of view. He whistled and smoked, but I did not give a response. With the advent of dawn came the sound of a cuckoo bird and the promise of a new day on the road.

When I got to the Americans' home in St. Andrews, I told them of my adventurous night sleeping in the haystack and being woken by the cuckoo bird. Both of them were excited by my being the first person to hear the cuckoo. It was duly reported to the newspaper and printed in the next day's issue. Apparently, it is considered invaluable good fortune to report the first hearing that season of the cuckoo! When I hitchhiked back the following day, I had instant responses to my request for a ride as I was identified as the guy reporting the cuckoo. The night before, I attended a performance of *Bell, Book, and Candle* at the playhouse. When the curtain came down, I mingled with the performers. A young actor asked me to walk and talk with him afterwards. We strolled the quiet town, our footsteps echoing on the slate sidewalk. He asked me to sleep with him, but my shyness tinged with fear prevented such intimacy. It seemed like I was missing out on participating in a more active life, yet my inner restraints did not permit more.

It was time for me to get back to London. Someone in my growing network had offered me a Wednesday matinee stagehand position at the Court Theatre. There was a manpower shortage after the war that created the need for matinee temps to do stagehand work without needing a work permit. With plans to leave London shortly, I felt this opportunity was worth doing for one performance.

Laurence Olivier was performing there in *The Entertainer*, which was a further inducement to accept this temporary work. Getting to watch this great actor from back stage was truly a remarkable experience. He arrived early and worked out by himself various aspects of his performance, which was fascinating for me to observe. This was a great privilege for me, as were the experiences of my getting to the little theater in St. Andrews, the cuckoo bird, and the propositioning actor, as well.

Soon it was time to get back to Paris and the Cité Universitaire to return some luggage I had borrowed from a kind Danish student. My useful Eurail pass permitted a trip to the south of France for a very brief stay before it was to expire. I desired to investigate the charms of Nice and Cannes before returning to London and book passage to the USA.

I checked into a youth hostel near Cannes. The first day was spent sunning on the famous beach there and admiring the lovely people. Most astonishing of all was a young man in a brief white bathing suit. He was taking the sun near me on the sand, and I instigated a conversation. This Adonis was an American who was a ballet dancer with the famed Ballet Russe de Monte Carlo. My mind raced back to Moira Shearer in *The Red Shoes,* as well as to the Diaghilev productions starring his beloved Vaslav Nijinsky at this same Monte Carlo theater earlier in the century. My new friend was a link to this overwhelmingly romantic history. I yearned to have more of his company.

During the conversation, I revealed my plans to leave in two days for Paris and England to book my return to America. Also, I mentioned my staying at the youth hostel. He suggested I leave the hostel the next day and stay with him for the final evening in Cannes. I was thrilled at the proposal. It was agreed that we would meet, after his performance in Monte Carlo, at the bar of a local Cannes bistro, where he was an habitué.

This would mean I would have to check out of the hostel, to avoid paying another night's rent, and I would wait for many hours for my balletic prince charming to return from the theater in Monte Carlo. Feeling nervous, I confided to the kindly manager of the hostel my plans. He gently warned to me how precarious this arrangement seemed. Yet, I was determined to carry through my decision to spend the night with a man, finally, especially this beautiful and talented young one!

The following day, with luggage in hand, I purchased a ticket to a movie so that some of the waiting time would be spent comfortably watching a sketchily intelligible French film. Though improving daily, my French was less than fluent, which was not as vital for understanding the film as it was when my trouser leg got caught in the seat in front of me. Someone sat down and pinned the fabric of my trousers in his seat. I did not know how to explain the problem, so I sat cross-legged until he finally got up and freed my trousers. This added to my nervousness, but I felt every discomfort was worth the efforts to keep my assignation.

I appeared at the bar just before the appointed hour, but my young dancer was not there. I waited over a Pernod that I sipped very slowly, not easily affording another one. Finally, I managed to convey to the bartender for whom I was waiting. He knew the dancer and assured me he would appear after his trip from Monte Carlo.

Though late, the dancer finally showed up. Others in the bar joked with him about keeping this innocent prize waiting. He seemed a little surprised I actually kept the rendezvous but took me back to his apartment. With gentleness, he suggested we sleep in separate beds. I do not think he wanted to get involved with breaking in this virgin. He had anticipated an adept bed partner, but at his apartment I confessed my total lack of experience. To avoid complications, we spent an uneventful night. I was somewhat relieved of my anxieties, but disappointed. After my last night in Cannes, I departed in the morning as virginal as I had entered. However, this travel experience broadened me enough to move beyond the barriers I had been brought up with. I began to realize that the real world was very extraordinary and I was ready to explore it.

Ruth Warrick from A Guest in the House.

Upon returning to England, I wasted no time in booking passage to New York. It was fortunate for me that I had waited until the last moment because the famed SS *Île de France* was unexpectedly sailing, having finished necessary repairs. It was a scene from *Gentlemen Prefer Blondes*, when my tender approached in the foggy night. Suddenly, out of the dark appeared the gaily-lit ocean liner, with large light bulbs spelling out her name just as in the stage production, inviting us to board and set out for America with Lorelei Lee and friends waiting to greet us.

Little did I realize this was to be a "ghost voyage," since there were very few passengers aboard due to the sudden departure. The ship had to journey to New York promptly. Passengers were booked for the return journey. The glamorous public rooms, adorned with tapestries and etched glass paneling, were filled

Mlle. Clandestine's engagement party to an Italian duke in New York City.

with French lilies, nodding with each wave probed by the prow of the ship. The beautiful carpets invited walking upon, but the vast spaces were nearly empty of people. The sparse passengers were constantly treated to gratis champagne as one of the many efforts of the cheerful crew to please those few who chose to cross on this unusually quiet voyage.

On perusing the guest list, my heart leaped when I saw the name "Ruth Warrick." She was one of my favorite movie stars when I was a kid. Aside from *Citizen Kane*, I remembered seeing her in *The Corsican Brothers* and *Guest in the House*, as well as several others. I even had a postage stamp sized photo of her from a miniature-size collection of Hollywood stars, acquired from some forgotten source. I cautioned myself when I met this glamorous actress that I would not share my childhood fascination with her, as it might indicate the aging process all actresses avoid. The next night, when first class passengers put on their formal attire for dinner, I did it, too, but in my tourist class stateroom. I had borrowed a tuxedo from a friend's relative in London to escort a young lady to a formal party before leaving for this voyage with promises to return it later. To sneak into first class, I had to swing out over the open ocean past a barricade. I found Ruth in an emerald green silk dress. She agreed to dance with me and before I knew it, I blurted out as an ice-breaker, "You used to be my favorite actress when I was a kid!" She graciously accepted the compliment, and our friendship began. It was to last until her death, almost forty years later.

Highly intelligent, spirited with good humor and always beautifully turned out, Ruth made all of us feel privileged to be aboard this gracious ship. A few days out into the ocean, invitations arrived at various staterooms inviting the guests to attend a reception in Ruth's suite honoring Mlle. Clandestine. Upon arrival at the door of the suite, I saw, leaning against the wall, a life-sized mannequin with blond wig and rouged nipples spied through a filmy negligee worn over black lace skimpy panties. In her right hand, she held a pistol pointed downwards. In the other hand was a small bouquet of violets. It was a startling sight to behold!

The purser arrived and demanded, with good humor, to know who this stow-away was; the ship's doctor claimed to have administered all necessary inoculations for entry to America; and the captain and every man there was charmed by Mlle. Clandestine, who had recently been rescued from a barbed-wire fence at the Marché aux Puces, on the outskirts of Paris. Close up, she was very lifelike with many moveable parts, including her fingers. Ruth's husband had requested she bring back a French maid, so here was the result! (The antique revolver in her hand was another of his requests.)

On a subsequent evening, I escorted Mlle. Clandestine to dinner in the first class dining room, followed by dancing afterwards. She needed to be balanced on my feet at all times, as the only way for her to move was through my direct assistance. My frequent forays into first class deepened my friendship with Ruth and made for a very memorable voyage back to America.

A Russian aristocratic émigré artist, Maria de Kosenko, who was on board with us, was inspired shortly later, in New York, to plan a party for the engagement of Mlle. Clandestine to an "Italian duke." This duke was a rented male mannequin, complete with evening attire. The celebrants enjoyed the event, leaving the newly engaged couple embracing on a settee while they went out to dine. Mirthfully, they returned and swore that the two mannequins had tousled about in their absence!

Sedately traveling in cabin class was the handsome, elegantly attired writer, Gordon Merrick. His books were very daring for that time, as they all had gay themes and explicit sex, *The Lord Won't Mind* among them. He and I spent some pleasant times talking together. Gordon was from the Philadelphia Main Line, and he had very sophisticated experiences with elegant social circles and the aristocracy of Hollywood. He showed me gold cufflinks given to him by one of the film heartthrobs of yesteryear, Lew Ayres. It all intrigued me.

Our last night out before docking in New York City, I was with Gordon, but what transpired was a blank and remains a mystery. I awoke in my third class cabin with most of my dinner clothes off, and the bed greatly rumpled. Having had much to drink that night, I had a blackout and did not remember Gordon departing . . .

I went to visit him in New York City to have him autograph a couple of his books I found at local bookstores. His small apartment was very far west, almost at the Hudson River, in a commercial area. It surprised me that he would not be living in a more up-market location. When I entered the studio apartment, his "roommate" was showering, with the parted curtain inviting clear viewing. The young man was gorgeously built and obviously not shy about showing off his attractiveness to strangers. I was too intimidated to let the situation develop into anything, and I left shortly after Gordon signed delightful inscriptions into my book. And that was that...

Years later, when I mentioned to Ruth Warrick that I had been a virgin when she met me on the *Île de France*, she expressed surprise and said she never would have guessed.

*A family portrait: George, Flo, Helen, Bob-Eric standing
with parents seated.*

Chapter 3

THERE'S A PLACE FOR US

An orgasm at last! Wow! This thrilling, long-overdue experience opened an ever-widening boulevard of sexuality inviting exploration. As a late bloomer, I was thrilled to finally have this erotic explosion shortly after I settled back into New York City. It was a direct result of my search for Rosemary Banks, a struggling actress I knew from the summer before. A mutual friend advised me she had moved from the West Side to East 74th Street, between First and Second Avenues. Though I did not have the exact address, I searched each bank of bells of every tenement until I hit upon her name. Excited with triumph, I climbed up the three flights of stairs, through the dingy hallway, to her door. We screamed with delight upon seeing each other!

Rosemary had given me twenty dollars before I sailed for Europe to buy her a bottle of French perfume. It was her way of giving me much-needed spending money. I surprised Rosemary with the specified fragrance, Écusson. As I had no place to live in the city at that point, Rosemary introduced me to a theater director who lived on the floor directly below her. He was preparing to leave the next day for an out-of-town engagement during the impending summer.

Royal Hubert was going to direct a summer stock production and was glad to have someone such as myself sublet his minimally furnished apartment. He was engaging and attractive, and maybe ten years older than I, but who wasn't? We spent this night before his departure enjoying our spontaneous mutual attraction. I was over-ripe for the plucking, and he did not need much to seduce me into the sheeted fields. My ejaculation was instantaneous when I felt him inside of me. He told me it was normal for that to happen on the first time. It was a surprise; it was wonderful; it was marvelous!

Also living in this tenement was a gay couple, one of whom was rehearsing a theater scene with Rosemary for her Uta Hagen class at the Herbert Berghof studios. He was very much like Van Johnson, and he took a particular interest in me. Before I knew it, we were engaged in a very sweaty, hot summer tussle.

The dam of my repression seemed to have broken, and I was carried away with the flow. How regrettable and disappointing for me, when he dutifully returned to his lover waiting in their near-by apartment. Just new to the scene, I learned it was how open gay "interludes" worked.

It was easy to get a job serving food, soft drinks, and desserts at the counter of various local Walgreen's drugstores. The tips were good and I did not need much to keep me going financially. I enjoyed the variation in

Ruth Warrick (seated) and young hopefuls
(Steve, Helen, Rosemary and me).

changing locations and customers according to the management's requirements. At an Upper West Side counter, I was thrilled to serve Diana Adams, whom I saw so often dance Balanchine ballets at the City Center. At a Times Square location, during the early hours, hookers would take a break and get a pick-me-up. Sometimes that was literal. Once, a guy asked me where he could find an easy lay. I indicated a usual customer sitting at the end of the counter. She took him across the street to her cheap hotel and the request was filled.

As the hot summer progressed in New York, and the director returned to claim his apartment, I decided to go to Provincetown on Cape Cod. I did a brief stint on Long Island as a Good Humor man, selling ice cream to suburban kids. This was not a very satisfying way to earn a living, turning corner after corner ringing musical bells ad nauseam to attract customers. It was very lonely living in a cheap room on the nowhere outskirts of Riverhead, and a far cry from the liveliness and natural beauty of Cape Cod. The appeal of sea-washed beaches and the colorful town of Provincetown induced me to finish out the summer in a better atmosphere. I got a job at the Moors Restaurant as well as an inexpensive room nearby on Bradford Street. The money to go to graduate school would be better earned there, though I was not certain it would be enough. (The thought of student loans, if they were available then, or scholarships did not enter my brain.) What was enough, by far, was to be out in the ocean breezes, walking along the dunes when not working hard as a waiter. I felt very happy to be in such a carefree environment, making money and new friends.

Having entered into the lion's den of active sexuality, my notion of myself began to change. Though I had heard people say I was attractive, I truly did not believe it deep within me. Enjoying the physicality of my work as a waiter together with being in nature, exercising by walking long distances along the ocean, inspired me into believing in myself more. I was aware that people noticed me when I walked down a street, and I began to understand that I had an attractive vitality together with natural good looks that would be admired as well as desired.

The season was coming to a close. I loved the vigor of being twenty, being trim from demanding work, and being bronzed with hair bleached by the sun and sea. I even had some money saved. All this felt wonderful, but I knew my cash fell short of the amount needed for graduate school expenses. My hopes that my brother might help me with the balance needed did not work out. He and his distant, disapproving wife were not supportive of my plans and held their money in closed fists. My sister, Flo, had an alcoholic husband who created a constant drain on financial resources. It was up to me to work this tuition puzzlement out.

Carnegie Institute agreed to postpone my attendance for one year, for which I was very grateful. However, it was truly disappointing to put off until the next September my going to graduate school. It was time to organize my life. I had to earn more money. Flo suggested that I brush up my typing, as she had done at the YWCA on Lexington Avenue, to enhance my office skills. She had worked at U.S. Plywood Corporation at an earlier time, so I decided to apply there, too. It was nicely placed on West 44th Street, near the theater district. I could imagine leaving work, getting a bite to eat, and then continuing into a theater for a performance. The corporation owned the entire building; it was about five stories high, but not very wide. I would guess it was built just before the war, around 1940. It sustained a modest employment roster of perhaps fifty people.

The employment officer was an attractive young man who thought I could be a useful addition to the company. I had to take an entrance exam, but the officer made it clear that he would give me extra time to deal with the test and help me pass all the necessary requirements. This was not necessary, as the test was not difficult. It was leisurely administered in a corner of his office. When it was completed, I scored a high passing grade. After an interview with my future boss, Ilsa Marum, the executive secretary to the export department head, it was decided that I could start the next day. In celebration, I was invited by my new pal in the employment office to join him after work for drinks and dinner. I acquiesced, and even agreed to stay the night at a near-by hotel with him, so we would be convenient to the office the next day. . . . This was very merry and gay! I felt a little like Barbara Stanwyck's character in *Baby Face,* naughtily making my way upwards in the business world.

Through an ad in the *New York Times* real estate section, I found a pleasant room for rent on the top of a building on East 76th Street, near Lexington Avenue. I loved the view from the large roof terrace of the cupolas of the Saint Jean Baptiste church on the corner, as well as of the spacious panorama of the city all around. Though the bathroom was shared by some other men renting what were once extra maids' rooms, my room was comfortable and inexpensive. Also, there was a respected privacy and quietude that made for a well-behaved fraternity atmosphere.

If I kept things low profile, it was possible to entertain, both on the enormous terrace as well as in my tiny room. That winter of 1957, while sitting through a Queens College Christmas performance of Handel's *Messiah,* I became aware that the utterly desirable baritone soloist, John Reardon, was continually eyeing me from the stage. When I went backstage to greet my college friend, Helen Athos, who was a violinist with the orchestra, John introduced himself. It seemed polite to invite him over for a Cinzano. Though I found him charming and alarmingly good looking, I was put off by his hirsute body. No preference for a physical type had developed in my mind, but I learned furry was not it. However, we continued a restrained friendship until his untimely death.

Each morning, I would walk— through the man-made wonder of Central Park—to work at U.S. Plywood, stopping to feed bread to the ducks in the lake. A St. Francis-in-the-making, I enjoyed the atmospheric walk through that part of Manhattan. During the snowy winter months, I felt an urgency to feed the birds around the lake, as I imagined that foraging for food in the snow would be a great challenge for my feathered friends. I would help them through this rough period. How great it felt to stretch my legs in walking the significant distance from the East '70s to the West '40s. With the city bordering the edges, the different views through the park—carefully planned out by Frederick Law Olmsted—were lovely, whether dusted with snow or abounding in green with the advent of spring. These long walks stimulated reveries of Paris. There seemed a perceptible connection between the two cities, especially on snowy days. My happiness at achieving my modest sexual freedom during these walks added to the exhilaration. I felt alive and well, in tune with nature and the pulse of the city.

Ilse soon became Illa, and a growing friendship between us developed over the years to come—long after I departed for graduate school via summer stock. She shared a comfortable apartment with another German woman, Margot Carey. Both of the women, in their fifties, were a refugees from Hitler's Cologne, Germany. Illa was very plain looking, with glasses, and unaffectedly direct in manner. She smoked lots of cigarettes and had a distressing cough as a result. Despite her modest appearance, she had a biting humor that never ceased to amuse me. Margot was more Dietrich-elegant with an attitude, sporting blond hair swept into a French knot. Unlike Illa, Margot was always turned out in a smart dress or suit. They both welcomed me often into their cozy, European-flavored home. Margot was proud of her Emil Nolde watercolors, and Illa had a gorgeous etched colored vase from Bavaria I would have been very pleased to own. The women plied me with their home cooking, often influenced by German recipes. Though they did not drink much, there was always scotch, wines, and liqueurs to embellish the meal. My libations there were many and much enjoyed. The women became like aunts to me, making my life in the city more agreeable. On one occasion, I had an extra pair of trousers with me when I arrived for a dinner with the ladies. At an appropriate time for departure, I took the elevator down to West 69th Street, forgetting to take my other trousers with me. Illa opened her eighth floor window above me and loudly shouted "Bob, you forgot your pants!" They sailed slowly down, having filled with air almost like a balloon. We wondered what the neighbors thought! This friendship with the two women was to carry on for many years to come, long after I quit U.S. Plywood to prepare for a summer working at the Lakes Region Playhouse.

My transformative European jaunt was under my belt as well as the summer of working at odd jobs. Now, after U.S. Plywood hours, I immersed myself in the cornucopia of New York's performing arts scene. The dance world was abundantly blessed with thrilling works produced by American Ballet Theater, New York City Ballet, and Martha Graham, as well as works by my soon-to-be-friend Alvin Ailey. Zizi Jeanmaire and her husband, Roland Petit, had titillated me with their Ballet de Paris while I was in France; now they appeared on Broadway. On one occasion, while waiting to be admitted to the dressing rooms backstage, Roland Petit pointedly came to stand directly in front of me, gazing deeply into my eyes. It reminded me of the intimidating interchange I had with Sir Michael Redgrave at Cinecittà. I did not encourage him further but explained I had an appointment to see one of his dancers. Through my acquaintance with André Prokovsky from Paris days, I managed to insinuate myself into meeting and fraternizing with those dancers. In contrast to the straight and dull André, the other dancers from the Ballet de Paris were gay and lively. I was intrigued by their off-stage antics and delighted to be in their company.

It was backstage where I met Sylvia Tysick, a young ballerina from Canada, who was to become a long time-friend. She was a good friend of one Petit's dancers, and we managed to get together when she was not in Canada, as a featured dancer on a CBC television show.

The London Festival Ballet came to town, too. John Gilpin, the principal dancer, and his mentor, Anton Dolin, joined this coterie of dancers with whom I spent idle moments in awe and admiration! I invited all of them for a drink on the terrace of my "penthouse," and I have a photo of us having a merry time there, with the cupola of the church in the background. Dolin introduced me to Alexandra Danilova backstage in the theatre where she and Tony Roberts were appearing in a play. "Choura," as she was called, was a Russian-born classical ballet dancer who performed for Diaghilev and had been in a common law relationship with George Balanchine. Choura appeared often in my life in the years to come, acquainting me with other Russian dancers and regaling me with fascinating stories from her balletic history. She had a cute way of describing the Balanchine connection as "I was, how do you say? . . . his 'common' wife."

*Anton Dolin, director of the London Festival Ballet (right) and his premier dancer,
John Gilpin (3rd from left) join dancers from Ballet de Paris on my terrace.*

One thing led to another, and the circle of acquaintances active on the stage
grew à la six degrees of separation into ever widening proportions. I was honing
my networking skills, and my celebratory drinks were increasing with the fervor
of my expanding horizons.

A chance meeting in Manhattan reconnected me with Lucia Pisacani, a
Queens College student who had graduated the class before mine. We had never
clicked in school. She was very academic minded and seemed overly serious; I
was fraternity driven at one point, then theater obsessed later. Now, we found
each other very good company. We often sent each other funny cards or letters
in envelopes decorated in colored whimsies of our own inventions. With growing
frequency, we had fun either in sending each other things or going about town.

Lucia appeared more sophisticated since college days. Her brunette hair was worn straight to the shoulders, the ends gently curled. She had an attractive, slim figure and often wore becoming, fitted outfits, usually navy blue with ¾" heels either blue or black. She enjoyed a quiet elegance. Her large dark eyes were lively in accordance with her easy smile. Her handsome carriage was agreeable with my own presentation to the world. We made a nice couple.

We began going to foreign films and having meals together. Often, Lucia came to visit me to have a Cinzano in my penthouse room before going out for a meal. She met Henry, who lived just across the hall from me, and the three of us would enjoy stimulating conversations about books or recent stage productions or world events. It was great fun and spending time together became a natural pastime—so much so that our shared experiences nurtured a quickly budding romance.

In sharp contrast to my times with the agreeable and stimulating Lucia were my lunches in the Central Park Zoo with Dr. Frederick Stern and his coterie of young actors and dancers, all of whom he treated free of charge. (This bit of charity afforded him a rich source of voyeurism, for sure!) The group was very merry and redolent with flirtations. I expanded my acquaintances in the theater world, especially with an Englishman who was personal aide to the then-star of *My Fair Lady*, Edward Mulhare, the replacement for Rex Harrison. Noel Davis invited me to visit backstage, often in the star's dressing room. On one occasion, I was offered a glass of whisky and soda while sitting in Edward's dressing room. In came Sally Ann Howes, his co-star. She asked if anyone would like a glass of champagne. Noel indicated that I didn't need one as I had a scotch in hand. I quickly suggested that the scotch was in my left hand, but my right hand was free! Yes, my alcoholic tendencies were becoming unleashed at an alarming rate!

Though it was enthralling to participate with Freddy's boys and be backstage with Noel, soaking in the tuneful, hit show in operation, it was also pleasurable to spend lots of time with Lucia, trying to make the mantle of straight-hood a comfortable fit. Perhaps it was my ingrained Lutheranism together with the social pressures of the time that expected/demanded me to be straight, along with what I thought was a sincere, budding love for Lucia, that motivated me. Our relationship was growing stronger and the question of marriage became a reality. I felt that with a commitment to Lucia, my other fanciful thoughts would diminish and disappear. Accordingly, I rented a ground floor apartment in an East '70s tenement that we could use after the knot was tied. Upon leaving my bachelor's pad; the die was cast.

One white lie was to grow into a big crimson one. We skirted the notion of my being gay, but tacitly acknowledged the possibility. I did not mention Noel or Freddy's boys at the zoo or the summer stock director who induced my first orgasm, or . . . rather we both enjoyed each other's company over dinner, a foreign film or stage production. Sex was only vaguely discussed, both of us agreeing not to indulge ourselves in it before marriage. (It was so Doris Day—after she became a virgin!) We hoped for the best, ignoring warning signs from within as well as the outside world.

Lucia showed me a poison pen letter her family had received about my unsuitability as husband material. I had met them in their apartment over a storefront in Forest Hills, Queens. They were a simple Italian couple from

Abruzzi, Italy, who came to make their way in America. This letter sealed their disapproval of me, causing a rift of sadness for us all. We were both shocked at the vicious intentions of the perpetrator, but it brought us closer together. My mind explored the myriad possibilities of who the sender could be. It was typed on a machine with a couple of faulty letters, which was a clue but hard to follow up on. I contemplated my mean spirited sister-in-law or the young guy who rented a room in the same house where I lived when at Queens College, who bought my very expensive tape recorder, and sundry others who might have wanted to make problems for me for whatever reason. Many people knew Lucia's last name and that she lived with her parents in Forest Hills. The address was easy to obtain. Was it someone I knew while at Queens College, or a more recent

Lucia and I cutting the wedding cake.

acquaintance? Possibly it was a colleague of Lucia? My brain worked overtime seeking out enemies.

Despite cautionary words from her good friend who worked in her office, whom I had met on occasions, Lucia and I proceeded to make plans for a simple Justice of the Peace spring wedding ceremony. It was held in Yonkers with Flo as matron of honor and Henry, a floor mate from my penthouse days, as best man. My brother, George, and his wife, Ellie, attended, as did my father and mother. As expected, no one from Lucia's family attended.

After the ceremony, we all went to my East 75th Street apartment for food supplied by my mother and lots of champagne. Champagne became my answer, remedy and solution to everything. When we were left to ourselves, we went to the Russian ballet film of *Romeo & Juliet*. This was our "honeymoon" and perhaps our first marital mistake. We should have taken a real honeymoon, away and alone. Maybe then we could have established a better physical relationship, breaking down my frigid response to women. In the past, I had some frightening experiences with women forcing themselves on me. Near rape events with many cougar and co-ed, hungry, determined women lusting for me made me very psychologically distressed when approaching intimacy with females. Lucia was different and I trusted her. We loved each other and enjoyed each other's company, but my fumbling attempts in an alcoholic haze on our wedding night were a failure. We had a big bed problem to overcome.

Lucia and I planned to move to Pittsburgh in the fall of 1958, so that I could finally go to graduate school and get my Master of Fine Arts degree in theater directing. She would keep her job in Manhattan until then, while I worked at the Lakes Region Playhouse in New Hampshire doing summer stock to enhance my professional life.

The time quickly arrived to leave for the two-month-plus summer commitment. It was exhilarating to get settled into a routine, with new acquaintances sharing the making of theater in this small locale on Lake Winnipesaukee in New Hampshire. The young apprentices were from various places, but all had hopes of pursuing some sort of future in the world of theater. The Lakes Region Playhouse had a successful running record for more than a decade. Each of the five productions billed for the summer had a well-known star, or was a popular musical or comedy suitable for light summer entertainment. Situated away from the town, the white clapboard theater probably sat about 400 people. It was close to the lake so summer folk, transient tourists, and some local residents made up the audience.

Summer stock performers and crew.

I was paid a weekly sum, more than enough to cover all living expenses with some money left over. I rented a modest studio bungalow within walking distance from the theater. It had a screened porch allowing visitors to sip ice tea or something stronger, while talking and visiting.

Most of the work at the theater began promptly each morning. We were kept busy making the scenery, the props, and focusing the lights. All costumes were brought in by each transient company of performers. After building and painting, there were technical rehearsals. Each play had a single set and ran for two weeks. The director had previously blocked the stage movements and business, which was put into effect at each theater along the booking. Often, he was not there at all during the run. Sometimes, someone came along to monitor the performers in following the prescribed directions set by the director. Some of the productions recruited help from the crew at the theater to perform small parts or duties. I played the glib, loquacious private in *No Time for Sergeants* and the dresser for Hal March in *Cat on a Hot Tin Roof*, for example.

One of the most looked-forward-to attractions was the production starring the incomparable, legendary Tallulah Bankhead. The great day arrived but the

Star was hours late. The entire stage crew at the Lakes Region Playhouse for the upcoming production of *House on the Rocks* waited, and waited, with mounting anticipation of finally getting a good look at an icon of theater history—Tallulah Bankhead.

As famous for her theatrical antics as her outstanding performances on stage and screen, she continued to capture the attention of audiences far and wide. After playing Regina in *The Little Foxes* and giving a memorable performance in the film *Lifeboat* more than a decade before, Tallulah's career devolved into a sex and alcohol sodden parody of herself rife with outrageous camp.

Tallulah at summer stock.

Tallulah arrived with a police escort. She had met the cops in a bar on route to the summer stock playhouse. With a flurry of activity, she burst through the front door and strode through the house to the stage. Even though it was summer, she wore a mink coat that was soon flung on a chair on the stage. This vintage actress, after mounting the stage, proceeded to slink around. Glancing at the spotlights to make certain the jells were her specified bastard amber and lavender, she checked to see if the cigarette boxes were filled with Craven A, then she swept into the wings to descend to her dressing room to deposit her makeup kit, and quickly departed.

Everything we had imagined of her was verified—larger than life arm gestures, a deep, gravelly voice with dramatic tones, and a total conviction of her being the star. The two weeks of performances were going to be a romp, indeed.

Tallulah was full of surprises. One was that she placed her makeup on ice. Applying it very cold, she believed, tightened the skin. I wondered how long that could last under the heat of the stage lights, but that was her ritual, and, for some brief time, I would like to think that she felt transformed. Without the aid of a wig, Tallulah appeared on stage with her hair the same as it was during the daytime—shoulder length, slightly waved. She had a mannerism of sweeping her hair away from her face with her right hand, often accompanied with a deep chuckle or a Dah-h-h-ling."

It did not surprise us that Tallulah enjoyed her bourbon. There was a lovely young female apprentice to whom Tallulah took a shine. She requested that this girl bring her things, including a glass for her refreshments. This was done with great trepidation on the girl's part. Also, one had heard about Tallulah's aversion to wearing clothes. She often stripped completely when in her dressing room, leaving the door wide open. It was difficult not to notice the abundance of body wrinkles that came with advancing age.

"Son of a bitch" was her term of endearment for me. When she heard my voice back stage, she got excited, thinking it was a dear friend of hers who had arrived to visit her. "Oh, you Son of a Bitch!" she would exclaim in her deep, exaggerated theatrical voice when the error was realized. I adored this moniker of distinction, however, and enjoyed fooling her.

House on the Rocks was packaged to travel around, hence there was no need for rehearsals other than some technical adjustments. Tallulah was always prepared before curtain time and created no Diva-like scenes. She took her time preparing for her entrance, and, once "on," gave the audience and crew the delight of her presence. The play was hardly outstanding, but she was weaving her magical touch into the theatrical evening. I neither remember the plot of the drama, nor the other actors in the cast. It was all TALLULAH!

During the first act, a record was played on the on-stage phonograph as part of the stage business. The song was sung on the record by Tallulah: "Did I remember to tell you that I loved you . . . to tell you I adored you . . .." I spent idle moments singing this to myself, dreamily relating to the play and the actress. (This was not unlike my singing Denise Darcel's song after she gave me her Channel No. 5 drenched key at the Paramount Theater when I was a teenager.)

During the last act, Tallulah wore a crinoline under a long black gown. She usually rushed downstage to take her bow, lifting the skirt in her excitement to receive the enthusiastic applause. When lifted in front, the crinoline tilted upwards filling with air. Dimly revealing her thighs, it hinted that the star did not wear underwear! It was done is such a flurry of spontaneous good humor that, in the thrill of the moment, those sitting in the front rows might be too startled to be offended or register what they had indeed seen. Somehow, it was befitting the outrageousness of the star. Her performance was that of Tallulah the personality, not Tallulah playing a part. Unlike her earlier career, people came to see her playing herself.

Tallulah enjoyed the services of a maid, who tended to her when Tallulah was not in the theater. On occasions, the maid and I enjoyed some conversation through which I had hoped to glean some understanding of the Bankhead mystique, but without success.

Tallulah was a woman needing attention. She was also highly addicted to both cigarettes and alcohol. Throughout my life, her plight was something I tried to avoid in my existence, though my own attraction and growing dependence on alcohol threatened a firm grip on me at that point. I wanted to avoid the excessive drinking I had witnessed in my father. I swore it would never happen to me. Yet, I noticed how much easier it was for me to be with other people, especially prominent people, when I drank. To my consternation, I used this crutch increasingly to overcome my insecurities.

The same shyness that kept me from contacting Alice B. Toklas in Paris prevented my visiting Tallulah at her East 60s town house during the'60s. I walked past it on occasion and was aware of her probably being alone within. I did not feel adequate to request her attentions. She had imparted to me a sense of the larger-than-life outlandishness one could fill an existence with, together with an implicit admonition about alcohol abuse, which should have raised a red flag to me. I chose to revel in her behavior and adopt it as my own, bolstered by a flow of alcohol that was to continue for at least another couple of decades.

Alcohol consumption played a major role in the life of Veronica Lake, as well. She appeared in a production of *Cat on a Hot Tin Roof* that summer at the Playhouse. Her Maggie was unique: Along with her stage husband, Brick, she played it on crutches, having broken one leg prior to production. My entree into her company was to secretly secure for her cans of beer. Despite her husband's request not to give "Ronnie" any alcohol, her cajoling won me over. I was appointed the dresser for Hal March of TV talk show fame, who played Maggie's husband, Brick. Hence, I had every reason to be available back stage during performances and to slip her a "fix."

Our special relationship won me the invitation to visit Veronica Lake and her husband at their lakeside retreat one day. Enhancing my networking abilities, my interest in the visiting theater personalities was intense. Because I was criticized by my stage crew colleagues for making friends with the star, a promised ride to deliver me to the lakeside rendezvous did not materialize. I had to walk the distance, all dressed up to socialize with the Hollywood legend. Ronnie no longer looked the way she had on screen, with long platinum blond tresses brushed to one side almost hiding one eye. Now, her hair was bobbed and an uninteresting blond. Her figure had filled out, no longer the sylph temptress. Her voice was still quite haunting and unique. However, unlike all the other stars who had come to the Lakes Region Playhouse, Veronica Lake treated us all to a closing night Bar-B-Q on the lake. She had a generous nature and was very vulnerable, as well. When she turned her head to a certain angle in the firelight, I could see the Veronica Lake from Hollywood days. I was thrilled, and so grateful to her.

Veronica was later to take a job at the George Washington Hotel in the Murray Hill area of New York as a waitress. Down at the heels, abandoned by her last husband, she was available to attend parties as a fag hag and garner drinks in exchange for being scorned as a fallen Hollywood star. How I detested those insensitive queens, feeling superior to the ill-fated movie actress on the skids. I disdained attending these gatherings. Worse was to come in Chicago, where she was beaten up by a mob for owing money. It was a complete extinction of a star who once shone so brightly on the Silver Screen.

Every two weeks, another production would be "on the boards." On occasion, a director would commandeer my services in a speaking role. I would protest that I was not an actor, but I was assured that the director's talents would take care of it all. One time, while kneeling on the floor fastening something, an actress asked me what my middle name was. I told her "Eric," to which she suggested, "Never use Bob again!" Dazzled by this glamorous woman, I became Eric for the rest of my journey.

This same actress had flirted with me, but was obviously very taken with a young leading man, Wyatt Cooper. Wyatt had very strong southern charm, and he induced me to suspend my shyness by visiting the room where he slept with a couple of other actors. Highly determined, I steeled myself to do what did not seem at all in my nature. Stripping nude, I wore only my raincoat and proceeded to seek out my obsession. At his bedside, I slipped out of my raincoat and lay down beside him. We had a quiet, but thrilling discovery that dark New Hampshire night, careful not to disturb the other sleeping actors.

There were other sensual adventures during that summer stock summer. However, daily work assignments in preparation for the next incoming show and the various jobs during the performances kept me very busy. While working backstage, there was one very attractive young man from the Midwest who captured my imagination. Handsome, blond and well-built, David Halliday was always singing Tony's songs from Leonard Bernstein's *West Side Story,* which recently opened to great success in New York. "There's a Place for Us" was a constant favorite. (It gave further significance to the Broadway performance when I attended it after the summer, and later still in London as David's guest when he played Tony, the lead! "There's a Place for Us," indeed!) David had arrived in a hearse he converted with his girlfriend into an amusing vehicle. They both worked on the tech crew. I assumed this dreamboat was straight, so my attentions were focused elsewhere. I was the only apprentice in our group who made an effort to befriend and hang around with the cast of the various shows and was criticized by my peers for being a "star fucker." This did not deter me from getting as close as possible to those wondrous stage folk.

The iconic Groucho Marx became a focus for my attention during the run of his theatrical vehicle. He brought levity to the playhouse, but made sure others did not vie with him in that area. A supporting actress had devised a costume addition that she felt would create a mirthful outburst from the audience. During a dress rehearsal, I was joined by a few co-workers to sit in the audience to watch. When the actress made her entrance, we all guffawed loudly. Groucho eliminated her amusing costume as a result! Clearly he was the generator for laughs, not the supporting actress!

That same actress invited me to a festive luncheon planned by Groucho for his cast members. Groucho had his real-life young wife there, as well as the middle-aged woman who played his wife in the play. During the meal, a fan approached

Groucho, expressing his admiration for the great comedian, and extended his hand. Groucho looked at the proffered hand, placed a napkin over his own hand, and shook hands! Groucho then introduced his stage wife as his real wife, adding further humor to the event.

A very serious tone was added to the season's offerings with James Mason appearance together with his daughter in a little known melodrama. When not acting, much of Mason's time was spent playing the piano. He was taciturn and did not invite friendly conversation.

Aside from the amazing, dominant Groucho Marx, the stellar James Mason, and the bewitching Wyatt Cooper, it was Veronica Lake and the inimitable Tallulah Bankhead who were the major attractions for me that summer. These two actresses utterly captured my complete attention while they were in residence.

The summer stock season was drawing to a close with a play featuring Ann Sheridan. I nodded to her as I took an early leave to drive to Kennebunkport for a cheerful holiday with some friends. I recall eating raw oysters, reclining on some rocks by the ocean, while Noel Davis sipped champagne out of my navel. He and other friends had driven up to New Hampshire to collect me for a jaunt to the ocean. Following that, we drove on to the Shakespeare Festival in Connecticut, where I was to meet Lucia after a busy summer apart. My traveling companion had deposited me there, but first shaved my crotch and applied anti-crab lotion. It was his perverse way of indicating proprietary privilege. What an astonishing way to greet my new wife, and what a foreshadowing of things to come!

With my head buzzing from the star-filled escapades during the summer, Lucia and I moved to Pittsburgh. We found a small apartment over a store in the Schenley Park area, walking distance to school. Lucia was very disappointed by our living in apartment over a store. It was a distasteful remembrance of her family's apartment in Forest Hills. However, seeing how the price, space, and location were so desirable, she assented to the arrangement.

The drama school was in the same three-story, dark red-brick building housing the Art Department on the top floor. Trees and lawns surrounded all the buildings, creating a pleasant atmosphere. My graduate work in directing commenced, and Lucia found office employment in downtown Pittsburgh, not dissimilar from what she had been doing in New York. Lucia and I were full of hopes for a bright future, even though there was no improvement in our sexual compatibility.

As well as classes in directing, I had theater courses including costume history, lighting techniques, make-up practice, acting and movement exercises, and reading great theater literature. There were plays produced in which I was expected to act, and additional directing projects I had to create as part of my training.

Carnegie Tech had probably a few hundred undergraduate theater students, but only ten Master of Fine Arts theater students. Being slightly older and a graduate student gave me a certain cachet and distinction with the undergraduates, which stroked my ego. Both students and faculty assumed that I came with assorted distinguished credits. Mary Morris, long associated with Eugene O'Neill as his mistress, was the prominent acting teacher. As I knew how to walk and position myself on stage, she used me as a model; because of her confidence in my abilities, she cast me in her production of *The River Line*. Mostly, I was adept at innuendo and name-dropping to bolster my sense of accomplishment. Being married further created an aura quite confusing to many on campus.

My thesis was to be on the Noh Drama, created for the Japanese elite. In college I had read about this recondite drama with interest. I had viewed a film of Noh Drama at the Museum of Modern Art, which stimulated further investigation. I had seen Kabuki, but that was not as compelling to me. The department head disapproved of my choice of thesis on the grounds it would not serve me in my future career in the theater. It suited my sensibilities, however. Studies in Zen, the tea ceremony, and other esoteric Japanese practices were part of understanding this form of drama; they filled me with a peculiar satisfaction. I took to walking at dawn along the railroad tracks, contemplating nirvana while picking cherry blossoms.

These studies and activities at school did not help nurture a happy marriage. Lucia managed to attend one performance of a play that I had directed, *X*, about retribution to Nazi informants. Her response was warm and supportive, but resentments were fostered by both of us. She knew that working on theater projects took priority over our having dinner or a movie together, always. That "always" seemed really too long and continual time for her to wait. Our relationship was not gelling properly.

Efforts to cement our marriage seemed fruitless. Much of the trouble was due to my resistance to being married and the distractions at school. I had not been unfaithful to Lucia while in Pittsburgh, but I was constantly tempted. I had hurtled into marriage expecting a miracle to change me, but I acknowledged to myself that I did not want to change. As Christmas approached, I yearned to get away from both married life and Pittsburgh. Noel had suggested we spend New Year's Eve together in New York. Lucia did not care to go to New York for just a few days, and a longer period such as I planned was too long for her to leave her job. She got Pittsburgh Symphony tickets for the time I planned to be away, so I accepted the invitation to stay at Edward Mulhare's apartment with Noel. I got on well with Mulhare, who would be there part of the time but on holiday the rest of it. I imagined Noel would involve me with the colorful people in *My Fair Lady* and other glitterati on the New York scene. Little did I know there would be a tremendous event in store for me—one that would alter the course of my life!

Leonard Bernstein, the dynamic conductor of the New York Philharmonic and composer of *West Side Story, On the Town,* and later *Candide*, together with serious concert pieces, had just returned from a triumphant tour in Russia. He was the talk and the toast of the town. Fifth Avenue shops had blow-up photos of him in windows, and he was honored in a welcome-home parade packed with much of New York.

Noel carefully explained to me how the handsome conductor/composer was a great friend of the opera star Jennie Tourel. She had helped him early in his career, and he was invaluable to her career once he was established. Mme. Tourel had invited Noel to bring me to tea in her West 58th Street apartment.

Always agreeable to meeting a distinguished performer, I put on my best behavior and paid court to the great lady. Everything about her seemed round: her plump fingers with several rings, her cheerful countenance, and her full figure. She regaled us with amusing stories about her earlier career. Once, she was engaged to perform a role familiar to her at an opera house, but without rehearsals. Her entrance was from the door of a horse drawn carriage, and when she was blinded by the stage lights, she had moments of deep concern about not having any vision with which to perform her role. The diva entertained us with snatches from *Dido*

Leonard Bernstein introduces himself.

& Aeneas. "When I am laid . . . laid . . ." she sang, enjoying her innuendos.

I was charmed, and then very excited when she invited us both to attend a supper for Maestro Bernstein to be held here in her apartment. Edward Mulhare was invited, as well, but would be out of town that night. He suggested we take his close friend, Jean, a beautiful young woman who was the wife of a Canadian conductor.

The three of us went to the supper, full of anticipation over meeting this compelling legend in his own lifetime, Leonard Bernstein. I was determined to make him take notice of me amidst the adoring throng. Perfectly attired in dinner clothes, the living/breathing god saw us enter and approached. When he greeted Noel and Jean, I turned my back on him purposely. When I heard him ask Noel, "Who's the guy?" I knew I was on the right track, and with false bravado spun around with a bowl of nuts in my hand. "Nuts, anyone?" I queried.

In *sotto voce,* Noel said shortly later, "I think he wants a four-some . . . " Jean and I moved ourselves over to the den, where the Maestro had a clear view of us. He was seated on a couch with everyone crowding around him, many sitting on the floor at his feet. We ignored them all and danced cheek to cheek to soft music on the radio. He glanced at us appraisingly. Jean whispered in my ear, "I think he wants a three-some."

After supper, I noticed Lenny leave the room to visit the bathroom. When he returned, he came over and sat next to me. Drenched in cologne, he clutched my inner thigh as a young Israeli woman sang some songs *a cappella*. I knew then he did not want a four-some, or a three-some. He wanted a two-some!

It was a puzzlement how I could maneuver Lenny away from his worshipping crowd. There were several Russians who didn't want the evening to end. Our hostess seemed relieved when the last of us left with Lenny, and she requested we not keep Lenny up too much later as he had a concert the next afternoon at Carnegie Hall.

The Russians, Noel, Jean, and I followed the Maestro around the corner to the Osborne, where he and his wife, Felicia Montealegre, had an apartment. He also kept a separate studio there, which served as an excellent place to continue our revels. I was impatient about how the late evening, now early morning, partying would resolve itself? The Russians held out until the very last gasp. Sadly, we had to disperse, but the Maestro asked Noel and me to sit in his box at Carnegie Hall later that afternoon at the concert.

Back at the apartment, Noel was enraged over my showing such attentiveness to Lenny, ranting about my bad behavior towards himself. All those drinks and heady excitement caused me to feel nauseous, especially under the barrage of insults from Noel. He seemed pleased when, in distress, I vomited into his toilet, but then furious when I moved into Edward Mulhare's vacated bedroom. I locked the door behind me, ignoring his rattling of the doorknob and demands to open up.

Later that morning, I called a friend to request a bed for the evening, as I would not tolerate any further verbal attacks from Noel. We partook of a coffee and some light repast in a frigid atmosphere and dressed for our appearance at Carnegie Hall. I had packed my clothes and checked them before entering Lenny's box at the concert. I felt very proud to be sitting in the Maestro's box as his guest. My sense of arrival into the glamorous world of celebrity was tremendous.

After the concert, we greeted Lenny in the Green Room and congratulated him on his conducting. At the moment when I was to leave, I felt let down: He said nothing to me about getting together. I turned and started to retreat from the scene, when Lenny called me back. He said he would like to call me later. Thrilled and excited, I informed him of my new contact number and was startled when he made no attempt to write it down. What if he did not remember it? What if...?

Early evening, the phone rang and my host announced it was Leonard Bernstein for me. What a fabulous memory the great man possessed, but then again, a conductor was used to memorizing scores. Why not remember a telephone number? He regretted he would not be able to see me later in the evening because his doctor told him complete rest was mandatory. The conductor had, unbeknownst to the audience, suffered a mild heart attack while onstage. Shortly afterwards, I learned that Jennie Tourel blamed me in particular for precipitating Lenny's heart attack by encouraging non-stop partying until the early hours prior to his concert. He did not lose his place in the score while conducting, but would not be able to pursue his overactive life for the immediate days ahead. Lenny was off to an island in the Caribbean.

I suggested being in touch when next I was town, and wished him a speedy recovery. It was a bitter disappointment, but did offer me a strong sense of validation. I was thrilled that a stellar personality could take an interest in me sexually, and maybe even become a friend and colleague. So much so, that I decided then and there, in all fairness to Lucia, I would ask her to file for a Mexican divorce. I was not going to be the straightened out, dutiful husband we both had thought possible. She deserved to pursue a happy, complete life with a real husband. Perhaps her future would be more fulfilling with the benefit of children. I felt I could best pursue my path on my own, being available to the attentive world I was discovering. After my graduate work was completed, I could apply my networking to begin a pursuit of a rich theatrical career.

I had been skating on thin ice to fall through a hole into the cold waters of Reality. A sense of blame and guilt gnawed at me in the immediate years to follow. I had involved Lucia in a compromising situation, despite both of us hoping for some magical resolution. When I could manage it, I wrote Lucia a note that enclosed a check for $1,000, which was worth considerably more then in the Sixties than now. I suggested she use it for something other than practical things like a dentist bill, groceries, or other everyday expenses. Rather, I recommended indulging herself in a trip, a new ensemble, or something frivolous. She responded with a sweet letter thanking me for gifting her, but it was quite unnecessary. Lucia said we were both so young and both were responsible for the breakup. While I was being overwhelmed by Lenny, she developed a friendship with a lighting design student, who is now one of Broadway's most successful designers. She told me at the breakup that she had called Noel and managed a meeting with him. I presume he gave her an ear full, from his prospective. She wished me well in the missive but included a suggestion of considering professional help if I found the going too difficult in the future.

Lucia proceeded to engage herself in two marriages and lived in Poughkeepsie. Our notes gave some closure to our failed relationship. One day years later, changing trains at Harmon-on-Hudson to visit my family, I noticed Lucia with two boys in their early teens. She smiled at me and extended a gloved hand, stating "I'm Lucia." "Yes, I know," I stammered, surprised. The boys eyed me with curiosity, as we exchanged some brief words. She looked trim, and well-put together (still in navy blue)

Leonard Bernstein loved his wife, Felicia Montealegre, but he craved the physicality of men sexually. He left his wife to live with a man in 1974, then returned to his dying wife in 1977, full of guilt. He emotionally relied upon his wife, but physically needed his male lover. This mirrored my situation.

Recurring memories of dynamic Lenny.

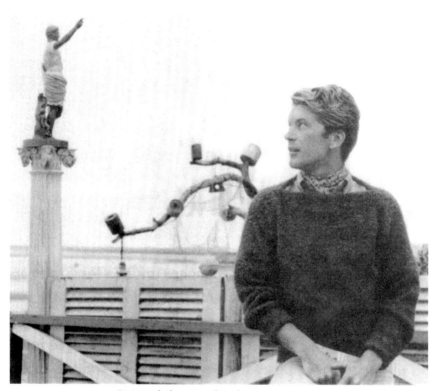

Rising tide from Jones' Locker, Provincetown.

Chapter 4

ELUDING LA DOLCE VITA

A Mexican divorce in February of 1960 was not expensive, but there was some cost involved. To cover the divorce expenses with enough left over for a bottle of champagne, a salami, and orchids in the spirit of Zsa Zsa Gabor, I volunteered myself as a guinea pig for a study being conducted by the University of Pittsburgh. After Lucia left Pittsburgh to file for the divorce, I moved into a rear ground floor apartment on Forbes Avenue, near the main entrance to Carnegie Tech. My next-door neighbor, Audrey, was a Ph.D. student at the University and knew about this experiment in boredom. She suggested that my participation would remedy my financial needs. I would be paid to go into isolation for three twelve-hour days, with a day in between each session.

There were a number of participants in this unusual experiment in boredom, but I suspect very few, if any other than myself, went the entire three days. I carefully prepared myself to be in a totally blacked out room for twelve hours at a time. I knew there would be no movement, no visibility and no sound during this period of time. What I did was create three different projects, which I could gear my mind to work on in the dark.

I thought constructing mentally an entire historic panorama of man since recorded time would be an enormous challenge. It was amazing how lying still in the oblivion of darkness seemed to stimulate recall in the brain. Things, places, and people I did not realize I knew sprung to mind. My creating a time line from the beginning of recorded time was aided by stored knowledge about ancient rulers and important places. Puzzled by seemingly unfamiliar names, I resolved to check on this recalled information in the library when I was released from the room.

That first evening after twelve hours of darkness, I carefully crossed busy Forbes Avenue, oblivious to the significance of red or green lights, having been removed from the reality of the world. There was a short term disconnect with the world around me each time after the isolation session. Sensing the danger of blindly crossing the busy street, I cautiously made my way to the school's library to check on some of these names my mind offered to my growing time line. Indeed, my mind had conjured up accurately facts untouched for years. It was an amazing discovery!

The second project I worked on was directing a stage production of *Cyrano de Bergerac*. I felt free to cast anyone I wished, living or dead. Anna Magnani played the baker's wife; Marilyn Monroe was given the role of Roxanne, etc. It was enjoyable to play with these performers in my imagination and give direction to the script.

My third project was more personal. I tried to recall faithfully everything about my family and their interactions with each other. This examination of family relationships was easier to perceive in the still, darkness of the room. It, like the other two challenges, was absorbing to me, though my perceptions of the family inter-relationships revealed how scanty my knowledge was in reality. I had not spent significant time directly living and relating with my family. It was all so hit or miss and casual due to our apartness. However, all were efforts significantly worthwhile.

Each of the three rooms was different. After arrival in the morning, I would be shown the room with the lights on. I would sit on the cot and then walk over to the bathroom to locate the toilet, and return to the cot. An orange juice was given to me before I lay down, and the lights were extinguished. When the cot quivered, I knew that a tray had been slid in on tracks under the bed. I could then decide when and if I wished to eat the bland, white bread cheese sandwich, drink the carton of milk, and have the packet of cookies. I was permitted to sit up to eat or to go to the toilet. Otherwise, I thought I was to lie still. I did not discover until it was over that it was permitted to change my prone positions; I stayed on my back at all times.

Aside from eating or visiting the toilet, the only effort I was allowed to execute was to push the button on a small, black metallic box I could hold in my hand or keep by my side. It had a wire connected with the box on the ceiling overhead. If I pushed the button, a different result would occur in each room. One room had a device that moved over-head while blinking a red light; another day in a different room, the light would alternately blink red or white; another day in yet another room, the light might just blink red in a stationary position. I did not feel any of these blinking boxes to be particularly interesting, so I only pressed the button when I wished to feel a cause and effect created by me. It was comforting to know how an action on my part in this sensory deprivation environment could create a visible result. My thoughts relating to my projects were far more interesting, so I seldom pressed the button.

My first minutes on the first day in the darkened room were filled with tension. I did not know what to expect and felt unprotected in a weird atmosphere. Even though I had been assured I was in a safe environment with nothing other than what was explained to me going to happen, my confidence in the situation wavered. I imagined white flashes in front of my eyes, but decided this was an illusion. Was there something in the orange juice causing this sensation? Or, was it fear stimulating the phenomenon? Settling into the situation, I relaxed and began my excursions into my projects, never to see the white flashes again.

After each session, I was asked to write down my comments on the experience. I really found the experiment fascinating, though I did not believe this was an exploration for use as a device in space ships to amuse the crew, as I had been told. The astronauts would have been dim-witted to be entertained by these blinking lights.

This evidence, that my mind could hold such an amount of information ready to be called forth from past experiences, was astonishing. I was pleased by how I could maintain a calm, even comfortable endurance of sensory deprivation. It intrigued me. The staff seemed impressed as well. I think most of the other guinea pigs ran out of there after a minimum exposure, as I never saw anyone else after the first day. It would be interesting to do the experiment again, but I do not have the discipline to attempt it on my own.

Since my Valentine's Day divorce, my life took on a zesty and busy balance among school activities, explorations into the gay bars near school, and rarer forays into downtown Pittsburgh. One evening, after one of the performances I gave in *The River Line*, I was surprised to be visited by the American couple who had been so kind to me in St. Andrews, Scotland, reminding me of the cuckoo bird episode. They were visiting someone else at the school, but while attending the play, they recognized my name on the program and came backstage to greet me.

My two directing projects were less than brilliant. The first was a medieval morality play, much too esoteric for either cast or audience to relate to; the other was an OK drama in Hitler's Germany. My acting scenes were also foolishly chosen and poorly acted, but I got an A for my theater costume class, in which I felt much more comfortable.

Because my apartment was very close to the railroad tracks, I enjoyed dawn walks there, contemplating my Noh Drama studies and Zen. My neighbor, Audrey, who occupied the front portion of the ground floor where I lived, became a friend with whom I could share confidences. She was a PhD candidate at the nearby University of Pittsburgh. Though she was majoring in speech pathology, I could hear her through the kitchen wall when entertaining a friend, making mistakes in pronunciation. It infuriated her when, from the other side of the wall, I would correct her nasal "a's" as in "can't." But, on some mornings, she was enchanted when she woke to find her sleeping body covered with blossoms I had picked during my dawn walks. Knowing she never locked her door, I slipped in quietly to deposit springtime to the sleeping maiden. On other mornings, I might be struggling back from a night of debauchery, or "bedauchery."

After the first of the two years in the Master of Fine Arts program, I wavered as to how I could find the courage to pursue a career as a director in the theater. It seemed as daunting as what an actor would face in gaining success in landing a role in a play. My shyness was tremendous, even though I had gained some acceptance from the mighty and stellar. My growing sexual freedom did not diminish my insecurities about self-esteem. I sidestepped an immediate commitment to a life in the theater by spending the summer garnering money by working in Provincetown at the Moors, a popular restaurant where I had worked two summers earlier.

To earn the best tips required thoughtfully focused energy together with a warm flirtatious attentiveness. I was considered attractive and available as well as a professional server. It was permitted for a customer to request a particular waiter. When possible, I encouraged diners to ask for my table when booking or coming in for a meal. One night, I had half the restaurant wanting my services! This was funny, but a highly pressured situation. There was a mad rush to please everyone, and other waiters pitched in at my urgent call for help where possible. It was reciprocal in that whenever a waiter was overwhelmed, his mates would jump into to assist—thank goodness! I thoroughly enjoyed the attention and prided myself on the service I could provide. It was akin to being "the belle at the ball."

In Provincetown, it was easy to be in love with being gay. Where there was strong repression of gays elsewhere around America, here there was a flamboyant in-your-face atmosphere of gay exuberance. There were so many playful men, both on the beach and around town. On Saturday afternoons, the Moors had a sing-along with a piano player. After hours on the beach, crowds of men and women poured in to swill down cold beer and sing their hearts out, usually to some gay theme. "I Enjoy Being a Girl" or "Take Back Your Mink" and other Broadway musical numbers were easily camped up and sung full throttle. The place pulsed with enthusiasm and merriment. Wearing the boat necked blue and white horizontally striped sailor shirt prescribed for the staff, I sang along while distributing bottles of beer or other libations, and pocketing large tips.

When it became closing time at the bars downtown, it was clear that many stragglers were thirsty for more. One time a guy who had trouble meeting people asked me to invite some men up to his place, which was diagonally across from the Atlantic House, one of the most popular gay meeting places. He stocked his bar with bottles of booze and anticipated entertaining thirsty strangers rounded up by me. Outside his doorway leading upstairs to his apartment, I lounged at closing time. As guys sauntered by, I asked them if they wanted to have another drink. If so, they could give me a dollar entry and go upstairs to party. I believe I supplied the lonely host with a room full of die-hard party makers, while modestly increasing my coin of the realm savings.

It may have been my bone structure and youth that captured the attention of Robert Hunter, a major artist working in Provincetown that summer. Juggling my free time between waiting tables at the Moors and helping Larry Jones make repairs to his amusing guest house, "Jones's Locker," I posed for Bob. I felt a vitality and surging energy at Provincetown that enabled me to work at these three jobs and keep everyone happy, as well! All of this insured a growing stockpile of money to be used on another European trip in the fall. My decision now was not to return to graduate school. I rationalized that there was time enough later, if ever, to figure out how to best approach developing my career as a theater director. Now, I wanted to relish the moment and drink deeply in the fountain of life or from many a bottle of what-ever who-ever offered me.

Being cherished and adored with constant stroking made me feel radiant and important. Larry Jones invited me to parties down the Cape and permitted me to drive his Gold Mercedes. One time, under the influence, I drove straight across the roundabout at Orleans. I met the most influential gay men from various parts of the country, who would congregate at Jones's Locker, especially at the annual costume party. Larry introduced me to Boston Brahmin, Nathaniel Saltonstall, who always requested my table when at the Moors. Later, on a couple of occasions, we entertained each other with lively conversations in his plush apartment on Commonwealth Avenue in Boston. He had been trained as an architect decades earlier, and he shared his views on art and changing society with me. I felt comfortable with this aging, plump man, as I knew he had a proclivity for young Latino types. Hence, we could enjoy friendly visits without the hassle of hidden agendas.

Larry Jones, a retired naval captain, became a dear companion. He taught me to gather driftwood planks on the beach and then make flooring out it by using a sledgehammer to straighten the warping. A sledgehammer! Who could have imagined me swinging a sledgehammer? It was so Victor Mature-ish. Larry was creative in decorating his guest house and inventive in keeping it functioning. It was amazing it had not been condemned for faulty wiring or other building code violations.

His longtime lover, Jamie Spilman, was philandering somewhere, probably in the South. Jamie would appear suddenly and then go off again, traveling with his pet monkey and its drag complete with a jeweled tiara. Jamie and Tallulah Bankhead had a lot in common behaviorally. He was a sometime boyfriend of Eugenia, her sister, as well. I adored and admired him for his warm flamboyance.

Jamie Spilman wit his pet monkey.

These were days before Stonewall, the gay liberation movement, and AIDS. There was a vibrant and exciting flowering of gay life in Provincetown in contrast to elsewhere. The camp was fervent and effusively over the top. I felt in the midst of it all, center stage. It was liberating not to worry about finding the courage to pursue a directing career in the theater or about fulfilling obligations in married life. I was young, attractive, and free to expend my energies in the fascinating, colorful world around me, framed by the Atlantic Ocean and the lovely sand dunes of Cape Cod.

Jones Locker was on the shore of Provincetown harbor, adjacent to the Shore Galleries. One fine day, as I was swimming during high tide in front of Larry's place, I saw him on the deck of the Shore Galleries talking with a woman whose hair was pulled back into a bun, smoking a cigarette. Larry beckoned me to come out of the water and join them. I was about to meet a stimulating person who was to become a lifelong best friend, Nina (Juanita) Micheleit.

Nina claimed I looked like a Greek god, when I emerged from the water onto her deck. Sun bleached locks framed my smiling face, betraying how I felt on top of

Nina Micheleit in Shore Galleries, Provincetown.

the world. Bronzed and glistening with salt water, I merrily greeted this woman, who was managing the art gallery for her brother-in-law, Bob Campbell. She had a very straightforward manner of engagement, often tapping her cigarette ashes into a seashell. Nina wore her gray streaked hair pulled up and tied casually on top of her head, gazing at you with an open, earnest but warm glint in her large eyes.

My rented apartment, also on the waterfront, was nearby. Nina and I were to spend many an after work evening on the deck there, scotch in hand, discussing and even suggesting solutions to the mysteries of the world while the buoys clanged, tides changed, and the lighthouse across the water blinked under starry skies. . . . Years later, when we visited together in Florida, we still analyzed the metaphysical problems that dared miraculous solutions, but now, we know better than to suggest an answer.

Before leaving for the Cape, I had developed a relationship with an artist in New York City. Douglass Semonin was a very dear and caring friend, but I could not see us committing to being long-term lovers. He was an excellent designer of wallpapers and a fine artist, who encouraged me to share his ground floor apartment off Stuyvesant Park on East 16th Street on occasions when I was in town and desired his company. It was evident to me that our relationship would never be what he wanted. I treasured him as a friend, not a lover. When he came to visit in Provincetown, we had strained words; they hung heavily between us. He decided to go for a walk along the low tide flats, and I had to get to the Moors for work. I wrote him a note asking him to go over to see Nina at the gallery. Nina agreed to talk with Douglass, who had great regard for her. She managed to help him get over the parting of our ways with her gentle, caring manner. We were both grateful, and we developed a continuing devoted friendship with each other.

When I departed for Europe in September of 1960, Douglass presented me with a silver and gold Tiffany cigarette case, engraved "Prince Eric Gustav" at my sailing aboard the Liberté. (A few years later, Douglass painted a full-length nude portrait of me. It took me a couple of years to notice that there were six toes painted on each foot. Douglass claimed that royalty such as the Bourbons often had six toes or fingers.)

Douglass Semonin.

After being so very impressed by the elegance, charm, and beauty of the *Île de France* the voyage before, it was natural for me to want to experience further French hospitality crossing the ocean for the second time. The *Liberté* had been converted to a troop ship during World War II, but the French had managed to restore her to an impressive grandeur and elegance. I fingered my new Tiffany cigarette case with studied nonchalance while bidding farewell to my parents, Douglass, and other well-wishers, sipping champagne at a table in the grand salon. They descended the gangplank, and I gaily waved good-bye to them all on the dock, streamers flying downward, band playing...

From working all summer at three jobs, I managed to splurge on a cabin class ticket, an upgrade from my first crossing in tourist class. After my guests who came to see me off departed, I quickly perused the first class list of passengers. To my delight, Hermione Gingold was listed, as was Mrs. Claude Dauphin. I recognized the famous French actor's name, but wondered who his wife might be. Little did I realize how much Norma Eberhardt Dauphin was to instigate herself into my life in the near future. She stayed in her stateroom the entire trip, so I did not meet her until later in New York at a party.

Hermione Gingold was very familiar to me through her many comedic roles on the screen and on the stage. *Gigi* came foremost to mind: She and Maurice Chevalier singing "I Remember It Well" and her trying to counsel Leslie Caron's youthful character in love with that gorgeous Louis Jourdan. I looked forward to meeting her in the impending future.

There were a few first class passengers I would spend the most time with, however. One was a handsome, conservatively dressed woman from Ohio, who

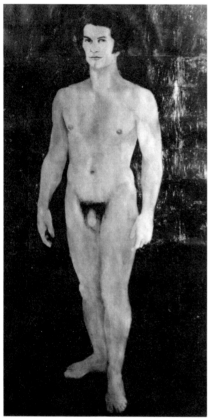

had stood next to me at the railing as the steam ship pulled out of the harbor. We began a conversation in which I discovered she was going to be attending the Cordon Bleu in Paris. She hoped to master the art of cooking so as to please her husband at home in Shaker Heights. Becoming a master at sneaking into first class, I was always glad to see her. She introduced me to others on board, comprising a pleasant group of fellow travelers. It took some cajoling, however, for this jovial group to gladly accept Hermione Gingold to join us. As much as I found the comedienne amusing, they found her vulgar. I did succeed in having the actress with us on some occasions.

Though my plans were to go directly to France, Hermione convinced me to disembark with her at Southampton and train together to London. She assured me I could continue to Paris shortly thereafter, and it would be a great favor to her to keep her company. When a personality of this magnitude prevails upon a starry eyed youth, what else could be done than to alter plans?

Portrait of Eric by Douglass.

With her prevalent underbite and in her strange English accent, she requested my advice on what to wear into London. Should she wear leopard? Coat, hat, and handbag? I told her that I thought that outmoded, but, lo and behold—what did Hermione appear in at the disembarking? Leopard everything!

We had a compartment to ourselves on the train into Victoria Station. I helped her with her lines for a movie she was to make with Marlon Brando. I sipped some cognac to settle my nerves, while trying not to be obviously fascinated with her taking out and putting back into her mouth a set of upper plates. Upon arrival at the station, she was very agitated. She stepped out to a flurry of flash bulbs and press men; I stood behind her, supporting her star status. After what seemed an eternity, she turned to me and asked me in front of her press people, "What is your name?" I felt very belittled and shocked. How could someone to whom I had extended so many continual kindnesses over the week aboard the ship lose the name of her escort?

I had agreed to accompany her that evening to a very glamorous event in her honor at a famous hotel. Simmering with annoyance, I waited until the last moment to call to tell her my dinner clothes could not be ready in time. I would not be available. In retrospect, I should have finessed that better as I could have met some interesting contacts by attending. It was cutting off my nose to spite my face.

Rather, I spent the time with adorable David Halliday, the lead of *West Side Story* in London, and my friend from the Lakes Region Playhouse. It was far more thrilling being his guest at the theater, experiencing his performance as Tony, and later being with him in his apartment and sharing his bed, than escorting the graceless actress with the faulty memory and the bad manners.

It was my dancer friend from New York, Sylvia Tysick, who had the idea of my staying with David. I arrived backstage at *West Side Story* to announce my arrival in London to Sylvia. She was playing the role of "Anybody's", and was delighted I was there. However, her place was tiny, so why not bunk with our pal, David? Truly a delicious idea! We happily agreed to a night together after his performance, but he was going somewhere the next day for a Sunday outing. It was a most surprising night, and a most agreeable one at that! So much for David being straight, as I had thought for so long!

It was a brief stay with David, but other adventures were to follow immediately. Before leaving for Paris to spend my birthday there, I went to view paintings at the wonderful National Gallery on Trafalgar Square. As at the Metropolitan Museum in New York City, a Sunday afternoon strolling through great art is an inducement for men on the prowl to score. I was getting used to men showing an avid interest in me. I knew I was a curious young man from the Bronx, who sounded like Noel Coward.

With the backdrop of great master paintings, two men engaged me in interesting conversation, followed by an invitation to enjoy a drink together. I liked the red-haired man who professed to be an actor. The other man was a theater director and very nicely mannered. They both were pleased to learn I was on my way to celebrate my birthday in Paris. The director was flying to Paris and would be there before the time my train pulled in. Could he meet me at the station, and take me for my birthday dinner? He would arrange, as well, for me to stay where he was booked. I saw how his plans could be quite delightful. The actor was going to come in some days to Paris, too. He would like to join me and suggested I stay at the same place the director had booked, keeping the room for his arrival. It seemed very agreeable and fortuitous, or was I being very naïve and foolish?

The director departed for his flight to Paris; the actor invited me to dine with him. After a delicious fish dinner at Sheekey's on St. Martin's Lane, there was time for us to catch a performance of *Oliver*, playing next door. The actor asked me to join him for the performance, which I was pleased to do. First, we stopped at the adjacent theater to pop into the dressing room of Alan Bates, star of another show. I was familiar with his work and pleased to meet him in person. He said he was envious of my going to Rome. I mentioned I had participated in a film a couple of years ago as a bit player and was planning to meet with the noted Italian film director Franco Brusati there. (Douglass had been in touch with Brusati and arranged for this meeting.) It was very satisfying to hear the lead of a London play and an international film star being envious of me!

Adorned in garments festooned with pearl buttons, Pearlies—who have long since disappeared from the theater scene—were doing their sidewalk entertainment outside on the street as we entered the theater for *Oliver*. The evening was enchanting. We went to the theater bar during intermission to have a pre-ordered drink, as one can still do in London today. Then, I was off with farewells and promises to meet as arranged in Paris soon. The night train and ferry, followed by connecting train into Paris, permitted me to ponder these thrilling, wondrous events. It seemed I must be charmed...

London, itself, had an inherent charm. This was before all the tall, modern, glass buildings began to appear. There were still abundant aspects of Victorian England. I was pleased by the crescents of whitewashed buildings, all with columns at the doorways— no structure too high so that sky and clouds could not be enjoyed. It had a gentle but sturdy ambiance.

That was left behind so now I could journey on to France. After walking into the street from the Paris train station, I saw my newly found friend waiting for me! We dropped my luggage at our hotel, which was more of a pension than a hotel. As it was my birthday, he asked what I would like to do. One thing I loved doing upon arriving in Paris was to view the Seine from one of the bridges. He suffered that with me, then took me to a very elegant *boîte* where we could have a drink. I asked for a Pernod, which he thought *déclassé*. But, I was determined to do what reminded me of my not-too-long-ago student days in Paris.

He spoke of an invitation for us to spend the weekend at a famous person's chateau, but first he wanted me to go to the theater to hear a friend's one-man performance. If it was not Gilbert Bécaud or Charles Aznavour, it was someone similar. After one act of this, I asked to leave and have some dinner. It was rude of me, but I was young and headstrong about celebrating my birthday the way I wanted to do it. We went off to a grand restaurant, instead of a bistro as I suggested. Clearly, I was being difficult. Being in the magical city of Paris, redolent of earlier memories, I felt as I was the birthday boy, I could be permitted to enjoy simpler pleasures. It was generous of him to want to take me to up-market places, but those were not the joys Paris held for me. Vainglory and pomp was not what I wanted, nor feeling I could be bought by enjoying them. Rather, I had hoped for something earthier, vibrating in the pulse of the city. A growing dislike for my host was developing. The evening was less than smooth, and no further mention of the chateau visit was forthcoming. He left the next day, alone, and I waited a couple of days for the actor to arrive.

With the actor was an LP of *Oliver* to remind me of our enjoyable musical theater evening together in London. What a pleasure to see him! We liked doing the same things, and he was indulgent of my whims. Our interests meshed nicely, making for a memorable Parisian sojourn.

Our couple of days were much more felicitous than those with the director. He took me to Boeuf sur le Toit, a gay cabaret featuring gorgeous transvestites. One was invited to join us at our table to sip champagne. That evening, I learned that these lovelies were officially licensed to appear in public as women. Leaving the club at an early morning hour, I noticed a very young Winston Churchill chatting with a few people waiting for a cab. He was the grandson of the real thing, identical other than age (and weight)! In the mingling of the departing people on the street was the most gorgeous Alain Delon. Truly I was in the world I yearned to be a part of. . . .

My dear actor friend returned to London while I took a train to Rome. I found an agreeable pensione in the Margutta area, close to the previous one on my first trip to Rome. Enjoying an *osso buco* meal one day in a trattoria, I saw through the plate glass window two faces peering in I recognized! They were Susan Berns, daughter of the owner of 21 Club in New York and her friend Danielle Weill, a fashion model. Susan and I had many friends in common and saw each other often around New York. They were as surprised as I was, and we joined together for a mirthful lunch.

Susan Berns models with Eric in Corinth ruins.

The two recent graduates from Bennington were doing their first tour around Europe. I was stunned to learn that Susan had purchased a new Lancia Flaminia, with intentions to drive it to Greece and back. She did not know how to drive but was going to take lessons in Rome! Quickly, I saw how we could be of mutual assistance to each other. I would gladly drive them, if they would cover the costs involved in the drive. It seems a win-win for all, so we planned to get on the road the next day.

Around 9 a.m. the next morning, I met them to begin our odyssey. As I got into the car, I spotted a white garbage truck further up the road slowly coming in our direction. Driving along the Corso in Rome, I noticed that the garbage truck seemed to be following us. It took a while for me to realize that it was not a white garbage truck, but it was our white trunk door that had sprung open that I had viewed in my rear view mirror! We stopped to rescue the arm of a mink coat; it had been trailing behind us. Once it was back into the trunk, we secured the latch and continued on our merry way.

Every so often, I would stop and ask directions in my basic Italian. Often, "giù" was expressed in the reply, indicating "down there." One of the girls finally asked me how the people knew they were Jewish! ("Giù" sounds like "Jew.")

We headed towards Naples, and I eventually drove the car onto a ferry bound for the island of Ischia. That evening, we visited a popular drinking establishment to peruse the action. I decided to separate from the young women, to encourage them to do their thing, and sat myself at the bar fingering my Tiffany cigarette case. A young man approached and announced a Prince so-and-so desired my company. I glanced over at the overripe with age, plump prince and turned my case around for the youth to read, "Prince Eric Gustav." Haughtily, I said, "This prince isn't interested!"

While in Ischia, I had hoped to meet someone for whom I had a note of introduction from Don Hagerty, a Provincetown friend. Don kindly wrote that I was Lady Brett's son, which indicated I had the spirit of being her son if she were to have one. Unfortunately, his friend was not in Ischia at the time. Don's famous brother was Press Secretary James Hagerty in Washington DC, which duly impressed me.

The weather was overcast, so we left the island, driving across Italy to get the ferry to Greece at Brindisi, truly the anus of the country. It was a dusty and dingy town with only a communist parade to indicate any activity. Once aboard the ferry, we settled into our cramped, hot staterooms for the overnight trip to Piraeus, the port for Athens. A leering, obnoxious crewmember acting as steward made lascivious advances, which repulsed me. I propped my suitcase in such a way that no one could enter during the night, but a bit of air could circulate. After a brief stop at Corfu, we sailed on towards Athens.

The young women checked into the 5 star hotel on Constitution Square in Athens, while I settled for a 2 star hotel on the lower corner. Near my hotel was a bar where I went for a cool drink. While there, a burly man approached me and engaged me in conversation. It turned out that he ran a brothel on the outskirts of town and thought I would be a remarkable addition to his stable for special customers! I often conjectured about the "what if"—but remain relieved I did not muster any courage or interest in investigating this flattering albeit dubious proposition.

One evening, I drove the car to the location of a famous gay bar, Tria Delphia (Three Brothers). There I encountered a most adorable Greek sailor who could not speak English but had a gentle, sweet manner. I invited him back to my hotel room without ever managing to have anything happen. Neither of us could come to grips with the situation. We were both too shy, evidently. I drove him back to his base, and could not help noticing a search light following the car in and out again. A similar inaction occurred when I visited Vouliagmeni Beach outside Athens. A young Greek talked me into walking up the beach to a secluded area, where he suggested we investigate each other. I did not have the courage to go along with his intentions, because I thought he might be a hustler. My pride would not allow me to pay for his services.

The confusion in Greece was not limited to sexual encounters. I had heard that Jayne Mansfield was making a movie in Athens, and I saw her with her husband at the hotel bar where my friends were staying. She was very attractive and less extreme in demeanor than I had expected. I thought it a great idea if I could get involved with the filming as an extra, even for one day. Fortunately, I met someone who told me he could arrange this for me. When all was set, it turned out to be

Athens at La Plaka: A night in the old town quarter with student friends.

for another film being done in Greek. It was not the Mansfield film, so I backed out of the deal. Greek being the working language seemed an obstacle, and the small amount of money to be earned was not worth the effort. I would rather see the great sites and experience the liveliness in Athens during the short time we would be there.

The Plaka is an old area of Athens within view of the well-lit Acropolis. I met some Greek English-speaking students who took me there for a very merry repast. Retzina and ouzo flowed; our laughter was non-stop. Like all students, we enjoyed much discussion of current events and movies and exchanged travel notes. It was a colorful visit, happily before pollution of the city became so obnoxious.

My two American friends and I continued our tour around Greece. We had time to gander at wondrous ruins, monasteries in various states of abandonment, and other points of interest before heading back to Rome, from which the car would be shipped to New York. I finally was planning to bite the bullet and summon the courage to arrange a meeting with film director Franco Brusati.

Brusati responded to Douglass's request to meet with me while I was in Rome. We met for an apéritif in the lobby of the Excelsior on the Via Veneto. This esteemed director—winner of film festival awards for *Per Vedere Venezia*—had a young American man with him, whom I took to be one of his playthings. After some conversing in English, Franco announced that I should not consider being an extra or bit player again when I had the makings of a leading man. He extolled my looks and photogenic qualities. He would make me a star!

This terrified me, mostly because I felt I was to be his toy boy in my quest for stardom, which I was not convinced I wanted nor did I think I was equipped to deal with it. If I could overcome my great insecurities as an actor, I would not choose to be a star but rather an actor dedicated to serious roles, away from the diet of glitz demanded of stars. I believed that stars are victims of their fame, which is corrosive to the soul. That is one of the reasons I tended towards wanting a career as a director, where I could apply my creative energies with a more salubrious lifestyle. Another reason was that I have a directorial mind, very different from that of an actor. Franco was not unattractive; but without allure, I simply did not feel any interest in a sexual liaison with him. If I felt an attraction to him, it is possible I would have consented to a brief interlude. However, it would not have involved an exchange of favors for a film career. The "casting couch" did not appeal to me. I politely thanked him for both the drink and his vote of confidence in my potential future under his guidance. I had to think about it—but not much.

My pensione was close to the Via Veneto on a side street. I returned there confused and in emotional turmoil. On entering, a young Englishman glanced at me and gasped in amazement. He remembered me from the theater's lounge in London at *Oliver*, and he recounted my exact conversation that he had overheard! The world seemed to be getting very small indeed. What were the chances of someone in London hearing some talk among strangers, then going to Rome some time later to meet that very person he was eavesdropping on—and living in the same pensione?

Fellini's *La Dolce Vita* was showing at a movie theater near-by. I decided to indulge myself in this popular movie maker's examination of contemporary Roman life. With the implications of Brusati's proposition resounding in my head, I found the film greatly disturbing. Because it seemed to spell out my fate if I remained in the city of decadence, I rushed back to my room with the determination to flee the city the next day. I packed hurriedly in the morning, forgetting my cream-colored silk pajamas under the pillow. I left a packet of money to cover my room charges, and, at the nearby American Express office, I booked a passage on the S.S. *Constitution*, sailing from Italy to the USA. My Lutheran teachings of basic decency were saving me from utter degradation. Though baffled and frightened to the core, I knew I had to seek refuge back home.

However, the American ocean liner displeased me. I thought the food in tourist class not up to par, and the staff were determined to keep me from sneaking into first class. In a huff, I jumped ship when we arrived in Cannes and booked a seat on a Spanish flight to New York with the money refunded by the steamship line.

Grand tour begins: Louise Schacht, a friend bids the boys farewell.

Chapter 5

THE BIRTH OF THE DAVID DYNASTY

Going directly to Montrose to visit my parents seemed a good place to sort myself out after this European sojourn. Over breakfast that first morning, I was perusing the New York *Daily News* and saw on the front page a large photo of handsome Wyatt Cooper, with a covering story of his marriage to Gloria Vanderbilt, the "Poor Little Rich Girl." Fascinated, I eagerly read every word, the morning following my return to the USA. I remembered this sexy man pictured in the newspaper—I had last seen Wyatt on my visit to his shabby West Side theater district apartment, when I asked to use his typewriter to create my curriculum vitae. I kept my clothes on that time, with never a mention of our bizarre, thrilling night in New Hampshire. This was just before I left for Europe, earlier in the year—for the second time—still trying to find the formula that could best help me break into my theater career.

In following years, I would greet Wyatt and Gloria on occasion, walking with their two young boys on the East Side streets were we all lived. One of the boys was to later throw himself out of their upper floor apartment at United Nations Plaza; the other, Anderson Cooper, went on to become a popular TV news journalist, who recently outed himself publicly.

While in Vienna that previous trip, I had stayed briefly with someone I had met in Spoleto. He introduced me to the cabaret star Greta Keller. Greta told me she had taught Marlene Dietrich how to sing, and I had heard they were an item at one time. In appearance and voice, they resembled each other. It was rumored that Hitler, on his climb to power, had taken quite a shine to Greta, a nice Jewish girl with great looks and talent.

When she arrived in New York that autumn, I met with her and discussed my professional problem. She kindly set up an interview for me with someone at the prestigious William Morris Agency. My interviewer invited me to meet him at his Upper East Side apartment that evening, so we could go out and discuss my future. When I arrived, it was clear I neither liked him, nor was willing to discuss what he was really interested in doing with me.

This nice albeit selective and proud boy, virtue intact, rented a very simple, walk-up apartment on Third Avenue near 83rd Street and found a very dull office job while trying to figure out "What next?" Perhaps, even, that elusive career with the theater? The Fickle Finger of Fate worked her wonders.

Going to work during rush hour, I boarded the Lexington Avenue Express subway from 86th Street to Grand Central Station, where I noticed the glances of a very tall, handsome, slim young man who was also very crushed in the mob. We looked at each other from a small but packed distance, knowingly, but were soon dispersed in the Grand Central disgorging, each disappearing into the crowds.

That very night, with nothing better to do, I went to the Loew's 86th Street movie house to see a horror film. I loathed horror movies, but the other movie house was showing something even less appealing. It was a good feeling to be out of the tiny apartment. I sat in the balcony in an aisle seat. During the gory unraveling of the plot, I happened to look across the aisle. There he was again! This made me believe in kismet! He looked at me and smiled. Promptly, he got up and came over to sit next to me, saying something like, "Is this scary enough for you?" I was charmed, but how could I guess that, down the road, this engaging man was capable of being scary enough for anyone?

We had coffee later, and even later, he climbed my stairway to the sheeted fields. We both liked what we discovered and began a nocturnal habit, but at his place on 81st Street near Madison Avenue. His roommate was greatly discomforted by our activities and kindly moved out. I moved in, relinquishing my sparse, recently rented apartment.

David Wallace and I became more closely intertwined with each day and night. With me being 25 and him 26, we seemed to complement each other, spinning dreams and aspirations together for a rosy future. He was disenchanted with his job at Lehman Brothers, and my office job held no interest beyond the paycheck for me. This situation was to change. David's father was Bess Wallace Truman's brother, so President Truman was "Uncle Harry." When Bess's other brother died, David was about to come into an inheritance, which would happily start us along the path of fulfilling some dreams. Concurrently, my grandmother died, leaving me a small amount of money. Between the two of us, we immodestly speculated on a "Grand Tour" in the old fashioned sense, to be followed by some entrepreneurial investment, such as an antique store in New York, upon return. It seemed a natural, if grandiose, decision for two young gay men in love. The idea of being in love was new to me, and thrilling to savor. I am certain my step was lighter and I moved with a swagger; my head was twirling with joyful matters; and my eyes saw the world as brighter and more colorful. It felt so grand and exciting

Eric with the Trumans at their 219 North Delaware home.

to be alive! (He was to become David the First—in a dynasty of Davids—later to be dubbed David the Cruel.)

David had a Siamese cat named "Kitty." She was ineligible to participate in the Grand Tour, hence we contemplated finding a happy new home for Kitty. To facilitate her cherished son's wishes, Christine, David's mother, agreed to take on the cat for the year we were to be abroad doing our enriching tour. Since she lived in Denver, and with thoughts of film stars boarding the 20th Century Limited, we would take Kitty by train to Colorado, stopping off to see Aunt B and Uncle Harry in Independence, Missouri.

We had met once before, at the triplex apartment of the newly elected President and Mrs. John F. Kennedy (at the Carlyle Hotel on Madison Avenue between 76–77th Streets in New York). This New York residence for the President and Jackie was furnished with treasures chosen by the First Lady and her favorite decorators from the nearby antiquarian French & Company.

While the Kennedys were in the White House, this elegant eagle's nest was lent to Harry and Bess Truman when they came to visit their daughter, Margaret Daniel, who lived around the corner on Park Avenue and 77th Street. Senior Editor of the *New York Times*, handsome and brilliant Clifton Daniel and their two growing sons completed this cosmopolitan family.

The Trumans invited David and me up for an afternoon visit. Though seemingly composed, I was very nervous about meeting this historic figure and his wife. Interestingly, I did not notice any Secret Service men in the lobby or around the apartment when we arrived at the Carlyle Hotel. Bess sat in an easy chair in the living room, with her back to the plate glass window overlooking Central Park, from a high vantage point, and the west side of Manhattan. She looked exactly like her photographs, wearing a two-piece medium blue suit and permed blue-white hair. Harry sat on her left and was instantly gregarious with us. He beamed an easy smile, wearing a nondescript suit, with his shirt open at the neck. Guessing that Bess would not like the smoke, I tried to restrain myself from lighting a cigarette. Nerves got the better of me, and I decided to puff on a cigarette even though I was not usually a compulsive smoker. Bess's countenance did not reveal displeasure, but I felt it.

Conversation was strained, especially when Mrs. Truman asked if we would like something to drink. I sensed that Baptist Bess meant water, so I declined with thanks. "I would be glad to go to the kitchen to get some water," she said. "Those boys don't want water," good old Harry piped up, "they would like something stronger."

Bess explained that they had just arrived in New York with no time to get supplies in, but Harry lightheartedly said, "A lot my girl knows." Taking me by the arm, he led me into Jack Kennedy's small den. On the desk was the famous red phone linked directly to the Kremlin. If I picked that up, Khrushchev would be on line! Wow! And, next to the desk was the famous rocking chair that the president was often photographed sitting in. Harry reached in behind some books and extricated a square bottle that seemed to contain liquor. I followed him into the kitchen where three glasses soon had liquor poured into them over some ice cubes. So, that is when I became "Wild about Harry" as the song goes. . . .

Bess and Harry Truman later played hosts to us, when we stopped by for a few days in Independence, Missouri, on our way to Colorado. Anyone on board the train, who might have looked out of their windows when the train pulled into Independence, would have seen Mr. President standing by the open door of the driver's side of the Blue Lincoln Continental. On the other side, stood resolute Bess Wallace Truman. I suspect few people made the effort to pay attention, however. It was a thrilling moment for me to see them waiting there for us, or in particular for ME, as I chose to flatter myself.

We proceeded to motor over to 219 North Delaware Avenue to the Trumans' attractive homestead. It was a comfortable, unpretentious house with a Victorian flavor. The dining room, for example, had a glass display case with the Truman's White House porcelain dinner service. Otherwise, it was an ordinary room where we enjoyed plain but tasty meals without pomp or fuss. The aging black cook/server was the same one that went to the White House during the Truman administration. When Bess was preparing to become First Lady, her servant was driven by her friends in an open car to the Independence railway station with a banner, "Our First Lady to the White House."

Life was casual in the Truman household. We dressed in day clothes of sport coat and tie for dinner; David and I shared a twin bedded room with bath. (It did not seem to matter what relationship David and I shared other than we were friends and planning a trip together to Europe. What personal views Harry and Bess may have had about us were never indicated.) The time spent in this Midwestern, middle class environment went quickly.

Baptist Bess was firm about the one-drink-a-day practice. However, in the privacy of Harry's den, a libation might quietly appear on the sly. Harry and I really enjoyed sitting in his den, talking about various subjects, all of his choosing. David had cautioned me about not intruding my own subjects in conversation, or disagreeing when in the company of exalted personages. (I remembered that during the Vatican audience with Pope John XXIII, but forgot it when keeping the Queen Mother of Romania company at Sir Harold Acton's in Florence, resulting in her cane banging on the marble floor while she stated she was just a blind, old woman—but that is another story.) I realized in retrospect I should have done my homework before this visit. Through subtle insinuation, without asking a direct question, I might have been able to learn many interesting things from this world-wise man who had helped shaped the 20th Century.

I felt a warm regard and respect for Harry S Truman, and he imparted some very useful advice during our den talks. He told me it was a good practice to read a few books at the same time, to keep the mind activated and challenged. I follow his advice to this day. Also, he suggested it was important to walk a lot every day, but to walk with purpose. I enjoyed his kindly good humor and easy manner; he made me feel comfortable in his home.

One day, Uncle Harry walked purposefully down Delaware Avenue towards the Harry S Truman Presidential Library and Museum with us boys, amicably chatting. There may have been Secret Service men around, but I was never aware of them. He took us around the library, recalling various incidents relating to the exhibits, often referring to his wonderful Margaret and Bess, as well as the enormity of the Hiroshima decision.

This was a recurrent thought in Harry's conversation. He expressed sadness at having had to drop the atomic bombs on Japan. I heard him exclaim his remorse over his decision a few times in my brief stay at the Truman home. I could not imagine what an awful responsibility it is to make such a decision, and how it could haunt one for life.

There are a few things in my curious life that I would have avoided doing if there could be a replay. One was what happened while lunching with David and his aunt Bess at a country restaurant outside of Independence. In those alcoholic-in-training days, my compulsive behavior was making deep inroads. Aunt B., David, and I sat at a table, enjoying lunch at this eatery, when a woman came up to her to chat. I had been drinking a daiquiri, which had evaporated much too quickly. Knowing our hostess would not countenance consumption of another drink, I slyly indicated to the waitress to bring me a refill. It was a tasteless thing to do, but compulsion took over. Mrs. Truman was not amused when she realized what I did behind her back. I can still feel contrition upon recollection. She had kindly taken us out for lunch, but I had broken the rules of my otherwise generous hostess.

Later that evening, both Uncle Harry and David indicated an intention to make an early evening of it. Harry asked me to please sit up with his girl, as she intended to see their daughter on a television talk show. Unfortunately, I was seated next to Bess and could not see her face clearly without swiveling around in an obvious fashion. I would have been fascinated to note her expression when Margaret went into detail about how she outsmarted her parents, when she wanted to go out on a date while at the White House. I could see Bess sitting serenely with ankles crossed, and I think she had a vague smile on her face, while she was being discussed on television by her daughter. I was the only one in the world who could have been witness to her reaction, but peering over my nose peripherally as I was, my sightline was limited.

A heldentenor's venue: Red Rocks near Denver.

At this early stage of television, the guest was often asked to participate in the promotion of a sponsor's product. Margaret was handed a carton of Camel cigarettes. She quickly tossed it back to the announcer, not wanting to endorse the cigarette manufacturer. It was startling to see, and delightful for me under the circumstances, sitting alone with her amused mother in Independence.

While packing to leave the next day on our final portion of the train journey to Denver, Harry came into the bedroom I had been sleeping in. He asked if we would like to have the two leather belts that the president of Mexico had given him. They had rancher buckles—one set had gold and silver with small rubies inserted. A "T" was engraved on the buckle. David and I quickly accepted the gift, and David gave me the fancier buckled belt, which I still treasure, but with updated belts to accommodate waist size changes.

The Trumans drove us to the railway station and gave David a package containing a walleyed pike to give to David's mother. It had been retrieved from their freezer, the same freezer that had been the subject of some scandal years earlier. It probably had to do with a bribe, but I could not recall the details of the event. Again, I wondered how many people on the train were looking out of their windows to see Mr. President and Mrs. Truman standing beside their blue Lincoln Continental. Mindfulness is a marvelous discipline. It can reveal amazing things in everyday life.

David's mother and younger sister, Margo, joined us on jaunts outside of Denver. After we went into the Rockies to visit historic mining towns, we went south to Colorado Springs and the Garden of the gods before it was time to head back to New York in preparation for our European tour.

Convinced we had the world on a plate, David and I dipped into our newly found funds and booked first class passage aboard the French Line's SS *Flandre*. (Smaller than both *Liberté* and *Île de France*, it had a special French charm and intimacy that was very agreeable.) A young woman who took over the lease on our flat on East 81st Street recommended we look up an artist friend from Bennington, living on the via Margutta in Rome, when we got there. She asked us to entertain "poor Karen." In my mind I put "poor" and "artist" together with the resolve to help this unfortunate girl.

Before the ship even pulled out of the harbor, I found myself face to face with the attractive, vivacious, white-mink clad young Egyptian woman, Leila, who had come just a few days ago to buy some furniture we were selling in advance of touring Europe. We

Two Bennington girls at the farewell party.

merrily embraced and did a dance around with champagne glasses in hand, to the amazement of my family and other friends on the pier who had come to see us off. Music played, streamers filled the ever widening space between dock and ship—a lovely, emotional send off to new experiences.

The crossing was fun filled, with Leila and me dancing and cavorting about like two delighted children. David and Leila's rich American husband, Bill (whose occupation or source of wealth was never revealed), watched us with tolerant amusement. On board was Monsieur Andouzfari, the president of the French Line. When he learned from the Captain of the ship that David was the nephew of President Truman, our libations on board were complimentary. President Truman's effort, years before, to help the crippled French line's *Normandie* in New York harbor was gratefully remembered with this gesture. We lifted many glasses to Uncle Harry!

Clearly, our Paris stay would include numerous good times with Bill and Leila, who lived on the ultra-chic Quai Bourbon on the Île Saint Louis in the heart of Paris. Chic and lively, Leila inspired riotous outings to colorful, offbeat night spots, while Bill indulged her extroverted behavior and quietly picked up the tab. One of many memorable occasions was etched in my memory. The Rue de Lappe near the Bastille had a couple of *bal musette* dives frequented by hookers, pimps and very commonplace working class people out for an evening of drinks and dancing. One

Arrival in Paris to the hotel on the rue de Rivoli, near the Louvre and Tuileries Garden.

evening, we four entered into one of these crowded, smoky establishments. I feared for my life, but Leila went on ahead. She removed her white mink coat and threw it down on the sawdust floor. Leila shouted a very loud "Une!" Someone then replied "Deux!" and another cried "Trois!" This was a request for the band on the balcony to play a *java*. Leila had taught me this earthy dance on the *Flandre*, so we commenced our flamboyant movement on the dance floor. I grabbed her ass with both hands, and she put her arms around my neck as we quick stepped, rocking side to side like lascivious sailors, bodies close together, around the floor. Once in a while, I would reach up to take one of her hands, clutching it in mine and bring it to her ass. Gripping her hand, I would swing her about until we crashed into each other front-to-front, simulating an in coitus position. We thought it enormous fun!

These merry days were later extended to Cannes, where they had a sprawling apartment in the Palais des Pins, overlooking the very expansive Mediterranean. An excursion into Nice, which at that time was more of a fishing village than the mini-Miami Beach it is today, was charming. At a pleasant seaside restaurant, Bill arranged with the owner to move some tables away so that Leila and I could dance to music playing. Voilà! A dance floor was created for our own use. On one occasion, the Bill and Leila Hart generously lent us their lovely place when we were in Cannes and they were in Paris. After many forays about France with them, David and I departed for Italy with the firm promise to meet again either in New York or Paris. This promise was fulfilled many times over in the years to come.

This is where "poor Karen" comes into the story, as well as Dame Joan Sutherland. Hollywood was filming *Cleopatra* in Rome concurrent with our stay there. Both David and I were friends with Richard Burton's personal aide, another Richard, and his partner, Jim, whom we had known slightly in New York. The stars of the film were always being given tickets to any major event happening in Rome. Richard Burton's two tickets inevitably ended up in my possession, as neither the star nor his aide wished to use them. It seemed to me very sweet that Richard Burton went home to his wife, Sybil, and their children on the via Appia Antica after a busy day of filming, rather than attend the opera, or the concert, or whatever. It was wonderful that David and I benefited by attending these events. Sometimes, I would take Karen, if David's interest was not keen. It was not until we returned from a tour of Greece and Turkey that we became aware of the truth of the matter, as the famous cable to Hollywood declared: "Burton plucking brains out of Taylor!" (No wonder we never saw Elizabeth at any of the events that we used Burton's tickets for!)

"Poor Karen" was wined and dined by David and me. We had a very lively time, going about Rome in her old VW bug. The surprise, I much later discovered, was that Karen was the heiress to the Sears Roebuck fortune, and her Rosenwald family had a remarkable book collection outside of Philadelphia, now in the Library of Congress. The only thing poor about Karen was that she was in Rome without her Bennington friends, who thought of her as "poor" because she was alone.

Gala on the Flandre: *Leila and Bill Hart with David on right.*

As an aside, this is this same Karen who, upon return to New York, invited me to escort her to the wedding reception of her friend, Shirley Chaplin, when she married young Broadway producer Hal Prince. The event was held on the St. Regis Roof. This champagne-drenched extravaganza exposed me to many glittering personalities of film and stage, not the least of whom was Rita Hayworth. She and I made an embarrassing exhibition of ourselves on the dance floor at my instigation.

Karen did not like to dance, but she encouraged me to invite others to dance with me as often as I liked, as she was content chatting with friends. When I danced Arlene Francis around, she inquired if I were an actor. "That's 10 down, Arlene," I said as though on the hit show "What's My Line," on which she was a featured panelist. Betty Comden assured me that she was not married to Adolf Green as we took a turn around the floor, with me having suggested the contrary. Gail Lumet and I did some fancy footwork causing me to comment to her that she should be on the stage. I did not know she was the dancing star of a Broadway musical, and that her mother was Lena Horne. Lena Horne, who looked incredible in a svelte black gown and with a hairdo that wrapped some of her hair like a veil around her face, declined a dance with me but gave me "a rain check." On and on, shmoozing the glittering guests continued until late arrivals sat themselves at my table. Several people had departed, so these seats were available for Zero Mostel and Gary Merrill (just divorced from Bette Davis) escorting the unmistakable Rita Hayworth.

Unlike the gowned and jeweled guests and underneath a sable coat, Rita wore a simple in-town-for-shopping sheath dress with a long gold rope necklace. She seemed lost in her thoughts while Zero and Gary prattled on, so I dared to get up and approach her with the offer of us dancing together. She seemed confused and glanced over to Gary Merrill for advice. "Don't bother them in their discussion," I said putting out my hand to her to join me, which she did. It wasn't until the distended belly of the love goddess pressed against my cummerbund that I realized how under the influence she was. It was impossible to lead her, as she was not responding to my strong leads, so I thought I would give her the chance to lead me. Nothing! I resorted to trying conversation, swaying in place. "I knew one of your husbands . . ." I ventured. "Wishh one?" "Ali Kahn," I replied, hoping for some interesting comment. "Oh, him . . ." Rita replied, with the sweep of a limp wrist. Her sadness was touching.

This was tough going, so I thought it time to end the effort. "If you don't want to dance, let's sit down." "But, I love to dance," Rita assured me. "Well then give me a smile," I requested the intoxicated film icon. She gave me a half-hearted smile. "Oh, give me a frown," I said in mild annoyance. Rita really frowned, then broke out into a huge smile to our mutual pleasure.

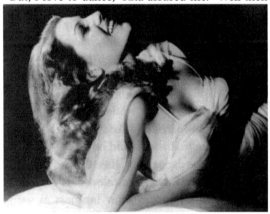

Who knows or can explain where I sometimes get zany, sometimes inappropriate notions. Certainly they are hatched after generous amounts of

Love goddess, Rita Hayworth.

alcohol, but the direction my mind takes is startlingly outrageous. Just like Mickey Rooney and Judy Garland spontaneously made a show in the barn, I decided that Rita Hayworth and I should do a floor show. Trouble about that was that there were too many people dancing around us. (The other trouble that did not enter my mind was that we were both drunk and quite incapable of creating a fabulous terpsichorean display. Had I so soon forgotten that she would not follow any lead of mine?) "Let's knock the fucking bores off the floor," I suggested. "Wha..yeah, fuckin' bores . . ." she replied. We proceeded to elbow and bump with our hips those dancing around us. When they saw who it was abusing them so, they sat down. Maybe the throng expected to see Rita Hayworth do a spectacular routine. If so, they were disappointed. We shuffled around the now empty dance floor. Lester Lanin, who was familiar with my frequent appearances dancing to his popular music, looked at me with a puzzled expression as the band played on. Happily, Gary Merrill made his way over to us and firmly advised Rita to sit down, much to my relief. The party was over and I was deeply embarrassed.

Burton's tickets provided another memorable experience. The opera world during the '60s was abuzz with the extraordinary voice of newcomer Joan Sutherland. This *bel canto* artist was going to sing in Rome at a concert in conjunction with her conductor husband, Richard Bonynge. They had never appeared together before, so this was an historic performance. It was one that many of us in attendance would never forget, especially when Joan Sutherland walked down the narrow aisle to the front of the stage, pulling down music stands ensnared by her emerald green tule gown. It was so flared that there was no room to permit easy passage.

The audience laughed, clearly viewing the path of destruction. Roddy McDowall was particularly raucous in his guffawing behind me. To make matter worse, when the diva turned to leave up the same aisle, those musicians without the forethought to firmly hold on to their stands found them toppled again.

Twenty years later, when I recollected this incident to the now "Dame" Joan Sutherland, I thought she would chuckle about it. I discovered that a great diva has the knack for instantly dealing with such things by simply not acknowledging anything has been said. Not a flicker, not a hesitation—on with conversation, completely ignoring the comment. This takes lots of discipline.

Thanks to the assistance of Catherine Hawkins, a young English woman I had met on the last trip in Greece with Susan and Danielle, we secured an apartment in Rome. By chance, she had been staying in the same hotel in Athens that I was booked into. Catherine was affiliated with the Food & Agriculture Organization (FAO), an international organization in Rome linked with the United Nations. The newly found apartment was just beyond the portal at Piazza del Popolo, where Queen Christina entered Rome centuries before, one block off the Tiber River. The apartment was going to be our home base of operations, with forays into Spain and Morocco, France and Switzerland, and the many fascinating cities around Italy.

This was a very special time to be living in Rome. It was before economic measures shut off much of the lighting as well as the fountains during the late hours. I loved walking home from some event to the sound of water splashing and the clip-clopping of horses' hoofs, viewing the beautifully lit architectural wonders of the Eternal City. Then, in the early hours of the morning, melodious bursts of song could be heard from the purveyors of vegetables, fruits, or whatever was being sold door-to-door.

Before departing for Europe, David had arranged, through diplomatic sources, to secure a private audience with Pope John XXIII, who was invigorating the world with his concept of setting up the Ecumenical Council for the better rapport between religions. Our audience with the Pope would involve only a handful of people, in contrast to mass gatherings held weekly for the crowds of visitors to the Eternal City. As there was an official invitation to be collected at a Vatican office conveniently located in central Rome, I suggested I would stop by to get it before our papal audience the next day.

I entered the office and announced I had come to collect the invitation to meet the Heavenly Father. "Yet another Protestant," the Irish priest mirthfully declared. "You mean the Holy Father, as you are much too young to be seeing the Heavenly Father!"

David and I collected various mementoes at shops near the Vatican for the Papal blessing requested at our meeting. These items would be dispensed to friends or interested relatives later on. We entered the Vatican with mounting excitement, invitation in hand. The beautifully attired Swiss Guard escorted us through impressive Renaissance hallways, leading into the marble chamber where the Pope would grant us the audience. A few other people quietly assembled in a semi-circle, anxiously awaiting the moment His Holiness would appear.

When the Pope walked slowly into the room, I was surprised at how ill he looked. Almost immediately, His Holiness inquired who would like to speak French, then English, then . . . With each foray into another language, Pope John XXIII seemed to grow younger and more lively. His pallor improved with his growing enthusiasm. He was a joy to behold, and I had the notion that he forgot he was Pope!

After we departed His Holiness's company, David and I got special permission from the official on hand to visit the Etruscan tombs under St. Peter's Basilica. At that time, the remains of St. Peter were also kept there and we joked about hijacking them. They have since been moved to another resting place, but the Etruscan altars and tombs are probably still intact in their subterranean resting place.

When not being outfitted on the Via Condotti in the best tailor shops, we made efforts to visit many churches of architectural and artistic interest. Trips out of town to Hadrian's Villa and the Etruscan tombs north of Rome compensated for our dropping out of the tedious Italian classes at Dante Alighieri Society. Previous readings about the construction of Saint Peters and Michelangelo's creation of the Sistine Chapel prepared us somewhat for the actual viewing. However, the immensity of Saint Peters could not be appreciated fully until actually roaming about the interior. It needed several viewings to absorb the magnificence of it. The vastness of the Vatican Museum was unexpected and exhausting. Since our visit, the Sistine Chapel frescoes have been restored, but they were very impressive before this work. Putting the enclave of the Basilica and other buildings and the sculpture and painting together, Vatican City impressed me by its mighty treasure trove. The world would be much poorer without it, but one has to be impressed and perhaps cynical of the power of the Catholic Church to amass such wondrous holdings.

David and I fastidiously studied our guidebooks and read about Roman history with enormous pleasure. We shared the experiences of viewing Roman ruins or great masterworks at the many museums, both in Rome and in various other cities. Florence, along the Arno River, with its Renaissance art and architecture, totally blew our minds, as did the mysterious city of Venice, seemingly afloat, full of winding alleys, art-filled churches with clanging bells, and singing gondoliers gliding along the canals. It was thrilling to see so much history and beauty and share the awakening awareness of it together.

David had a prodigious knowledge about classical music, particularly opera; I had a broad awareness of theater and ballet. We made a great team as culture mavens wandering around Italy, in Vienna, and even Barcelona, where I was introduced to the zarzuela being played as our ship pulled out to bring us to the island of Majorca for a tour.

It seemed as though the cornucopia of delicious delights was ours for the sampling, which we did with gusto! We learned from each other as well as from the cultural worlds we were relishing. This was truly a grand tour, with few blemishes. Even my sliding off the Matterhorn while trying to ski in icy conditions did little to diminish our enthusiasm. There was every chance I could have been killed instead of temporarily incapacitated. I pulled ligaments in both legs, but had a glorious view of the famous mountain from my bed in that quaint town, Zermatt. After our return to Rome, David bought me, through an FAO discount from Catherine, a silver Dunhill lighter to remember the Matterhorn incident.

One further long-distance trip that was particularly fascinating began with the ferry from southern Spain over to Morocco. We were intrigued by the Arabian nights atmosphere in Tangiers but maintained a careful guard up, especially when visiting the *souks*. Neither of us wished to become white slaves or be robbed, as we feared was commonplace there. (David tended to be a worrier and more pessimistic than I.) A very affable young Dutchman changed money for us and seemed available to show us around. It was clear he would have happily agreed to a threesome, but that was something totally foreign to us. With his experiences living there, we learned something of the city before returning to Spain by ship.

I purchased a white- and black-striped *djellabah* as a useful souvenir from Morocco. We were planning to go to Malaga and stay at the Alhambra Palace Hotel, adjacent to the famous historic palace. I saw myself inspecting that great Moorish palace, appearing in my djellabah like an apparition from the distant past. However, that had to wait until our last day there; I was taken ill with some stomach disorder and bedridden for three days under the hotel doctor's orders. I could hear the bells jingling on the goats outside on the mountainside, and could see the walls of the famous Alhambra from my bed, taunting me. I yearned to get up and dress up as a Moor, striding the palace grounds, which David obligingly took photos of when I could finally stroll around.

Although the Alhambra Palace was a luxury hotel, the prices at that time seemed do-able. Things in Spain cost much less than elsewhere, especially when compared to the United States. Consequently, we could savor the comforts of high-ranking Spanish hotels without breaking the bank. We relished a couple of delightful days in Andalusia, with its dazzling whitewashed walls and windows filled with bright red geraniums, then went on to Madrid. The Palace Hotel and the

Grand Hotel in Madrid, near El Prado Museum, enjoyed a huge expanse between them. Small trees were planted in nicely spaced rows; they have since grown up to maturity, now hiding the hotels from each other. We booked into the Palace and enjoyed the luxury of its wonderful appointments.

One evening, after returning from a scouting trip around shops to buy decorative items for the projected antique shop we wanted to open in New York, I changed into a purple silk robe acquired in Rome. A knock at the door interrupted my way to the bathroom to take a shower. A good looking young porter stood there, looking me over. He said something in Spanish and ran his hand over my crotch, completely shocking me. I closed the door and told David, who said I must report him to the management. David was fearful there might be a robbery as retribution for my rejection of the fellow's advances. I disliked getting the porter into trouble, but I dressed and went to the lobby to consult with the manager. He seemed distressed, but promised to handle the situation.

Back in Rome, Christmas was advancing, with shops and avenues decorated for the big annual celebration. Policemen standing on their podiums directing traffic began to have boxes of *panettone* or other seasonal delights left, as holiday tribute, at their feet. The lines grew longer than usual at the post office, as many people wanted their Christmas gifts sent off. In Rome, respecting a queue is not a practice commonly observed. One pushes, shoves, and gets in front of one another ruthlessly. Often, when one finally gets to the front to speak with the counter attendant, one is told he has been in the wrong line and has to go to another window. The biggest crowds gather at St. Peter's for Midnight Mass, but many go to other famous churches of their preference like Santa Maria Maggiore. It is a night of great celebration and pomp, smells and bells.

A crowd is a perfect place for one of Rome's prevalent pastimes, pinching! Many people, not exclusively women, get their bottoms pinched. It comes with the territory. As each sewer cover proclaims: SPQR. That may have stood for *Senatus Populusque Romanus* to the ancient Romans, but today it indicates *Sono Porci Questi Romani*, or "All Romans are Pigs!"

The Romans have a unique method of celebrating New Year's Eve and getting rid of junk. Anyone with a car makes sure it is parked under cover, as torrents of stuff are tossed at midnight from balconies onto the street below, while other celebrants shoot rockets across the street and into the air. It is not safe to be on the street or even on a lower balcony. To avoid hurdling toilet seats and rockets, safety remains within the walls of the house. After the crashing of thrown objects subsides, a tentative peace reigns, until the pre-dawn street sweepers and cleaners arrive to gather up the broken glass and assorted objects hurled from above.

When David was not cooking up a storm from a multitude of fresh comestibles obtained from various outdoor markets around Rome, we might be found in old section of town, Trastevere, or the area below the Spanish Steps in one of the many lively eateries, or in the Piazza Navona dining with Karen, Richard and Jim, or Catherine.

On occasion we would attend gatherings in apartments around Rome. One of the most attractive belonged to Peggy Guggenheim, who lent it to the famous photographer Roloff Beni. I had met him on my initial visit to Rome. He was a neighbor in New York of a mutual good friend and artist, Louise Schacht, who kindly made the introduction. The penthouse overlooked impressive Roman ruins and was perfect for entertaining. Framed blowups of Roloff's photographs used in *The Pleasure of Ruins* by Rose Macaulay decorated the walls, as most of Peggy Guggenheim's famous collection was in her museum in Venice. I later met Peggy Guggenheim on a subsequent trip to Rome. Mink coat open, she rushed into the apartment, clutching her small dog and claimed that she had nearly been raped. I could not imagine why anyone would want to bother as she was so out of shape, with her face bloated and blotched from alcohol abuse—a veritable wreck of a woman.

David and I had been to a screening of *The Pit and the Pendulum* the afternoon before Beni's party. We were amused to see the leading actress, Barbara Steele, sitting in the theater near us, watching herself. More astonishing was to meet her at Beni's gathering. She was wearing a scanty black dress and complaining of getting a cold. I could see why Ms. Steele would invite a cold with the lack of warm clothing in a chilly season.

Catherine had an old Morris Minor convertible that took us on odd jaunts. The most amusing one was transporting to our apartment a Christmas tree secured in the back seat of the open car. We sped along a wide boulevard, with Catherine proclaiming how she loved to hear the sound of wind in pine needles. She was about to retreat to England, where plans for her wedding to an Italian count were being put in order.

We had decided to go to Paris and buy a Peugeot that we could later ship to the USA when we departed, as a car would be invaluable upon our return. In the meantime, we could break it in so it would not be a new car, thus avoiding import taxes in USA. A tour of the Loire was deemed to be enchanting as would be a visit to London and environs. Catherine suggested we join her in England. We could drive around Lorna Doone country with her before her wedding, since we would not attend the ceremony later because of other plans. The idea of such a trip shocked Catherine's parents, who felt it inappropriate for the bride-to-be cavorting around the countryside with two young men just weeks before her wedding to someone else. We thought it great fun to have a local girl show us about. The three of us spent one very chilly night in an old inn near Bristol, conducting a scary séance in a downstairs sitting room full of hideous antiques. We frightened ourselves into believing that the carved gargoyles in the furniture were coming to life. Aside from this, our outing was resplendent in Devonshire cream and strawberries, with lots of accompanying laughter.

Leaving Catherine to turn her attentions to the parade of Alpha Romeos soon wending their way northwards from Italy for the big wedding day, David and I prepared to set off on a trip to Greece and Turkey. We motored south to Rome, stopping off to see some of the places we had previously missed in the cornucopia of delights in France and Italy. After returning from Turkey, we arranged to give up our Lungotevere apartment and head to Venice, where the Peugeot and our ever-expanding luggage and bundles of decorative objects would be loaded on to the MS *Vulcania* for the ten-day ocean voyage to New York. With these arrangements in place, we were ready to experience Greece and Turkey.

This second go-around in Greece was very different from my first visit with the two young women. David and I stayed in fancier places, exploring museums and searching out shops that might have curious objects to sell in our shop-to-be.

So that we would have ample time to see the wonders of Athens and its environs, we arranged a round trip flight to Athens from Rome (instead of driving). Attendees from all around the globe were to arrive in Athens for a royal wedding a couple of weeks after our arrival, creating a tight availability of hotel rooms. This prompted us to book passage on a ship to tour the Aegean, with visits to Crete, Rhodes, Ephesus, Pergamum, the monastery on the island of Patmos, and Istanbul. Each day we made trips to the various points of interest, returning to the ship for dinner and to sleep. There was so much to see and try to absorb. It was fascinating but tiring, even for active young men like ourselves.

An enormous amount of energy had been directed to investigating Europe. We had managed an audience with the remarkable Pope John XXIII, had a wardrobe of elegant Italian silk clothes made in the best shops on the Via Condotti, and enjoyed our notions of the princely life, dipping in and out of culturally-rich Italian cities such as Milan, Verona, Florence, Venice, and Rome. We had taken a good look at France, England, Switzerland, Spain, Italy, Morocco, Greece, and Turkey, picking up lovely objects along the way for possible re-sale when we returned to the United States.

We drove our recently purchased Peugeot around Europe, so that it qualified as a used car when imported to America. Having savored many amusing and fascinating events while abroad, we began our move back to our new life in New York. Final preparations were made to depart from bewitching Venice for a ten-day crossing to America, after what we considered a triumphant, almost year-long Grand Tour.

The MS *Vulcania* was to be our floating home as we steamed westward through the Mediterranean, then across the Atlantic Ocean. This Italian line ship had been purposely run aground during World War II, to save it from being stripped of its elegant fixtures and accommodations while being converted into a troop ship. The first class dining room was three stories high, with painted rondels and murals; oriental carpets and carved wood panels enriched the atmosphere of utter luxury aboard this famous ocean liner.

With not a hint of modesty, we booked Suite A and had our car in the hold. Three uniformed attendants awaited our arrival at the door of the suite, as did a case of champagne ordered in advance (at sea price). I remember requesting firmly that the two male attendants remove the carpets, since we had our own, and hurling our carpets down into place on the floors. I had the maid remove the artwork from the walls, as we gaily hung our own pictures! While sipping chilled champagne, I rummaged through the trunk we had delivered into the bedroom. It had been stored for some months and contained pre-Via Condotti clothing now deigned unworthy of further use. I had a porthole opened and threw some of these garments out into the Adriatic Sea. My sense of drama was heightened by the champagne and the supreme luxury of living in this wonderful suite. I felt like a Zelda Fitzgerald, or Lady Brett in *The Sun Also Rises*.

Our presence on board did not go unnoticed by our fellow travelers. Sometimes, we would invite worthy guests to dine with us in our private dining room in the suite; however, when we chose to use the first class dining room, we reserved a table for four, so that we could invite others to join us if we wanted company; sometimes we did not appear in the grand dining room for dinner for days on end. Breakfast was always in bed, brought by our three attendants, who entered singing Italian opera. Lunch was often poolside. When we did appear in the dining room, it was in sartorial splendor. With our shimmering silk suits and impeccable dinner clothes, we seemed to be visiting royalty to the more mundane travelers.

Once back in Manhattan, we leased a one-bedroom apartment in a nice townhouse off Fifth Avenue on 72nd Street. Some of the Spanish furniture, carpets and paintings came in handy, furnishing the empty space that was to be our home for several years.

We had returned from our Grand Tour to a Camelot atmosphere. A sense of pride and enthusiasm swept America when the young John Fitzgerald Kennedy was elected to the White House. The previous atmosphere of dowdiness was replaced by a modern, streamlined vivacity, capturing the imagination of the nation. Both young and older Americans engaged with the dynamic duo of Jack and his glamorous wife, Jackie. A new energy was injected into the country, with a promise of a brighter tomorrow steered by its youthful leader at the helm.

The First Lady and her favorite decorators created a New York residence for her and the president in a triplex on the top floors of the Carlyle Hotel on Madison Avenue and 76th Street, where David brought me to meet the Trumans many months earlier. This was just up the street from where we now lived. On the ground floor of our building were the offices of Dr. Max Jacobson, a.k.a. "Dr. Feelgood," famous for ministrations of painkillers and "speed" to wealthy patients. The president was known to have had serious back problems and resorted to the attentions of this doctor.

One afternoon, when exiting my building, Jackie was jaywalking across the street, directly in front of me. A Secret Service man was on either side of her, warily investigating the surroundings, but they were too preoccupied with their surveillance to be aware of what the lady they were protecting was doing at this time.

Jackie fastened her eyes upon me, alone on the sidewalk facing her. With a demure smile on her face, she continued to stroll towards me. Riveted best describes my state of mind and body at attention. I have been cruised by many individuals in my life, but I never had such a thorough undressing as the First Lady bestowed upon me. Though very embarrassed, I was flattered that she thought me worthy of such an intense perusal. This was an unexpected perk from living in this fashionable community that I now called home.

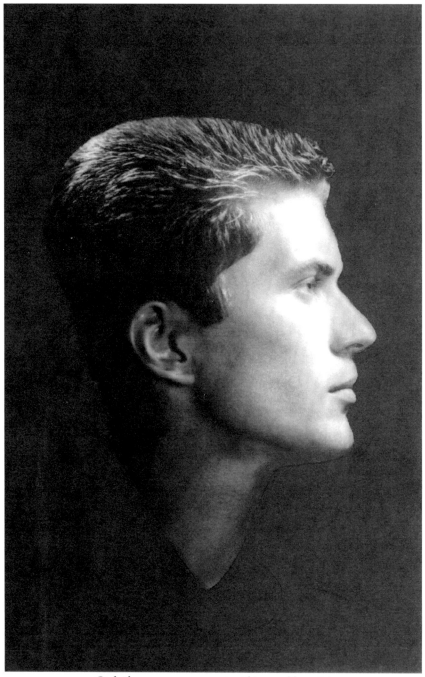

Go forth, young man – an astonishing world awaits!

Chapter 6

IS THE SUCKER PAYING FOR THE CALL?

As this Prince was not inclined to use public transportation, I canvassed the neighborhood for a likely place of employment. The very dignified Parke-Bernet Galleries were easily in walking distance from my home and very prestigious in both the arts and social circles. Being well-spoken, nicely attired in my Italian suits, and intelligent with office skills, I was hired to handle dispersing information to the inquiring public, whether on the phone, in person, or by mail.

Sandy (Eunice) Carroll, the manager of the business office, interviewed me; we hit it off immediately. Her warm, nurturing personality encouraged confidence and made for a friendly working environment. Sandy wore glasses (unless going to a function) and relied on a cigarette burning in her ashtray constantly. She was a regular gal with an easy demeanor. She seemed pleased by my appearance and background.

The Galleries were located directly across from the main entrance to the Carlyle Hotel on Madison Avenue. A well-mannered doorman in a green uniform with matching hat attended to opening the glass doors into the marbled lobby. Elevators straight ahead delivered visitors to the second floor, which housed the administration and business offices as well as curatorial offices for the rare book department and the jewelry department. On the third floor were the spacious viewing rooms, with the auction room to the left. When visiting either of these two floors, one encountered a noticeable hushed atmosphere as in a museum. The painting and decorative arts and antiques departments shared space on the floor above, the fourth floor.

The ground floor uptown corner featured a pleasant restaurant useful for visitors to the Galleries. Parke-Bernet did not have a cafeteria for its employees, so I would either go home for lunch or visit a neighborhood eatery with colleagues. We all tried to look neat and well-dressed. There was not a hint of blue jeans anywhere.

The first desk in the front of the office, one floor above the entrance to the building, was assigned to me. It faced the long, wide hallway towards the elevators, rest rooms and telephone operators' room, which was across from shipping, where customers picked up their purchases. I had direct observation of everything transpiring on the public sector of the floor, and everyone coming though could not help but notice me, as well.

I was often the first person to come into the offices. It was good to get work out of the way, so I could go to the floor above—where the auction room and two large exhibition halls were located—in order for me to acquaint myself with what was displayed and on the block, and with whomever was floating about. My outbox was filled before many employees arrived, something Leslie Hyam, the English founding president, was quick to notice. He admired my work ethic, and manner of dress and speech. Unlike his stony expression for many of the other personnel, Mr. Hyam always had a warm greeting for me.

With earnest enthusiasm, I fulfilled all my duties to everyone's satisfaction. Leslie Hyam noticed upon his arrival that I was always early and busily engaged in dispensing orders for catalogues and handling requests pertaining to estimated or realized prices on items in the many sales. My manner with customers who came to the counter was favorably registered by the hierarchy there. I often spent my breaks in the auction room, learning about provenance and values of the prized objects that passed through the hallowed portals.

This expertise would come in handy if and when David and I ever opened our antique shop. At this point, we felt the financial outlay would be too costly. Getting our feet more firmly established on the scene seemed a wise choice of action. In the meantime, we used much of the furniture we bought in Europe, together with the decorative items in our apartment. Some we sold to friends or acquaintances, or gave as gifts for weddings and birthdays.

Greta Garbo sometimes came into the exhibition rooms to enjoy the beauty of the displayed objects. One day, she spied me across the room and asked the manager in her attendance, "Who is that beautiful young man?" Momentarily, I was escorted into the film legend's presence. Upon hearing my name being Gustafson, she uttered it was the same name as hers before it was changed. "You could be my nephew." The reader will soon discover how it came to pass that I was to claim Garbo as my aunt on two prestigious occasions!

Jackie Kennedy was another frequent visitor, sometimes coinciding with Garbo. I had the preposterous notion they planned it to happen that way. Garbo, in her white sneakers and blue raincoat, could enjoy her supposed wish to be alone, while Jackie enjoyed the notoriety. It probably was not so. Garbo could hardly avoid being spotted just because she dressed so casually, devoid of any fashion sense in a place full of well-turned out people. Also, it should be noted: if Garbo went unnoticed for very long, she would compulsively do something to call attention to herself.

People are funny creatures. The same syndrome applied to Martha Mitchell when I danced her around the MOMA (Museum of Modern Art) dance floor later, during the Nixon era. She told me she hoped the press did not notice her, but as we passed them she said something to them to attract their attention!

"Aunt" Greta

Working at Parke-Bernet was fast moving, high pressured and usually fascinating to a person such as myself who was interested in improving his knowledge of art, antique furniture, and rare objects and books. The promenade of social figures always added zest to each day, as well. It was an ideal pedestal for me to see and be seen. The experiences there strengthened my ego and give expression to my place in the scheme of things.

New York University's Graduate School for Advanced Studies in Art took over the Doris Duke mansion on Fifth Avenue at 78th Street. Two prominent students there became colleagues of mine. Iris Love of the Guggenheim family was engaged in archeological work in Greece and Turkey, making international news with her finds at digs. A friend of mine working at the United Nations as a guide, Karen Gilmuyden, introduced us at the auction house. Karen was Norwegian and Greek heritage, but from a family living in Turkey. She knew Iris through Greek and Turkish connections. The other student was the very handsome Philippe de Montebello, who often came into the auction house, and worked with the master painting department at the Metropolitan Museum after his graduate work was completed. He eventually became the director of the museum.

I saw Iris on various social occasions and soon met her attractive sister, Noel Gross. Noel liked to lunch at the 21 Club, and would invite me once in awhile to join her. As a gay man, I guess I was considered safe, and her husband would not object. One evening, at a formal dinner party on Park Avenue, the woman whose place card was next to mine startled me. "We met at the 21 Club today!" I was nonplussed, as I had not been there for weeks. She asked if I knew Noel Gross and explained how Noel was there with someone whom she introduced as me. I eagerly telephoned Noel the next morning to thank her for the lunch I did not share with her. Poor Noel was very surprised to be caught out. Had a few days gone by after the lunch, my dinner partner probably would have forgotten the name of Noel's male guest. Apparently, Noel thought by going to a well-known place no one would suspect she was with a lover, especially if he were given a gay identity. It would be thought too audacious to really be with one's lover at a popular watering hole. Alas, she was mistaken— what a wonderful Manhattan tale.

Ysabel Aya de Salgar in her 955 Fifth Avenue home.

During the summer of 1962, David and I opted to rent a small cottage on the middle dune on the northern side of The Pines on Fire Island. This cottage had vistas of both ocean and bay. Parke-Bernet offered its employees the summer off at half-pay, if they wished, since the galleries were closed for the season. I thought it a splendid opportunity for us to enjoy Fire Island's sea breezes and famed beach life. David would leave the Midtown office of Diamond Match Corporation, where he did promotional work, to come out on Fridays and return Monday mornings to resume work in the city.

The Pines in the early '60s was a mixture of straights and gays. It was more upmarket than its neighbor, the older, very gay and cute Cherry Grove. This was just before the grandeur set in, and it was still a very merry place for summer frolics, less soigné than it was to become. Though more sophisticated than Cherry Grove, The Pines was still simple, without swimming pools and sprawling show-off homes.

Our lives on Fire Island were populated with interesting people, one of whom was to become a very long-time close friend, Ysabel Aya de Salgar. Ysabel was staying there for only a short time and brought two Colombian maids with her. Though one maid would have been enough in her modest beach house, Ysabel wanted her girl to have company. She was unique in having a servant in residence there, never mind two.

We met when our neighbors, Walter and Ruth Loveland Stane, gave a party. I began conversation with a tall, slender, and elegant woman who had a dark Hispanic flare. At one point, we glanced out of the plate glass window facing the

Tennessee Williams with Dr. Ruth Loveland and Walter Stane attending the New York premiere of MGM's Lord Jim *starring Peter O'Toole; one of my promotional stunts.*

David's birthday: Eric, David, and the maid, Cleo.

ocean. Two party guests were in a close embrace outside, which caused Ysabel to exclaim, "It looks like they're fucking!" It startled me to hear someone I had just met make such a comment. This was only a hint of what I might expect in future encounters.

After some minutes of curious conversation, Ysabel suggested I stop by the next morning for some refreshment. I arrived and was given some "hair of the dog that bit me" the previous night partying. It surprised me that a Bloody Mary with beer added could be tasty, and I drank it dutifully.

We had a merry conversation, at the end of which I invited Ysabel to come with David and me to a Cleopatra-themed costume party that evening. We were going as scantily dressed slaves and bearing torches. Henry Fonda's ex-wife, Susan, was the hostess. What I recall most about the event was strolling about the boardwalks the next morning, noting with amusement the debris from the revelers. Bits of costumes and discarded under garments had been strewn about in abandon.

So began the journeys between 16 East 72nd Street and 955 Fifth Avenue (just north of 76th Street), as Ysabel and I upgraded our friendship. Ysabel did not pass through life unnoticed. Although she loved classical music, she detested the opera. Often, someone would mistake her for Maria Callas. Ysabel would feign great regard for the vocal talents of the Greek diva, and insist that, although they were friends, she would never appear on stage with Callas.

Her long, black hair was always pulled straight up and wrapped around what she called her merkin. Her bun was worn on top of the head, Buddha fashion, rather than in the back. Often, her main adornment would be an authentic pre-Columbian gold piece on a gold chain around her neck. Sometimes, she preferred a triple-strand pearl necklace with a ruby and diamond clasp. Another standard piece of her jewelry was a gold bracelet created with a centipede-like flexibility. Her tailor-made clothes were form fitting and sometimes low cut in the back, showing off her statuesque figure. On occasion, she threatened to wear a dress backwards—tits out!

Allegra Kent Taylor (Papagena)
and Eric (Papageno) at the opera party
devised by David and Eric.

Apartment 11-A was a floor-through with a gorgeous view west over Central Park, towards the Hudson River. Coming from the elevator hall into the entrance hall—with black and white large squares of marble on the floor— one could see the bar with black light straight ahead. Coat closets lined both sides of the hall leading to the main salon (living room) on the left, with the expansive view through the plate glass window. Very long, '40s-style gray sofas set behind thick-glass-topped coffee tables on marble bases provided seating. A pale beige baby grand piano stood on the left, in front of floor-to-ceiling mirrors. Across from it on the right was a long black-lacquered record album case with phonograph/radio installed within. Above it was one of the four large Jean Miró ink on rice paper drawings that he created for Ysabel some years before. A thick gray rug covered the central portion of the room. There was a very '40s feel to the room, inherited from Art Deco. It was comfortable and created for pleasure.

To the right was the dining room with a semi-abstract mural on the right wall. The elongated table had glass bases supporting a long, thick simulated lapis lazuli top. At the far end of the room, on the left, were curved windows facing Madison Avenue as well as the swinging door into the kitchen and maids' room. Sliding doors on the left closed the dining room from the guest room or library. A glass case showed pre-Columbian pieces intermingled with a clay replica of the penis of Eunice Gardiner's lover. Above, "Fatso" sat on top of the case. This large pre-Columbian terracotta statue was a fantastic addition to the room.

The other room in the front of the apartment, Ysabel's bedroom, had sliding Japanese panels at the windows, a purple oval bed, and art deco chests of drawers in front of a mirrored wall. Two more black ink Miró paintings graced the wall to the right of the bed. There were two bathrooms between the library and her room. Her bathroom had painted murals suitable for Cleopatra's loo; mine, the guest bathroom, was done up as an Etruscan tomb. It was an exotic environment with taste and verve befitting its owner.

Ysabel was born in Colombia. Her father was the generalissimo of the Colombian army and her mother, who was very Eleanor Roosevelt-like in stature, was named "Woman of the Americas." During the Kennedy Administration, her mother endorsed the work of the Peace Corps in Colombia. Unlike free-spirited Ysabel, Doña Maria was conservative and utterly lady-like. Her world was restrained and elegant. Her other daughters were living lives somewhere in between Ysabel's flamboyant world and the proper world of her mother. Beatriz, closest to Ysabel, but always correct in behavior, remained in Bogota, while Cecilia chose to live a *bon bourgeois* existence in Paris, away from the constraints of home.

Always a rebel, schoolgirl Ysabel, at a French convent school, was made to memorize poetry as punishment for bad behavior. As a result, all her life, she could

Nannette's Stock Club birthday celebration for Eric.

spontaneously spout lovely poetry in Spanish, French, or Italian. Usually, this happened after several libations while sitting quietly with me. The air became filled with her spontaneous recitations. Art, gypsy dancing, and classical music thrilled her, just as the opera appalled her. Artists often wanted to paint her, and some of the most famous were her friends. She enjoyed the bohemian camaraderie of creative people and did not suffer the company of the pompous or self-important.

Other colorful visitors to our summer cottage were the irrepressible Leila, who claimed her father was an Egyptian pasha, with her husband Bill Hart, with whom we had cavorted on the *Flandre*, as well as in France. Timothy Baum appeared, a cohort from my first ocean voyage in 1957 aboard the SS *United States*. He confessed having scraped the fender of Noel Coward's Rolls Royce in the ferry parking lot. Timothy lived in our neighborhood in Manhattan, and I would see him on occasion.

Back at Parke-Bernet, an amusing attraction was added to my daily work life in the form of debutante Nannette Cavanagh, daughter of the deputy mayor of New York. She had no office skills but was a sweet tempered girl who hoped to please me as my first and only assistant. One of the first things she did was to sit on an open ink pad in her Channel styled skirt. Though she was obviously a political arrangement between Mr. Marion, the vice-president, and City Hall, I enjoyed having her around. Soon, I began escorting her to charity balls, and we would bring back bouquets of floral arrangements, taken from our table the night before, to decorate the office. Our frequency at the society balls increased my familiarity with influential people, many of whom visited the auction house.

It was amusing to call David late one afternoon from the Junior League to ask him to wait on a specific corner of Park Avenue, where we would pick him up. Nannette's aunt, Barbara Cavanagh, had recently married Mayor Robert Wagner. The mayor, Nannette, and I were leaving the Junior League, and the mayor suggested dropping us off at some function being held at the Waldorf Astoria Hotel further south. David was going to join us, so the Mayor's limousine stopped to pick up an astonished David, who had been expecting us in

Phillip and Eric drive around in style.

a taxi at the appointed street corner. What a pity this was not an official jaunt, as we might have had a police escort. As it was, riding with the mayor in his limo was a hoot! We then continued with the mayor on our mirthful way.

One dashing man about town who came to Parke-Bernet with some frequency was Philip van Rensselaer. I remembered reading about him years earlier as being a favorite of heiress Barbara Hutton. Later, he showed me the ruby and diamond cufflinks she had given him. Whenever he was short of cash, he would hock them and always retrieve them when cash permitted. His brother Charles wrote the society column as "Cholly Knickerbocker" for the *New York Journal-American*, and Philip was often mentioned in the press, as well. We struck up an acquaintanceship. Philip was working on another book, *House with the Golden Door*, and did not type, so I agreed to be of assistance some hours a week. Both of us laughed a lot during the writing of the book, especially when I helped to dream up erotic situations for his heroine, Cherry Towers. He kindly gave me vodka to help keep the wheels grinding. After a few hours, he would invite me to lunch with him and his brother, Charlie. I thought it glamorous to share time with this notorious playboy, and to be part of the social life the two brothers were so familiar with and worked to immortalize.

Andy Warhol frequented gallery openings and special events at Parke-Bernet. This gave me an opportunity to stay in touch with him. We had met before he became so famous, when he was a designer for shoe displays at Bergdorf Goodman. A colleague there introduced us, and over the years we continued to have some exposure to each other. He was living in a brownstone in the Upper East '80s, then moved to a ground floor apartment on Lexington Avenue. Andy invited me in one day to see something in his bedroom. Passing through the kitchen, I met his mother, who had a glass of booze at hand and seemed to be signing the back of a painting of his. In his bedroom, I noticed his wig stands, each holding one of his wigs in varying states of messiness.

From what I remember about this ground floor apartment, Andy certainly did not collect antique furniture. The place was nondescript and messy. The only conversation we really shared was about mutual friends we had in the past, what they were doing, and what had happened to them. I do not remember ever talking about art. I avoided talk about his work, as I thoroughly was appalled at his put-on with Pop Op stuff. Andy knew he was hoodwinking the public, and they deserved it for taking his stuff seriously. His work reflected the nothingness he saw in contemporary society. What I objected to more was the wreck he and his cronies made at lovely dinner parties. People would congregate in a beautiful Park or Fifth Avenue apartment to enjoy a civilized dinner, only to have it disrupted by the scruffy Warhol mob. His carryings on had an antisocial aspect. He seemed taciturn and was most comfortable when his "factory folk" were around him, doing drug-inspired foolish things.

Andy Warhol's first silk-screened portrait in the series that included Jackie and Marilyn was of taxicab heiress Ethel Scull. Ethel had been introduced to me during the summer David and I rented a house in Amagansett. She often invited me to escort her to some event, when I was not going about with Nannette on my arm.

Thanks to my contacts, David was busily engaged in a public relations stint that was later to become his career. Together with Mimi Strong, they generated publicity for the opening of The Barge, a new discotheque in Bridgehampton on Long Island. David invited Ethel and me to join Michael, Prince of Hesse, in a helicopter ride, arriving at the Barge with a battery of photographers and film people to record our landing. We were to be lotus-eaters, coming in for fresh pleasure. A hitch occurred when the helicopter did not arrive on time to take us airborne out over the Atlantic Ocean, in order to return and descend for the press. The Prince left after waiting a little bit, but Andy Warhol arrived with his groupies. He gladly joined us for the thrill of the ride, but was dissuaded from bringing anyone with him. The cabin only seated three people aside from the captain.

Having consumed significant amounts of celebratory champagne, I felt aggressive towards Andy, who was sitting on my right and blandly ignoring everything. I turned to Ethel as I placed my hand on the door handle just beyond Andy's crotch and said, "I have a good mind to throw this pink and white asshole out into the ocean!"

Ethel sniffed, as she often did, and said, "That's too good for him." I froze, puzzled, and she continued, "The press below would capture his death for posterity.

Eric with young Maria, the extraordinary Dalí, his Gala, and Ysabel.

It is too good for him!" That made sense to my besotted brain, and I released the handle. Andy sat stunned, not saying a word. When we landed, he disappeared into the blaze of flashing bulbs, not to be seen again that day!

The best thing to come out of that event was the spark of a friendship between me and Sheldon Rich, the producer of the documentary being made about the Barge. Rich and his South American pianist wife, Alicia, were going to begin a chamber music festival in Santa Fe in the near future, but soon he would agree to help me move some of my things when I departed the 72nd Street apartment. But, I am getting ahead of myself . . .

David seemed to be relieved not to be caught up in my social whirl, as he preferred listening to opera records or reading at home, or so I thought. He never complained about missing me when I was on the town, and our sexual relations were still active, though more relaxed after the initial few years. Though easy on the eye, David was sometimes clumsy socially and a bit of a lead balloon in a downdraft if he was not entranced with the social ambiance. Having Betsy Forbush's "cockeyed optimism," I overrode many alarm bells giving inklings that something was awry. Also, being the gregarious one in the partnership, I often introduced him to people I had met. On occasion, they would invite him to something or other. I did not take the time to analyze the extent of his friendships.

Eric emerging.

Parke-Bernet engrossed and enthralled me, and my growing man-about-town status after hours was often enmeshed with the prominent clients. My engagement calendar was full, both with personal commitments David and I made with friends and the fabric of social events I found myself sewn into. It was this non-stop twirling that stimulated me. There was always something intriguing on the program, usually with interesting people—art events at galleries and the museums, opera or ballet performances, and dinners with visiting doers and shakers.

In the midst of all this activity, a reporter from *The Boston Globe* asked to interview me while at a party at Didi Auchincloss's Park Avenue apartment. Shortly thereafter, splashed across the front page of their society section was a picture of me leaning across the lap of a Yveta Love (no relation to Iris or Noel), smoking a cigarette and looking quite dissolute. I was quoted as daily filling my days and nights with non-stop events—luncheons, cocktail parties, dinners, charity balls, the opera or ballet, and a late night club. Though it was an obvious exaggeration, it was enough to choke my Lutheran aunt in Lynn, Massachusetts, who felt New York was a pit of sin.

Meanwhile, my work at the auction house took on greater dimensions. With time, clients came to rely on my judgment and information about items for sale. One man, who lived in New Orleans with his special lady, asked me if I could bid for him on several 20th Century paintings coming up at auction. He was unable to attend but would be very pleased if I could secure the art he desired. It occurred to me that, with a telephone in the auction room, we could confer on each item as it came on the block. He was thrilled with the idea and committed to work with me by phone during the entire sale. This had never been done before. Usually, a person might be on the telephone line for one or two items, never for the entire length of the sale. When I spoke with the gruff vice president, Mr. Louis Marion (name changed from Marioni, it was rumored), about this prospect, he asked, "Is the sucker paying for the call?" Once I assured him the cost of the call was covered by the client, I got the go-ahead. The fast pace of the sale made the telephone transactions highly pressured, but we succeeded in getting him a couple of paintings, and I dissuaded him from buying some others I thought too high priced. When I revealed this to the executive vice president, Mary Vandergrift, she was very satisfied with my handling of the transaction, and remarked on my making a client for Parke-Bernet for life!

Art News wrote it up as a first in the art world. (This was only one of a few firsts I would create in my ever-expanding career.)

All kinds of wheelings and dealings began to reveal themselves to me during my years at Parke-Bernet. One of the most astonishing and amusing had to do with the visit one morning of two parish priests from the church Louis Marion was affiliated with in Westchester County. Louis Marion's son was the auctioneer, when two lovely crystal chandeliers came on the block. I happened to be at the door of the auction room when the gavel descended along with "Sold!" There was no chance for anyone to bid on them in that split second after the priests raised their paddle for them. Shortly after the chandeliers found their way to the parish house, the church held a raffle there for a Lincoln Continental Town Car. Imagine how fortunate it was when Louis Marion won it, and then sold it for full price to Parke Bernet, so they could give it to their new president, Louis Marion!

The distinguished Leslie Hyam had recently committed suicide, leaving instructions for his secretary to be kept on and for me to be made vice-president! Louis Marion, now the president, did not like this at all. He resented my relationships with the high-class customers and museum curators he could not achieve because of his crass behavior. He called me "the Duke" as a rebuke to my elegant demeanor. The suicide note was supposed to be a secret, so I did not mention it when he called me into a meeting together with Mary Vandergrift. Rather than promote me to an executive, he suggested that I learn to be an auctioneer, as he himself had been, after working his way up from the mailroom. Stunned, I stammered, "but I am not you, Mr. Marion." Knowing he and I would never get along, I proceeded to tender my resignation. No mention was made to the suicide note and I departed. Mary Vandergrift was saddened, believing I was a natural for the auction world. I am certain Louis Marion was delighted to be rid of me.

Sotheby's of London bought Parke-Bernet Auction Galleries shortly afterwards. Before my departure, I was in the business office, when I heard someone from Sotheby's ask where the "living room" was located. An audit was being done on the firm's assets before Sotheby's purchase. The large bill being investigated was for "installation of air conditioning in the living room." The "living room" was in Louis Marion's Westchester home! Mr. Marion was soon to leave Parke-Bernet to set up his own appraisal service, a few blocks south on Madison Avenue, taking his secretary with him. He should have done quite well, with his access to the top dealers and major people in the auction world. He was as crafty as he was crass; a tough customer with a flushed face, in expensive blue suits. Immersed in non-related work and impending trips away from that scene, I soon lost all interest in the fate of Louis Marion.

My final suggestion to Mary Vandergrift was to consider setting up a lecture series and a concert series in the auction room, when it was not being used. It would be a cultural enrichment for the community and a good will gesture, as well. For a small admission, many people would come into the otherwise forbidding-

Tribute to the Old Met. Above: l to r Eric, costume designer Elizabeth Mongomery (Motley), Dr. Berger with his wife, actress Anita Louise.

Right: Nell Webster, Maria Zaheri, Jeremyn Davern.

seeming, elite Parke-Bernet Galleries. It would familiarize them with the facilities, and their small entrance fee would give them permission to be there, possibly inducing new customers as a result. As I was departing the hallowed halls of Parke-Bernet, Desmond Guinness had been invited to talk on Irish architecture, and some chamber music concerts were planned.

I thought I wanted to try working with a museum, although shifting from a commercial venture to a significant museum position is very irregular. I was not schooled for museum work as Philippe de Montebello was, but I went to an interview with the director, James Rorimer, at the prestigious Metropolitan Museum of Art. He startled me by putting his leather boots on his desk, as though showing them off to signify—what? An S&M leather fetish? I did not feel comfortable becoming his assistant anything, so I looked elsewhere.

The Museum of the City of New York was looking for an assistant museum administrator. Carlin Gasteyer, the administrator, seemed to think I would do nicely in this position. It did not take me long to know how very different the museum world is from the auction world. Everything went at a snail's pace, with me dozing at my desk constantly. I wanted and needed more liveliness, more people around, and more challenges. Carlin claimed I brought Camelot to the stuffy museum. The male curators began to improve their sartorial appearance, possibly because of my verve in dress. As usual, I made new acquaintanceships. The most interesting one was with the Italian Consul General, His Excellency Vittorio di Montezemolo. Vittorio attended a luncheon of crêpes and champagne to celebrate an exhibition opening at the museum. He became a regular in my growing circle of friends. Despite Carlin being a wonderful, warm friendly soul, this bland environment was not for me.

My cohort from SS *United States* days, Timothy Baum, had worked for years with Janine Walkenberg at the Galerie Moderne at Brentano's on Fifth Avenue near Rockefeller Plaza. Janine knew firsthand of my work with Parke-Bernet and suggested I work with her. To afford me, she and the president of Brentano's created a double job for me, which would enhance my salary significantly. I would help her at the Fifth Avenue gallery, as well as organize exhibitions and inventory for the other galleries in Brentano's stores on the Northeastern seaboard. This was far more challenging than museum work, though I had learned a great deal about museum collections, and this would come in handy later on.

An interesting benchmark in my career was about to happen at the Galerie Moderne. My *Tribute to the Old Met* in 1966 began my career of dealing in theater designs. Many New Yorkers were saddened to hear that the old Metropolitan Opera house was going to close for demolition, with a new house to be built at Lincoln Center. I thought of my great-great aunt, Christine Nilsson, appearing at the Met's inaugural opening night on October 22, 1883.

What art could I put onto the walls of the Galerie Moderne at Brentano's to commemorate the history of the Met? Maybe the costumers and set designers had drawings or designs for exhibition and sale? I called their union and began my search with the names given me. Many designers sincerely wondered if anyone would really pay to buy these designs, which were usually given or thrown away post-production. (At state-run houses in Europe, the designs were property of the house.) I followed up my phone calls to the half dozen designers by arranging to see and select their designs for framing and mounting on the gallery wall. It was a time of exploration for all concerned in this new venture. Beni Montresor was participating in the first season of the new Met with his designs for *The Last Savage*. Those, together with earlier opera designs, were chosen for exhibition, as well as work by other, more seasoned designers.

I was confident they were the last of the collectibles. Were they not attractive, the right size for modern apartments, inexpensive, and redolent with sentiment? Some were by internationally renowned artists. The president of Brentano's gave me the go-ahead to mount this showing of costume and scenic designs, *A Tribute to the Old Met*.

While I was working on assembling these original designs created for Met productions, little did I realize my life was going to take a sharp turn. Maestro Gian Carlo Menotti asked me to visit him at his New York apartment, as a result of this theater design exhibition. He cajoled me into planning a design gallery at his Festival of the Two Worlds in Spoleto, Italy, for the summer of 1967. The maestro charmed me into the idea with extravagant promises of assistance in promotion and logistics.

Though the task of bringing an inventory of costume and scenic designs to Italy for the festival season was daunting, there was an ominous atmosphere at home that deeply troubled me. It seemed a portent of things to come in all aspects of my life. . . .

Rudolf Nureyev,
my Tartar bête noir.

Prince of Dance, Danish Eric Bruhn.

Chapter 7

THE SEVEN-YEAR ITCH CAME EARLY

By 1966, very dark, threatening storm clouds were brewing over my head at the 72nd Street apartment. David and I were in serious trouble. We had loosened our commitment to each other. When I was tempted to stray, I did so with utter discretion. No one knew. There was no public evidence from me that anything was amiss between the two guys on 72nd Street. I believed in privacy being maintained. Any dalliance was dispensed with quietly. This could not be said of David.

One memorable dalliance was with the great and very beautiful Danish ballet star, Eric Bruhn. We met at a gathering on Gramercy Park. He and I had a lengthy, interesting conversation I did not want to terminate. David had gone home, or at least left the party, indicating he was going home. I suggested that Eric and I have a dinner together, somewhere in the neighborhood. He readily agreed and we went to a place that I remembered Ethel Merman frequented. Still dazzled to have the attentions of a man many considered the Prince of Dance, I suggested calling a friend of mine, who lived in the neighborhood, to request a bed to use for the brief time we had together. It was a daring thing for me to do, but Eric's attraction overpowered my sense of commitment to David. We finally walked home as the garbage trucks were rumbling about the city streets and the rosy fingers of dawn were becoming evident. We walked fingertips to fingertips, still in quiet conversation. Eric lived in the next building to David and me on 72nd Street. His partner, Rudolf Nureyev, was waiting for him; David was waiting for me. Our interlude was private, unpublicized, and discreet. David, however, flaunted his new attachment for anyone to see. Twice, his height-challenged, red-headed decorator crashed dinner parties hosted by David and me, much to my utter shock and humiliation.

An open relationship was not possible to discuss, as David was petulant, imperious and ill-tempered. He was above having any conversation about our deteriorating situation.

I began to consider David cruel. At least, he was cruel and insensitive to me, disregarding the extraordinary years we spent together, avidly sharing the world of opera, the Grand Tour and later international travel, as well as exploring the glamorous social world of New York. We were perceived by many to be the perfectly turned-out attractive couple, enjoying all the best in the world. How easily the facade was crumbling.

The eruptions of turmoil and strife happened the previous summer. We had rented a Victorian house in Amagansett on the south shore of Long Island. "21 House" was on a corner property on the Montauk Highway and Windmill Lane, just before entering the small village. Unlike the beach cottage we rented in the Pines at Fire Island in 1962, where we met the Colombian dynamo Ysabel Aya de

Cabaret entertainer Hugh Shannon visits "21" House with Betty Metcalf (Marchesa Bugnano).

Maria Zeheri and Eric frolic on Amagansett beach.

Salgar, and where our Egyptian friend Leila and her WASP husband visited us, as well as Timothy Baum from the SS *United States* ocean voyage, this house had several rooms for guests. We enjoyed having many friends visit us. To celebrate the close of the summer season, David and I planned a large dinner party for about 20 people. We were pleased to have legendary torch singer Libby Holman attending, together with art collector Ethel Scull; both had summer homes in the area. Cabaret entertainer Hugh Shannon and other long-standing friends from New York City came out for the event, as well.

All was very friendly with merrymakers mingling on the lawn, drinks in hand, anticipating one of David's marvelous meals. It was twilight as we were about to go into the house. I noticed someone who was not on the guest list, or at least not on my guest list, cutting across the lawn towards the assembled guests. I realized this was the fellow David had recently taken up with in New York. Now, amidst my friends, he was openly attending our dinner party, disregarding any feelings I might have on his being there.

To avoid welcoming him, I soft-pedaled the situation by asking Libby Holman to join me at the main dining table inside. Outraged and tense, I felt hurt, with no idea how to combat the situation. Dear Libby took my hand and said, "I don't know what is troubling you, but it will be OK." She picked up the Dunhill cigarette lighter that David had given me almost seven years before after I slid off the Matterhorn. She spoke of how both she and her great actor friend, Montgomery Clift, gave each other matching lighters like this. We talked briefly of Clift's residency on Fire Island and about more general things. Libby helped see me through this awful experience, while all my other good friends at the dinner, who knew me much better than she did, were not aware of what was going on, at all. I presume that David introduced the intruder around and had him sit away from the main dining room, where I was. Gratefully, the dinner ended and the guests departed. David left as well—with the red-head! Cowardly, he called in the morning to inform me that his friend would be by shortly for the keys to the car so they could return to New York City. I was staying another day and would return with other friends. I left the keys on the dining table and went for a long walk on the beach. The keys were gone when I returned.

The height-challenged, red-haired decorator intruded himself again, when David's mother came to visit us in the fall. Since the summer, he had phoned the apartment on many occasions, and David spent many evenings out, presumably with his new friend. He made another appearance at the party David gave for his mother. Margaret Truman Daniel was there to greet her aunt, and many mutual friends of ours were on hand for the occasion. When the intrusive decorator appeared, I appealed to David to have him leave. With a very short temper, David threatened me with the carving knife he was using to slice the roasted turkey at the buffet table. I do not know if guests were aware of this interchange, but I backed away. This was a different David from my partner on our Grand Tour. He was unhappy with his job and resentful of my glittering social life and fascinating work environment. It was a devastating, intensely shocking moment of truth for me. The menacing knife brought back the terrifying times from my youth, when my parents pulled knives in their violent battles. Though I could hardly bear it, as soon as arrangements could be made, I would move out. It had been useless to speak of the situation with David. I had to leave and establish my own territory and continue getting on with my life. The Seven Year itch came slightly early. . . .

Before I could manage the move, and after a tempestuous argument with David the Cruel, I rushed out of our 72nd Street apartment to flee a few blocks up Fifth Avenue, seeking comfort from Ysabel, my Colombian friend. Gulping down a scotch, I sat in her large Art Deco living room with tears streaming down my face. I announced that after nearly seven years together, I had to leave David.

"No, darling, you cannot," Ysabel stated to my astonishment. When I asked her why not, she exclaimed, "Where else can I get such good meals?" She then proceeded to chalk up pros and cons on an imaginary blackboard on her wall between the fireplace and her "pre-" Botero. (Pre-Botero because the figures were not the bloated ones in his later works.)

Yes, I imagine Ysabel and many other friends would miss the sumptuous meals so elegantly prepared by David. My careful table arrangements greatly complemented the cuisine, to be sure. I used David's grand lace cloth placed over a colored cloth to show the beautiful patterns when spread over our Spanish refectory table. Our green Venetian vase full of flowers—in the center of David's fine china and sterling silver flatware, with gleaming crystal stem glasses—made for a glamorous dining setting. The candles in the overhead chandelier completed the stage picture. I mindfully chose the place card settings. These were resultant to the Tiffany-engraved dinner invitations I had sent out ten days before. Course after course, the guests wined and dined in warm geniality. All that was to end. Ysabel was right in protesting that I could not leave David. Clearly, my cooking efforts would never compare to his feats of delicious delights! (Some of which were picked up from his White House visits, others through studious interpretations from various cookbook attempts.) *Tant pis*, I hurt too badly to remain a victim much longer in the 72nd Street apartment. Clearly, I was not going to solve anything that evening, but at least Ysabel and I could share some drinks and good company together. This was a bonding destined to support many years of abandoned, delirious madcap adventures ahead.

Something had to be done immediately about my living conditions. David's new attraction was aggressively wanting to move in with him. I was desolate but proud. I would move out quickly to avoid any further crushing conflict.

Counterpoint to this traumatic situation was a stimulating, exciting event, the direct result of my successful endeavors at Brentano's with the theater design exhibition. The director of a theater design gallery in London heard of my exhibition and suggested we meet to discuss a partnership for a design gallery in New York. I knew the immense expenses involved in opening and running a gallery in New York, but thought I would audition the Englishman by suggesting we do a joint venture in Spoleto, Italy. He and his partner loved Menotti's proposal to help originate a gallery of designs for the upcoming Festival of the Two Worlds in Spoleto. They would provide the designs from their London gallery, and I would provide my time, labor and expertise in running it. It "seemed" like a very attractive arrangement to all of us.

David II and Eric in the hills of Sicily.

Chapter 8

BON VOYAGE ON YOUR ROAD TO OBLIVION

I found a charming apartment located on Lexington Avenue in the 80s. It was on the front of the first floor, above ground level, in what once must have been a mansion. The mahogany carved doors into the apartment were very tall, opening into a lofty room with a molded ceiling, from which I hung a wrought iron chandelier we had purchased in Spain years before. (The purchases from our Grand Tour had been mostly given away or sold; those remaining I left with David, with a few exceptions.) There was a marble fireplace with a tall mirror over it.

I was liberated from the oppressive tension filling the 72nd Street apartment and able to reconstruct a viable life for myself. The upcoming summer promised a vibrant couple of months in Italy, running the design gallery as part of the Festival of Two Worlds in the enchanting old section of Spoleto. A poet I had met wanted to rent my newly fixed-up apartment when I departed for Italy, which freed me from having to pay rent during my absence. It was a welcome fitting together of pieces into the puzzle of my current situation. I had vacation time coming from Brentano's. My notice of resignation was tendered to take effect afterwards, so that I could remain in Europe. A very aggressive directrice had taken over the Galerie Moderne, when Janine Walkenburg died a couple of months earlier. We did not click very well, so I had plans to move on somewhere even if this Spoleto venture did not come along.

Nell Webster, a youngish acquaintance with financial means (presumably an inheritance), expressed an avid interest in joining the Spoleto escapade. She claimed to want nothing out of the gallery operation financially, but was excited about the promise of an adventuresome, colorful summer in Italy, playing hostess to the gathering of international visitors and performers. I had met her through Marianne van Rensselaer Strong, who ran a publicity office as well as Entree Unlimited, a business to help well-heeled clients, who had recently moved to New York, find their way around socially. "Mimi" introduced these clients to each other as well as to society acquaintances, and suggested charity events she was involved with that they could attend, making it a win-win situation.

Nell wanted a career as a cabaret singer/dancer. Patton Campbell, a theater design friend of mine, created outfits for her. Sporting a pixie red hair-do, she projected a southern California sunniness à la Carol Burnett. We enjoyed dancing together and singing "Hush Up! Don't Tell Mama" from *Cabaret*, which was a popular hit on Broadway. It promised to be an amusing summer in the hills of Umbria.

La Bella Italia beckoned. The two of us flew to London to meet the two English partners, Peter Wright and David Hepburn. My instincts told me that David, a dancer by profession, was sweet and did not seem threatening, but that I needed to keep an eye on Peter, a shrewd charmer. My eyes, however, were out of focus from the tsunami of booze I consumed. They invited us to a reception to be held at their design gallery in Chelsea. At the gathering, I ran into ballet star John Gilpin, whom I had entertained with Anton Dolin and the French dancers on my large terrace on 76th Street some years before. A New York acquaintance was giving me a cocktail party at his Mayfair flat the next day, so I asked John and his wife to join us. I suggested we all have dinner as my guests at a popular restaurant on the Kings Road afterwards.

The Mayfair drinks party was very festive, but our table at a new "in" restaurant awaited Nell, our host, the Gilpins, and myself. John offered to give me a lift in his sports car; it only had room for the two of us. He cajoled me into stopping for a fast drink at a club he enjoyed visiting. At the door was Countess Patsy Jellicoe, with whom I engaged in lively conversation. She invited me to bring Nell to partake in what turned into a wildly merry Kings Road luncheon in the company of one of the Guinnesses two days later. With great delight, I accepted her invitation. Upstairs by the pool table lounged the very beautiful, god-like Terence Stamp, who had recently won rapturous acclaim for his *Billy Budd* performance on screen. The club was very gay, and one just could not tear oneself away after one drink! This was a real escapade to be fully enjoyed. John assured me that our friends were probably just arriving at the restaurant and would be ordering drinks as well, so why not have another glass of ambrosia—then another seemed to follow easily, as well. I was on the merry-go-round called "Fabulous." The "demon rum" riveted me in the moment, erasing all else. At a point when it seemed rude to appear so late for dinner, we decided to wait a bit, enjoying the lively atmosphere and flow of alcoholic beverages. There was a carefree carelessness in our altered state. When we got to the restaurant, I was appalled to find it closed. We really had stayed too late at the club. John, flying high, suggested driving to Cornwall to a house he had there, but that seemed a bit too far.

We settled on meeting in the afternoon of the next day. In the morning, replete with guilt and a throbbing hangover, I went to see our American friend in Mayfair, who had been stuck with the dinner bill. Nell reported to me how John's wife was very worried that we had been in a traffic accident, since we did not call to explain our absence. I brought flowers to our Mayfair acquaintance, who coolly took my sincere apologies together with the cash for the dinner expenses the previous evening.

John and I finally got together the next afternoon, in the gallery director's vacant apartment where I was staying, but the result was not nearly as thrilling as the expectation. Phlegmatic and perfunctory might best describe it. Somehow, the glamorous premiere star on stage did not translate well into the bedroom environment.

However, Patsy Jellicoe's luncheon the next day was hilarious with Nell and Lord Iveagh Guinness. We roared with laughter and naughty conversation, mostly instigated by our hosts, describing their misadventures in social situations. I noticed Doris Love, a social columnist for *Lo Specchio*, being turned away from the half-empty snooty restaurant. Possibly the management did not want a woman dining alone, or did not want someone they did not recognize, or just did not like something about her. She spotted me, and was obviously miffed at being rejected.

Noticing the charming flower children along the Kings Road near the restaurant left an added pleasantness to the day. It was my first introduction to the notion of peace through offerings of daffodils from the hands of these young people. (Too bad the outcome of this movement introduced the scruffy, ill-kempt hippies!) This was Nell's and my last engagement before leaving for Italy. It was almost ruined by her forgetting her passport where she changed some money. We realized this blunder and managed to backtrack to retrieve it, still laughing about the madly amusing luncheon party.

The Wright/Hepburn gallery assistant was to come with us to Spoleto to help carry, hang, and sell the inventory of designs. It was obvious that he was to keep an eye on things for his bosses, as well as to be useful to the operation of the gallery. The London partners and I were to divide the profits—banked safely in London to avoid both Italian taxes and international red tape—or so I was told. As a partner, I was not salaried but was responsible for banking all monies in London. Peter Wright would come midway through our exhibition's run to collect the cash and checks from sales and return to London. The rest of the profits would travel with the assistant at the end of our exhibit. He was also to tend to the return of the unsold inventory while I went on a holiday to Sicily. We agreed that I would go to London after my sunny sojourn to receive my portion of monies earned and

discuss what future we might have for a New York venture. There was never a
written contract between us; we had a gentlemen's agreement concluded with a
handshake.

Thanks to a friendship that began at the Museum of the City of New York's
luncheon with Vittorio di Montezemolo, Consul General of Italy, I was able to
get our drawings through customs without putting a bond on them. Vittorio had
given me the name of a high placed government official, together with his phone
number, should any difficulties arise. We claimed the art was for exhibition, not
sale, but legally a bond should have been placed on them to make certain what
went in to Italy came out again. I was aware that I was "stretching the law" but
persisted strongly in my lie, perhaps making a deal with the devil. (This was not
an honorable thing to do, but I was to discover at the end of this sojourn that
there is no honor among thieves.) The customs official balked at letting the designs
go through without bonding them as was the usual procedure. I told him to call
the official if he had any further objections. Or, I would use his official phone
and make the call myself, if he continued to object. He backed down, passing us
through with no further problems.

Maestro Menotti had secured a rent-free apartment large enough for all three
of us, as well as free gallery space just off of the piazza. Though the charming Gian
Carlo Menotti managed to set us up and initially introduced us to some of the key
players, his support diminished once the festival got under way. To his credit, he
did make sure I quickly met someone who was to become a prominent addition
to my life. This was the Texas benefactor to the festival, Robert Lynn Batts Tobin.
Though only one year older than I, he affected a much older stance, including
streaking gray his mop of hair. A tall, thin man always carrying a cane, he had, like
me, a penchant for both alcohol and extravagant manner. I was delighted by him
and further pleased that he was an avid collector of theater designs.

That same day of our meeting, after many luncheon libations and enthusiastic

Il Duomo in Spoleto.

conversation, some of us strolled about
the adjacent grounds of the restaurant. A
most elegant, soft-spoken, and humorous
gentleman greeted us there with his
younger companion. We joked about
whether or not to buy this place with the
lovely view of the town. Il Duomo on
the plaza below, with the 18th Century
Teatro Caio Melisso, looked like a
picture postcard. I assured charismatic
Samuel Barber that this would be a good
investment, indeed. It was thrilling to
meet this famous composer, and I was
aware of his longtime, earlier liaison with

Menotti. I had hoped I would have more conversations with Barber. That did not transpire as he left Spoleto shortly thereafter.

The charming gallery on the Via del Duomo attracted many people and garnered press attention. I organized gallery parties to celebrate the Stuttgart Ballet and Ingrid Bergman—who had strong Italian connections and, like many performing artists, was attracted to the Spoleto offerings—and various opera stars. Sales were brisk and I relished being in this lively Umbrian ambiance of narrow cobblestone streets and vintage hill-town architecture.

One of the many delightful people I met at this colorfully magnetic gathering place for international culture mavens was Mrs. Walker Long from West Virginia. Eloise was a member of the Metropolitan Opera's National Auditions. She sponsored auditions for her area and would come to New York to participate in the events surrounding the finals at the Met. A tall, slim, bespectacled woman who always wore a black band across the top of her bottle-blond page boy hair style, Eloise was full of lively enthusiasm, good humor, and energy rare for a woman of her advanced age.

Festive events, romantic flirtations, performance-going, and gregarious dining produced a non-stop whirl of a season. I was panting from the utter indulgence and seeming financial success of this summer in enchanting Umbria. My networking with famous performers such as Thomas Schippers and pianist John Browning, as

Robert L. B. Tobin joins us for the Spoleto gallery opening.

well as international patrons of the arts, was highly successful. I felt myself gaining a significant position in this fascinating artistic world, both as a curator/art dealer and as a participating personality. Amidst all the goings on, I made time for the attentions of two Italian admirers. One was a retiring, attractive young man from nearby Fano, who was innocent and sweet. He seemed very appreciative of the emerald silk jacket I gave him as a remembrance of our times together. It was made for me on the Via Condotti, when I lived with David in Rome during the Grand Tour. The other amour was a flamboyant playboy aristocrat, who sped me about in his car on impromptu adventures to the sea, to Etruscan burial sites, and once to enjoy sex on a desanctified altar in an abandoned hillside chapel. I felt the same exuberant energy I enjoyed in Provincetown, when I was working at my three jobs and playing into the night.

I went to explore Sicily before going back to London. Through Philip van Rensselaer, I had met the two Niscemi princesses, Maita and Mimi, in New York. Mimi designed a line of jewelry and was about to marry Alexander Romanov, a pretender to the Russian crown. I had met him at a drinks party the UN girls Karen and Allegra gave, as well as at a popular East Side gay bath. The women owned a famed palace in the elegant outskirts of Palermo. The classic novel and great Visconti film *The Leopard,* or *Il Gattopardo*, were based on their family history. Maita had suggested that I drop in for a visit when in Sicily. I did go to see the palace, but only Mimi was there. She had received a letter for me from Adrian Moore, a fairly recent New York friend. He wrote to express regrets at being unable to join me. He and I had been planning to tour Sicily together. After a pleasant tour of the palace, which still showed scars from Allied bombing during the war, I decided to train to the foot of Taormina and taxi up the mountainside to that famous town overlooking the sea and great Mt. Etna. The map indicated Cefalù, a colorful fishing village, was on the way. It seemed a good stopping off place to visit, according to my guidebook.

Sitting in the train compartment while waiting for the departure, I regarded with curiosity the burly, good looking man who came in with some luggage, which he put into an overhead rack. Behind him was a young man, smiling and thanking him in exaggerated, poor Italian. The slim young man looked at me with a warm acknowledgement and stepped into the hall to have a cigarette. As he seemed to have difficulty locating a match, he asked me if I spoke English and asked whether I had a light for his cigarette. I gave him a book of matches and joined him in the hall. David Scott Melville was originally from Zambia, but was now living in Taormina. The muscular man who had deposited his luggage was the houseman for an Anglican priest whom David was visiting in Palermo. The priest officiated regularly in a Taormina chapel, but had taken a few days off to tend to matters in Palermo.

As Cefalù was fast approaching, I suggested to David that we jump off for an overnight in this lovely seaside village. I would cover the expenses, and we could proceed together the next day to Taormina, where he could be my guide. He readily agreed. We enjoyed a walk around the old town and a late afternoon swim in the crystal clear waters of the beach. Our comfortable hotel room overlooking the sea provided a nurturing environment for us to blissfully engage in a night of exploration.

Taormina, especially with an attractive and enthusiastic young guide and host, made for a compellingly romantic interlude. The few days flew by, with the prospect of London ahead. I did not know if I would meet David—this enchanting keeper of fantail pigeons—again, but hoped so. He lived in a tiny place above town with a breathtaking view of Mount Etna, spewing forth red lava streams into the star lit nights.

Eric at Naxos Beach.

My future seemed brighter as I planned my return to New York via London. However, the English partners had plans of their own waiting for me in London. As soon as I disembarked from the plane, I saw both of them gravely awaiting me at the airport. It would have been normal for one of them to be there, but both seemed unusual and signaled trouble.

I was taken to a restaurant, where they announced plans had changed. We were not going to be partners, after all. Peter, the older, craftier partner claimed that the expenses in running the Spoleto gallery and travel back and forth had eaten up the profits, which I knew to be an outrageous lie. The gallery and apartment had cost nothing; the same was true of my unstinting labor. I was firmly and coldly informed that there was to be no money forthcoming for me, at all. It was obvious that nothing I said would change this decision, so I put up no argument. With restraint, I remained cool and non-confrontational, which seemed to upset the partner whom I believed to be the real perpetrator of this shady deal. He excused himself from the luncheon table and got nauseated in the men's room as a result of my calm demeanor, which had rattled him. He expected and wanted a fight, but got upset when I coolly announced I was glad to be able to return to the most enchanting David, whom I had met in Sicily. No recriminations were forthcoming from me. I felt murder in my heart but gave no hint of discomfort or disappointment.

(When I was a little boy climbing out of my bedroom window to escape the violent fights my parents had, I developed this helpful defense mechanism to protect myself from stress. This was one of those occasions. Despite my tearful flight to Ysabel after a bitter argument with David, I handled the rest of the breakup with David with cool reserve. My cool was called forth now in England.)

The partners casually mentioned that my New York acquaintance, Nell, the gallery hostess, was going to meet Peter in Cannes during the coming weeks. This was a surprise, but I remembered her professing a liking for the partner I considered devious. She and I had discussed his lack of ethics dealing with the theater design artists: cheating on framing bills and "missing" designs. Nell was no fool. She certainly was not traveling all the way to Cannes for sex with him. That was out of the question. What was she up to?

Perfunctorily, I was deposited in an inexpensive hotel near Earl's Court after they severed ties with me. Stunned by the betrayal, I was further astonished to see John Richardson leaving the same hotel later that day. I knew him from his New York days, when he was an auction executive, then the author of a book on Picasso. In some circles, he was known for his S&M activities. Once, at his apartment in New York, I noticed the belt that he was wearing had holes punctured all around it. He explained it could be used around someone's neck when needed. His phone rang many times and I heard him confirming a meeting for that evening. John suggested I might like to join them. The realization of what kind of gathering it was going to be was evident, so I retreated to the safety of David Wallace's company on 72nd Street.

Now, the shock of my partners' treachery caused me to retreat back to Taormina, Sicily, with almost the last of my cash reserve. I felt comfort in the idea I could lick my wounds and injured pride in the close company of David Scott Melville.

David was very surprised and seemed genuinely delighted to see me. He noted how I had left for London seeming like a prince, but came back changed, troubled, and damaged. It was evident my finances were diminished, but that was to be dealt with another day. Short of cash did not mean short of resourcefulness. We resolved we could overcome the problems at hand together, hungrily enjoying the warmth of each other.

I wrote to Nell, bringing her up to date. When she met with one of our former partners in Cannes, I suggested she try to get some money for herself, as I did not want them to keep all of what I had earned. I would feel better if she had a share. A blue envelope arrived, addressed to me in Taormina. It had the embossed blue imprint of the luxury Hotel Carlton in Cannes. It contained a tart, deeply upsetting response to my note, "Bon Voyage on your road to oblivion!"

It was devastating to receive such a vicious blow while dealing with depression and financial distress. My naiveté was tremendous. Having shared a vital and a joyous optimism with my "friend" Nell Webster when embarking on our Spoleto summer, the betrayal was bitter. I never could have dreamed up a worse scenario.

Being with my very desirable David—as well as thrilling at the utter beauty of Mount Etna in the distance, spewing forth red, glowing lava—as well as the therapeutic hiking up and down the steep mountain to the lovely beach, with refreshing dips in the crystalline, blue sea—gradually helped me regain strength and self-confidence. As Rilke proclaims: "That which doesn't kill you, strengthens you!"

It now was very evident to me that Nell, who had claimed in New York she desired only to play hostess in Spoleto and "wanted nothing" out of the business, had linked up with the London gallery owners behind my back. This effactually eliminated my participation in the New York venture. With this now as clear as the crystalline blue sea, and after her unforgivably brutal response to my note, I developed an iron resolution to return to New York and open a gallery before they did! How this would be accomplished by nearly penniless me, without a gallery and only a small clue about rounding up a large, impressive roster of designers, seemed to demand a miracle.

The sojourn in Sicily nurtured a robust return to New York to work miracles.

Chapter 9

Catching a Tiger by the Tail

Before this miracle could happen, I needed to beef up my constitution and mend my emotional wounds in the lively company of my new companion, David Scott Melville. Born in Zambia, but traveling around looking for adventure and searching for his path in life, he enjoyed his twenty-something years as a free spirit. His sparkling blue eyes, easy smile, and trim physique assured him of being noticed by the world around him. David got great pleasure raising fantailed pigeons and living in a simple cottage above Taormina, with an unobstructed view of Mount Etna. His financial support came from a stipend sent by a German fellow, who was working in Sardinia. Their relationship was obviously coming to an end, sped up by my appearance in David's life. In a very short time, he was to become David the Second, in the newly created dynasty of Davids.

Our life in Taormina was populated with interesting expatriates from both the United States and England. Each Sunday, we would attend the Episcopal service held by a personable gay priest, who quickly shed his robes at the end of the service for mufti in order to enjoy martinis at whichever location the group chose. The members took turns playing host, and lively afternoons followed. The partying often went into the evening, becoming more ribald with the passage of time.

One day, David and I packed a couple of sandwiches to enjoy later on the beach, down below in the colorful seaside village of Lettojani. I spotted an older gentleman, standing at the edge of the sea and looking out at a small craft approaching. On board, I recognized a famous French actor, Jean Claude Brially—whom I had met in Spoleto the month previous—together with Romolo Valli and an American actor of *Barbarella* fame, John Phillip Law, whom I knew from the United States. The beautiful American recognized me and waved. (We had been together on a few occasions as the guests at parties and dinners given by noted psychiatrist Ruth Loveland and her husband Walter Stane in New York.) David and I were within a short distance from the man on the shore, who remarked that, since I seemed to know his arriving guests, would we please join them at his villa for lunch? David and I secreted away our soggy sandwiches and joined Gayelord Hauser with his attractive male visitors.

The internationally well-known Gayelord Hauser was very much remarked on in Taormina. He and his life partner, Brownie, were long-time residents at his spacious, grand villa on the Lettojani beach. Hauser was the world's leading proponent of nutrition and was known to be the advisor to the stars in Hollywood on diets. His fame and fortune helped him avoid problems with the local police regarding his lively interest in local under-aged youths. His generosity supporting neighborhood charities smoothed over much scandalous behavior.

This trio of handsome young actors from America, France, and Italy made for a lovely luncheon party. Gayelord mentioned that Rita Hayworth had recently stayed with him, and Greta Garbo was expected soon. I could not restrain myself from bursting forth with "Please send love to my aunt . . . ," which caused a few astonished looks. Living sparsely, David and I were not used to the flow of quality alcohol. It made me tipsy and argumentative with our host. He grew and pressed his own olives, which he professed made the healthiest oil. I claimed vegetable oil was unquestionably better. Our host was a world expert on the matter, but I challenged him. Recently, there had been lots of hype in the States about the virtues of vegetable oil over olive oil. The alcohol obviously spurred me on to undiplomatically contradict my host. After graciously feeding and wining us, he departed from the table early. Doubtlessly, he was incensed at this ingrate boor. Brownie took over hosting the luncheon gone wrong, for which I realized my blame in retrospect.

The flow of libations in Spoleto had magnified the problems of my drinking. It had already increased during the David the Cruel era. However, I still did not heed the warning signs or register the dangers of my excessive, wanton drinking of alcohol. The resulting habit of unattractive compulsive behavior had not yet become unacceptable to me, nor had the dulling of my wits as far as people like Nell Webster was concerned. On the contrary, I felt such a surge of uniqueness when under the influence that I scoffed at any kind of regulation. I was above all that and thought I was in total control. I was different—golden, glowing, and a wonderful adornment for the more mundane world— or so I thought!

Sunny days were gaily indulged in on the beach, often with various Europeans vacationing there for the summer. Until I could re-enter the art world awaiting me in New York, David and I would rummage through the heaps of broken pottery shards discarded centuries ago by the ancient Greeks or Romans, or dip our lithe, bronzed nude bodies into the sea, and make love.

We would manage to live off the land until I could manage to scrape enough

Sunny days with new friends on the beach.

air fare together to return to New York and get back into business. Fortunately, I had some artwork in my sub-let apartment. I arranged to sell it to a couple of friends in New York. Literally, I had to wait until I saved up enough postage money to write to both the Italian consul general (who liked a fine ink and wash rendition of a jockey and horse I had framed on my wall) and to Dr. Ruth Loveland (who admired a Cocteau drawing I owned). Both works of art were sold to these friends. It was enough to get David and me to London, then New York.

It was a happy occasion when David and I could give up scraping mussels from the rocks on the shore, scrounging tomatoes and figs from farmers' gardens, and watering an old German professor's roses for coins to buy pasta and purchase postal stamps to write my friends about acquiring the art work for sale. David's German friend in Sardinia sent rent money and something for the bird food once a month, but our other needs were now nicely addressed.

Having networked with a few of the BOAC ground hostesses by entertaining them on their previous visits to New York, I was able to get LoRaine, Diane, and Maureen to shoot our vast amount of luggage on board without our paying overweight fees. David had all his worldly possessions in assorted suitcases and boxes, and I had my luggage from London, Italy and Sicily. It was a delightful boon to have our checked stuff on board, and a great way to begin our American sojourn. When time for our departure came, arrangements were made for David's fantail pigeons to be tended to by the landlady, until the German friend returned to Sicily.

Upon arrival, we stayed with a friend of mine who had worked for me at Brentano's Galerie Moderne earlier that year. Silvia Gronich had a large enough apartment on East 79th Street for us to have a merry reunion. We used the bedroom her daughter occupied before going out on her own.

Enchanted by David, the daughter began to visit very frequently. They spent much time together while I was out sorting out our future plans, and I suspected they were involved with more than talk. My Colombian friend, Ysabel, found David interesting enough to try him out for a brief session, too.

One afternoon, we had a startling conversation in Ysabel's living room. David wanted to get a status in America allowing him to stay in the country. Ysabel suggested that he marry Silvia's daughter, who found him so spellbinding. To my surprise, he absolutely refused to consider such an option because she was Jewish. Ysabel, high-born Catholic, daughter of the general of the army in Columbia, stood up in fury. She announced that her father was a rabbi, and her grandfather was a grand rabbi. How dare he speak against Jews in her home. He was to leave immediately. She pointed to the door and dramatically said "Get out!" He sheepishly returned to his Jewish hostess, Silvia, until Ysabel simmered down. I really loved Ysabel for her intolerance of intolerance, and her dramatic method of expressing it. Her heavy indulgence in alcohol often obliterated any gentler means of expression, making for colorful, startling theatrics.

Ysabel's antics did not go without censure from some quarters. My friend Dickie Ransohoff, whom I met in Spoleto, resided off Fifth Avenue on 81st Street. She once said no room was large enough to accommodate both Ysabel and me at the same time. Presumably, she meant that when both of us were together in high spirits (90 proof, or better), the dynamics were too overpowering to endure.

Dickie featured heavily in my survival at this period. She precipitated the course of events that eventually resulted in the miracle I had wished for. Though I was getting a small amount from the sub-leased apartment, I did not want to impose us at Silvia's apartment indefinitely. I needed a steady income to support both David and myself.

I was coming from the Metropolitan Museum of Art one fine day, when I heard a voice calling from the French windows of a town house. It was Dickie. She warmly invited me up for a visit. Petite, with short-cropped hair and the ubiquitous cigarette in hand, this middle-aged woman sat me down to a cup of tea in her Francophile sitting room. On hearing my plight after leaving Spoleto, she brightened and suggested I contact a friend who was looking for an art gallery director.

Eureka! After a long interview with her friend, and after seeing the large gallery space on West 56th Street just off of Fifth Avenue, we really talked turkey. My credentials from Parke-Bernet, the Museum of the City of New York, Brentano's Gallerie Moderne, and the gallery in Spoleto more than filled the bill. This was a co-operative gallery, meaning each artist contributed a set amount each month in exchange for exhibition space. I viewed work by each artist and knew some had potential I could work with, and others I would want to edge out.

Most importantly, I proposed two conditions taking on this daunting work: One was that I be allowed to live in the back room of the gallery. If I did not have to pay rent, I could keep my apartment on Lexington Avenue rented out to the poet. I would install a refrigerator and hot plate, as well as a daybed/sofa for sleeping. There was little heat and no hot water, but I was willing to forfeit comfort in exchange for making the gallery work. The board agreed to this unusual proposal, all of them being artists with a bohemian nature. Importantly, they were desperate to have a professional take charge of their gallery without paying a commensurate salary. The second and equally important demand was that I be allowed to operate, in conjunction with the art exhibitions, a display for sale of original costume and scenic inventions for opera, ballet, and theater. I offered the co-op a percentage of the sales.

The back room, my living space at night, would have an on-going theater design exhibition, while the front had the co-operative artists' work. However, once in a while (by careful scheduling) in the front gallery would be a large exhibition of theater designs, with the back showing representations of the gallery artists.

Details were worked out and the miracle was achieved! After a few months of feverish preparations, I set up The American Center for Theater Designs at the Capricorn Gallery *one week* before the "other" gallery opened off of Third Avenue in the low 60s on the other side of town!

Beverly Sills' addition to my "Hall of Fame."

One board member was the life partner of Jean Rosenthal, the famous theater lighting designer. Jean devised the special lighting for the gallery, the only gallery in New York to have such an appropriate distinction. Naturally, Jean and her partner knew every theater designer of consequence in America. Access to these prominent artists quickly formulated an impressive roster for the opening exhibition. What an entree! Endless hours were spent contacting designers, then choosing designs for exhibition. I employed my expertise, developed at Brentano's, for framing each design and hanging them as attractively as possible.

From my earlier years on the art scene in New York, I knew how to generate a great deal of publicity for our opening. The media were quick to respond to the stellar names involved—Oliver Smith, Freddy Wittop, Miles White, and José Varona, to name only a few. They had created costumes for Mary Martin, Ethel Merman, Leontyne Price, Dame Joan Sutherland, and Beverly Sills, and they had decorated the stages of the Metropolitan Opera, Broadway, and other top venues in America. All this work could be viewed at the gallery I was now running.

My contacts, together with the enthusiasm of the various designers in spreading the word (to sell their work), created a very successful start to our American Center for Theater Designs at the Capricorn Gallery. Robert L. B. Tobin, my friend from Spoleto, attended and bought lavishly. So did other Americans I met at the Festival, as well as many people who responded to the enormous publicity.

The cooperative artists at the gallery had not been very supportive. At first, they did not like sharing their space with theater designers, until the significant amount of sales and the recognition the exhibition brought to the gallery impressed them. Often their work sold as a result of someone coming in to buy a theater design. It was a win-win situation, and it made all my previous suffering almost worthwhile. The accomplishment also gave me great satisfaction. It was another vindication of my professional ability.

David the Second was on hand for the opening. He tried to be helpful in dealing with the inevitable problems. It was clear this was not his forte, and he soon opted to help a friend of mine sail his boat down to Florida through the inland waterway, seducing the attractive captain en route. Helena, the owner's lover, blabbed to me long distance blow-by-blow information. This did not sit well with me, but I decided to give him a second chance when he returned a month later. The gallery would close for the summer, and I got the brainstorm to create an exhibition of designs in conjunction with the opening of the new opera house in Santa Fe, New Mexico. The previous one had burnt down mysteriously but, through generous financial donations from Robert L. B. Tobin and other benefactors, the venue would open for the summer season of 1968. After crating up selected designs and arranging with designers at the Santa Fe Opera to include their work in the coming exhibition, David and I headed west.

Capricorn Gallery opening. Eric with David II and a friend.

The "other" gallery had a splashy opening at their location near Bloomingdale's, just east of Third Avenue. Their prices were reported to me to be higher, and little fuss was made over the gallery. It went along quietly until I eventually heard no more of that operation. Peter Wright had found some project outside of New York City—upstate, I think—and disappeared into oblivion. There is not a clue about what happened to David Hepburn. Nell is probably still on East 57th Street, waiting to appear in the starring role of a cabaret show.

After arriving in Santa Fe, I discovered that Margaret Jamison had the most prestigious gallery in town, so I paid her a visit. She inspected some designs and suggested a more appropriate place for an exhibition would be at the gallery of her friends, Bill and Bernie's Collectors Gallery, off the Old Santa Fe Trail, near the oldest church.

David helped me organize and hang an exhibition of designs at the Collectors Gallery. We were quickly assimilated into the vibrant summer whirl of activities in Santa Fe. With one exception, all the designers participating in the opening of the new season had works of theirs in the exhibition. I had purposely not invited Rouben Ter-Arutunian to show his beautiful designs. He had signed up with "the other gallery" in New York instead of with me at Capricorn, which I considered treasonous. Rouben very much wanted to be included in my Santa Fe showing but I stuck to my guns. Like everyone who would listen to me, I had told him of the treachery following my Spoleto episode. Perhaps it was their East Side location, the London gallery connection, or Peter's smooth salesmanship, but Rouben chose to show there.

One day while I was sunning by the pool at the Casa Loma Apartments—where David and I had rented a studio apartment and many of the opera crowd lived—Hans Werner Henze and his young companion entered the pool area and sat down nearby. The famous German composer was having an American premiere of one of his operas performed in Santa Fe that season. The two men, assuming I did not understand Italian, began speaking about me in most lascivious terms. My Italian may not have been fluent, but after a couple of stays in Italy, it was not difficult to understand their meaning. Quietly amused, I stood up and entered the pool. They commented in Italian on how hot the water must have just become with my body immersed in it. I said nothing.

Shortly thereafter, I was exiting a performance during an intermission at the opera. One of the company's lead sopranos was on my arm. We encountered Rouben with Henze and his friend in the aisle. Rouben invited us to join them at the Opera Club so he could talk with me. I looked at Henze and his friend and said in perfect Italian, "Thank you, but perhaps another time," and swept up the aisle. Amused, I was certain they realized I had understood their provocative comments at the pool.

Rouben, not to be outdone, created a one-man exhibition of his designs elsewhere during the opera season. I felt I had maintained my principles, and the brief opera season progressed successfully. My exhibition was well received, garnering good press and generating healthy sales.

The members of the gay community were like vampires thirsting for fresh blood when new young men appeared in town. We were no exception and were promptly invited to many gatherings. Though it seemed clear that we were a couple, since when did that discourage the lechery of others? Sometimes, if I was tending the exhibition, I would encourage David to go and enjoy the events. Our opening night of the design showing was very well attended, resulting in many brisk purchases. Shortly thereafter, Bill and Bernie suggested David might be attracting serious attention from others, while I was busily working at the gallery. It was a meant to be a kindly warning, which I pondered.

At a post-opera gathering at the Casa Loma Apartments, I was invited to go for a swim in the pool by one of the stage directors at the opera. We left the gathering of singers, musicians, and friends to splash about under the full moon. In what seemed like casual conversation, the director gossiped about the new boyfriend of one of the affluent guys in the group. His description of the young man from Africa was a precise fit for David. The penny dropped and I felt mortified, fighting back tears. I remember clutching the side of the pool trying to gather composure. Bill and Bernie had tried to warn me about something everyone in town seemed to know but me. David was aligning himself with a new lover! It was someone who could keep him in style, and would soon build him outdoor cages with exotic birds for him to tend . . .

We had long planned an exciting rafting trip down the rapids of the Colorado River, when the exhibition ended in some days' time. It was David's birthday, and I thought it a perfect gift for him to experience this unique opportunity in nature, which we both loved very much. We peacefully agreed that our relationship had run its course, and we would officially separate at the end of this river adventure.

The Kennedys had recently done an abbreviated version of this trip, bringing much attention to the new vogue of shooting the Colorado rapids. Our river trip with Hatch Expeditions was to last ten days, but a series of dangerous mishaps and other circumstances reduced it by one day. There were two rafts, each with a boatman to steer and advise the passengers of safest maneuverings over the challenging rapids. There were about six people to a raft. The boatmen were to build the campfires and cook our food, as well as supply information about the glorious Grand Canyon—its history, geology, and indigenous Indians.

It did not take us long to realize that the boatmen were not giving us correct information. The young, burly boatmen made up stuff on a whim. As some of us left our watches back on shore with our other belongings, we were never sure even if the correct time was given to us. They invented information about rock formations and anything else we wanted to know. At mealtime, there was a most unattractive surliness. Once, one boatman threw a frying pan of food down onto the sand and told us to "eat that shit!" We discovered they were feasting on the best grub (including caviar) and giving us the rest.

Their workload was overwhelming them. Not having enough rest between runs encouraged them to drink increasing amounts of hard liquor to keep going. We suspected they indulged in some drugs during the night. It became a nightmare unfolding with each day. An attractive lesbian couple firmly

Shooting the Colorado rapids.

turned down their sexual advances, increasing their irritability and aggressive bad behavior and rudeness. A couple of accidents occurred, making the trip even more perilous. One person had to leave the group to receive medical assistance when we got to the small hostel on the canyon floor; another older man had to be flown out by helicopter after he punctured his foot after leaping off a waterfall.

At one point, the boatman ordered that a case of beer be flown in to them by helicopter, which infuriated all of us, who were feeling deprived of proper attentions and better food. No one dared to complain strongly, but I did raise my protest enough to be threatened by them. The lesbians came as my protectors when I had to go to answer a call of nature in the bushes to assure I was not attacked. Why didn't David do something? Instead, he buttered up to the bullies, saying I was a bit mental. He even helped them secure the case of beer when it was brought by the helicopter. I had resisted fully realizing it before when David gave many indications of his unworthy behavior. Now, Mildred Pierce's fight with her daughter, Veda, came to mind. I remembered vividly Joan Crawford as Mildred saying, "Veda, I'm really seeing you for the first time, and you are cheap and horrible!" I came to accept how much David lacked character and was ruthless in furthering his own interests. It was another knife in my back. My foolish self-deception was finished.

Though tempted, a group of us thought it was unwise to loosen the rafts during the night in an effort to indicate to overhead flight surveillance that something was amiss in the canyon below. One day, when a raft got stranded on a bank, we found a half-gallon of bourbon while having to unload the craft. My traveling companions asked me to get rid of it to help keep the boatmen sober. I did my best to "get rid of it," but had to throw some of the remains into the Colorado, alas. The boatmen were supposed to keep an eye on the rafts during the night, as floodgates were opened at odd hours up river, causing a sudden rise in the tide. After some hours, the tide would go down again. Then, the rafts were stranded if not moved in time. This needed attention during the night, but the boatmen slept through it.

We had all paid a large sum of money for the river run, but ended up doing a lot of labor to keep the rafts afloat. Under the hardships and offensive behavior of our captors, we decided to beg them to return us a day early. With enormous relief, we did get back early, and again the lesbians were my bodyguards on land until we could depart for our individual destinations.

All of us promised to be in touch with one another, sending copies of our correspondence of protest to the owner of the business, the prominent Senator Orrin Hatch. He sent each of us a letter indicating surprise at our complaint, saying that no one else had complained! We had substantial verification from all the other members in the group, which was to go to an Arizona lawyer of great reputation. He was the father of one of the lesbians, but he had a heart attack and died before we could proceed. It was determined not to pursue attempts at further legal action and to go on with our lives.

David and I proceeded to Las Vegas, where I would spend a night, while he returned to his new paramour in Santa Fe. I caught the extravagant floor show in a casino there, where an acquaintance was appearing as the lead dancer, and then returned the next day to New York to await the arrival of a shipment of designs from Santa Fe and to continue my gallery operations.

The Whitney Museum had planned a major retrospective of Georgia O'Keeffe's work. I had two tickets to the opening reception, and I invited one of my gallery artists, Nathalie Van Buren Marshall, to accompany me. Nathalie had become a great friend, and I admired her art tremendously. She considered O'Keeffe's work to be a major influence on her own work and held her in the highest esteem.

We attended this important art event early, because Nathalie had to take a train to Connecticut, where her teenage children would be waiting. There was a snowstorm anticipated, so she felt it urgent to be home in good time. The vast exhibition enthralled us. As we were descending in the elevator, we commiserated on the lost opportunity to see O'Keeffe. Then the door opened onto the crowded lobby, and I noticed the great lady coming in through the revolving doors. Crowds thronged around her as she resolutely made her way, like an ocean liner parting the waters. She advanced, looking neither left nor right, oblivious to the crowd. Closer and closer this magnificent woman came, until she stood in front of me! She put out her hand and said, "You are my friend." I was astonished, as were a vast amount of onlookers, many of whom knew me and probably wondered how I managed to have this distinction. There was every possibility that Nathalie peed in her pants when I introduced her to her muse. This was an historic event for both of us.

Having lived in Santa Fe, I was familiar with not only this major artist's work but also her environment. Georgia O'Keeffe lived in Abiquiu, just under one hour northwest of Santa Fe, New Mexico. Her house sits on a bluff overlooking the vast northern New Mexico landscape, captured in her many paintings. When the weather became too hot in the summer, she would retreat a short distance north to Ghost Ranch, where she kept a cabin both for living and painting.

A very private person geared for concentrated hard work of painting and sculpting, she had a wall built around her home and gardens, to discourage casual drop-ins, as did her young assistant, Juan Hamilton. In the ensuing years, Hamilton became more than an assistant to the aging artist, whose eyesight was failing. Relatives of O'Keeffe, friends, and her lawyer became increasingly concerned by his presence and influence upon her. Just before her death, she was moved to a house closer to the hospital in Santa Fe. I had stayed there as a guest of Howard Hook some years before. The intriguing story of Hamilton's staged "wedding" there and his efforts to manipulate her estate are worth the effort to read in the biography of her, *Georgia O'Keeffe*, by Roxana Robinson (Harper & Row, 1989).

Surprisingly, when I ran the Jamison Gallery in Santa Fe, there was a paucity of O'Keeffe's work available. She had turned her back on Santa Fe, partially because of the rebuff she received when she offered to paint some murals in the St. Francis Auditorium, contiguous with the Museum of Art, just off of the plaza. It was determined that there was no need to consider work done by a woman to grace those walls! Female artists were considered second-class citizens during that period. One can only wonder what the auditorium would have been like with Georgia O'Keeffe's murals resplendent on the walls!

Although the great lady and I had the fortuitous meeting at the Whitney retrospective of her work, I felt I should honor her privacy by never intruding upon her. If we were to have another incidental getting together, that would be very welcome. We both had lots to keep us busy, so I let Providence weave the web. There was no subsequent meeting, though I did have a private tour of her Abiquiu property years later, when I wrote an article about it for a New Jersey newspaper chain.

Back in New York City, a major theater design exhibition was in the making at my busy gallery. I had asked a few distinguished women to play hostess for the event. It was to benefit the Damon Runyon Cancer Fund. One of them was Beverly Sills, the soprano wonder at the City Opera, riding the crest of enormous popularity. This was a long distance from those earlier years when I, dressed as a torero, received an orange from her, a gypsy vendor, during the first act of *Carmen*. Beverly arrived promptly in mink and a simple cocktail dress to find me in my casual pre-event attire, not having time to get into black tie. Her good humor and easy manner carried the day. Those attending came to see the exhibition and meet Beverly, not me. She was gracious to lend her name and presence to the event, for which I was very grateful.

A few days before the benefit, I had called Tallulah Bankhead to urge her to attend. I thought that would add publicity value. She gently told me that she could not speak long on the phone. Her doctor had advised her against abusing her condition. Emphysema had limited her activities, and besides, she elaborated, it would mean getting her hair done and doing other preliminary amenities for making an appearance. Tallulah rambled on about that dreadful Jamie Spilman, taking advantage of her sister, Eugenia. (She did not realize I was very fond of Jamie and considered him a friend.) *One hour* later, I thanked her, even though she would not be in attendance. I hung up the phone, vastly amused by this extraordinary, extravagant character.

Capricorn Gallery. Miles White and Eric with Ysabel and her visitor from Spain.

The exhibition was comprised of framed original costume and scenic inventions by the notable designers Oliver Smith, Donald Oenslager, Miles White, Ming Cho Lee, José Varona and Freddy Wittop. These prominent talents from the theater, ballet, and opera world attracted luminaries such as Leontyne Price and Ethel Merman, to name just a couple in attendance. A major failing on my part as host and organizer was not having a photographer for press coverage, as well as to take photos for my gallery's file and my own album. The work to get the opening to happen was overwhelming, but I did manage a couple of photographs. There were many photo ops lost, however. Curiously, neither Price nor Merman attracted notice from the other guests. Hard as it is to believe, it was only when the nicely turned out Ethel Merman in a white suit and carefully curled hair of a reddish tint exclaimed, "Eric, where is Miles (White)?" that anyone realized she was there.

Jovial Francis Robinson, Condé Nast's Leo Lerman, and many more culture mavens enhanced the Gallery's event. Even the statuesque Ysabel appeared in a svelte black/white/brown long dress, adorned with one of her famous gold Pre-Columbian eagle pendants. It was very gratifying to have masterminded this auspicious gathering and to have launched so dramatically a significant venue for theater arts in New York.

Not only collectors but also curators from various museums and university collections were attracted to this treasure house of designs. As the director of the theater design exhibitions, I began to help form or update collections for the Museum of the City of New York, the Cooper-Hewitt Museum (the National Museum of Design), the Library for the Performing Arts at Lincoln Center, the Harvard Theater Collection, and others. My efforts were recompensed by grants or funds raised by the various institutions.

It was interesting to note how acquisitions from my gallery exhibitions generated different responses in the curators or representatives of the institution. Curators are very protective of their holdings, sometimes guarding them from the public they are supposed to assist in research. On occasion, I felt their resentment in what they perceived as an intrusion, even though I was expanding their collection. Some curators are arrogant and openly hostile to someone else updating their collections with donated additions. I found this surprising, and mean spirited. Perhaps it made them appear conspicuously unproductive in developing the holdings; the additions always pointed out areas in need of updating. Curators can lapse into laziness and a smug sense of self-importance. I was not always popular, bearing enriching gifts.

A very impressive windfall came my way when Arthur Birsh, the publisher of *Playbill*, the magazine distributed in New York theaters, hired me to prepare a proposal for a series of collectible books featuring theater designs. Because I was aware of what was in all the major theater designers' portfolios or at the back of their closets, and I knew what was in museum and library collections, as well as tuned into the whereabouts of designs purchased through me, I was in the unique position to accomplish this task. The collector, Paul Stiga, who professionally worked as a consultant to product promotion, had suggested me to Arthur. Paul would get a huge compensation, equivalent to mine, for writing up my findings and proposal. We worked well together, compiling a list of possible collectible books: *Diaghilev and the Ballets Russes, Norman Bel Geddes and Modernism, The Theater of Max Reinhardt*, and so on.

A fascinating all-expenses-paid trip to the University of Texas at Austin permitted me to inspect the fabulous collection of theater designs housed in one of their libraries. Then, in San Antonio, I was invited to go through the vast collection belonging to my friend Robert Lynn Batts Tobin. How amusing it was to come across some of the designs that I had sold him over the years. This collection is now at the university in Austin in a museum dedicated to his memory.

Knowing the Harvard Theater Collection might hold some source of interest for my Playbill project, I arranged with Jeanne Newlin, its curator, to visit. I spent the morning going through the collection's holdings. Over lunch, I expressed surprise at a few things in their possession that would have been meaningful in my specific quests, which I had outlined to her beforehand. I asked the curator why she had not told me about them, to facilitate my search. She protectively told me she thought I would find them. (If I had not, then her little chickadees would be undisturbed in their nest of archival boxes.)

Thanks to my warm relationship with Lisa Taylor, the director of the Cooper-Hewitt, and with Thor Wood, head of the theater collection at the Library for the Performing Arts, curatorial interference was kept at a minimum. Their curators' egos may have been bruised, but the collection grew in stature, thanks to my perseverance.

Paul Stiga continually encouraged me to present and promote theater designs. Aside from his collaborating with me for the *Playbill* project of collectible books illustrated with theater designs (which never came to fruition), it should be recalled that he bought his first design, Beni Montresor's *Last Savage*, from me. It was the first design I sold at *A Tribute to the Old Met* in 1966 at Brentano's Galerie Moderne. He encouraged me to curate special design exhibitions in various venues. *New York Collects New York* opened at Pace University in lower New York in 1978; *Costume & Scenic Designs* at Klapper Library, Queens College in 1970; *The Alvin Ailey Design Collection* at the New York City Center in 1975; and *Twentieth Century Scenic & Costume Design* at the Cooper-Hewitt Museum (National Museum of Design) at the Carnegie Mansion in New York in 1976. (Programs, publicity, photos, and other ephemera relating to all my theater design exhibitions are archived under my name at the Library for the Performing Arts at Lincoln Center: T-Mss 2011-066 and JOB 07-35.)

Interspersed with curating exhibitions and helping to form permanent collections, I busily gave lectures and seminars at various museums, libraries, and universities, both in the New York area and in Denver, Boulder, Miami, and

New Orleans. Invitations with honorariums were gratefully received; my vigorous networking precipitated many of these lecture engagements. The lecture topics were "A History of Theater Designs," "Twentieth Century Costume & Scenic Inventions for the Opera, Ballet & Theater," and "Designs for the Court Theaters of Europe."

It was in 1980 that I created my most prestigious—and the largest—exhibition ever held in the Main Galleries of the Library for the Performing Arts at Lincoln Center. It took more than one year to get it up and going. "Designs for a Prima Donna: Dame Joan Sutherland" was the triumph of my curatorial career, leaving trauma and disappointment in its wake.

A sybarite dances in "A Night in Tunisia," a German movie filmed in Hammamet.

Chapter 10

1+1 MAKE MORE THAN 2

Tunisia seemed a very attractive option for spending part of the summer of 1969. Both Ysabel and I had contacts there, and neither of us had been to this exotic locale in North Africa. The art galleries were traditionally closed for the summer in New York, which permitted me the freedom of travel and further networking. On the way, we would visit Rome and Tuscany, dropping into Spoleto for a visit to the Festival of Two Worlds, where I had labored, played, and savored the joys of Umbria just two years before. The dark memories from the gallery misadventure were kept at bay, not to interfere with this Italian sojourn. It amused me how wonderful these plans were. Unlike the year David and I spent on our Grand Tour as innocents abroad, looking and absorbing the touristic wonders of foreign travel, I would now be cavorting with Ysabel, a habituée of the international scene, well-seasoned with years of experiences living at the top. No longer a novice tourist, I would be experiencing daily exposure to the lofty lifestyles of the rich and famous. I felt like a young man graced by the Gods. Who would have thought the bright boy from the Bronx, who spoke like Noel Coward, could have put such a program together?

Prince Angelo Lanza had invited his long-time friend Ysabel to visit him in Rome. We agreed to reconnoiter at his penthouse on the Via Margutta to begin our Italian adventure. First, I wanted to visit Hamburg to see José Varona, who was there working on designs for a new opera production. It was a part of Germany unknown to me and close enough for me to pay my initial visit to Sweden, birthplace of my parents, as well.

It was auspicious and in league with all the other blessings in my life so far that in the opera circle in Hamburg was a visiting young Swedish aristocrat. Like many

Swedes, he was not the stereotype blond but brown-haired, slim and intellectual-looking with his horn rimmed glasses. He was quietly handsome and reserved. Björn Bexelius insisted I stay with his family during midsummer's night, when I told him of my plans. Also, he agreed to come with me to a lake location north of Stockholm that I had read about with mock pagan midsummer festivities. His father, doctor to King Gustav V Adolf, would be just back from a holiday with his mother in Italy. Björn and his sister would pick me up from the Grand Hotel in downtown Stockholm for the drive to the family retreat. After a couple of days with the family, we would depart for the mock pagan celebration. It was very enticing.

As planned, Björn and his sister, Ilse, arrived at the Grand Hotel in the center of Stockholm in their sedan, to drive me north for about an hour to their home on a lake. Much of Sweden is covered in scrub pine and stands of white birch, with slight indications of a hill now and then. The landscape is subdued in a pleasant sameness, with only a rare attempt at the dramatic. Many of the houses and slatted fences along the country road are painted a particular dark red. Björn explained that the color is a natural derivation from a pigment local to that part of Sweden. Their house was large but unpretentious, with emphasis on being comfortable. I was quartered in a spacious, simple guest cottage, independent of the main house, in the garden.

My biggest concern about this visit was how his upper class family, with their built-in snobbery, would respond to someone with such a commonplace name as mine. A nagging familiar "less than" feeling was in my thoughts. Sometimes, a small country, diminished from a larger, more powerful state, produces fierce social attitudes. Their name, Bexelius, had the Latin "ius" ending, indicating social status. With Greta Garbo, who originally had the same last name as mine, I resolved to use her adoption of me as her nephew as a device to further my standing. Then, there was my relationship to Christine Nilsson, a Swedish heroine of the opera. My thinking was that advancing erudite conversation about the arts or my intellectual and professional achievements would not be as effective as establishing direct ties with these Swedish icons. Knowing inspiration would not fail me in fostering further acceptance, I enjoyed the Bergmanesque scene to the utmost. The family, with its elderly female retainer, and I heartily partook of the delicious meal and avid conversation under the trees, overlooking a placid lake in the glow of midsummer night.

Observing the various small boats at the dock beside the sauna, the sought-after inspiration burst forth! Swedes can overcome their snobbishness, if a surprise diversion enters the equation. I announced during the progression of the dinner that we should partake of a sea battle afterwards. "A sea battle?" voices queried. "Yes," indicating my suntanned hostess, I said, "You can be the beautiful princess in captivity, and you"—indicating the distinguished doctor—"can be a slave rower." I suggested two teams using various small crafts available. One of the younger daughters made an eye patch and declared herself Admiral Nelson, who would be my adversary. With astonished mirth, all changed into bathing attire after the last morsel was devoured at the table. Lots of splashing with overturned boats and delighted squeals were heard as the battle progressed.

After a session in the sauna, we retired to the house to change into appropriate attire for coffee, chocolates, and Mozart. Shortly, the ladies appeared in long dresses, with careful attention to their appearance. Only an occasional damp sprig of hair was testament that something unusual had happened just before—nightfall never came, only a stillness when the night birds stopped singing and the morning birds began. The moose ceased calling, but an occasional mosquito prevailed. When my friend and I were about to disappear into the guest cottage at an appropriate hour to retire, I noticed the curtain in the room of the eldest daughter move when I glanced up. Clearly, Ilse was observing us, and I had the notion that she wanted to change places with her brother, Björn.

In the following days, we proceeded to the festival on the northerly lake, which was purported to be pagan. We drove in Björn's car for probably a couple of hours past more pine trees and the ubiquitous white-barked birch to the site. Much of the carryings on had recently transpired, with much litter left about as witness to the event. Björn pointed out the unusual housing there. The small farm houses were built above where the cattle were kept. It was an economical way of keeping both people and animals warm during winter months, with no need to construct a separate barn. Bjorn and I continued our outpouring of affection, which had taken us through our midsummer night at his family's country retreat. However, without the protection of a cottage interior, mosquitoes had a feast, with so much unprotected flesh on our lakeside blanket.

Shortly thereafter, Björn and his sister, Ilse, took me to the home of a lovely young Huguenot woman who lived in Stockholm. She prepared a wonderful dinner for us, washed down with much wine and lively stories. Some of them had to do with my great-great aunt, Christine Nilsson. By the end of the meal, it was decided that we would taxi out to an outlying park, where there was a statue of this singer. The hostess selected another bottle of wine from the wine cupboard—one of superior quality— in honor of the occasion, along with the floral bouquet from the table. At the door, the thoughtful hostess returned to fetch a couple of candles in holders for this sacred event.

The taxi driver did not approve of traveling with an opened bottle of wine onboard, but we promised to leave the cork in it until we arrived at the toasting spot under the statue. He was delighted to partake in this merry group's escapade, especially as he had proposed to his wife under my great aunt's statue some years earlier.

A mist was rising from the water around the park, making it very dramatic and romantic. However, a mystery ensued when the statue could not be found. The driver was certain of its location, but it wasn't there. A call to the police station established how the statue had recently been taken away for cleaning, after pigeons had left years of their droppings upon the diva's head!

Christine Nilsson

Someone in the group impertinently suggested we go over to honor Jenny Lind's statue nearby, instead. No! Resolute, I encouraged the celebrants to enjoy the wine while sitting on a nearby bench by candlelight (even though the midnight sun provided plenty of visibility), offering a toast to the art and life of Christine Nilsson.

I departed Stockholm and flew to Rome, where I was to meet my beloved Ysabel. My rented car seemed to know the way from the Leonardo Da Vinci International Airport to the gate of Angelo Lanza on the Via Margutta without hesitation. My having lived in Rome, and once on the Via Margutta, helped. Upon pulling up near the gate, the headlights illuminated Ysabel, as she was about to exit. I could not believe the timing was so perfect. There she was in her silk black and white patterned blouse, adorned with her triple strand of pearls with the ruby clasp. I recognized the familiar green silk trousers and white sandals, as well.

"Where have you been, darling?" Ysabel asked, as though it were perfectly natural for me to arrive at the gate the moment she was leaving. "Angelo gave a party for both of us. I wrote to you informing you of it, but you only arrive now when it is finishing." Ysabel had sent a letter to me at the Grand Hotel in Stockholm, which I had long since vacated to stay with Björn. Anyhow, here we both were, ready for a celebratory supper at a local restaurant below the Spanish Steps in advance of our upcoming summer together.

Dear Ysabel had gone around earlier in the day to each shop whose provisions had been ordered for use at the party. She did not want her friends to pay for the party given for her, so she paid each bill. The prince had a title but no money.

As we were to stay overnight with Angelo, it was a very kind thing to do. Poor Angelo had a serious mishap the next morning, alas. The elderly fellow had been in the water closet and, while pulling the chain to flush the toilet, his false teeth fell down into the drainage, lost into the sewers of Rome!

It was a high-octane series of episodes that filled our Umbrian/Tuscan days.

Driving around hill towns, sometimes visiting friends, investigating museums, and enjoying delicious food stuffed with white truffles, we enjoyed lots of wine and amusing places such as the Bomarzo Sculpture Park, where Dante's sculpted mouth of hell admonishes, "Lasciate ogni speranza voi ch'entrate," and also Etruscan tombs.

Thanks to connections Dickie Ransohoff had in Spoleto, we managed to rent a small villa outside of the charming town for a week or so. It was surrounded by fields of countless red poppies, which we found enchanting. The tiny villa had almost no furniture, but we had a riotous (literally) time there. In the refrigerator were ice cubes, a few oranges and lemons I brought, and nothing else. Secured bottles of Italian vodka, Cinzano and Campari awaited our attentions on the counter top.

Lasciate ogni speranza... Eric with Ysabel in the "Mouth of Hell" at Bomarzo sculpture park.

Each morning, the Princess would stretch and, upon arising, call for her "Caw-fee . . .me caw-fee." I would hasten to the kitchen, where I would cut a slice of orange or lemon, slip it into a glass with some ice, and add varying portions of vermouth, Campari, and vodka. Before her cool shower was finished (we did not have hot water), she would call for another "caw-fee." So began our Spoleto days. After our tasteful outfits for the day were selected and donned, we placed our empty glasses down in the sink, and headed towards our trusty VW bug. It was a short distance to the piazza, with time permitting for an official Negroni as a prelude to entering the Teatro Caio Melisso for the noonday concert. Well, YES, we were certain we could manage a Negroni before the performance . . .

Parking in high spirits was always less of a challenge, and the VW bug managed to squeeze into unusual places, usually acquiring another scrape or bend in the fender. Stone walls, iron gratings and other obstacles left their marks on the dear vehicle. The accumulation of traffic violations grew in volume, but we paid no heed. In those days before computers, foreigners could ignore paying tickets on rented cars.

Our daily appearance in the piazza became a point of general interest to many seated there. Ysabel and I often exchanged items to make our fashion statement notable. Breezily, we would arrive with a flourish to summon dear Giovanni to bring us our "usual" as we "chatted up" the familiar faces. After the noonday concert, there was pre-prandial jockeying about to see who was lunching with whom and where. It seemed like such civilized fun for this Bronx-bred fellow!

Our most memorable lunch was at a country inn. It had a pond with lovely swans swimming about. Dickie was with us, as was the handsome Austrian assistant to Maestro Herbert von Karajan. We met at the box office the night before. He had just arrived in Spoleto and had no ticket, but I secured one for him from the press officer, when I explained who he was. An invitation to stay with me after the performance was accepted. Ysabel, in her room, called us in before we bedded down. Both of us were naked, and she thought it would be very nice if he would let her warm her hands on his abundant male endowment . . .

The Umbrian charm of the pondside inn, together with the chemistry between the Austrian and me, caused me to exclaim after the bill was paid, "Andiamo a letto, subito!" Our foursome quickly rose unanimously, knocking over the rush chairs in our haste to exit for afternoon pleasures. The startled diners heard my call to the sheeted fields and were astonished at four gleeful lotus-eaters hastening to partake of siesta delights. As we approached Spoleto, I sent the two ladies on, while my new pal and I disappeared, blanket under arm, behind a lush thicket.

Later, Gian Carlo Menotti gave a formal reception at his hillside palace while we were in residence. He could not help but notice Ysabel in Spoleto and had great expectations his charm could encourage her to become a big time supporter of his Festival of the Two Worlds. Ysabel was wearing her turquoise and gold sari outfit with a solid gold pre-Columbian eagle pendant around her neck. A large amethyst and diamond ring together with the gold centipede bracelet completed the aura of taste, elegance, and wealth surrounding this extraordinary woman.

I introduced them when the maestro came over. Though Menotti had helped me set up the design gallery a couple of years earlier in Spoleto, I did not think he was aware of the treachery that resulted, nor did I think it appropriate to bring the unpleasant subject up at this festive gathering. When he discovered that Ysabel was from Colombia, he informed her that his mother was Colombian. In a friendly manner, she matter of factly informed him that she knew. "She used to be our cook." The grandeur of Gian Carlo shrank as he struggled not to choke. Though her intention was not to belittle him, he was so used to playing the grand *seigneur* that this revelation shocked him. I am certain he was hopeful no one else heard her comment and that it would go no further to diminish his image.

These sunny days passed quickly with a few memorable moments. One afternoon, Ysabel and I entered a small theater to see a South American production.

Gian Carlo noticed our fruitless search for seats and rose to his feet with his companion to offer their places. We gratefully acknowledged his thoughtfulness but were soon distracted by a rustling movement in back of us. Someone else had just come in and been given seats directly behind ours. Very soon, we became aware of very strong body odor. Ysabel indicated with the wagging finger on her lap that a no-no was happening. When the lights came up for an intermission, we both turned to investigate the perpetrator of the offending smell. There was a very animated Anna Magnani holding court, earthy and disheveled and true to her image!

Ysabel, for a change in program, suggested an outing to Lady Sarah Spencer-Churchill, involving a motor trip around Tuscany. At this point, Sarah's father had died, and her brother had become the Duke of Marlborough. I remembered from my David days on 72nd Street, attending the dance Sarah gave her brother on the occasion of his engagement. Noni Phipps joined us, but both her mother and her husband, Tommy Schippers, stayed in Spoleto. We all agreed that Perugia was the hill town to aim for, as it was famous for its food. It was a lovely ride, peppered with Ysabel's diverse commentaries. She much preferred lively conversation to gossip, and everyone participated. The scenery and company were perfect.

Another event I shall always remember from this Spoleto visit was the quiet one-on-one that I enjoyed with Willem de Kooning. It was midmorning when I spied him, sitting by himself in the sun in front of the cathedral on the piazza. I greeted him and we sat chatting. He was shy and a bit befuddled, but we managed

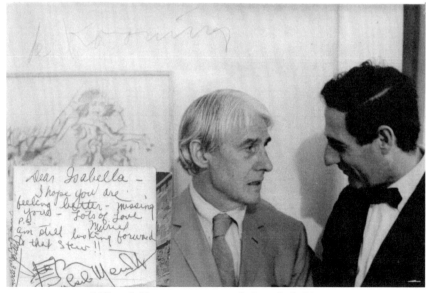

Willem de Kooning converses with Gian Carlo Menotti.

a gentle rapport. It was indeed a rare treat for me to share time with this world-renowned artist. I mentioned that Ysabel and I were having a cocktail party the next afternoon at our little villa in the nearby poppy-filled countryside. I told him the guests would include opera star Justino ("Gus") Diaz, who was performing at the festival, as was his lovely wife, ballerina Anna Aragno. Both had agreed to attend, as did soprano Muriel Greenspon, a friend from the Santa Fe Opera, appearing this Spoleto season in Menotti's *The Medium*.

Though tempted to enjoy some drinks with us, the rattled man was abruptly taken away from my company by one of his appointed keepers, who had momentarily lost sight of him. Somehow De Kooning had evaded those appointed to keep a life-saving eye on him. His alcoholic drinking was frequent and was to be discouraged. My influence was certainly not to be permitted.

These hedonistic Italian days came to an end, when these two international lotus-eater club members, insatiable for fresh pleasures, flew across the blue Mediterranean to the coast of Africa. The Tunisians warmly greeted us, once we departed from the sunny, merry Italians. Through my gallery dealings in New York, I had met a few Tunisians who avidly suggested I visit their country during the summer. Ysabel, as well, had friends who had villas there. The Sindbad Hotel in Hammamet was to be our home for the coming weeks, promising superior delights. It was the meeting place of the glitterati in the vicinity. Unlike the *La Dolce Vita* lifestyle in Rome that I so reviled, this happy atmosphere, with good friends in a beautiful setting on the sea, promised me stimulation, yet safeguarded me from lurid threats of compromising, soul-corrosive involvements—or so I told myself. Perhaps I was growing more attuned and wiser in dealing with the seductions of worldly behavior? I was certainly diving into deep waters where *louche* sharks doubtlessly swam amidst the scintillating beautiful people.

I was marveling how, if I squinted, the dreams of the boy from the Bronx and

A visit to the Dougga Ruins, Tunisia.

the exotica of the Hollywood films set in Arabia overlapped with Tunisia. After exposure to Ysabel and my many experiences in Europe over past decade, I felt I could maneuver myself more securely in the rarified world of the super rich. Constant jollification was becoming a norm for me.

Shasha Guiga was the acknowledged Perle Mesta of the area. She knew everyone and was married to the minister of tourism, who was a cousin to President Habib Bourguiba. The cast of characters was dazzling, with an interesting program always on hand. Stellar in residence was the Countess Carla Cavalli, whose daughter Marina, Marchesa Ferrero de Ventimiglia, kept her company. They had their own staff, and had a huge tent erected on the beach for their exclusive use, *Kema Karla* (Carla's tent). Vivid and colorful, Carla was beyond rich, with vast Tuscan landholdings, as well as being the mistress of the owner of a major liquor company, perhaps Cinzano. In contrast, Marina was retiring, shrinking from her vocal, commanding mother. Marina was married to the cousin of Gianni Agnelli, who directed the Fiat empire, in conjunction with her husband.

The blond duo of mother and daughter presented a charming contrast to each other in age, height and deportment. They enlivened the community around them—lovely Carla, with her animated conversation, and demure, pretty Marina, looking adorable. Marina claimed we were twins because our cropped hair had the same habits of self-expression, defying any amount of combing. One night, Marina and I paddled a rowboat out a short distance from shore under a starry sky. We wanted to escape the continual conversation of the group assembled and enjoy the quietude of the evening. Even though Carla's voice could be heard across the water, we enjoyed the atmosphere. Marina surprised me by breaking her pearl necklace and dropping some of the pearls into the sea. She claimed that this was special food for the fish who were protecting us. Since that night, Marina and I

Eric adoring Ysabel in Hammamet, Tunisia.

have used the fish symbol in giving each other gifts. (Marina claimed Lloyd's of London kindly covered her loss of the pearls!)

France's champagne king, Nicolas Feuillatte, had a large villa down the beach. It was here that Ysabel and I attended a celebration lunch honoring the American men landing on the moon. All was very festive, and towards the end of the meal, Nicolas informed us that next Friday, Gian Carlo Menotti and Greta Garbo would be arriving as his guests by yacht. Having had a snoot full of champagne, I could not resist it. I asked him NOT to give my greetings to "Gian Culo" but lots of love to Garbo—from her nephew! The guests regarded me with fresh eyes.

Nicolas had a gorgeous young Frenchman, Patrice, in residence. In his early twenties, Patrice told me it was his desire to return to France to get his sister. Together they would travel into North Africa, where he wanted to be kept by some enormously rich Berber out in the desert. He seemed to want to become a sex slave, presumably, with his sister joining him in the endeavor. The notion that this ravishing young man fantasized giving his life away in this manner fascinated me.

After departing the feast of a luncheon at Nicolas's Technicolor villa, Ysabel surprised me by suggesting we go into business together. Not imagining what business Ysabel might possibly consider undertaking, I waited to hear her notion. Inspired by the American astronauts landing on the moon, Ysabel thought it a chance in a lifetime to cash in on their needs. Imagine how successful a whorehouse on the moon would be, she explained. The men would welcome such a diversion. Only Ysabel would conjure up such an idea, I thought to myself.

Though there was often a gala event at one or another villa, the biggest event that summer was the birthday party given by Carla Cavalli on the occasion of her birthday. Beautifully made up with carefully-coiffed blond hair, the glamorous hostess appeared in a cherry red chiffon gown, wearing ruby and diamond earrings, bracelet and ring. Outside her tent, standing on the edge of the dance floor constructed for the occasion, she glanced down the beach at the approaching cavalcade of camels, torch-bearers, and slaves bearing gifts. They slowly advanced, with Carla swaying on the dance floor in avid anticipation of receiving these exotic guests. Nicolas was dressed in potentate finery on the lead camel, followed by a veiled Dior model, Yvonne, who was a house guest, with Patrice veiled in oriental slave drag on the camel behind her.

Other guests arrived more traditionally, driving through the gardens of the hotel or walking along the beach. The tables set up around the dance floor and in the tent were filling up; one of the three orchestras hired began playing Tunisian melodies. Western dance music and rock were to be played by the other orchestras as the evening progressed. Many guests were dressed in Tunisian attire. Ysabel wore a lovely embroidered long jacket—made of pale green linen with white embroidery—and matching trousers. I borrowed a royal scarlet red robe with gold trim from a newly acquired Tunisian friend, under which I wore what was to become the "famous" gold lamé bikini that was divested from Ysabel's undies collection.

Music blared much of the night. The fireworks were displayed as a special gift from Marina (much to Carla's annoyance as she hated loud explosions), and liquor flowed unceasingly, leaving some guests passed out in the surrounding bushes at dawn.

During the party, I had taken a strong liking to the American attaché, whose home was in the souks, the native enclave down the beach. A flood of drinks later, I woke up in bed snuggling next to what I thought was Ysabel's arm. "How hairy it is," I thought in the dawn hours. Opening my eyes, I realized I was not bedded with Ysabel, but with the American attaché. Though it was very agreeable to be in the sheeted fields with this darling man, I had a predicament: how to get back to the Sindbad during daylight with nothing on but a royal robe, a gilded bikini, and a borrowed, valuable Buccellati bracelet that I had borrowed from Marina. Getting through the Arab quarter unnoticed was a huge challenge.

The safe return of the solid gold Buccellati bracelet to Marina concerned me. I did not want to risk being robbed. Wearing the outstanding gold-trimmed robe would call much attention to me. After a warm farewell to my adorable host, I braved the brilliant sun, with blinding reflections off of the ancient walls. Quickly, I pulled the robe around me and headed for the beach. Once on the sand, I rolled the robe up, with the bracelet securely wrapped inside, and ran in my gilded bikini back to the Sindbad. Ysabel was vastly amused by my "hairy arm" tale, before we turned our attention to the next glittering event. Providential morning libations in conjunction with food and swimming in the sea helped dispel traces of hangovers, so we could embrace the day ahead with fervor.

One evening, we attended an exhibition of Tunisian dancing held in a courtyard of the Sindbad Hotel. Seated in the circle around the performers was a young male beauty beside a much older gentleman. Body language revealed that they were together. The attractive youth noticed me and held me with his long glances. He mumbled something to his companion and got up to walk into the garden. I followed. We had a brief conversation, long enough for me to learn he was guest of Binkie Beaumont, the famous London West End theater producer. It was determined that a "matinee" in my hotel room would be very agreeable the next afternoon. We both returned, separately, to the dance program, feeling particularly uplifted by the impending assignation. The next day was my new friend's last afternoon in Tunisia, so he gave me his fetching white bathing suit that I had admired, together with his address in England near Windsor Castle.

Though my stay in Tunisia was ongoing, Ysabel was soon scheduled to fly to Spain to visit with friends. The German television personality whom I befriended in Spoleto, Freddie Biolek, was soon to arrive in Hammamet. Freddie would stay with me in the bed Ysabel vacated. He was going to produce a film here, featuring one of Germany's top actors as well as France's aging Jean-Claude Pascal. The filming involved a Hammamet party atmosphere, with me appearing as a sybarite who would execute a Tunisian dance.

I again borrowed Marina's bracelet. It was a great compliment to the gold bikini, now worn under a short white silk *djellaba* turned sidewise so my right arm was completely exposed. The djellaba was draped to carefully expose much of my tanned body and the gold bikini. Two Berber silver necklaces completed the outfit. I wore the broad circled necklace and clutched the other in my left hand, clinking it like a cymbal, marking each beat of my *poésie de movement*. In my right hand was a spray of jasmine. The look on Jean Claude Pascal's time-worn face when he saw me was full of annoyance and anger. He had a robe tightly buttoned to his chin, reaching to the floor. His make-up was thick to help hide his aging. He viewed me semi-naked, tanned without make-up, youthfully prancing about, and he fumed! Perhaps the obvious difference in age irked him; perhaps he felt I would steal any scene we both were in; perhaps . . . who knows?

A bar had been set up for the partygoers' indulgences during the filming of the bacchanal. I imbibed dutifully. Getting a refill, I stood next to the English girl who was infatuated with my American attaché. She arrived to be with him but had no idea about my relationship with him. She asked me if I knew of any kind of employment that would be suitable for her, as she did not like her current job in London and wanted a change. What I said was very naughty of me, in my desire to be rid her, clearing the field for my friend and me to enjoy life together. "Yes, Ysabel and I were thinking of opening a whorehouse on the moon, and you would be perfect for it!" I swung away pleased with myself and re-entered the party scene ready to do my dance for the cameras. It went very well, with only one retake. Afterwards, I regretted being so tacky by resorting to such wild, wishful thinking to offend the young woman. The Devil Drink "screwed up" my head, again!

My personality was developing a duality. Frenetic playing with willful abandonment, in a flow of alcoholic excess, contrasted strongly with my energetic, disciplined professional pursuits. With the Tunisian idyll finished, it was time to switch gears and apply myself to more serious matters.

It had been a richly entertaining summer, but the fall art scene beckoned in New York. Both Capricorn artists and my theater design enterprise needed reactivation. I prepared an exhibition of international theater designs to open in December, with Capricorn Gallery artists shows before that. I attended the usual museum and gallery openings as well as social occasions, refocusing my energies from the sybaritic to more mindful matters involving my career in the art world.

A young Dutch woman—whom I knew from the United Nations circle of hostesses—invited me, while I was in Italy, to a "Spanish" party she was giving that fall in New York. I attended with Maria, a young Spanish woman I knew from this UN group. I had noticed a good-looking Iranian guy at the party, who seemed to be ducking into the bathroom on occasion, leading me to believe he was on a drug trip. At one point, after being annoyed by his attentions to Maria, I told him to "fuck off." He got incensed and really started getting abusive. He was dissuaded from arguing with me by being led off to another room by the Dutch hostess, who turned out to be his girlfriend. It seemed a good time to take Maria home; she lived in the next building.

For some reason, I returned to the party briefly. When I was then quietly trying to depart, a Greek girl called my name and the Iranian saw me. I was rushed out the door by the hostess and taken by an elevator down to the ground level. I was very peeved at this fellow. When I was about to hail a taxi, he came out of the building with two other Iranians. I thought how ridiculous for me to run away in a cab. Unlike my normal tendency to avoid physical conflict, I decided to let the taxi pass and try to reason with the angry Iranian. Before I knew it, the two guys had me pinned to the sidewalk and the Iranian was striking blows to my face, nearly ripping out my left eye. He got up from me and walked away, the two accomplices following. One murmured he was sorry . . .

Blood was splashed across my pleated dinner shirt and my head was needing attention, so I returned to the apartment. The doorman made believe he saw nothing unusual. The Greek girl opened the door and swooned when she saw the mess I was. My shirt was removed, and a couple of girls worked on cleaning me up. After resting a bit, a male friend of theirs took me home in a taxi, recommending I seek professional attentions in the morning.

Tyrone was a largish, orange cat given to me some weeks earlier. He lived with me and slept on my bed. After I got into bed with the lights extinguished, I drifted into a troubled stupor with a snoozing Tyrone by my side. Above the two walk-in closets, behind my bed and set out into the room, was a shelf on which I put large, outsized books and a delicate glazed ceramic sculpture from Spain. I put it up high, out of the cleaning woman's reach, for safety. Below it stood a floor lamp.

During the pre-dawn hours, a loud crash ensued. My outsized Henry Moore sculpture book obeyed gravity by falling straight down, knocking over the floor lamp. The sculpture, on the other hand, made an arc, landing close to me with only one armature snapped off, miraculously. I do not know what caused the disturbance or why the sculpture flew over to me with minimal damage to its fragility. A psychic later explained to me how I was in shock and subconsciously wanted something close to me that I valued, such as the sculpture. My energies carried it to me, disturbing the book in doing so . . . maybe?

The angry Iranian turned out to be a nephew of the Shan of Iran. He was a student in upstate New York, and he left the country shortly after his attack on me. At first, I could not understand why the Dutch girl claimed not to know who he was, especially when it seemed she was his girlfriend. She was shielding him until he could leave the country.

During these weeks, there was great tension at the Capricorn Gallery. The elevator was not operable; the owner of the building wanted to increase the rent, and he made use of the space difficult in every way possible, including cuts in heat and hot water. I decided it was time to move the operations uptown to Lexington Avenue, in the low 90s. I found a two-story space there propitious to a gallery

Portait of Eric by Lotte Lichtblau after the beating.

operation. At first, the entire board of five agreed with me, until I announced that the Jean Rosenthal lighting would not be appropriate to install there. The installation of efficient track lighting—rather than labor with the cumbersome installation of Jean Rosenthal's creation—seemed a wise decision. I wanted to leave it behind, but the partner of the deceased lighting genius would not hear of it. She wanted it taken along, in tribute to her deceased beloved, or have the gallery stay with the Rosenthal lighting where it was. Another agreed with her; both wanted to remain in the old space. A compromise was made. Those whom I wished to have join me in the new venture could do so. The two board dissenting members and other artists I did not wish to bring along could continue as Capricorn Gallery.

In retribution for my parting from two board members, the physician/husband of one of the board members cancelled an appointment to treat my head injury, after I had made the trip to Long Island to see him. When I arrived in his office, I was told that he could not see me! It was rude and unprofessional to punish me in this way, especially since I needed his special medical attention. The two objecting members went on to indicate that they thought my injury had caused some brain damage, as evidenced in my determination to leave the 56th street space. Much unpleasantness resulted. Had they forgotten the attention I garnered for the gallery and overlooked the fact that they did not have a board majority in the decision?

It was courageous of me to try to attempt running a two-pronged gallery operation independently, without the safety of the co-operative set-up. Though the theater design sales could bring in a fairly steady source of income for my Compass Gallery, the promotion of emerging artists was less certain.

It was urgent that the rest of the world knew about the existence of this new Compass Gallery, located north at where the compass points from the hub of galleries on 57th Street or Madison Avenue. My good friend, Rita Simon, artist and writer for art magazines, collaborated with me to garner attention by creating a couple of group shows as opening exhibitions incorporating well-established artists. With gracious cooperation from their well-known galleries, one of each artist's works would be incorporated into the themed exhibitions. *Beyond Realism* and *Outer Spaces, Inner Limits* were the first of these shows, featuring work by both known artists and the artists that I was beginning to promote. This generated interest in the public and stimulated critics to cover the events.

It was unfortunate that Ysabel was not on the scene to add her encouragement to this daunting venture. Because of money problems, she had moved to Rome to a small rooftop suite that I had enjoyed previously, located near the foot of the Spanish Steps. It was an economic measure, countering the cutting off of the monthly stipend that her long-time benefactor had arranged for her for many years since they ended their relationship. Ysabel had planned to marry Andy after getting him setup importing Colombian Coffee. He became a millionaire; his daughter married her son just as it became possible for them to wed. That was now out of the question, so Andy married the young, beautiful divorcée of Fernando Botero. Ysabel sub-let her Fifth Avenue apartment, moved to Rome, and helped some local hookers upgrade their underwear by giving some of her own supply. I was glad that I snared the gold panties before this transpired! Ysabel was caught in a whirlpool, and, perhaps, so was I! I missed her at the opening of the Compass Gallery.

The Compass Gallery was across from the 92nd Street YWCA. It was on ground level, with a floor above for exhibition as well. In these spacious two floors that traversed the length of the building, I agreed to sub-lease the back of the ground floor to an acquaintance for his contemporary art gallery, which he named the Blue Moon Gallery. I used the front space for small sculpture and theater designs. The second floor was ideal to accommodate large paintings, with its high ceiling and light spilling in from the front and rear windows. A door in the back led to a terrace, just above the back of the ground floor. I used this upper floor for my living space at night. My Lexington Avenue apartment, rented by my poet friend while I was in Italy, was now a painting studio of my friend Rita, who took over the lease. All these arrangements made my finances stronger, so that I could tackle the challenges of running a new art gallery.

Lotte Lichtblau, an artist who was one of the original supporters of my running the Capricorn Gallery, had strongly encouraged me to branch out from the clutches of Capricorn's negative forces. Lotte had long inspired me on my path as gallery director, and encouraged me to trust myself in matters of art. Through an unending dialogue, whether in her studio or living room, Lotte guided and helped me develop my judgments over the years, consoling and encouraging me through difficult periods. We shared time together ruminating over art in Altaussee, Austria, on two occasions when summer circumstances were favorable, as well as at her summer home in upstate New York.

Stalwart friends like Rita, Nathalie, and Lotte helped me enormously in this transition period into independence. Oliver Smith, the dean of theater designers, confided in me that it was "better to leave those women" at Capricorn, and urged me to be on my own. Another good friendship had developed through being in the gallery world. John Barker, an editor for ARTS Magazine, often visited and wrote about my exhibitions. He became part of a nucleus with Lotte, Nathalie, and Rita in supporting my efforts.

Rita was my constant companion at either museum or gallery openings, as both Lotte and Nathalie had family commitments. It was at one Whitney Biennial that I invented a new artist on the scene. Stairways connected each floor of the museum. At the landings midpoint between floors there was a green marble topped bench. Rather than take the elevator between floors, I walked down from the top floor. After viewing much "stuff" I felt to be ridiculous, ugly, and lacking any sense of art, I decided to make a statement. Removing the NO SMOKING sign from its frame above the bench in the stairwell, I turned it over and wrote with my marker pen:

AFTER THE PARTY
Glorietta Trash
Mixed media
1970

On the green marble bench were plastic cups in varying stages of being finished, some on their sides; a couple had a cigarette butt inside. A Doubting Thomas, with a personal supply, had finished a tiny liquor bottle, leaving it with all the other detritus. This small *objet trouvé* I placed artfully with the cups and thought it made a wonderful statement, both about the state of art in the exhibition and an after-party scene.

Very pleased with myself, I joined Rita and some artists-around-town. There was a big women-in-art movement being pushed that evening at the Whitney. Women were going around blowing whistles and being annoying. With the focus

Left: Eric as a sphinx by Rita Simon. Right: Eric with Rita Simon.

on women in mind, I announced that I, too, had one of my pieces in the museum exhibition, but as women seemed to get the emphasis of attention this year, I used a pseudonym: Glorietta Trash. My work could be viewed on the landing in the stairwell! Rita caught on what I was doing, and joined me in the put-on. Later, to other artists, Rita would bring up Glorietta Trash and her California background. We both would talk about this fictitious artist with great earnestness. I no longer claimed her as my invention but as a West Coast talent. A curious painter asked Rita about Glorietta, and she replied. "Oh, yes, I know her and though her work is interesting, I would never want to show with her." Glorietta Trash entered conversations during the following days, when Rita and I would visit various artists. It got to the point where an artist, not wanting to seem ignorant or out of the loop, also claimed to know Glorietta Trash. It became too exhausting to continually breathe life into her, so I announced that Glorietta Trash died in a car crash on the freeway near Santa Monica!

Clayton Cole, who was surfing along in this hippy-influenced period, enjoyed visiting my gallery and having long conversations with me about art and the crazy world around us in New York. He had a small but art-filled apartment on East 73rd Street, where he would entertain an assortment of curious people. At one gathering there, I had the pleasure of meeting the famous Brooklyn Heights artist, Paul Cadmus, who sensually captured the muscular physiques of sailors and stevedores in varying states of undress. Though Clayton wrote a column for *SCREW* Magazine, once featuring me as the "apricot, gash-gold vermilion prince" in the art world, he obviously had a trust fund to support his lifestyle. Sometimes, he accompanied me to the Janis Joplin, Jimi Hendrix, and Andy Warhol factory cast of characters' watering hole near Union Square, Max's Kansas City. Late hours found us straggling back uptown, sometimes with company collected along the way. During this period, I gave up living at the back of my gallery for staying with Ysabel, at her kind suggestion. She had returned from Rome with a sense of firmer financial footing. We were both living illusionary existences....

I found it amusing to have hippie-looking clothes tailor-made while living at the Fifth Avenue apartment and carousing with the unwashed descendants of the lovely flower children. It was make-believe to me—a way of life not held close to my heart. I much preferred alcohol to drugs and people in formal wear to sloppy attire. I was never an authentic hippie but more of a playboy, astray from what I perceived to be a higher social plane. Clearly, my hippie excursions were only occasional, while I enjoyed and indulged in the more conservative and elegant environments as further assurance that I had "arrived."

Holly Woodlawn appeared on and off during this frenetic period. I had met the transvestite star of *Trash* at a Museum Of Modern Art event. She invited me to the opening of her cabaret act in a West Side bar, Reno Sweeney's. From a florist friend, I presented her with a wrist corsage of an anthurium, whose pistil penetrated a white lily. With many colored balloons placed in a tall plastic bag, I

Holly Woodlawn, star of
Andy Warhol's movie, "Trash".

slipped in a favorite 8 x 10 picture of me autographed to her. It was a very effective presentation and prompted her to send me a gushing letter kissed with her red lipstick. On a note inside, Holly scrawled, "Eric I love you madly!"

After her show, Holly and I decided to go for a drink at a gay club. This was followed by another drink at another club, ultimately leading to her East Side walk-up apartment. Though intoxicated, I could make out, in the dim light by her bed in the center of the room, a pallet adorned by a sleeping young man. Holly and

I were not compatible playmates, so I decided to take a bath in the tub, which was in a direct line of vision from her bed. I noticed her watching me in the bathtub as the young man got up and came over to fool around with me. Lots of alcohol and exhaustion make recollection dim. I do not remember when I left the "Spick and Span-ish" (one of Holly's favorite phrases) environment, and it was some years until I saw Holly again.

One afternoon at some gathering, I noticed how much more put together she was. Her dress and manner were more subdued and tasteful than I remembered. We got along very nicely, which induced me to invite her up to my place. Despite attempts, nothing sexually successful transpired this second time around; it was un-momentous until it was time to bid Holly goodbye at my doorway. Standing nude and offering polite words of farewell, I was surprised when she demanded, "Aren't you going to see me into a taxi?" It seemed implausible for me to get dressed and go downstairs so unnecessarily and indicated in the negative. Holly gave me a strong slap across the face and blurted out, "You are no gentleman!" To which I stated, "You are no lady!" as she stomped away.

So ended my contact with any of the Warhol cast of characters. Bridget Berlin, Joe Dallesandro, and even Edmund Gaultney (who left running R.C. Gorman's Taos gallery to join up with Andy in the Factory) were a small part of the past. My threatening to throw Andy out of a helicopter over the Atlantic Ocean helped finish relations with this Pop Art icon.

As debaucheries continued, along with rampant drug use, AIDS became a constant concern for everyone. We all knew people who died of one or the other, or just disappeared. Clayton Cole had moved to Mallorca, where it is believed he committed suicide. My move to the Compass Gallery—a distance uptown—moderated many of my activities in the downtown world centering around Max's Kansas City and lowlife haunts as well as in the realms of the establishment art world around 57th Street and Madison Avenue.

My reputation in dealing with costume and scenic renderings and advising for the updating of museum and library collections created the possibility of my becoming an appraiser in this field. This is something that I had never considered, and, after appraising the estate of designer Boris Aronson, I avoided further entanglements, no matter how much financial gain was involved. The executor of this famous designer's estate invited me to lunch at Sardi's, to coax me into taking on the arduous task of cataloguing and appraising every drawing in Aronson's studio, representing a lifetime in the theater. The worst part of this challenging task was the detail of cataloguing—indicating size, title, medium, and market value. I did not enjoy the time-consuming tediousness of the mammoth task. Although I was handsomely paid, I wanted my talents to be put to better use. Creating an exhibition and promotion and interaction within the gallery resulting in sales were more to my taste. It was flattering to be considered the authority in artistic matters, but I would like to leave the cataloguing details to a librarian.

The young duke returns to Sicily with me from Tunisia.

Chapter 11

FOLLOWING THE ITALIAN ARMY IS HELL

The advent of summer invited me to leave the woes of running a gallery until the autumn, while I returned to Europe and Tunisia for another dip into that intoxicating land of exotica/erotica. Karen's roommate from UN days, Allegra Kent Taylor, was back in London. She was always a particular favorite of both David Wallace and mine. I thought she resembled Catherine Deneuve. Slim, blond, and blue-eyed, with a warm proper English manner, Allegra charmed me with her hospitality and friendship. I shared with her my enthusiasm for Sicily and in particular Taormina, where I planned to visit on my way to Tunisia. There was an overnight boat service between Sicily and Tunis. Allegra thought she would really enjoy a holiday in Taormina with a current beau.

Josette Stielle, a Belgian woman I had befriended in Taormina two years before, had invited me to visit in her new villa. It occurred to me that Josette might enjoy going to Hammamet with me, as Ysabel had the previous summer; she could rent Allegra her villa while we went to northern Africa. And this is how it all worked out. . . .

While in London, I delivered a plaster cast of a head executed by Bianca, Princess of Löwenstein. Bianca was a great friend of art critic John Barker, part of my Compass Gallery coterie of friends. Bianca and her American husband kindly invited me to stay with them, partially as a thank-you for delivering her artwork. They had a flat on the Embankment Gardens in Chelsea. Each day, Bianca and

I would open and later close a pub. We enjoyed drinking together and sharing stories or notions about life, the sort of conversation intelligent drinkers partake of with very serious intent.

In the next building on the Embankment Gardens an Irish woman ran a very low-key brothel. I was introduced to her and given a room there, when Bianca and her husband needed to go on a trip, and their flat was not available. The bawdy house room was very pleasantly decorated and comfortable, with barely a clue as to what really went on there. (Another neighbor in the building, on the other side of Bianca and who was about to become a great friend, Katya Douglas, was astonished when I told her about the brothel in her neighborhood.) This accommodation was to serve me very well in my future visits to London. The area along the Thames was ideal—it was attractive with colorful local history; the price was reasonable; and the notion of living in a brothel was irresistible! But—hush up, and don't tell Mama!

My return to Taormina was very different from my visit there a few years previously, when I lived off the land, suffering poverty and humiliation from the Spoleto fiasco. During that trying period, I first met the lively Belgian woman, Josette, who was always a continual source of amusement. With good humor, she enjoyed a vibrant life in Sicily, far removed from the dull existence in Brussels. Having convinced her husband that Sicily was beneficial to her health, she would spend only the winters with him, their son, and her mother in the hostile Belgian climate. Josette managed, through her sensuality, to engage attractive Sicilian men, not only to get her villa in operable condition, but also to stimulate her leisure time.

Lustily, we both set off for Hammamet, once Allegra and her beau were installed in Josette's villa overlooking Taormina, Mount Etna, and the beautiful Mediterranean. Shasha enthusiastically greeted us at the Sindbad Hotel, measuring Josette against the inimitable Ysabel. Though there were no Carla Cavalli and daughter Marina there this season, some of my previous acquaintances were there. The American attaché was there briefly, and the darling actress from the Comédie-Française, Denise Noël, had taken a house in Hammamet.

One day, a fashion show was planned for the visitors as a special afternoon's event. Though I did not fancy the show, I noticed a slim young man, in outrageous toreador pants, staring at me. He resembled a youthful Gérard Depardieu, although less tall and with a less prominent nose. Eventually, we began a conversation. Giorgio Sanfelice di Bagnoli was an Italian visiting Hammamet with a couple of good friends. One was an attractive young woman around twenty-one. Verde Visconti was the niece of the famous titled film director and granddaughter of dress designer, Elsa Schiaparelli. Though lovely and pleasant, Verde seemed disapproving of me. I felt she was trying to control those whom Giorgetto befriended, and I was not her idea of a good companion for him. Some young Italian women with privilege can be very smug and unkind. The alarm bell was probably set off by the Angel of Mercy to warn both of us, but I did not choose to hear it. . . .

Young Giorgetto told me he was a student but was about to join the regiment in which all the men in his family served. As national service was required, he was going to get his duty over with ASAP. The comandante was a great friend of his father, and being in Italy, his connections allowed him the privilege of picking where and when he was to be based. In the winter, he chose to be in Caserta, since it was close to the family palace in Naples. Later in the year, he would go to the mountain army base, to avail himself of the nearby country home owned by his land-rich family. It was a fantastic notion to me how this young private-to-be could determine the way he would do his required military service. Doubtlessly, I was impressed by his ancient noble family and felt flattered when he bestowed such interest in me, ten years his senior and from another, much humbler background. I instinctively knew that, as an American, no matter what I achieved, it would never mean anything to him! While sitting all afternoon sharing lengthy conversations about ourselves on the beach, I tried to dissuade Giorgetto from considering a relationship with me, because of age and background differences. These differences do not mean as much to Americans as they do to upper class Europeans, where lines are carefully drawn up, daring intrusions.

Reluctantly, I fell under his romantic spell. Our early, very fulfilling sexual escapades grew into an intense relationship over the passing days. Despite my warnings that we should avoid going too quickly, or making any commitment, Giorgetto persuaded me to rush forward with him into strengthening our bond. He was partial to Americans and I suited the young duke's needs—for the moment. Despite Verde's disapproval of me, we spent each day and evening together. Sometimes Verde came on an excursion with us to a remote beach or village to watch a Berber wedding, but she maintained a distance. It did not deter Giorgetto's pursuit of me. I was enchanted by his infectious smile and sense of humor. As I mentioned before, his slim, compact body reminded me of the young, nude Gérard Depardieu in a film with the provocative Catherine Deneuve. Giorgetto, though in his early twenties, was no newcomer to lively sex. I was beguiled and seduced.

Josette was no slouch. During my preoccupation with the *duchino*, Josette found in the souks of Tunis a very handsome young Moslem, who was glad to put aside his wares to be with Josette when we returned to Taormina. Giorgetto joined us. The four of us bought matching outfits to wear, while parading down the main street of Taormina. Josette had her "prince" and I had my "duke" to show off to the amused townsfolk.

My head was completely turned around by the intensity of this affair. My new Italian sandy-haired lover plotted our life together. I could easily imagine my closing down my gallery in New York—it being drained of its operating funds and my energy—in exchange for a life of bliss with Giorgetto in Italy. Giorgetto thought it a wonderful idea. I could live in Caserta while he was based there, and someday we would occupy the small house an uncle left him in the hills outside Rome.

Clearly, I convinced myself that this decision was well-based. Back in New York, I not only had seen the handwriting on the wall, I could read it! Impending financial ruin was threatening me and my gallery. Impetuously moving to a location akin to Siberia as far as closeness to the hub of the art world had only gained me a freedom from the unpleasantness permeating Capricorn Gallery. I had sensed the gallery scene would move, but it went south not north as I counted on. Paucity of sales had to be acknowledged. Though good publicity was garnered, the public shied away from the journey north to visit. Giorgetto's enthusiastic persuasion together with the intoxication of being by his comely side overwhelmed a frantic me.

There were matters in Rome, partially to do with school and family, keeping Giorgetto at home after returning from Tunisia via Sicily. However, he was diligent in sending letters and often sent telegrams, as well. Nino Peluso del Giudice was a friend Josette and I had spent time with in Taormina. We called him "Titano," as he liked the idea of being a titan. Titano was impressed and fascinated by the mail I received daily while staying with him in Milan. He became intrigued by Giorgetto, and later was to go out of his way to meet him (and probably seduce him, as well). I had agreed with Giorgetto that we would imitate—in writing letters—a tennis ball's flight back and forth. These missives would arrive constantly while I was traveling across Europe to my final destination, New York.

The flow of correspondence continued with regularity, creating a substantial collection of Giorgetto's outpourings to me. When I returned to New York, I was determined to close down the gallery and divest myself of everything that was not needed for my transfer to Italy. Escape from the two garrulous women at the Capricorn Gallery to the creation of the Compass Gallery had seemed mandatory for me to establish a professional freedom. Now, I had convinced myself that closing the Compass Gallery was becoming a necessity for survival. Its location forecast a grim future, which I had been unwilling to accept in my determination to get away on my own—the sooner, the better—as there could be some recouping of my investment, leaving a sum for me to take to Italy to use on my venture into a compelling amorous relationship.

My plans were disturbing and seemed capricious to some of my friends in New York, especially the artists I handled. With determination spiced with willfulness, I packed a good sized *bauli* (trunk), with a box of silver flatware, a woolen quilt, some framed photographs, and whatever favorite items I would find necessary to continue life anew with my *duchino* in Italy. It seemed fittingly glamorous, dramatic, and utterly romantic, but it exchanged professional ambition for what might be considered an insane diversion into escapism fueled by alcoholic immersion. The nurturing attentions from Giorgetto seemed preferable to the harsh impending failure on the New York art scene.

My landlord kindly released me from the balance of the lease on the art gallery, so I was busily tying up loose end in readiness to return to my beloved in

Italy. Ysabel had sub-let her floor-through Fifth Avenue apartment and was living abroad again for the duration. Nathalie had moved to Florida with a new husband. Supporting my decision, Rita was impressed at my disposing of everything to follow my heart. My family in Montrose was not unduly surprised by my leaving the US to move to Italy, since I had never spent much time with them and seemed to be always going to and from Europe. I stored some things with them and departed to my new life, with the trunk shipped by boat to Rome awaiting further instructions.

Caserta, slightly inland from Naples, has an interesting history, involving the king of the Two Sicilies and his marriage to the sister of Marie Antoinette. Their palace has pretensions to being a diminutive Versailles. Few tourists ever venture to Caserta, but there is also a large army base. This is where Giorgetto chose to begin his army career.

Privates are not allowed hot water for showers, so Giorgetto rented a small apartment near the base in which to retreat for this luxury. The other luxury was me, installed and prepared to amuse my private when he could get off duty. In the beginning, I quite enjoyed having this unusual arrangement; it permitted me to explore the vicinities around Naples by bus or train.

Each morning, I would go to the nicest cafe to order a double black coffee, a vodka with Campari and orange slice over ice, and a delicious, Italian-style brioche. Day after day, I stood at the same counter and had the same menu. Not once did the man behind the counter inquire who I was or what I was doing in a place so far removed from tourists. There seemed to be no curiosity. Even drinking an alcoholic mixture in the early morning did not stimulate speculation, or so it seemed . . . Perhaps in such a small town, it was known that the private with a noble name had an American with a penchant for alcohol tucked away. In my mind, I imagined myself to be the Simone Signoret's cast-away character in *Ship of Fools*, wandering foreign ports of call, needing the sensual to anchor life and find happiness . . .

It was thrilling to hear army boots ascending the staircase when I least expected it, followed by a knock on the door. Giorgetto often had amusing stories about his fellow soldiers. Once, going back to base after our intimate interlude, approaching the entrance to the camp he saw two guards doing a waltz together accompanied by a transistor radio. Another time, while going out on a march in the countryside, some soldiers stopped to pick wild flowers. Little wonder Italy has never won a war.

Christmas and the New Year were approaching. I had brought a dozen presents from America to give my darling Lucertola. He had given me a small bronze lizard treasured since his childhood. Hence, his nickname became "Lucertola," Italian for lizard. He called me affectionately "Papera Grassa,"—fat duck—because I tended to waddle, or so he claimed.

Giorgetto had leave for some days over New Year's, so we decided to go to Capri. I had been to Capri with Nell during the Spoleto gallery visit, but summertime on that fantastic island is far more romantic than in the winter rains. Giorgetto and I rented a tiny apartment overlooking the beautiful Faraglioni rock formations, with the churning sea below. It was on the property of the sister of Thomas Mann. She wore black in remembrance of her dead Italian husband, but we were not encouraged to have dealings with her.

When I divested myself of many things to go to Italy, I kept my two fur coats and a fur jacket. One fur coat I got through a promotion deal with a leading furrier in Copenhagen. Trying to heal the deep wound left from David the Cruel's bold-faced transgression, I hired him to do some PR for my first gallery, hoping that encouraging him in business dealings would normalize our communication. We both lived in similar circles within the strata of New York society, and after all those special years together, I thought we should have a civil relationship. David had managed to convince the Copenhagen client that I was prominent in the social whirl of New York, and that it would be good publicity for them to have me photographed around town in their pin seal coat. The Norwegian raccoon coat I bought from Clayton for only $100 when he was moving to Spain; the very used jacket was a gift from a friend in New York who tired of it.

The furs came in very handy on Capri, as our place was cold and damp. Giorgetto laughed at me for dragging fur coats around with me, but we put them to good use. The weather was mean, and our spirits tended to flag under the cold dampness.

We attended a party held at a large home owned by a countess long known to Giorgetto. Many of his friends were there and a merry time was had, though I sometimes lost the nuances in conversation as it was all in exuberant Italian. The lights across the harbor to Naples were visible when the rain desisted. I was informed that life on Capri went on quite nicely during World War II, with much food and livestock provided by Anacapri, just above the town. However, sometimes the explosions of bombs around Naples could be seen from this distance. It was a grim reminder that there was a bitter war going on, somewhere out there.

New Year's Eve was a bust. We went to a club in Capri where he was well known. When I complained of the noisy, smoky place, he suggested I walk home and he would meet me soon. I left but waited in a doorway out of the rain across the road, to see what he might do. A previous lover was at that club, but Giorgetto said he was going to walk a girl home after I left. Indeed, he had the girl with him when he departed. Noticing me, he came over to tell me how crazy I was to hang around in the rain. Why would I do such a foolish thing? He walked the girl home then came back to our little place with me. I did not think it was behavior for a lover to adopt on New Year's Eve. Annoyances like this began to pile up.

Back on the mainland, we could occasionally attend a film. After watching a showing of *The Garden of the Finzi Contini*, we had a very serious disagreement. I maintained that the Italians should be ashamed of their behavior toward the Jews in World War II; after all, they were fellow Italians. Giorgetto calmly asserted that they were not Italians; they were Jews. It was clear that though we had mutual sexual satisfaction, our attitudes about things were very different. I began to question the wisdom of my having abandoned my homeland and my career in favor of following the Italian army and a willful, spoiled youth. The little apartment began to get smaller, and my waits for boots clicking on the staircase got longer. Finally, it was mutually agreed that I return to the USA and my life there, at least for the time being. I had my trunk full of dreams and hopes, unopened, returned to America. Daily, I obsessed over Giorgetto and missed Italy very much.

Ysabel was still out of the country, with her apartment subleased. With no apartment of my own, I accepted a kind invitation from Osborn Maitland Miller to stay at his large West Side apartment near Columbia University. Informally known as "Uncle Monkey," he liked my company and needed a drinking buddy. It was his niece, Diana Rose Miller, who introduced me to him. Diana and I met in Greece on a tour bus together with David. When she came to New York on one of her free trips as an employee of BOAC, she would visit David and me, as well as Uncle Monkey. Born in the late 1880s in Scotland, he was very badly injured in World War I, but he went on to become a leading cartographer and director of the American Geographic Society in New York. His gayness was quietly kept in a closet, but he liked having young gay men around for company. I introduced him to many, and some became great friends.

Uncle Monkey got this strange moniker for two reasons. When he sang as a child, he screwed his face up like a monkey, and later his nephew and niece could not pronounce Maitland and said "Monkey" instead. This was to be his term of endearment forever in the gay world in New York. It was in sharp contrast to his correct and proper manner in speech and dress. O.M. Miller was a charming gentleman, greatly admired and enjoyed by his professional colleagues and his acquaintances in New York.

One morning, over a few orange juice and vodkas, he revealed his never having

Uncle Monkey adores his Manx kitten.

Allegra Kent Taylor and Uncle Monkey visit Montrose.

seen Italy. As a frail aging gentleman, there was little opportunity left for him to do so, unattended and on his own. However, as I seemed to miss Italy and Giorgetto so much, why didn't he treat me to a trip to Italy and have me show him around that wondrous country at the same time? It was a thrilling notion—soon I would be able to see my darling "Lucertola" again!

Giorgetto seemed pleased by the idea of my return with Uncle Monkey, of whom he had heard so much. By now, he was in the mountains. We could take a train from Venice up to Merano. His camp was very close to there. The preparations were hurried because of my excitement, but I knew Italy well enough to know how to show Uncle Monkey the best things en route to Venice.

Our first stop would be Rome for a few days. Uncle Monkey was charmed by the city. We stayed at the Inghilterra Hotel, the same first stopping place David and I used some ten years earlier. The area around the Spanish Steps provided good restaurants within walking distance from our hotel. Taxis delivered us to specific sights, enough to give him a sense of the beauty of Rome, the Eternal City.

The first class train ride to Florence was comfortable, with an easy check-in to the Berchielli Hotel on the Arno. He could sit on the small balcony overlooking the river and observe the famous vista of the bridges and hillside of Fiesole in the distance. The Piazzetta and glorious architectural wonders of Florence were thrilling to the elderly gentleman, as were the special attentions we received in certain restaurants, thanks to the assistance of influential friends who lived there, people I knew from New York.

All was blissfully moderated with the joy of Venice ahead. Uncle Monkey had been fascinated since youth with railway timetables, so our creeping along Italy by train was particularly interesting to him. He was enjoying this adventure and anticipated with pleasure viewing Venice both from his hotel windows and walking along the canals. I had to pay careful attention to his balance on the *vaporettos* that took us around to various locations on the waterways.

Countess Gozzi (Elsie McNeil) usually entertained me at her lovely villa on the Giudecca when I appeared in Venice. This time was no different. She sent her motor launch to the Danieli to pick us up and later return us. She was very gracious, as always, and I think Uncle Monkey was very impressed by the luxurious treatment this important woman extended to us.

Before their meeting, Uncle Monkey was fascinated to hear about Elsie's shrewd dealings with Mussolini. During World War II, Mussolini decided to commandeer commercial ships for wartime use. The very clever Elsie McNeil, through marriage to Count Gozzi, was now the owner of Fortuny Silks. Knowing the dictator was very fascinated by postage stamps, she acquired a large collection to put on an oversized envelope addressed to him. In it, she requested an audience, so that she could plead her case and maintain her ships. Her high heels clicked on the marble floor of Il Duce's Roman palace; double doors opened *enfilade* as she progressed dragging a mink stole. Famous for her fabulous *belle poitrine*, Elsie seductively convinced Mussolini to permit no government interference with her ships plying their valuable cargo internationally. Her fortune was secure!

After a few days of small excursions around Venice, Uncle Monkey and I took a train to Merano, in the mountains, where Giorgetto was to meet us. The hotel delighted Uncle Monkey very much, not only because of its comfort, but also because he could enjoy hearing the mountain stream gurgling by from his window. In the meantime, I clutched at Giorgetto hungrily when we had a moment alone in my room. He pushed me away, informing me that he did not do sexual things while in uniform. I was stunned and deeply injured at his restraint. We went out for a walk and a drink to talk. I felt it was going to be useless hanging around this area, regardless of its beauty, if my Lizard was going to be so distant with me.

Upon returning to the hotel, I found Uncle Monkey enjoying a drink in his room, reading and listening to the water flowing by outside his window. I took a strong drink, and when he asked what the matter was, I announced we were leaving in the morning! "Oh, no!" He cried. He so enjoyed this environment but would agree if I felt so strongly. Back to Venice and our hotel there . . .

We no sooner got back to the hotel than the phone rang and it was the Lizard. Giorgetto took a chance that we would be returning to the same hotel in Venice, and he was correct. He was very upset I had departed and told me how much my leaving had made him unhappy. After hanging up, I realized how miserable I was, too. I resolved to return to the mountains as soon as possible. Uncle Monkey was surprised, as usual, but agreed to wait at the Venetian hotel until I finished what I had to do in Merano.

After getting off the train in the now familiar train station, I called the army base. I was informed my Private San Felice di Bagnoli was off base with other soldiers, in town for dinner. It was not a large town, so I quickly located Giorgetto, sitting with a half dozen soldiers in an open air garden restaurant. I sat across the garden in direct view of him. He was greatly surprised when he noticed me. After excusing himself from his colleagues, he came over to me. In a brief exchange, I asked him how he explained my presence to his companions. "I told them you were a friend of my mother." Upset, I gasped with despair. That sealed it once and for all. A friend of his mother, indeed! Our relationship was at a total end. Any future exposure to each other would be on a totally different basis. The intimacy was finished; only a polite sociability would be possible.

A friend of his mother, indeed!

Uncle Monkey and I returned from Italy having had a remarkable adventure, some of it poignantly sad for me. Time to move on and re-invent myself with only haunting memories to remind me of a black and blue heart. During this bouncing back period in New York, I called various friends to announce my whereabouts.

A telephone conversation with Margaret Jamison in Santa Fe opened a new vista for me. She eagerly suggested I go out to run her gallery, located just across from the La Fonda Hotel. Margaret had admired the quality of my art dealings both in New York and Santa Fe, and she thought I would be a welcome addition to her operation. Little did I realize how much would develop from her trust in my abilities.

Absorbing the mystique of "The Land of Enchantment."

Chapter 12

THEY ALL SAID MY IDEA WAS CRAZY

The remarkably beautiful town of Santa Fe, cradled in the Sangre de Cristo Mountains in northern New Mexico, has long been an attraction to painters and writers, as well as the wealthy, affording a glamorous second home for relaxation or easy socializing. Anthropologists and artists alike have valued observing essentially unalloyed living Indian culture on the pueblos in that vicinity. Hollywood personalities have moved there in great numbers and are referred to as Californicators. They bought up properties, raising real estate prices. In comparison to California, the cost of land here seems a bargain, but it upsets the balance of living costs for everyone else. It is a tri-cultural community, mingling Hispanic, Indian, and Anglo, with people choosing to be there, rather than having to be there.

A mariachi band greeted me and the twenty guests gathered at Margaret Jamison's home as a prelude to the lively lunch to follow. The carefree Mexican music was an infectiously joyous welcome to Santa Fe, setting the tone for the months to follow. Though I had been in Santa Fe for the opening of the new opera house and curated my design exhibition at the Collectors Gallery there a couple of years before, I had not deeply absorbed the mystique and immense wonderment of northern New Mexico. I had been preoccupied with the exhibition and the break-up with David II. This time around, my eyes and soul opened to the "Land of Enchantment." Previously I looked, but now I really saw—and deeply perceived the pulse of the high desert.

Margaret Jamison and her newly appointed director.

Part of the charm of living in Santa Fe was the exposure to the tri-cultural atmosphere. This was the result of a curious blend of local history. Four centuries earlier, the Spanish arrived in search of the Cities of Cibola. Their search for gold and their greed for land brimming with natural resources intruded upon the rich life of the Native Americans, who had developed their own flowering culture centuries before. The Pueblo Indians created a civilization that was greatly diminished and altered by the conquest of the Spanish. Their religious life had to be hidden, while they put on the mantle of Christianity to avoid retribution. The Spanish monks wanted to collect souls, while the soldiers searched for gold and free labor. In time, the conquistadores were vanquished by the American army, which was protecting settlers from the East and maltreating the Indians by denying their rights.

The Indians were placed on reservations, and their traditional farming and hunting lands taken over by the Anglo settlers from the East. Many promises were made to the Indians; most were broken. Those on the reservations today have managed to keep a few traditions alive, but many young have gone to live in cities to get better educations and earn decent salaries. Recent boons for the Indians have been the exploitation of oil and gas reserves on the reservations; another is the building of gambling casinos run by the reservations, garnering large profits. Some of these gains are siphoned off by Anglo ganglords, but the Indian treasuries have nicely increased, giving better bargaining power to the reservations and a higher standard of living for the people.

With the establishment of the United States government authority, towns and cities with connecting roads through the high mountain desert flourished. Art was among its greatest manifestations. The rich history of the Southwest and its wondrous vitality were caught on canvas by a long succession of talented artists. The Santa Fe and Taos area became a mecca for artists from the East, intrigued by the landscape as well as by the colorful Hispanic and Indian peoples.

Part of the mystique of northern New Mexico is the vibrancy of the festivals held at various Indian pueblos in the area. Santo Domingo's annual Corn Dance is the largest and perhaps most thrilling to attend. It seems like thousands of plumed, painted dancers with rattles chant their sacred rituals under the hot sun in the huge dusty plaza, equaling any Cecil B. DeMille spectacular. One group of dancers leaves and another arrives. Mother Earth seems to shake. In the distance, the 20th

A northern New Mexico pueblo.

Century Limited writhes by like a silver snake. I have wondered how many people looked out the window to see in the distance the exotic display through dance and chant of ancient communal prayer.

These dances are usually performed without much publicity, if any at all. Learning to understand the significance of costuming as well as aspects of the presentation of the dance and the role of the kiva—where male education is given in this matriarchal society—continues to intrigue me. Indians are very private about their beliefs. They never answer inquiries directly, so as not to diminish the strength of their spiritual medicine. Each time I stayed in Santa Fe, I read accounts of Pueblo life in novels by Adolf Bandelier, Oliver la Farge, Tony Hillerman, and Frank Waters, together with anthropologic studies by Bertha Dutton, Charles Lummis, David Roberts, and Hamilton Tyler. I was enriched by the findings. It melded with my knowledge of the Japanese medieval Noh drama I had studied in graduate school. I knew there was a universal force connecting the spirituality of the Pueblo observance with Japanese spirituality, and probably other beliefs, as well. There was comfort in the notion of a universality abounding in the spiritual life of the world. Perhaps this is a particularly important message for the time we are living in, suggesting a bridge of understanding between peoples? There has been such dissension tearing American society apart since the Korean and

Vietnam wars. Especially now, a healing to assuage the war damage caused by the Iraq and Afghanistan conflicts is urgently needed. We must be open to whatever healing balm presents itself, whether through our Indian brothers or elsewhere.

I knew the search for a spiritual enrichment and serenity was something my inner life needed after so many tumultuous events: my break-up with David after seven years, the Spoleto gallery treachery, the tormented David II episodes, and my impetuous closing of the Compass Gallery in its infancy to pursue an ill-fated liaison in Italy. There was no doubt in my mind that excessive alcohol consumption had precipitated much of the turmoil in my life. Alcohol had become my great friend, without which life was unimaginable. Counteracting its control over me was the succor achieved by embracing the spirituality available in Nature. Nature in northern New Mexico had always offered spiritual well-being. (Hippies relating to these natural forces arrived in droves during the '60s, dressing like Indians and emulating many of their life styles.) I, too, became impressed by the mystique of the land.

Margaret graciously lent me her white Tennessee walker, Nellie, to ride during the early morning hours before the gallery opened. Nellie was stabled at Winnebelle Beaseley's ranch in Tesuque, minutes north from Santa Fe. From there, I could ride the ridges of the foothills and through the arroyos, amidst fragrant piñon, blossoming chamisa, and Russian blue sage. I was constantly astounded by the natural high desert beauty around me, with vistas of forever under incredibly blue skies, during my rides on Nellie. I commissioned cowboy boots from the old bootmaker Ortega, in Burro Alley. With a white bombardier styled jacket

Irrepressible Winnie.

and the orange neckerchief from Giorgetto's regiment tied around my throat, I was convinced I was the smartest-attired horseman in northern New Mexico. Nellie did not like the smell from my morning libations, probably associating it with my pulling too strongly on the bit, which I was guilty of when under the influence. She would neigh her disapprobation yet dutifully prance out into the glorious landscape. This morning communication with nature propelled me, with heightened spirit, into the day of gallery transactions and the lunch break, often taken in the garden of the Compound Restaurant on Canyon Road, entertaining clients or artists.

The Jamison Gallery was prestigiously placed just off the plaza and across from the historic La Fonda Hotel, the end of the Santa Fe Trail. Though there were some other galleries, the important blue chip Western art was the drawing card at Margaret's, attracting collectors and dealers from far and wide, often from Europe. The famous masters of both the Schools of Taos and Santa Fe were available. These 19th century artists from the East were lured by the colorful landscapes and the native peoples in the Southwest. Most prestigious were Remington, Russell, Berninghaus, Blumenschein, Sharp, and Henri, to name a few. Included on the Jamison roster of artists were some contemporary artists, who faithfully painted the great Southwest in careful realism. Other galleries had similar local artists, but they carried a lot of shlock for tourists in their inventory, which Margaret disdained to handle.

It did not take me long to realize that there were many resident artists whose work went beyond postcard realism. Visiting their homes and studios, I was astounded by their daring break with realism. These young artists were harnessing the spiritual energy redolent in these ancient mountains and nurtured by the pueblos. Their adventurous work was vital and crowned with great artistic merit. However, they had no local market, because their art was considered too abstract and controversial for public tastes. I was dazzled by their output and believed it important to exhibit it, but Margaret had great misgivings. She felt her clientele would find it eccentric of me and wrong for her gallery to promote this type of modern art.

A notion began to formulate in my brain about art and nature during these early gallery days in Santa Fe. When I was a teenager in New York, I could easily see the sky from most locations around Manhattan. Before I realized it, the sky was diminished as more skyscrapers were erected to devour the sight of the heavens; traffic increased to a roar; and cement enveloped the city. Post-war break down in societal values; an increase in "recreational" drug usage; and a shift in taste influenced by television—all impacted the art world.

I am convinced that the artistic impulse is derived from an energy reservoir drawn upon by the subconscious of the artist. As with any reservoir, there are times when levels become low because of a drought. Having moved away from the art world in New York to the Santa Fe scene, I formed some startling conclusions.

The negative energy from the cement city of noisy impulses permeated and stultified the artistic life. Access to the reservoir of artistic impulse was impeded. Even before the '50s, artists went to the eastern part of Long Island or the end of Cape Cod for a jumpstart. The next generation continued this routine. Waiting for these inferior descendants were avid *arriviste nouveau riche* collectors desirous of buying their way into the establishment by donating expensive Pop/Op works to museums. These financial windfalls into the artists' pockets further corrupted the scene, by encouraging even more production of art of this ilk.

The master promoter of himself and Pop Art was Andy Warhol. Victim of being a city dweller but a fine craftsman, he was, I am confident, aware of the vacuous state of the reservoir of energy. He cashed in on it by promoting this nothingness to an easily duped public, who deep down related to his Campbell soup can to validate their own state of being. He had the same problem as his contemporaries, but turned it to his advantage big time. There was a much-trumpeted triumph in exploring the "cutting edge" and "avant-garde," which existed only in the minds of these trumpeters and those who did not know better. It had all been done before, and much better!

Paintings can have a modern, contemporary feel, such as the work done by color field painters. My favorite works are by Marc Rothko and Paul Jenkins. They please me aesthetically, but cutting edge is an expression implying the newest of the new. Forget it!

While artists in cities like New York and Los Angeles were drawing upon ever drier pools of inspiration, producing the anemic outputs of the Pop/Op artists and minimalists (not to be confused with color field painters), Santa Fe and Taos were nourishing artists relying on emotional and spiritual substance derived from the great natural world of the Southwest. I wanted to help these artists gain recognition and the financial success that comes with it.

Margaret and I did come to an agreement. We gave Fritz Scholder, a local artist boasting an Indian heritage (scant though it be), a one-man show. His work was bold, breaking the mold of the stereotype cowboy and Indian stuff and the pictorial realism usually shown in Santa Fe. The director of the Denver Museum of Art was planning a large opening of the newly renovated museum designed by the famous Italian architect Giò Ponte. In my usual fashion with kindred souls, I offered him a morning libation when he visited the gallery. I sat him comfortably in the private viewing room, while we discussed Scholder's work and the artist's daring use of color and form, breaking with realism.

Various paintings were brought out for inspection while we sipped, chatted, and contemplated the artist's startling treatment of the flattened, deconstructed Indian form with splashes of color on the canvas. The current craze was focused on the "First American," especially on works created in a contemporary style, but not too abstract, by American Indians. Though held at arm's length by the social elite in Santa Fe (an attitude soon to be diminished), Indians were "in" and the flavor of the day with the general public. However, Scholder went much further than other artists in abstracting an image. The powerful effects of color on simplified surfaces was soon to be imitated by other artists.

Louis, my newly acquired museum director friend, was fired up by what he saw and wanted to include a Scholder work in the opening exhibition of the Denver Art Museum. I pushed for one large painting in particular, which I had planned to purchase for my budding collection of Western art. Having it in a major museum exhibition enhanced its provenance, and potentially its value. When Fritz agreed to sell the canvas to me at a reasonable price, I was thrilled. My pleasure increased when I saw it installed in the new museum.

Though Fritz was only a quarter Luiseño (a California mission tribe) and raised white, he played "Indian" to the hilt, as it sold his paintings. His dress, haircut, and demeanor said "Indian." His fame was to grow to such proportions as an American Indian artist that the new Indian Art Museum in Washington DC has recreated, within the museum, a replica of Fritz Scholder's studio in Galisteo, NM.

The first few weeks in Santa Fe, I enjoyed living in Margaret's large house, which had been converted from the country club some years earlier. The swimming pool had been replaced by a large lawn with gardens bordering it, very unusual for Santa Fe at that time. Being high desert country, it was impractical to cultivate grass lawns demanding the rare commodity of water. Instead of filling a swimming pool, the water could be used on Margaret's grass and gardens. She did not take sun, and swimming was not a priority. Margaret was a very gregarious woman, born and raised in Oklahoma. She realized that her lifestyle as a gallery owner involved entertaining. What could be lovelier than having a group over for "sundowners" while mingling on the spacious lawn, enjoying the last rays of sun over the distant Jemez Mountains to the west, and the Sandia Peak fifty miles south? The vast expanse of God's country was resplendently displayed from her lovely, special garden.

An enormous oriental carpet covered the central area of the main room, and there were three contrasting types of pianos in different areas of the room. A magnificent silver saddle was displayed on a wooden saddle rack, with Indian pots, Hopi kachina dolls, many Western themed paintings, and other New Mexican items of interest placed around the periphery. A few bedrooms were entered from the corners of this vast room.

We both enjoyed having a relaxing drink after returning from a day at the gallery. *Southwest Art Magazine* was about to publish its first issue, and we were requested to submit an article on the history of the Taos and Santa Fe Schools of Art, samples of which were available at the Jamison Gallery. Sustained by libations, we enthusiastically put our heads together to write the article.

On occasion, after dinner, we would go to the La Fonda lounge, where Margaret was often asked to get up and sing with the band. "St. Louis Woman" was one of her favorites. She had a rich voice and temperament, well suited to singing the blues. Her blondish-red mop of curled hair and her very dark glasses to protect her weak eyes, together with her sturdy frame adorned in elegant garb, often with a western flavor, projected a colorful persona. She and I made for an unusual pair.

Margaret's husband, Bland Jamison, had died in her arms suddenly of a heart attack some years earlier. She opened the art gallery using the large amount of paintings in their collection as her inventory. Her keen interest in blue chip art helped establish her in the business. Bill, one of the owners of the gallery where I had the opera design exhibition a couple of years earlier, was her "Squeeze," but I was often her companion for nocturnal outings. (Bill and Bernie enjoyed a long-term partnership, but Bernie indulged Bill's special arrangement with Margaret.)

Upon returning from a night out, Margaret and I would sometimes sit at one of the pianos, with a nightcap. She would sing some of her favorite songs, usually melancholy and blue. Once in awhile, I was encouraged to sing along with her. I think she had the notion we could do duets in public places, like the lounge at La Fonda, but I did not respond with any enthusiasm. The late night drinking and singing the blues atmosphere reinforced my sadness about my recent breakup with Giorgetto. We still sent each other letters, but they were less frequent and more like friends sharing news. He had recently found another American to visit the family country house in the mountains. There were plans for his joining a famous jewelry house, Bulgari, when released from the army, and for his getting a Roman apartment adjacent to the hotel I used in the past.

A very comfortable house was located for me situated on the quiet Calle de las Animas (Street of the Souls). It had been a guesthouse on the property of a couple friendly with Margaret. Its size, inherent charm, and price were agreeable. It was a relief for me to have my own place since Margaret's housekeeper was complaining how since I moved in, it was "nothing but cans and bottles . . . bottles and cans."

I was pleased to be on my own, with an expanding group of friends and artists to entertain on my own turf. Trading a gold/blue silk shirt with silver togs—created for me by a costume designer friend the previous year—for a double bed painted

An "Indian" selling kachinas.

in a primitive style, I felt this was a good start to decorating my new home. Another friend was glad to donate a bed to the second bedroom. Other than these, I had few things to move in, but Margaret had a good suggestion. I could borrow her station wagon, drive to New York City and Montrose and bring out my remaining possessions.

Stunning events evolved while I was in the East. While visiting at Ysabel's Fifth Avenue apartment, Titano unexpectedly turned up from Milan. He and Ysabel decided to drive back to Santa Fe with me. They would be my first houseguests and could attend the opening of the Denver Museum of Art before returning east by plane—Ysabel to New York, Titano to Milan.

This was an important reunion for Ysabel and me. After writing back and forth, it was clear that she approved of my decision to close the New York gallery. She sympathized with the stress involved, but felt I had been saved by love, despite the repercussions of following my heart resulting in a breakup. Ysabel could commiserate, as she had left her husband and infant son in Colombia to follow her heart with Andy in New York those many years ago. In high spirits, we left thoughts of Giorgetto in the past and became excited about our adventure driving west. After my arrival from Montrose to her apartment, Ysabel looked out of her Fifth Avenue living room window, suggesting I look down upon the station wagon I had parked below. Laughing, she claimed it looked like I had used my mother's bra straps to secure items on the roof. During the time I was preparing to leave Montrose, my mother could not find proper rope to tie the cases on the roof but gave me strong cloth tape instead. It was a strange and amusing sight.

Ysabel looked adorable in the blouse and slacks, so reminiscent of our many pleasant times when she had worn them in the past. Without doubt, I had missed her very much. She had gone through one financial distress with another major one looming on the horizon affecting all the Aya women, none of whom took managerial care of their wealth. For now, those concerns were for another day. It was good that she was coming with me, and Titano might add to the flavor of the trip. It would be a pleasure to share the wonders of the Southwest with them.

My Milanese friend requested we speak only English, so he could learn to speak the language better. Unlike Ysabel, who made an attempt to amuse me while driving with interesting talk, his conversation was almost nonexistent. So we called him "Loquacious." It was naughty of us, but we decided we would employ theatrical improvisation by putting on a Swedish accent whenever possible and teach him to imitate it, thinking he was speaking American English. Stuckey's chain of restaurants became "Stoo-kee-s" and Oklahoma became "OO-kla-HOO-ma," with syllables rising and lowering in sing-song Swedish style. He became very proficient in his newly acquired language. Shortly after arrival, Margaret asked to borrow Titano as an escort to some social event. When asked what he had seen in America thus far by one of the guests, he rambled on with his Swedish accent, much to the astonishment of the listeners.

Another hoodwinking we pulled on poor Titano was to teach him our invented "American code of behavior" when making rest stops driving cross-country. At the first rest stop nearest the border, it was mandatory to park and have a drink to honor that state. If it was a large state like Texas, three shots would be appropriate. Delaware demanded only one, and so forth. Titano was befuddled.

He had no idea how long the trip from New York to New Mexico would be, nor had we thought it necessary to discuss it. His Italian road trips were usually an hour or two long, certainly not days. Going 2,000 miles was another story. It took three and one-half days. Sometimes driving ten hours each day, we would collapse into motel rooms to sleep and freshen up. We took the most rapid route on the fast Interstate 40, featureless and without tourist attractions. The emphasis was

Playfully donning tons of Indian jewelry, we posed for the tourists.

to get me back to work in the gallery as soon as possible. All of us sat in the front seat, making for tight company. The rest of the vehicle was jammed with books, records, clothes etc. At the end of our journey on the road, practicing "Swenglish" and toasting the states passed through, we got out of the station wagon, aching and hunched over like bears, dazed and more than slightly inebriated.

Both my guests had adjustments to make to life in "The City Different." The Indians around the Plaza amazed Titano, and he was challenged by the language so alien to French and his native Italian. Ysabel was appalled by the racism rampant in New Mexico and expressed her outrage. To the casual visitor to Santa Fe, the three cultures seemed to live together seamlessly. It was only on closer examination and after some exposure to life there that striations became obvious. Some rich Anglos, mostly from Texas, Oklahoma, and California, lived in a sheltered world of their own, barely aware of their Hispanic aristocratic counterpart. I was dazzled by these elegant personages, not unlike my youthful admiration of the lovely people I spied in the boxes at the Metropolitan Opera House. These were potential clients of the gallery and it was *de rigueur* that I paid appropriate attentions to them. While in their rarified world, I absorbed it but carefully walked the line between courtesy and personal protection of my own sphere of more liberal friends.

Santa Fe is noted to operate within a bubble. The anti-discrimination legislation in the early '60s did not penetrate into Santa Fe life until a few years later. Things generally seemed OK until infringements occurred, often unintentionally. An example of this happened during the period David II was still with me in Santa Fe. Margaret, her pal Bill, David, and I decided to go for a quick bite to eat after attending an opera performance. All of us were in formal attire, looking particularly elegant, with Bill wearing the currently fashionable Nehru jacket with white turtleneck beneath. We decided to go slumming and went to "Pansy's Diner" on commercial Cerrillos Road. A corner was selected for us to sit in, and we proceeded to move tables and chairs around to our satisfaction. Shortly thereafter, a scuffle ensued, with salt and pepper shakers flying, chairs thrown over, and fisticuffs. Detached, we watched as though it were a floor show. Only later, did we find out that some Hispanic ruffians resented our moving furniture, since they had been told they could not do it. They decided to attack us, but one man interceded and stopped them, with a fistfight resulting. He thought Bill was a priest, as the Nehru with turtleneck looked like a holy man's collar. To defend the church, he threw himself in the way to protect us!

Into the early '70s, the Indians were not treated as equal to the Anglos, sometimes not even permitted into the house. The Hispanics were a step below the Anglos but above the Indians, as well. This was most evident in some blow-in upper class Anglo environments, not unlike counterparts at the Southampton Bath and Tennis Club or the East Hampton equivalent on Long Island in New York. Distinguished Indian artists and writers helped change the stifling Santa Fe situation. I would like to think that Margaret's and my showing of Scholder and Gorman broke some ice, making for warmer relations between the races in Santa Fe. Now, decades later, the playing field is greatly leveled. There will always be someone gathering a clique to exclude others based on race or some other foolishness, but that is now politically incorrect and finally acknowledged as such.

Margaret was very prominent on the social scene in Santa Fe, entertaining at her gallery openings and at her house, which was geared for welcoming many guests for food and libations. Her sister, Betsy (Betty) Bennett had recently moved from Oklahoma to Santa Fe and was established in grand style on fashionable Camino del Monte Sol, a neighbor of Robert L. B. Tobin. Attractive and very rich, she was truly one of the grande dames of the town. During this era of social agitation among the tri-cultural community, the top Anglo social set entertained lavishly, turned out in beautiful attire and exceptional jewels. They set a tone of rich elegance and flamboyance, abrasive to both Indian and Hispanic activists. One morning, I heard a moaning in a flowerbed in Margaret's garden. I found her Pekingese gasping there, with slashes in her belly. She died before we could drive her to the veterinarian. The message was clear: Today it is your dog; tomorrow it will be you!

I did not practice segregating people from my home or life. Rather, I enjoyed both Hispanic and Indian friends, sometimes intimately. Both races had strong ties to the land with long family histories there. It was better for them to live within their heritage, withstanding racial pressures, than to move to unknown territory, cut off from their ancient history. At this time, Santa Fe had a very small middle class, but this was all to change when I later returned after an absence of some years. There

R.C. Gorman at home.   *(from the R.C. Gorman collection)*

were always a few necessary professional people, but nothing like today. Today the Anglo population looks more diversified. The desegregation movements have had good results here. Always the benevolent moderator, Santa Fe's high percentage of artists and artisans added immeasurably to the charm of "The City Different."

Early in my new career running the Jamison Gallery, I had concentrated on promoting the young artists whose talents I deemed important to exhibit. I had heard about the Navajo artist R.C. Gorman. His reputation was growing in Taos, so I decided to drive up there. R.C. owned his own gallery on historic Ledoux Street. As an Indian, it was the only viable way to have his art displayed and sold. He managed to commission Northland Press in Flagstaff, Arizona, to do a series of lithographs of his work. The Navajo Museum of Ceremonial Art (now the Wheelwright Museum) in Santa Fe had some of his lithographs on display. At this time, no commercial gallery in Santa Fe was exhibiting R.C. Gorman. Winneabelle Beaseley told me that, as a publicity stunt, she flew a biplane over Taos dropping red carnations and stickers asking: "Who is R.C. Gorman?" I was about to find out.

There are two roads to Taos from Santa Fe, each presenting a unique experience. The fastest is the low road along the Rio Grande River through fruit orchards in Velarde, climbing above the rocky canyon into Rancho de Taos—a place every artist has tried to paint, especially the famous church of St. Francis— before finally arriving in historic Taos. The high road to Taos passes into the Kit Carson Forest after going through the Hispanic towns of Truchas and Trampas—

with its beautiful colonial church—through Penitente country, and finally meets the main road entering Taos, with the sacred Blue Mountain looming behind.

R.C.'s gallery manager, Edmund Gaultney, was a charming young man from Georgia, who encouraged me to consider a Gorman exhibition in Santa Fe. Gorman and Scholder both had a friendly rivalry going, so R.C. thought it important to show at the Jamison Gallery, as well.

Gaultney admired an authentic pre-Columbian pendant I was wearing. I suggested giving it to him if he would convince R.C. into doing a portrait of me. R.C. agreed to come to Santa Fe to do this portrait on the condition that it be a nude. I was still in residence at Margaret's at the time. Margaret was away on a trip, and I asked the household staff to remain in the other portion of the house. The easel was set up in the gallery, where the mariachi band had welcomed me some months before, and a chair was placed in front of the easel. R.C. set down his glass of vodka on the floor by his side and indicated where I was to stand and what pose to hold. He worked quickly with his oil pastels, on occasion sipping his drink.

After some time holding my nude pose for the Navajo artist at work, I was told I could inspect the finished result. My face was drawn in a quarter profile, fully colored in, but there were only two strokes for shoulders and arms. One nipple was indicated; the rest was blank! It was amusing that I held this nude pose, when I could have been dressed and sitting. This was our first joke together.

R.C. was born on the Navajo reservation in Arizona. After service in the Navy, he studied art in San Francisco. He came to make his career in northern New Mexico, choosing the high mountain town space, and living quarters there. A flamboyant lifestyle developed as his work began to sell and his notoriety spread. Gorman's gallery parties were famous for crowds of rowdy, heavy drinkers, who often broke out into brawls. This was a completely opposite atmosphere to the gentrified Jamison Gallery events that featured serenading by guitarist/vocalist Antonio Mendoza while *hors d'oeuvres* were shared over polite conversation. Santa Fe was a distinct contrast to Taos, both engaging in their own way.

Over the years, R.C. and I always had time for many laughs over many drinks. He worked and played hard, gaining many hangers-on whose attentions he enjoyed. As a full-blooded Indian, R.C. strove for acceptance by the Anglos. He entertained lavishly and tried to copy Anglo upper-class material values, including the acquisition of a gold Mercedes. He built a compound to live and work in and as well as house his growing art collection, gathered on trips to New York and Europe. Miró, Picasso and Warhol were to adorn his walls. Future promotional efforts, such as billing him as the Picasso of America, together with the Jamison Gallery one-man exhibition propelled him to public notice and approbation in New Mexico.

Gorman harnessed his artistic energies and turned out paintings, pastels, and lithographs using the Navajo woman as a motif. A typical later work pictured a plump traditionally attired squaw sitting beside a bowl of red chiles with a simplified New Mexico landscape of sky and mesa in the background. These renditions were colorful and did not demand intellectual prowess. They were appealing and sold quickly to the public, whose interest in the exotic Southwest was greatly stimulated by the First American craze and the new hot tourist spot—northern New Mexico. The Navajo woman was to become his trademark and became ubiquitous in galleries around America, as well as in gift shops on notepaper or cards, and in housewares stores as napkins and even toilet paper! This was a far cry from the more serious work the Jamison Gallery exhibited in his early career. His early abstractions, based on Indian rugs, or his charming renderings of groups of Indians have more artistic integrity. The enormous public demand and financial success swayed the artist's output, encouraging repetition with slight variation to consciously increase his income and support his ever expanding extravagant life style. (My "La Marchesa, la Marchetta" profile on R.C. Gorman is archived at the Beinecke Library at Yale University in New Haven, CT, as well as here as an appendix.)

R.C. was caught in his own trap. Reliance on alcohol had warped his judgment and crippled his ability to function fully as an artist. Though he knew the work he was churning out was not up to the standards of his exhibition at the Jamison Gallery, R.C. felt compelled to continue turning out what the general public wanted, and what would keep his entourage afloat. He and Warhol shared this similarity. He tried to make himself believe he was having a good time doing it; no word from me or anyone else would have been countenanced. I felt great empathy for him, as I had been along a very similar path with my alcohol reliance before going to The Betty Ford Clinic. The crucial difference between us was my facility to continually re-invent myself as needed.

The atmosphere of Taos in those days in the early '70s was far more explosive than today's gentrified one. The Taos Indians were struggling to regain the sacred Blue Lake on the mountain. It was cause for a great celebration when the Blue Lake was returned to the Taos Pueblo during this period. Unlike today, it was common to see Indians around the plaza area wrapped in their blankets and sipping liquor from paper bags. Shootings and rapes were common occurrences around town. On occasion, there seemed to be something in the air that aroused deep emotions. I would sometimes feel the hair on the back of my neck raise, so then I knew it was one of those kinds of days. It was not something concrete, but rather something one felt. Taosaños attributed this uneasy feeling to the power of the Blue Lake on the mountain and its powerful medicine.

Around this time, R.C. had told me that he knew of two people who threatened to shoot me when I appeared in Taos. Some people harbored resentments after reading about me in Calla Hay's column "Pasa por Aqui" in *The New Mexican*. She mentioned my outlandish lifestyle in Santa Fe—the parties and outings with rich and famous—or, her updates on my travels. (Examples: Calla said it seemed as though Prince Charles was following Eric around California . . . Eric is flying in

Ysabel before the 100° martinis.   *Ysabel after the 100° martinis.*

from California on the private plane of Douglas Campbell, etc. . . .) Calla enjoyed talking about me in her column because she felt I was good copy. She gathered the latest information from various mutual friends or from me directly when I spoke with her, either on the phone or in person. Her running coverage made me seem a world traveling *bon vivant*, guaranteed to garner resentment in some of the less fortunate fellow New Mexicans.

Calla often told me she "was stuck in Santa Fe." I had a T-shirt with that phrase imprinted on it, and I gave it to her as a Christmas present. I believe she enjoyed my travels vicariously and empathized with my compulsive partying. She was very fond of her bourbon, priming her as a perky party guest. She and Ysabel made for lively company when Ysabel came to Santa Fe and Taos. R.C. made two oil pastel renderings of "the Princess" during an outrageous day in Taos. He called them *Before the 100-Proof Martinis* and *After the 100-Proof Martinis*. They are a witty statement indicating the effects alcohol has on the partaker—the grooming becoming less perfect with each drink. This was the same day that "the most memorable Pee" transpired, startling even Ysabel!

Virginia Dooley, R.C.'s Girl Friday and facilitator for some of his social events, had prepared a lunch for the three of us when we visited R.C. in Taos. This followed the flow of martinis at Cynthia Bissell's home nearby. While all of us were enjoying the repast, Edmund Gaultney, his gallery director, tried to pass around a microphone into which each of us was to describe our most memorable pee. At the same time, Edmund's boyhood friend, who was visiting from their hometown in Georgia, decided to photograph us. It was very Andy Warhol-ish and I found it the Southern Belles annoying. I waited until it was R.C.'s turn at the microphone, then stood, unzipped my trousers, and peed into the nearby zucchini bowl. "Virginia, take that bowl to the kitchen!" was our host's command, and both camera and microphone were put away. A more restrained luncheon group finished their meal; another unusual day in Taos neared its completion, as R.C. finished his two renditions of Ysabel.

The diverse and colorful atmosphere of northern New Mexico has been a natural nesting place for eccentrics, or those not seeking to maintain the norm. For decades, the most adorable and conspicuous character thrived in this locale— Winneabelle Beasley, a Wellesley graduate from the East Coast.

Migrating westward after World War II when—as a WAC— she flew in planes for repairs planes in England that the RAF deemed unsafe, Winnie freed herself from a marriage to an Italian and brought three sons to a horse ranch in Tesuque, just north of Santa Fe. When not on her motorcycle with sidecar, Winnie was on horseback, leading visitors on rides through the foothills of the Sangre de Cristo Mountains.

She offered a special rate to those working at the opera, organizing pleasant trail rides and giving instruction to improve riding skills. It was on one of these rides I met a quiet, attractive young woman who rode at the tail end of the group. Frederica von Stade began her early career with the Santa Fe Opera and developed into an international star. She was always modest and pleasant with those around her. Over the years, my respect and admiration grew for this talented mezzo-soprano, who wore her diva-hood so quietly. Consequently, I wrote a couple of newspaper stories about her for a New Jersey chain of newspapers. She kindly wrote me notes of thanks, and we managed a few pleasant social moments together over the years to come. "Flicka," as she is popularly known, is a native of New Jersey, and we knew many people in common, including Christine Todd Whitman, a future governor of New Jersey.

Winnie had great generosity of spirit. She was known to offer a snack of leftovers after a ride. However, she was not known for the sanitary care of food. Often when returning from the trail, if she did not find an interesting pot shard or arrow head, she would bring back a snake to keep in one of her cages. Plenty of mice caught on the premises kept her snakes well fed. Winnie would proceed to fix food after depositing the snake in a glassed box cage, but forgetting to wash her hands. Sometimes, the food's shelf life had long since expired, but she was oblivious to such trivial details. On occasion, I would bring an edible for our after-ride gathering as a self-protective measure.

One day my phone rang. It was Winnie on the other end. This pixie-like, Imogene Coca character invited me to a dinner where her "pr-r-roper and gr-r-

March 27, 1995

Dear Eric,

Thank you for your long lost letter which I finally recieved and for the wonderful article that you wrote. You have been so kindly attentive over the years and I appreciate it very much.

It's always wonderful to see all the terrific things that you are doing and with such gusto as well.

Thanks for many kindesses to me.

Lots of love,

Our friend Flicka: Fredrica von Stade.

rand friends" would be in attendance. She requested I not use four letter words while at the dinner. Nonplussed and amused since I do not use four letter words, I accepted. I knew I would have to devise something in retaliation for her accusation.

Her "proper and grand friends," all of whom I had known for some time in a casual and comfortable manner, gathered in her sitting room with drinks in hand. In a discussion with Louise Trigg, head of the Arts Council for New Mexico, I told her of Winnie's request. She said she never knew me to use four-letter words, but even if I did, so what? Inspiration burst forth! I asked her if she would use a four-letter word at the table when I gave the signal of a raised arm conductor style. She agreed, and I proceeded to ask every other guest to cooperate in the same manner. They all thought it was an amusing idea. I was vastly delighted. The taste of revenge is so sweet.

As the dinner progressed, our hostess, sporting multi-colored false eyelashes and red velvet hot pants, stood up. She looked at me and asked if I would like seconds. I smiled back at her sweetly, and lifted my arm into the conductor position. Expletives exploded around the table with everyone using a four-letter word except for me! Winnie looked confused, and meekly continued to offer seconds . . .

Winnie and her snakes.

Drugs and alcohol mingled freely with the daily experience of the prodigious natural energies of northern New Mexico. It was thrilling to see and feel the pull of this magical place, which works like a drug in itself. Young people got involved in the Native people's traditions, trying to adopt these ways into their lifestyle. The pursuit suited hippies that moved in from California and the East Coast as well as poor artists striving to soak up the atmosphere to reproduce its essence into art. Adobe building blocks were made for construction of their version of a kiva, or spiritual meeting hall. Peyote buttons were consumed in group ceremonies, imitating the Indians. Leather-fringed frontier clothes together with beads and feathers were the vogue. Drugs interfered with my alcohol consumption, so I stayed away from these events that were usually held on private property, out of town on a ranch, or farmland away from the eyes of Johnny Law. There was a fervor for imitating the ancient Indian way of life and relishing Mother Earth. Organic herbs and vegetables were cultivated. Back to nature was the theme of the day. This was a very sharp contrast to the ultra elegant life the glitterati of Santa Fe society were enjoying. I relished jumping back and forth between the divergent lifestyles, enjoying the best that each had to offer me. This aspect was not unlike my life in New York, swinging from Fifth Avenue or Park Avenue to Union Square or the West Side docks, always in the company of Johnny Barleycorn.

Probably the biggest summer attraction in Santa Fe was the opera. This popular venue was started by John Crosby, founding general director, in 1957. He owned the land, and Robert Lynn Batts Tobin, along with other benefactors, built an open-air theater for the operatic performances. In 1968, the new house replaced the old structure after it burned. Crosby began a tradition of annually performing a Richard Strauss opera, which he would conduct. Each year, a new opera would join the ever-expanding repertory. Aside from the visitors it attracted from diverse parts of the globe, the performers, directors, conductors, designers, and stage crews created a lively milieu and mix of personalities. Winnie's ranch was a great gathering place for many of these people. Parties at various homes and restaurants were held by or for the opera members, as well. It was very merry. David II was still tending his birds at the residence of his benefactor, although those days were coming to an end with the restrictions of bankruptcy proceedings. Fear not, David moved on easily.

Liquor was freely indulged in, especially during off times. This, on one occasion, led a band of us into trouble. Winnie loaded up her motorcycle with sidecar and another automobile to the hilt with celebrants out on the town. It was decided we might swing by backstage at the open-air opera house to see our friend, Leanne Mahoney, in the Costume Department. A Verdi opera was in progress. One of us, possibly me, for the drama of it, let out what was described as a blood-curdling cry. Though we were unaware of it, the cry carried into the opera house. It was a quiet moment on stage when this horrific sound was heard. The conductor thought perhaps someone had fallen down a shaft under the stage.

The next day, a great rumpus was led by the opera's crusty General Director John Crosby, who had not been at the opera the evening before. He was incensed at this abusive intrusion in the performance. No one could determine who let out that cry, so the off-duty opera staff that had been with Winnie were suspended. Happily, Leanne was free of any blame. Even though I thought it could have been me (my alcoholic recall was unclear), I was not reprimanded. The others were banned from the opera grounds, so I thought it wise to follow suit. For the balance of the season, I abstained from enjoying the glorious singing at the opera. The two young women on suspension directed their attentions elsewhere. They are still in Santa Fe today but engaged in other professional pursuits.

As the director of a prestigious art gallery, I enjoyed preferential treatment among residents and visitors. Some artists tried to curry favor with their charms and allure. I discovered, after the fact, that their attentions were more to achieve a gallery showing than any sincere sentiment for me. This situation did not present itself when I ran the New York galleries, odd as this might seem. Perhaps it was a mistake to socialize intensely with a potential artist. It placed me in an awkward position afterwards, when a professional relationship was to be adopted and their work rejected.

The beautiful Academy Award winning English actress Greer Garson lived on Forked Lightning Ranch in the Pecos with her super affluent husband, Buddy Fogelson. At a cocktail reception at La Fonda, we found ourselves together. She extended her hand and announced herself as Greer Garson. I acknowledged this obvious fact and gave her what must be the usual old-hand compliments. When she learned I ran the Jamison Gallery across the street, the actress commented on the large painting in the window of a cottonwood tree in an arroyo by noted artist Wilson Hurley. Greer Garson was locally notorious for being very tight with her money and always trying to get things at a huge discount. I feared this was about to happen but was able to dissolve any potential haggling over price. She thought the painting lacked a sense of humanity, and would be interested in acquiring it if the artist would paint a figure under the tree. I assured the lady the artist would never consider altering his masterpiece. The day was saved.

One of my favorite challenges in preparing for a new exhibition was the mindful hanging of the paintings, carefully working out the most effective lighting. Sometimes, I felt as though I were repainting the canvases with the choice of lighting. I usually did the hanging late at night, when not many people were walking around West San Francisco Street, so I did not feel prying eyes upon my every move. In the darkness of night, I could most effectively alter the lighting.

I tried to place paintings in dialogue with each other, creating a subtle harmony to be enjoyed by the viewer, often subconsciously. One memorable night, I noticed an attractive Hispanic man studying my activity from the street. After some minutes, I decided to engage him in conversation and invited him in. George Michaud was born in the area but lived and worked as an artist in Manhattan Beach, California. I took a needed break and invited him in to the lower level, where the bar was placed within an armoire. George's easy manner and sweet Hispanic demeanor pleased me very much. We sat in the private viewing room and enjoyed some mutual satisfaction at our initial meeting. He invited me to visit him when in Southern California, which I did on numerous occasions in years to come until his brutal murder.

George was a very outgoing, pleasant gay man. He had met an attractive pick-up at a gay bar and invited him to his home in Manhattan Beach. The man stayed for a couple of days, but at a certain point tied the nude George up and bludgeoned him, finally shooting him. It may have been astuteness of neighbors who put the police on the murderer's trail. The man was apprehended and sentenced to jail after his trial. While there, the murderer bragged to his cellmate about murdering his wife and getting away with that unsolved crime. The other prisoner, perhaps to curry favor for a lighter sentence, told the prison warden. George's murderer was brought to trial for his wife's killing and received a much heavier sentence, perhaps a life sentence or death penalty. George bequeathed to me a mixed media oil painting that I had once admired. I think of him each time I look at this work of art.

By Christmas, I had Margaret's assent to present a group show of young local artists. Many thought I had lost my mind, despite the popular Fritz Scholder exhibition setting a precedent and garnering a large amount of sales, and with the R.C. Gorman showing slated for the new year. Because of a ski accident involving three spiral breaks in my right leg, I held forth at the opening in a wheelchair. The governor and his wife commiserated with me, while a packed crowd experienced the unusual work of this group of local artists. The reviews were mixed, but, importantly, the ice had been broken. These artistic expressions could find viable venues in future, now that the first step had been taken to give them validity. Though many of these artists had taken up residency in Santa Fe as transplants from around the country, many were born to the land of New Mexico. Some were even from the neighboring reservation lands.

Santa Fe had a record snowfall that year. The winters were as long as the summers were short. Serious consideration had to be given to a work situation involving a staircase between the main gallery and my office below. None was friendly towards crutches or wheelchair. How long could I remain a semi-invalid, with a long rehabilitation time in front of me in an icy world?

Governor Bruce King commiserates with me.

The skiing accident happened on a sunny Thanksgiving morning, with perfect ski conditions. It was a very clear morning, when I spied the snowy peaks in the distance from my kitchen window and decided to go skiing. Louise Trigg had invited me for Thanksgiving dinner that evening at her ranch near Chimayo. There was time to go skiing, return, and get ready for the Thanksgiving feast. I rushed out of the house, postponing my usual morning "get me on my feet" drink. Because my skis had not yet arrived from New York, I would have to rent a pair. In haste, I foolishly did not check the bindings, which I always did in the past. When I took my spill on a perfect powder base slope, they did not release. This caused the severe spiral breaks. The ski patrol sent someone to retrieve me in a toboggan, which was a bumpy, uncomfortable descent. I had requested to stop at the inn for a drink to ease my discomfort, but I was brusquely informed that I was probably in shock, and alcohol was the last thing I should ingest.

When I arrived at St. Vincent's Hospital in an ambulance, I was in severe pain. Fritz's wife, Ramona, turned out to be my nurse. She administered a painkiller injection. I remember her commenting on how my face relaxed with each moment that passed as the medicine took effect. My first thought on realizing the extent of my injuries was not that I would not walk properly again, but that I would not waltz again! I loved to dance and found the Viennese Waltz gave me the utmost pleasure. It was grim to think waltzing was a thing of the past.

I called Margaret to inform her of my condition, and to request she contact Louise to cancel my appearance that evening for dinner. I also suggested she bring me white wine when she came to visit. I meant champagne but wanted to be modest in my request, thinking she would go for the bubbly. Not! Margaret appeared with chilled wine and extended her condolences on the accident, though I sensed how annoyed she was about this inconvenient turn of events.

I took a leave of absence from the gallery while I concentrated on rehabilitation. Although wheelchair bound, I could manage to give talks on Navajo culture at the Navajo Museum, where my pal, Bertha Dutton, was the director and a noted anthropologist. Bertha was aware of my having done extensive research into the American Indian in the Southwest. We enjoyed long discussions about my readings as well as her research. She thought it would be beneficial for me to spend a few hours now and then giving visitors a brief overview of Navajo practice and culture.

The one big challenge I had at the museum was when a group of Navajos came in to inspect the exhibitions. I was careful to diplomatically discuss their culture in vaguest terms, avoiding any distinct analysis of their sandpaintings, spiritual or medicinal beliefs, thus weakening their power. I opted to do a dull presentation rather than engage in anything the Navajos might consider inappropriate.

Navajo practices are kept private, away from Anglo prying. It had been explained to me that sandpaintings and weavings always had a mistake in them when they were used for viewing. The mistake kept the secret powers intact. However, when used for healing, perfection was demanded. The healing through sandpaintings depended on the accuracy of the carefully applied colored sand. The patient was placed on the completed, perfect painting, and friends and relatives then surrounded the person to be healed. Chants and music would be played while bits of the sandpainting was sprinkled over the area to be healed. A feast of a mutton stew would follow. The healing ceremony could last for days, and it was an expensive occasion for the host, who had to slaughter many of his livestock to feed the guests.

Ysabel convinced me over the phone to return to New York, where there were no steps. She had Shell (Concha), her Colombian maid, there to wait on me. All considered, I would be much better off there. After the Christmas show opened, I agreed I would go. Margaret was distressed to see me on crutches in the gallery, sometimes with my bandaged cast propped up on a chair. It disturbed her and thought it was not something a gallery visitor should be exposed to. Some people do not react well to the incapacity of others. Margaret was one of those. Though I had done much to help her in many aspects of the gallery operations, she concurred with me on my decision to return to New York.

I sold her some of my furniture and decorative items that she could use in the house she just bought in Tucson, where she wanted to live during the cruel winter months. My paintings, including the Scholder work shown at the Denver Museum of Art's opening, were sold back to the gallery at cost, and I was freed of all encumbrances to move back to New York.

What joy to arrive at Ysabel's door at 955 Fifth Avenue. I got out of the elevator on my crutches. When the door opened into the large black and white checked marble entrance hall, I took one step inside. The floors had just been waxed and I and my crutches went flying! So much for the safety of an apartment without stairs . . . welcome back!

It is interesting to note that the vacuum caused by my absence encouraged Elaine Horwitz, who had a gallery in Arizona, and others, to promptly open galleries featuring contemporary artists in Santa Fe. They cleaned up big time, now that the market was opened up. Before leaving, I met with three other people whose thoughts about the value of establishing contemporary art meshed with mine. We were in the process of setting up a syndicate to promote this art when I broke my leg. The time was ripe. I had set the scene, making contemporary art acceptable in Santa Fe. Today, Santa Fe has many such galleries and is considered one of the top three centers for contemporary art in America. And, they all said my idea was crazy?

The amazing Canyon de Chelly is an intriguing mystery.

A deranged savior appears in a new play at St. John the Divine, New York City.

Chapter 13

You Don't Need a Taxi, You Need an Ambulance

Zany, outrageous, flamboyant, and over the top might begin to describe the period following my return from New Mexico to the New York environment at 955 Fifth Avenue with Ysabel during the '70s. My alcohol consumption had increased into a high tide, while life expanded with equal force in the high altitude of Santa Fe. Upon my return to New York on crutches, Ysabel, Uncle Monkey and I kept the flow going full time.

As cosmopolitan culture mavens, we got into the habit of attending Wednesday matinees on Broadway. Each week, one of us would buy the tickets, another would spring for lunch in the theater district, and the third would pay the taxi rides each way. This avoided who owed how much to whom. It was a very agreeable way to pass a Wednesday afternoon.

The crutches were creating a bit of an encumbrance in getting around. Once, when leaving a Greek restaurant on Eighth Avenue, I caught up with my two theater buddies after I paid the restaurant bill. Thinking it amusing to make believe that I did not know Ysabel, I approached her as a mendicant and asked her if she could spare a dollar. She opened her purse, removed a bill and proceeded to shove it into my mouth. I staggered backward from the force of her action, nearly toppling over on my crutches. The passersby were shocked at the crazy woman's attack on that poor guy on crutches. We all found it a typical Ysabel invention, and very amusing.

After leaving the theater one Wednesday, I got into the front seat of the taxi with my two pals in the back tending to my crutches. The attractive driver was very amiable in conversation on our way to "955" and even revealed upon my questioning where he kept his money. Robberies of taxi drivers were much publicized, so I thought it interesting to know how he protected his cash. He gladly indicated which shirt pocket his stash was in. Much to his shock, I reached in and took all the cash as he was trying to concentrate on driving. It was an effort to deal with the demands of maneuvering in the traffic around him, so he continued to drive with a stunned look on his face. I passed the money through the little window where change was given to the passenger in the back. Ysabel was delighted to receive it; Uncle Monkey was abashed.

The driver hoped we were joking around, and I soon assured him we were. Did he play chess? Would he like to come up for a drink and a game? Yes, he was mesmerized by this wacky trio who certainly added zest to his day. Fortunately there was a parking space near the entrance to "955." As our chess game progressed, Ysabel was annoying in her kibitzing and suggesting moves for him to use to beat me. Finally, alcohol fueled my impatience, and I lost my temper, throwing the chess game on to the floor. Ysabel flared up and demanded I leave her apartment immediately. That was inconvenient as I was living there, but I decided to take refuge at Uncle Monkey's West Side apartment, which I had keys to. I took the taxi driver with me and departed. When we reached the street level, Ysabel was showering down upon us my clothing removed from the clothes closet. It was a very incongruous Neapolitan scene in this chic area of Fifth Avenue!

Gathering the clothes together, I suggested that my new friend drop me at Uncle Monkey's and come up for an interlude of pleasure. He had earlier indicated he had never participated in any homosexual activity but would consider it with me. Time was running out for the taxi driver on a long break, thanks to the interlude of the chess game. Another time perhaps, we agreed, as he drove off into traffic. Naturally, my clothes soon found their resting place back at "955." We chuckled over our taxi hold-up and planned our next matinee adventure.

To facilitate the healing of the breaks in my leg, my reliable stand-by friend, Nina Micheleit, suggested I go spend some weeks with her in Falmouth on Cape Cod. I could get therapy using an indoor pool she had access to at a fitness center, and there were salubrious walks to take around the area. I always enjoyed spending time with Nina, sharing insights into the condition of the world over a few scotch and sodas, or cooking up some healthy meal to gain better control on the idea of keeping our bodies in shape. During this period, Nina owned and ran a shop named "Paraphernalia." It started originally in Provincetown, but she moved it to Falmouth after the previous owner sold it to her. She found the "rag trade" a tough challenge, and was soon to disband the project.

During my visit with Nina, there was a mandatory visit to Provincetown, where we had met a few years earlier, contemplating the mysteries of the world. At that time, she was tending her brother-in-law's Shore Gallery, and I was engaged as a waiter at the Moors as well as helping Larry at Jones's Locker and posing for Robert Hunter. We always enjoyed a very warm rapport. I admired her down to earth philosophy and New England ethic towards life, which had to do with working hard, assuming a responsible life style, and fair play.

Walking along the sea at Provincetown's Race Point was a good test of my recovery progress. There was a long flat stretch of beach along the waters entering the Provincetown Bay. The real test was at Long Nook in North Truro. Those huge sea cliffs were one of my favorite places anywhere, however quite impossible for anyone to negotiate on crutches. At this point, I began to practice balancing myself to begin walking on my own, unassisted. I managed my first steps there without crutches, and was very pleased.

With the very long recovery period over, I could regain my usual activities around New York. I managed to secure a grant arranged by Chris Rohlfing, museum administrator, to help develop the theater design collection at the Cooper-Hewitt Museum, soon to become the National Museum of Design at the Smithsonian. While sorting through designs by various theater design artists at their studios, I selected appropriate donations to the Museum of the City of New York, the Harvard Theater Collection, and the Library for the Performing Arts among others. These designs were tax-deductible gifts from various wealthy friends interested in my projects.

Zeynep Turkkan, a long-time Turkish friend, introduced me to choreographer Alvin Ailey at a party for Duke Ellington, the popular composer and band leader.

Alvin Ailey, a most remarkable talent and warm friend.

Alvin and I talked about my work forming collections, and we discussed the possibility of making a permanent collection of designs created for the Alvin Ailey Dance Company productions over the years. I really liked him and wanted to help him get his wish. My efforts produced *Recent Acquisitions of The Dance Theater Foundation*, curated by me and exhibited at the New York City Center, in conjunction with the Alvin Ailey Dance Company's performance season there. I re-met Lena Horne at the opening performance and reminded her of the rain ticket she gave me for a dance while at Hal Prince's wedding.

I felt very cozy with Alvin. One evening he was visiting me when I was staying at the Wales Hotel, with Ysabel out of town and her apartment briefly sub-let because she was in a financial bind. He was helping me put pearl studs into my vest in preparation for my getting into white tie and tails to attend a waltz party. I suggested that we should consider going to bed together. He replied, "Whatever for? What would we do there?" So friends it was to be, nothing else.

I decided to make a brief trip to the Caribbean to visit my friend Hugh Shannon, who was playing the piano and singing his popular songs at The Mill on St. Thomas. I had stopped in Puerto Rico first to stay briefly with a friend who kept an apartment there, (Countess) Marguerita de Lema. We had enjoyed merry times in New York and East Hampton, some years before when I shared the "21 House" with David. She invited me down during the Christmas holidays, so I could not resist seeing both friends on this Caribbean junket.

Marguerita was giving a Christmas Eve party for some Spanish friends who had arrived on a ship, whose captain was part of her coterie. I had just met a couple of interesting young people on the beach, so I requested permission to bring them to the festivities. Marguerita assented to my inviting the English girl and the young American man. We spent so much time preparing for the gathering, with lots of attention to making a strong punch, that little time was left getting ourselves ready. The three of us decided to shower together to save time. The young woman had a mini dress with her that she thought would be festive to wear. I slipped on something gala and had another glass of punch in preparation for meeting the rather formal Spanish group. After they arrived, I asked my English friend to dance to something playing on the phonograph. She was slight in build, so I was able to show off terpsichorean techniques I thought remarkable. I lifted my partner, inadvertently pulling up her mini skirt revealing her nude crotch, which was eye level to the seated Spaniards. They abruptly got up and left the party. Marguerita rushed to her bedroom in tears. No words of regret soothed her distress.

The next morning, I booked a flight to nearby St. Thomas. Hugh was in good spirits, as always, and seemed glad to see me. His quarters were very tight, so I opted to rent a space on the beach nearby. During the splashing about in the blue-green sea with the mandatory refreshing drink at the bar, I met a most engaging young man from Boston. He was an Episcopalian minister, doubtlessly gay and entertaining. He had just arrived too, and agreed to share my living space until my departure the next day. I should have known that his name was David.

Rain clouds appeared, but we continued satisfying our thirst. It dawned on me that this could be a Sadie Thompson episode, and I enjoyed our lascivious time together even more! The next morning, my minister and I had eye-openers under the table's umbrella on the patio. Rain pouring down, it was perfect! The sinner and the preacher and RAIN . . . Yes, shades of Somerset Maugham and starring Gloria Swanson, or Joan Crawford, or Rita Hayworth!

I took a late afternoon flight to San Juan. Delirious from the debauchery and the Sadie Thompson episode, I decided I had enough time between flights to make an appearance in a gay nightspot outside of San Juan. I took a taxi there in very high spirits. David had made me feel as though I was on top of the world, and I glowed with sun and alcohol-splashed sex, stimulating an utter effusion of happiness when I entered the gay bar. It was the only time in my life that I had the experience of being like a magnet to those in the bar. I had seen Leonard Bernstein attract those around him, as well as the young Prince Charles when he was in California. Now I had an inkling of what it was like. I was glad I had a night flight to catch to New York, however. The energy I was emitting was draining me; I pushed my way out of the place, almost gasping for breath.

In later weeks, I arranged to see Nina and her sister Grace with a stopover to see the newly met David in Boston. He told me how a film crew had engaged him to do a bit part in a movie after I departed St. Thomas, but the rest of the time there was uneventful. Though a nice guy, my man of the cloth no longer inspired Sadie to reappear, so David III had a very short shelf life.

In New York, when not donning black tie for the opera or charity balls, I found pleasure in going on a toot with Clayton Cole to Max's Kansas City, where Janis Joplin and guitar-smashing Jimi Hendrix hung out, along with some of Warhol's Factory group. There were jaunts with Clayton to notorious gay bars, museum and gallery visits with Rita Simon, and diverse, often spontaneous activities with Ysabel—who had returned to New York—often involving gypsy dancers such as Lola Flores or José Greco.

Ysabel had a peculiar allergic kind of reaction when she smoked and drank simultaneously. Her face would stiffen, and her words became muffled and indistinct. By removing the cigarette, she would soon seem normal again. It startled and frightened people on occasion when this happened. Often, I would notice this happening from across the room and would hasten to take the cigarette abruptly out of her hand.

Imbibing vast amounts of liquor could produce a very unsteady Ysabel, as it would anyone. Put the cigarette smoking into the equation and a most unintelligible, unwieldy woman resulted. On one particular evening, I was trying to get Ysabel home in a taxi. She kept mumbling something indecipherable when leaving the party, as well as in the taxi. It was annoying that I could not understand what she was persistently trying to say. When we arrived at "955," with concerted efforts of the doorman, we finally managed to extricate her from the cab.

After her exiting the cab, the driver informed me, "You don't need a taxi, you need an ambulance!" I saw the wisdom in his observation. When I got her into the apartment, I finally got the message she had been trying to give me. "That is not my bag." I had picked up the wrong handbag when scooping up her mink to get her out of the party. Another taxi was hailed and I traveled a long distance downtown to exchange handbags, and return to an annoyed Ysabel. She did not feel any remorse or embarrassment about her condition, but thought I should have had better sense in getting the correct handbag.

Before sallying forth to some event, Ysabel habitually kept me waiting. After an exasperating lapse of time, she would appear and admonish me, "Come along, darling, I won't wait one moment longer!" I had to laugh.

Ysabel often was hostess to dinner parties, always on Thursday evenings. Her dining table accommodated ten people. Another half dozen could be seated at a round table set up in the contiguous library, whose paneled walls slid open when the room was not being used as a guest room. Following dinner, hordes of people arrived for after dinner drinks. Sometimes, the last of the stragglers did not leave until dawn, having been drawn into a game of chess with Ysabel or her professional chess playing boyfriend who never liked to leave. "Asparadropo" was Ysabel's nickname for him, which means sticky tape in Spanish.

One snowy evening, I was in a limousine arranged by an acquaintance to drop various people off after some gala opera event. I gave "955 Fifth Avenue" as m y destination. As it was Thursday, and I did not feel like going to the apartment where I was cat-sitting at that moment for a friend. I felt the need for further stimulation.

After the last guest left and the chessboard was put aside, Ysabel suggested it was snowing too hard for me to leave. Asparadropo suggested I slide the panels of the library to get the guest room prepared for my use. No, Ysabel invited me to stay with them in her purple oval bed, much to his annoyance. She had already slipped into bed and patted each side of her in the bed for us to occupy. I had my dinner jacket off and was slipping down my suspenders when Asparadropo began to object. So, I pulled them up in preparation to depart for the guest room. "Don't be silly, come here next to me," she insisted. Asparadropo stated that if I were staying, he was going. Ysabel said "Goodbye," as he stormed out of the room. My trousers were finally off when he reappeared, saying that she was being ridiculous and that I should be sleeping in the guest room. "Come along," she cooed to him, "come to bed and stop being silly." Finally, both of us were undressed on either side of Ysabel, thinking we could now settle in for what remained of our sleeping time. Quietly, Ysabel slipped her hands out on either side of her, placing one hand on each penis. "I like Eric's more than yours," she impishly announced.

The sheets went flying as the irate Italian lover jumped out of bed, pulling the covers off of us. Both of us, stark naked, stared up at him, as he ranted and finally exited the room. We pulled the sheets back up, but were soon de-sheeted when he returned to continue the tirade. After several sheets up and down, we three managed to close our eyes and catch some sleep.

A major exhibition of Van Gogh paintings was showing at the Brooklyn Museum. The director invited me to view this important event. Ysabel was pleased to join us for a simple lunch before, and then we were placed—admission free—in front of the crowd waiting to enjoy the paintings. The viewing halls were jammed with spectators. I was startled to hear Ysabel's voice announcing to the surrounding crowd, "The cameras are coming . . . the cameras are coming!" She indicated that a wide space be cleared in front of one of the prominent works of art. People obeyed, standing to either side while pulling out small mirrors to check make-up and combing their hair in preparation for a spontaneous appearance on television. While they craned their necks to locate the promised cameras, Ysabel placed me in front of the art work, put her arm over my shoulder, and exclaimed, "What a beauty!"

We moved on to another painting while the crowd maintained their positions so that the (fictitious) camera could get a terrific view of the painting we just admired. Happily, Ysabel did not repeat her performance, and I hoped that the director never heard of our escapade.

Ysabel had a great affection for artists. When she decided to give me a birthday dinner, she was especially pleased when I arranged for R.C. Gorman to be one of the guests. This Navajo artist and I had a long history of colorful events, enhanced by a river of libations. Ysabel had enjoyed meeting him earlier when she came to New Mexico with me and visited him in Taos.

Opera star Grace Bumbry would be in attendance, as well. We bonded at our first meeting at a reception at the Roerich Museum on Riverside Drive. Her escort was an intimate friend of mine who went off to become director of the Williamsburg Museum. Grace arrived at "955" to be greeted by me at the door, wearing a white see-through Mexican wedding dress. I had my famous golden bikini under it with the gold pre-Columbian eagle pinned to my crotch. Ysabel had a long white Mexican dress on, as well. I slipped the floor length fur coat off of Grace before she could flee and introduced her to her hostess. Ysabel gaily announced that she had read in the *New York Times* that morning about the standing ovation Grace had received at the Met. Grace smiled. Ysabel continued, "Of course, I sing much better than you do!" Startled by this comment, I distracted Grace by introducing R.C. Gorman, who adores celebrities. Grace was wearing the off-the-shoulder multi-colored gilded gown she had worn to the closing of the old Met. The Indian's brown finger touched Grace's black shoulder while he inquired, "Is that your real color?" I almost fainted, as Grace does not suffer criticism of her vocal talents or being black. "Yes . . . " she crooned in a rich mezzo tone. "Is that yours?" Whew, she had more humor than I gave her credit for.

The evening took many funny turns, but considering the cast of characters, it was only natural. Ysabel and Grace adopted a very competitive, but friendly kind

I judge Grace Bumbry the winner!

of jostling. At one point, I noticed the two women pulling up their evening skirts to determine which of them had prettier legs. The culmination of their competition was at a party Grace gave in her West Side apartment some weeks later. I arrived earlier than Ysabel, who was still fussing in preparedness, and I did not want to be late arriving at Grace's party. When I arrived, Grace asked where the *prima donna assoluta* was? Many major figures of the music world were there and speculated who Grace might be referring to. I parried their queries with "You will see." No one could guess her identity—Maria Callas was not in town, neither was . . . Finally, Ysabel arrived -- delayed because she had gone to the correct floor but went to the wrong apartment, where another party was under way. After enjoying a drink, she asked where Grace and Eric were. "Who is Grace? Who is Eric?" She thanked the other hosts and merrily proceeded down the hall to join us.

Ysabel had pulled her black hair up volcano style with jewels, lava-like, coming down the sides; a huge Hermès scarf, clipped at the shoulders with a brooch, covered her body stocking. Ysabel thought the nude male Grecian urn figures dancing around the scarf would titillate Grace's lascivious taste. When she entered, she claimed to have noticed how well Grace danced. Grace exclaimed, "Finally, a compliment. Well there is something better than I do than you, and that is, using a French phrase, Fucking!" The Swedish tenor, Ragnar Ulfung, known for his amorous proclivities, leaned in between the seated women and said, "Let me be the judge of that!" And so the gaiety continued through the supper. Later,

I noticed the distinct absence of both the women. Upon listening at various doors, I heard their voices in one of the bathrooms.

"Let him in," Ysabel said, "let him be the judge." I entered and Grace undid the bodice of her evening gown, revealing two large mammaries. I glanced at them and at Ysabel's breasts, then leaned over and kissed Grace's nipples, declaring her the winner! In the pre-dawn, I was half awake in Ysabel's purple oval bed and heard her murmur, "They were so big, they were so black!"

Grace Bumbry / Venus at The Met.

"Did I do the right thing? Kissing them?" I inquired. She sat bolt upright in bed, exclaiming, "It was mandatory! It was obligatory! You were the only gentleman there!"

I still attended dress rehearsals at the Metropolitan Opera House, where the staff mistakenly thought I was with the company. I would enter with bluff self-assurance through the backstage door and make my way into the house, having greeted the telephone operators and nodding to whomever seemed official and needed my salutation. There was a section towards the front of the auditorium for performers to view the rehearsal, and that is where I chose my seat.

When maneuvering backstage, sometimes it was necessary to take an elevator if I needed to find a locale other than entry to the house, such as a rehearsal room or dressing room. Once, on the elevator, I was told that last night's performance was wonderful. I mumbled some polite acknowledgement, but had no idea what the reference was or who I was mistaken for. Even at the old Met, Rudolf Bing would glance at me as though he knew me. It was a puzzlement, just as my self-identity was for me during these frantic years.

At a closed rehearsal for a Wagnerian opera, I did the usual routine, only to be stopped by an usher in the hall near the entrance from backstage into the house. He announced it was a closed rehearsal, so I retraced my steps back stage. A telephone operator looked at me and asked what the matter was. When I told her that the usher refused me entrance, she dialed him in the phone while exclaiming, "Doesn't he know who you are?" It was suggested that I return to the house, where I was duly admitted, but I seriously wondered myself who I was!

A very attractive man, whom I encountered at one of the many cocktail parties I attended on Park Avenue, engaged me in conversation. He mentioned that his wife Yveta often attended the dress rehearsals at the Met, as I did. She was given a pass by acquaintances at the opera and, being extremely fond of opera, enjoyed the experience very much. Robert Lincoln Love explained that his Czech wife was in Prague attending the funeral of her mother. As he was alone and had some chilled champagne at their penthouse apartment just a few blocks up Park Avenue, perhaps I would like to visit with him?

We had a few meetings before I actually got to meet the lovely, blond, long-tressed Yveta. She and I got along very well from the first moment, though I felt some guilt because of my clandestine relationship with her husband. That was valuable information for her to use later, when he decided to divorce her and threatened to put her, together with their two young sons, into reduced circumstances away from their Park Avenue home. I took Yveta's side in this mean divorce battle and was surprised she knew nothing of her husband's other life. When she married the conservative Malcolm Graf, a member of the Metropolitan Opera Club, I asked him if marrying Yveta meant I had to sleep with him, too. He was not amused, and banned me from their apartment! Methinks the lady protests too much?!

Yveta and I loved collecting celebrities, especially those at the Met. She was much admired by conductor Zubin Mehta, to whom I took an instant dislike, which was mutual. We both admired soprano Shirley Verrett, who joined us at a champagne fashion event given by our friend, George Stavropoulos, known in New York as the King of Chiffon. Since attending her Lady Macbeth performance at Sarah Caldwell's Boston production of Macbeth, with Bob Jacobson of *Opera News*, I had held Shirley Verrett in the highest esteem.

Also high on my list of very special talents was Jean-Louis Barrault, who was directing a Met production of *Carmen* with Marilyn Horne singing the title role. I had read about Barrault in my theater history books and had seen him perform "Bip" in the film *Les Enfants du Paradis*. Yveta knew little of his history but was thrilled he showed such interest in her during her attendance at the *Carmen* rehearsals. During a dinner party after a rehearsal, Yveta was mystified to discover one of the silk shoes she had slipped out of during the meal was missing. It was to reappear, full of flowers, when Barrault arrived at her party! I filled her in on his prominence, so when she gave a cocktail party for him, she would be more knowledgeable about her guest of honor. This was much more than her guests knew of him, as he was an unknown quantity to the young, hip social crowd. All they seemed to care to know was that he was a stage director at the Met. Barrault had never smoked pot and was pleased when Yveta assured him her friends could provide him with the experience. As I was the only person at the gathering who knew who this legendary world class talent was, I engaged him in conversation I thought appropriate. Soon the weed was being smoked, and I remember lying down on the carpet of Yveta's den hallucinating a sunflower growing out of my head, heavily leaning backwards. I opened my eyes at one point to see the great mime doing a wonderful performance for himself nearby, with no one noticing but me. It was very gratifying to observe his talent in this smoky confined area, and I considered it a special gift of a private performance just for me.

Thanks to the generosity of members of the Metropolitan National Council, I enjoyed many operas. Sponsors for young operatic talents from around the United States would gather at the Metropolitan Opera House twice annually, culminating in final auditions of their protégés. Eloise Walker Long, a member representing West Virginia, had visited my gallery in Spoleto. She always included me in her opera going when in New York. She stayed at the Waldorf Astoria Hotel, along with a couple of other distinguished older women on the council visiting from Michigan and Minnesota. I enjoyed hearing about their long years, rich in life's experiences in travel, music, and as witnesses to much of the 20th century's history.

It became a tradition for these three grand dames and me to stop at Peacock Alley in the lobby of the hotel for a nightcap, upon returning from an opera performance. One evening, there was a nice looking young couple sitting across from us. The young man commented on how fortunate I was to have three such attractive dates. "Oh, they are not my dates," I roguishly responded. "They work for me," implying that my fine ladies were really hookers. It was so astonishing how that outlandish comment worked magic on these pillars of respectability. They seemed younger just pondering my ridiculous notion. I could not resist following my statement with something to the order of suggesting that his young woman would be a good recruit, too. This generated general hilarity all around.

The ladies' estimation of me grew one evening there at Peacock Alley, when Zsa Zsa Gabor strolled by on the arm of Huntington Hartford. Both of them greeted me, which impressed the ladies. I knew Hunt from various parties around town, including a few meetings at Karen and Allegra's UN gatherings. Zsa Zsa and I had met first in California. Her acute, appraising Hungarian eyes scanned the three women and focused back to me with a knowing glance.

Opera going was further advanced with my good friendship with Robert Jacobson, editor of *Opera News*. He commissioned me to write a couple of articles for the magazine, one about my great-great aunt Christina Nilsson, who had opened the old Met as Marguerite in *Faust*, and the other covering the Metropolitan Opera National Council meeting in Boston. He invited me to the opera, sometimes out of town to Boston, Washington D.C., and Philadelphia. Bob had written a book, based on interviews with various opera stars, called *Reverberations*. He autographed a copy to me with the inscription, "To Eric, who reverberates more than anyone I know!" On a couple of occasions, I would venture down to 14th Street, where he lived in a walk-up, to prepare ratatouille, which he particularly enjoyed eating. Bob was easy to be with and had none of the attitude many of his colleagues assumed. He was sweet, gracious and quietly knowledgeable.

To gain some further coin of the realm, I put together a junket to Santa Fe in the mid '70s to visit Indian land, explore ruins, attend Pueblo ceremonials, and see the opera. Having lived there on two occasions—exhibiting opera designs in conjunction with the opening of the new opera house in 1968, and then in 1969–70 when I ran the Jamison Galleries, daring to show contemporary art—I knew people with interesting homes and ranches who would entertain my small group when we were not sightseeing. Visiting peoples' homes seemed a friendly way to get a feel for the Southwest. Also, at the opera, it would be pleasant for the visitors to see familiar faces. Eloise from West Virginia invited her daughter and her husband, who lived in Boulder, Colorado, to come on this trip, as did other friends from New York. This project was facilitated by my good and very affectionate friend, Alan Klaum, who had a travel agency.

There were occasions when I lived with Alan at his apartment on West 55th Street near Sixth Avenue. It was very thrilling to hear the "Iron Butterfly," as Renata Tebaldi was called at the Met, vocalize as I exited or waited for the elevator on Alan's floor. She lived in the apartment on the other end, but I often enjoyed hearing her from the hallway. We would meet sometimes in the elevator. On one occasion, I asked her whether she would autograph the photo in an album I had of hers, which she graciously agreed to do. I admired Tebaldi's elegance in appearance and regal stance, adding a diva's verve to the world around her.

Alan Klaum was a gentle person of my age, blond, trim, and with good manners. He enjoyed writing poetry when not engrossed in his travel business. He planned junkets for the benefit of the New York City Opera. One overnight trip was by bus to Washington D.C., where the group would enjoy a performance of the American Ballet Theater at the Kennedy Center, a trip to the zoo to see the pandas just arrived from China, and the splendid painting exhibition on loan from the Hermitage in St. Petersburg, on view at the National Gallery of Art. The number of participants required two buses. Alan would play host on one, and I would be the host on the second bus. Facility for a bar at the back of the bus was arranged, and each of us purveyors of the libations. I was to keep my earnings from the bar in my bus, which was an excellent incentive to push drinks.

Always ready to stimulate a party atmosphere, I got my bus riders very merrily partaking of the liquor. It was clear that my bus resonated much more rowdiness than Alan's did. Alan did not push his drinks, as he was a very sedate person of quiet dignity. My bar was empty upon arrival in Washington D. C., with a busload of vibrant celebrants; Alan's bar was barely touched and his passengers were noticeably quieter. Some of my passengers, who found the partying disruptive to their reading, opted to change busses at the stopover location midway; some on Alan's bus envied the liveliness on mine and switched, as well.

The second day presented a problem in our schedule. There was a long wait to see the Hermitage exhibition, so we had to decide whether to try to squeeze in the panda visit to the zoo or see the paintings. We had paid arrangements for both so why not enjoy both, I urged? I strongly advocated going to the zoo first, then trying to get into the exhibition. Those who wished to join me got on to my bus with a refreshed bar and enjoyed meeting the pandas. We hurried back to the National Gallery, where the line was indeed enormous. I hoped that Alan and his group were still inside enjoying the historic exhibition so that we would not hold them up too much. I hastened my group to the head of the line and announced to the guard that the rest of our group were already inside, and we had to join them. We were let in immediately, much to the chagrin of Alan's group, who were still waiting in line! When they saw us making our way to the front, some of them abandoned Alan and tagged along with us.

Alan had planned a Christmas/New Year trip to Salzburg and Vienna, again to benefit the New York City Opera. He had a German assistant who would be meeting us in Frankfurt to help lead the trip and who would remain at the end of it to rejoin his family in Germany. I was to go along to help manage the various arrangements. Ysabel decided that she would like to join us, as she was going to Rome afterwards and thought the Austrian trip might be amusing, especially since I would be there. Wisely, Alan had some misgivings but could hardly turn down a paying customer.

Our departure from J.F.K was seriously delayed, but a bar was opened for our pleasure as a distraction and recompense for the discomfort. Despite being the designated leader of the group, I could not resist having many bolstering libations to help pass the time. A woozy crossing to Germany was a dismal way to start this junket. The German guide and I did not coordinate well, at all. He shirked some of the duties, and opted to get better hotel arrangements for himself than I did. However, he was sober and more sedate than I was, with Ysabel often prodding me on.

In the tour group was a woman who distinctly captured my attention. Alice Fordyce seemed formidable and a model of discretion and taste. While Ysabel did not go on many of the side trips to monasteries and points of interest, Alice would link her mink clad arm into mine to assist her over icy patches on our walk about. Unlike her lively social sister, Mary Lasker, the famous hostess and benefactress for medical research, Alice was plain but tasteful, with a very sedate manner of respectability and propriety. I soon became her escort and even dance partner.

It was while waltzing at a *schloss* outside of Salzburg that Alice suggested I come to the Waltz Series in New York as her guest. When the tour was over and we landed in New York, Alice brought me into town with her car and driver. We made arrangements for our white tie and tails waltz evening, coming up in the next weeks, and parted.

Ysabel was stranded at the grand Imperial Hotel in Vienna, waiting for her passport to be returned from a fellow traveler who had shared her hotel room on the tour. For safekeeping, Ysabel had put her passport into Carol's locked suitcase but forgot to remove it when Carol returned to America. Eager to avoid prolonged costly payments at the five-star hotel, she would be glad to hasten to Rome as soon as possible.

Alice lived on the 11th floor at United Nations Plaza, the same building my dear Wyatt Cooper lived in with his wife, Gloria Vanderbilt, and their two sons. (Also in that tower resided Truman Capote, who had outraged and betrayed his grand social friends in his most recent book. His advanced alcoholism made my affliction seem petty by comparison. He and I never established a pleasant rapport. I felt repulsed by his drunken demeanor.) UN Plaza was seriously grand and sedate, and a perfect home for Alice.

Spectacular views of the United Nations and the gardens around it, together with the East River, filled the plate glass windows of Alice's lofty apartment. It was not long before my visits became a regular occurrence. When I was not escorting her to dances, Alice enjoyed playing anagrams with me after a simple dinner, followed by madeleines. We had developed a very warm friendship. Ysabel was living in Europe for the duration, so there was little distraction.

During this interim period while Ysabel was abroad, I was using a guest room at the Midtown apartment of my artist friend, Natalie Marshall. With her three children now living independently, she had moved from Connecticut to reside in the city.

Alice had a house in Little Compton on Rhode Island, directly across from fashionable Newport. She and her neighbors relished the simpler, less formal life from the one viewed across the waters over their trashcans. I enjoyed designing table arrangements for our dinners for two. It was a creative enterprise that amused us both. I also taught her to drink champagne in the morning, and how the larger the bottle, the better the taste. We dispensed with the splits completely.

One weekend, we went to the mid-Cape Cod to attend a performance of *You Never Know*, starring the eternal Kitty Carlisle Hart. We had a pleasant conversation in her dressing room afterwards. When Alice departed (with me following), the engaging star delayed me briefly with some comments. I was touched by her warmth. Shortly thereafter, back in New York, I had the delight to encounter the leading man of that production. His name joins the legion of nameless men in the annals of my personal history. However, I do remember the pleasures of his company.

Kitty Carlisle Hart and I were to meet on several future occasions. Most memorable was the program we shared at the Morristown Memorial Hospital in New Jersey many years later. This venerable star shared her colorful history in films and on the stage with the audience; I presented a trio of musicians performing a concert of classical music. We did two performances that day. During the break in between, she focused her energies doing meditation. I was impressed with her discipline.

Meanwhile I was beginning to show the effects of my overindulgences. As troubling to my self-esteem as my looks getting bloated was, even worse was that my heavy drinking had caused lesions on my hands and feet to occasionally erupt. I jokingly remarked that I had the stigmata, revealing blood oozing from my right palm. Sometimes, my shoes were painful to wear because the leather would aggravate these lesions, causing a leaking of blood. Alice kindly gave me a pair of her deceased husband's black velvet slippers, albeit too large, but far more comfortable than the irritating leather shoes. I was under a doctor's care to control the lesions and the bleeding, so I could function more normally. The doctor suggested I stop drinking. This did not seem an option, and life without my best friend, alcohol, I considered would be intolerable.

Alice surprised me one evening. We were in her chauffeur-driven car, headed for the Metropolitan Opera House for a performance of the Royal Ballet. Alice had the unusual notion to

Kitty Carlisle Hart joins me in concert.

attend the ballet and skip the formal dinner following, so we could go to a ball at the Plaza, where her favorite orchestra was playing. It would mean that we would arrive at the ball after the dinner was finished, resulting in our missing out on both meals but enjoying the ballet and later the dancing. Alice seemed the model of measured restraint, but her imaginative approach to spending an evening out on the town was unique. Being of a mindset to stay trim, her doing without dinner and supper fit the regime very well.

Princess Margaret officiated at the Royal Ballet benefit, together with her handsome husband, Anthony Armstrong-Jones, Lord Snowdon. As "God Save the Queen" was being played, the bouquet of yellow roses that the Princess was holding began to quiver. She noticed the cruising that her husband was directing towards me, standing facing them some yards in front; I knew she felt like swiping him with the flowers. Naturally, I was flattered by his investigative appraisal, and pleased that my well-tailored dinner clothes masked my bloated bulk. No one could notice my bleeding feet hidden in my dancing pumps.

Another unusual invitation from Alice involved attending the 80th birthday party for Josephine Baker, the black American dancer who went to France in the '20s and was an exotic sensation in the Paris stage revues. She was an icon in theater history. With the greatest enthusiasm, I wished to attend this benefit she was sponsoring to help needy children. Josephine Baker had a large number of adopted children herself, and she dedicated much of her energies to improving the lives of young children globally.

Famous for her dancing semi-nude in her heyday, that evening Josephine wore a black gown with see through panels around her waist and above her bust. It was demure in comparison to the costumes in her earlier life, but more appropriate for a woman of her advanced age. She sang a few songs, and then the guests danced. Alice and I did a Viennese Waltz when one was played. I noticed Josephine Baker standing on the edge of the dance floor watching us. Afterwards, she told me how well we danced, which was a special compliment coming from this famous performer.

One evening while I was enjoying my pre-prandial scotch in her UN apartment, Alice slipped a blue envelope over to me to read. It was written by Lila Tyng, a woman I had met while with Alice at the waltz party. She requested that Alice attend a ball she was sponsoring, and asked if she would bring the nice, young man from the previous party with her, as well? How nice to be considered "young," as I felt older than the "Big Fifty" that I was approaching. Alice asked me if it would please me to go, and I thought it would be very agreeable to see Lila again. She was very amiable and lively, and she danced well.

Exuberant Ysabel at home.

Canary Island Mardi Gras with Lila and "Charlie."

Chapter 14

YOUNGER THAN SPRINGTIME - IN 3/4 TIME

Lila quickly became more and more center stage in my life. It did not take long for Lila and me to begin going to dances together. I do not think Alice liked this very much, but I had enough time to go dancing with both of them. At one point, I remember Alice and Lila discussing how to best divide my dancing availability. They decided Lila could use me as a partner for the Waltz Series; Alice would avail herself of my escorting her to the charity balls and glamorous ballet or theater benefits. Neither of them thought to sound me out on what I wanted, but I was content with their arrangement, as I enjoyed the company of both ladies.

As well as the two-bedroom apartment at 480 Park Avenue, Lila delighted in her beloved Lu Shan located in central New Jersey, near Bernardsville and Far Hills. New Jersey to me was what it is to many people—a dubious place that smelled of industries lining the New Jersey turnpike with large oil storage tanks in profusion. Visits to her country retreat were to change my notion about the "Garden State."

Lila had been married to the publisher of *Time, Life,* and a series of other magazines. Henry Robinson Luce was a classmate of Thornton Wilder at Yale University. Lila knew Thornton from various social events and was introduced to "Harry" Luce as a result. During the Great Depression, Henry Robinson Luce built for his young wife and two sons, Henry III and Peter, a French-styled *manoir,* which many referred to as a *chateau.* It was one of the only great houses built in America during that time of deprivation, thanks to the flourishing *Time* magazine.

Lu Shan in winter.

This choice property, with a view over the surrounding valley, was carefully chosen by the young married Luces not only because of the view, but also for its being a convenient commute to New York. Most importantly, there was no income tax in New Jersey.

Lu Shan means Luce's mountain, or road to wisdom, depending on the inflection in three-dimensional Chinese. Luce's father was a renowned missionary in China, where Henry was born. Hence the Chinese influence. Lu Shan was filled

Serpentine wall at Lu Shan.

with antiques acquired by Lila and her mother while in Europe between the wars; Lila had directed the architectural designs to instill a French flavor. She laid out the gardens with a serpentine brick wall, serving as a backdrop for pink or white trumpet tulips and roses, and a squiggly path along the apple orchard, fragrant with lily of the valley among forget-me-nots and jonquils, as well as a maze of clipped box wood outside the Octagonal Library. Discretely tucked behind the lilac bushes, a rectangular fenced area was created to nurture a cutting garden of zinnias, asters, black-eyed Susans, and many other blossoming planting for use in bouquets within the house.

Henry Luce was never to spend one night in this remarkable creation.

Shortly after it was completed, the beckoning finger of Clare Booth attracted him elsewhere. What has been considered the American divorce of the century followed. Astonishingly, Henry was supposed to be a pillar of the Presbyterian Church, where divorce was not allowed!

Lila related to me that her first meeting with Clare Booth was at a dinner party at the home of their neighbors, Thayer and Laura Hobson, at 4 East 72nd Street. Lila was having a lively discussion with the man seated next to her, when Clare appeared between

Henry Luce makes a rare visit to Lu Shan.

them, literally cutting off their conversation. Lila said Harry showed an adverse impression of Clare on that first meeting.

Shortly thereafter, Elsa Maxwell arranged for a party celebrating Cole Porter's opening of *Anything Goes.* It was held in the Starlight Roof Garden at the Waldorf Astoria. Harry was bringing a glass of champagne over to Lila when Clare, sitting by herself, intercepted him by asking if the champagne was for her. He sat down with her as the lights dimmed, while Porter's tunes filled the rarified air. After requesting that Lila return home, he and Clare proceeded to leave the ballroom to pace the hallway, talking intensely for hours.

It was unthinkable at that time for a leader of the Presbyterian Church to divorce, then to marry a beautiful divorcée. It was shocking to many, and devastating to Lila. With not even spending one night at Lu Shan, their showplace home for their two sons to grow up in, Henry R. Luce asked Lila to divorce him. She promised her ailing mother, who was living there with them, that she would never invite Clare to visit this beloved home. She kept her word.

Afterwards, Lila suffered another disastrous marriage. Sewell Tyng owned a gold mine in Ecuador in South America and was the state attorney general for Thomas Dewey in New York. A plump man with amusing stories to entertain Lila's two young boys, he once exclaimed, after viewing Lila's array of shoes in the closet: "I married a centipede!" This marriage was short lived. For the second time in her young life, Lila was asked for a divorce. His alcoholism drove him to hole himself up in a hotel room with his girlfriend. They made a pact to drink themselves to death. He succumbed; she went to Alcoholics Anonymous.

Lila Hotz Luce Tyng, from Chicago, had been groomed to be a charming, lovely, social creature. Her mother, with the nickname "Muddy," had been long separated from her husband. A role model for Lila in taste and social behavior, she spent much of her later years in Lila's company. Lila was adept at ladylike chattiness. Also accomplished on the dance floor, Lila went to dinner dances continually, sometimes an astounding five in a week. Her growing sons felt her absence and resented it.

When I began to see Lila both in New York and in New Jersey, she was always aflutter with social activities, often with a gaggle of single men in attendance—all of them gay! More and more, I got drawn into her schedule of events; more and

Lila Ross Hotz Luce Tyng circa 1950.

more frequently I spent time at Lu Shan. Our friendship blossomed into a symbiotic relationship, which both of us needed very much. After Ysabel gave up her apartment and left New York because of financial distress, and Uncle Monkey went to live in a senior care establishment, Lila suggested I use the second bedroom at "480." We became like a brother-sister family unit, mutually beneficial. Ysabel told me how happy she was, knowing I had someone around me after she left the country to live in Colombia.

Ysabel's family were very distinguished oligarchs in Colombia. Neither the three daughters nor their mother paid much attention to the maintenance of the family fortune after the father died. Cousins had pilfered some of it, and the government had appropriated much of it, leaving the women in a precarious state seemingly overnight. Ysabel sold the apartment on Fifth Avenue that she loved so much. It was a bad time to sell, so she had to settle for a small amount. With the money from the sale, she retrenched with her family in Bogotá in a modest dwelling. Their country estate was sold; their palatial city residence gone as well. Cecilia, an attractive divorcée, returned from Paris, joining Ysabel and dear Beatriz, who had never left Bogotá.

Slowly, by helping Lila organize her social calendar, by becoming a reliable companion, and by assisting in directing her staff to cope with impending social events, I became an indispensable aide to her and meshed into the daily routine at Lu Shan and at "480." It was great fun for both of us. Our symbiotic life became immeasurably easier for her, and less of a challenge for me.

Perhaps it was the nurturing atmosphere at both Lu Shan and at "480," together with the ministrations of both doctor and dermatologist, but the bleeding lesions on my feet and the shocking "stigmata" on my right hand became a thing of the past. My expanding girth from continual indulgences from extravagant dinners and open bars was disguised by expert tailoring. It was internal disorders that troubled me. Taking "drying out" periods or cutting down on my alcohol intake was unsuccessful, only creating further stress. To hide these nagging battles with alcohol-induced malaise and insecurities, I was determined to

Lila when she was four.

make our environment even more lovely and special. I called forth my directorial and management skills to create a *mise en scène* that reflected exquisite elegance. The distinguished guests for dinner parties or a weekend gathering would discover a stunning environment, whether it be a remarkably beautiful table or enchanting floral decors, including flowers in the guest rooms. I inspected everything before guests arrived, chose the wines from the cellar with care, and prepared them for "breathing."

The seating arrangement took particular care. Place cards were arranged, after Lila and I discussed the best location at the table for each guest. We made certain a person with a distinct interest would have the opportunity of sitting next to a like-minded person, provided they had not been together at a previous dinner party at Lu Shan, which was easily checked in Lila's large registry annotating previous dinner parties. Sometimes, one guest with strong feelings about something would be seated distant from someone with opposing virulent sentiments. The dinner experience was to reflect gaiety and harmony, and was not a place for rebuttal or disagreement.

While I fussed and checked on details before the arrival of guests, Lila was freed up to annotate in her album for future reference—the guest list, seating arrangements, menu, and her choice of evening gown. After hair arrangements and make-up, she could slip into her gown for the evening and apply her jewelry and perfume. Then she would descend the circular staircase while cars began their way up the long driveway. With aplomb, knowing I had prepared all in readiness, the vibrant hostess would greet the guests in the entry hall looking cheerfully radiant, setting the tone for the evening.

I became adept at sitting at the other head of the table from Lila, leading conversation with a careful eye on which direction the hostess was speaking, so I could turn my attentions accordingly to my dinner partners. Unlike small dinners with general conversation, the hostess turned to her right to open the dinner, then to her left. Each guest followed the cue. Lila kept a minaudière in her lap. Within this small evening bag was a small cue card with various witty comments or reminders of short, amusing stories she could select if or when needed. After the guest on Lila's right gave a toast to her during dessert, I would gather the men together for brandy, liqueurs, cigars, or cigarettes in the library, while the women retired to freshen up. They were served glasses of water in the Louis XV salon, waiting for the men to re-appear. If desired, something stronger than water could be provided.

This structure encouraged four distinct types of conversation during the evening. It was fascinating to me. Lila and I shepherded guests who would not be seated together at the dinner table for conversation and cocktails on either the terrace or in the Louis XV living room, so called after the chinoiserie wallpaper, created for the king. During the Thirties, Lila and her mother, in the company of an antiquaire, came upon rolls of it, stored since the 18th Century in the original boxes, in an attic of a chateau in France. Clearly, it was meant to enrich the walls of Lu Shan. The original boxes were carelessly burned for kindling...

When it was time for dinner, Lila and her dinner partner began a procession

traversing the Gothic Room into the Venetian Dining Room. Once all were seated, the dinner conversation commenced with Lila choosing an opening topic; the third conversation of the evening followed with the men settled into the library, and women separated for their talk in the living room; finally, everyone joined together. It made for a diverse, thorough mixing of people with distinctly contrasting conversations, which helped make a brilliant evening in a remarkable setting.

Lila and her two angels in the Gothic Hall.

Murder was a popular

after dinner game, especially as the Gothic Hall and the Octagonal Library at Lu Shan were perfect backdrops for the "foul deed." There would be a drawing of cards. Whoever got the ace of spades was the murderer, whose goal it was to do the deed without any witnesses. "You're dead" is all that needed to be said. Everyone, upon cross-examination by the examiner, had to tell the truth, with the exception of the murder, who could lie to mislead the investigation. This seemed to be diverting for the guests, and Lila and I enjoyed it every time, as well.

On weekends, I would lead guests along the wiggly path towards the farm below for a bucolic walk. The large red barn, white cement milking barn and silo, and machinery barn were a colorful bucolic touch to the plowed fields and wooded landscape. Later, when I established Apollo Muses Center for the Arts at the farm, the guests were invited after lunch to attend the concert, art talk, and other programs. The options for entertaining guests were plentiful. The environment was built for pleasure.

The staff were excited by special events, such as a visiting maharaja or a concert recital in the large living room (a.k.a. The Louis XV papered salon), with the 1916 Steinway carved grand piano. They were noticeably relieved when all preparations went smoothly. At first, "interferences" were grudgingly tolerated when my "advice" helped make life easier for their mistress. Soon, I became essential to the running of the elaborate social life at Lu Shan. I am certain the staff looked forward to those times when Lila and I went away for writing retreats or on special trips, sometimes for months at a time. They could relax and work at their own pace, attending to chores needing attention while the house was empty.

Ever since my disappointment in realizing I would never pursue a career in theater directing, I had resolved to be living proof that "living well is the best revenge." I was determined that the arts would continue to nourish my life, and that I would always strive to become a Renaissance man. I wanted my life to be a work of art. I would continue to curate, consult, lecture, and even to write; my pursuits would abound. My activities would flourish amidst the stellar personalities in the arts, and include the movers and shakers in international society, as well. I improved my languages and kept myself aware of the significant cultural events influencing our times. What was happening not only in the world-at-large but also in the museums, opera houses, and theaters was carefully registered. Much of this took money or access to what money bought.

Often being financially strapped, I counted on invitations from Robert Tobin, Bob Jacobson, United Press International's Fred Winship, or the various ladies who asked me to escort them to the costly events well out of my means. Lila presented an on-going opportunity for my plans to flower. I enjoyed the comforts of in-town dwelling and country living with Lila, and no overhead. My everyday personal expenses were covered by a series of freelance commissions and stipends while I earned my keep doing what I did best: making fantasy reality by creating an elegant, lively Technicolor world for younger-than-springtime Lila to hold court.

Lisa Taylor and daughter visit us.

Paul Stiga, my first theater design customer, inspired me to curate an exhibition *Designs for the New York Stage*, which opened at Pace University in lower Manhattan in February 1978. This was a prelude to a larger exhibition *20th Century Scenic & Costume Design*, presented at the Cooper-Hewitt Museum, now the National Museum of Design at the Carnegie Mansion. It was on view for the month of April. Lisa Taylor, and her handsome, debonaire millionaire husband, Bert, gave me a celebratory dinner following in their huge Fifth Avenue apartment just blocks north of the museum. Lee Radziwill, charming sister of Jackie Kennedy, was on my left at the table. I was impressed by the quality of her conversation and liveliness. My success at curating this exhibition at the prestigious National Museum of Design and this sumptuous dinner with Lisa and Bert in their magnificent setting, together with Jackie's sister as one of my dinner partners, made me feel flushed with pride and rosiness.

My intertwined life with Lila took on increased dimensions. By now, Lila

Ann Luce and Oscar Murillo visit Taos.

called me "Little Brother" or "LB," and when in France I was her "Petit Frère." We traveled together with growing frequency, sometimes to Colorado to visit with her son, Peter, and his welcoming wife—the most adorable, sunny, and energetic Ann. Peter had built a house on the first ridge of the Rocky Mountains between Golden and Boulder, overlooking Denver in the distance. Ann delighted us with a dinner party in our honor. She was not only an excellent cook, but knew how to set a beautiful table. Sometimes we would drive into the Rockies for scenic trips. Both Ann and Peter had pilot's licenses, and both Lila and I enjoyed flying in their plane, as well.

Our trips included Bermuda, where we stayed with (Lady) Gladys Burney at her impressive Huntley Towers. This enormous edifice could have been a hotel. It had a huge dining room that easily accommodated enormous 19th century English gilt-framed canvases depicting sea battles. The oddity of Huntley Towers was that, aside from the suite of rooms Gladys occupied, and the one Lila had, no guest bedroom had a bathroom that functioned completely. I washed my hands and face in one bathroom, went down the hall for a bath, and into another for the toilet. Despite all bathrooms having complete fixtures, only one fixture worked in any of them!

Gladys had been a classmate of Lila's and married an English aristocrat. Her large blue eyes twinkled, especially when she looked at me and addressed me as "Big Boy." She drove us to her club for lunch one day. There I was introduced to the man who wrote the book, *A Man Called Intrepid*. With William Stevenson was the subject of his book, Sir William Stephenson, who had operated a successful spy operation in Rockefeller Center under Truman's directive for the British. Curiously, though unrelated, they both had the same surname, with a slight difference in spelling. We had an enlightening chat, and I realized the opportunity I missed by not knowing of him and the book when I spent time with Truman in Independence.

There was often a lively tension between Lila and Gladys. One early evening, standing near the pavement in the colorful town of St. George, Lila noticed a car backing into the space where Gladys was standing. Lila kept saying to her friend that a car was backing into the space where she was standing. Gladys insisted that cars were not allowed to be in that space. Finally, Lila and I gently, but firmly, lifted Gladys onto the pavement out of harm's way. Lila declared, "If you want to direct traffic, get a uniform!"

It was Easter. The night before preparing to attend Easter service at the local Episcopal Church, Lila created a whimsical, over-the-top Easter bonnet decorated with Easter eggs and various colorful flowers. She announced her intention to don it for the Sunday service in the morning, but chose to put it aside at the time of departure, wearing a modest, tasteful hat, instead—to our relief.

Her playfulness extended to harvesting some of the Spanish moss hanging on the branches of trees in the garden. After fashioning a beard with it and plopping a straw hat on her head, Lila appeared at the front door of Huntley Towers inquiring if there was a need for a gardener!

As a devout Francophile, Lila loved making jaunts to France. I did as well. We worked out a system whereby we could make each trip agreeable to us both. If car travel was involved, I would drive to the destination, saving her the expense of hiring a driver. This

Lila's Easter bonnet creation, Bermuda.

gave us the pleasure of picnics along the countryside, a mutual delight. Her friends in France slowly became known to me, and I was adopted into their circle.

We went on writing retreats where Lila worked on the biography of her mother, and I investigated materials concerning the court theaters of Europe, which I began writing about. Our lengthy retreats were sometimes to Costa Rica and often to Europe, with a concentration of time in France.

An idea to do research into the court theaters of Europe for a book began to germinate in my imagination. Surprisingly, there was no book on the subject, so I decided that, with all my experience in theater and scenic design, perhaps I could write one. It was enticing to discover no complete study had been written, but I wondered why? The private theaters of royalty fascinated me. These were not for commercial productions. They were used in royal circles to celebrate weddings and births, increase the prestige of the ruler, and strengthen the concept of the divine right of kings by presenting dramas promulgating divinities bowing to the ruler.

Research also could be accomplished in France while Lila spent catch-up time with her cronies. I pursued reading and collecting slides relevant to the productions of Louis XIV through XVI. (Through the good offices at both Versailles and the Louvre, I had slides duplicated or made from book illustrations of noted productions at Versailles and Paris.) I visited the papier-mâché theater of Marie Antoinette at Versailles as well as other portions of the palace grounds once used for theatrical presentations. Many off-limit places were opened to me thanks to an ever widening network. Alice Fordyce and her sister, Mary Lasker, helped open doors for me at Versailles; Lila and her best friend, Mary Hyde, introduced me to Sir Harold Acton in Florence, and various well-placed people in Paris.

I made further trips on my own. As the court theaters began in Renaissance Italy, I planned an excursion to the palace at Parma, followed by the remarkable palaces of Ludwig II of Bavaria after visiting Munich. While in Munich, I looked up a charming woman I had met with Lila at Lu Shan. She cordially invited me to call upon her when visiting Munich. Maria Theresa, a direct descendant of Empress Maria Theresa of Austria, added impressive momentum to my quest to experience the court theaters of Ludwig II. An opportunity to swing by this area presented itself when Maria Theresa and her husband drove me from Munich in their car. On our motoring away from Munich, she commented, in true Austrian fashion, on how much nicer the air was as we sat by a lake in Austria, where we were briefly passing through to get to the Bavarian castles.

Lila enjoyed summertime entertaining at Lu Shan. However, I had a very special invitation to Sweden to stay at Gripsholm Castle to further my research into the 18th century Swedish court theater of Gustav III. Some hours distant from Stockholm and Drottningholm Palace, the young king could tirelessly enjoy preparing theatrical productions employing the courtiers without interruptions from city distractions. This was one of Gustav III's favorite residences because of the rotunda theater installed in the tower of the castle.

I took my leave of Lila and went to say goodbye to Uncle Monkey. He had been put into the hospital because of a fall. He was desolated to discover I was leaving for Europe, since he was counting on my company when he came out of the hospital, even though he was under senior residence care supervision. I assured him I would be back before the end of the summer, and I cautioned him to be careful. He was greatly weakened by his advanced age and frequent binges with alcohol. A couple of hours before I left for the airport, the hospital called me to tell me that Osborn Maitland Miller had died falling down in the shower. I think he lost his will to live.

There was a call I wanted to make to the City Desk at the *New York Times* announcing this important cartographer's demise; a fast stop at the ATM to close his minuscule account; another call to the woman at the Protestant charity that financially supported his last days so that his cremation could be tended to, and it was agreed his ashes would be held awaiting my return. Then came a fly-by at the hospital to collect his few possessions there. It was a pressured pre-departure and one laden with deep sadness for me. Uncle Monkey was one of the kindest friends I ever had. I would miss him a great deal. Attempts were made to drink this sudden loss away; I arrived at the Stockholm airport a wreck.

However, the distraction of going to visit the palaces of Gustav III of Sweden alleviated my grief. Björn and his wife, Kerstin Mayer, were instrumental in getting permission from the king and queen for me to stay at Gripsholm Castle. I had met Kerstin when she sang with the Boston Opera; she was now a court singer whose request to Queen Sylvia on my behalf was very welcome. Björn was now running the National Theater in Uppsala, further bolstering my credentials as a worthy candidate for castle occupancy. A chance meeting in New York of a visiting Swedish scholar doing archeological work at the castle nicely completed the arrangement. I spent a couple of fascinating days at the Gripsholm. It still had scenery that had been hanging in the circular theater since the time of the enlightened King Gustav III in the 18th century. (Curators thought the scenery for Queen Christina would survive better hanging than rolled up.) It was in this theater that the young king, ever the enthusiast for drama, had play after play performed, often under miserably cold and damp conditions. Gustav wrote most of the plays himself, as was the case with *Queen Christina*. He used Swedish history to instill pride in national culture.

My bedroom originally belonged to the lady in waiting to the queen. Many items in the room were antiques from the time of Gustav III. The panes of glass in the windows overlooking the water below seemed of that period, as well as the bed. Agreeably, the linens were modern and clean. Decoration was at a minimum; perhaps many items had been removed when it no longer functioned as a royal residence. A space by the door was originally used for a servant to sleep. Happily, I had no need of one and I was delighted and honored to be there.

A thesis written by a researcher of Gustav III was lent to me while in residence. I devoured it and made great use of its contents on the evening a dinner was given in my honor at the castle. Young historians and curators arrived for this event, aware that I was doing research on the court theaters of Sweden and King Gustav III. With them was the *skål* master from Uppsala with a schedule of toasts to be used during the progression of dinner. Schnapps were to be used for toasting, and only to be consumed after a toast. I did not know I was expected to give an after-dinner speech until Agneta Hernmark informed me during an afternoon conversation sitting in the sun, sipping beer. It gave me very little time to prepare myself for this ordeal. Agneta was there to represent the king and queen. We hit it off immediately; she and I still maintain a lively friendship. She sat next to me at the banquet table and tried to control her amusement, listening to my outrageous speech to the gullible young experts in attendance. I could feel her leg next to me while I was speaking. It seemed to reflect through quivers her suppressed laughter at my antics.

As a start to my talk, I retold with exactitude the history of the castle. I was aware people who knew something of the matter would respond positively to information they could confirm as the truth. Wanting to infuse a sense of fun and a bit of the ridiculous into the evening's entertainment, little by little I swerved into improbable inventions. It was the sort of thing that Ysabel would have enjoyed enormously. I imagined Ysabel taking over within me in response to the academic snobbery I sensed in the guests. Though flattered by their special history, a devilment set in . . . .

Knowing how probably no one had read that morning's *New York Times* (and hoping no one wondered how I managed to read it), I mentioned the delight I had when perusing a lead story on the front page about the discovery of an ancient sailing ship sunk off the coast of Florida. Aboard was a water tight trunk containing papers relevant to the history of Gripsholm Castle. The listeners were all ears and nodded their heads when I recalled the history of the castle's land having been won by nobles gambling with the monks who had owned it previously.

My story began to lose credibility when I began to relate the tale of a princess in the tower overhead where we were sitting. She was frantic to alert her returning lover that hoards of Huns were surrounding the castle. At the time of my telling the story, newspapers were full of young people burning their draft cards in America and girls, seeking equal rights and liberation, burned their bras. I spoke of the princess running out of things to throw on the fire that she was using to send warning signals to her lover. In desperation, I continued, she threw her undergarments onto the fire. "And that, ladies and gentlemen, was the first time in history that a woman burned her bra!"

My studious audience gazed at me with growing disbelief. I wanted the guests to lighten up a little, as Swedes can be so dour in taking themselves so seriously. I soon sat down to enjoy yet another schnapps.

Previously, I had passed around my multi-paged program of the various toasts to be made during the dinner, with the request to the other diners to please write or draw something on the blank back side of the pages as a souvenir for me. It was interesting to peruse what was entered on to the program. One person wrote a cautionary note about the unreliability of the sincerity of others at the table; another drew a lovely sailing ship with kind words of welcome; and another drew a rune stone similar to the one outside the castle with phrases from a Verdi opera inscribed on it. Most puzzling was the picture of a partially open door with a light over it. In the morning, I was asked why I did not accept the invitation to come to that room after the party? (That was the meaning of the drawing, but I had not understood the intention.) It was a missed opportunity, but only for the moment. I visited the writer later when in Stockholm. The sojourn smacked of Ingmar Bergman's *Smiles of a Summer Night.*

My invitation to Drottningholm Palace and to the small, perfect theater for a production using the original machinery to move the scenery was invaluable to my research. In grand contrast to stern Gripsholm, classical Drottningholm's interior reflected the Francophile taste of Gustav III. This could be noticed in the extensive gardens surrounding the royal residence. Imitating the grand Louis XIV, jousting and theatricals were held there. The librarian at the palace was a great help in supplying me with relevant slides for use in my upcoming book and lecture series.

There were a couple of other Gustavian palaces to visit with Agneta Hernmark, who was fast becoming a treasured friend. Her knowledge and assistance in directing my further research made the balance of this Swedish experience priceless.

Natalie Marshall, the artist I introduced to Georgia O'Keeffe, was now living in Miami, teaching at the university there. When my manuscript for *The Court Theaters of Europe* was finally completed, she offered to edit it, create the layout and submit it to the press there for publication. I had made arrangements with the Library for the Performing Arts at Lincoln Center to have a reading and signing at the Bruno Walter Auditorium (October 1978).

Complications developed in Miami getting the copy into print, so I demanded it be shipped immediately to me in New York. Using Nathalie's layout, it was run off by a printer I had known for gallery projects, just in time for my talk at the Library.

Ruth Warrick kindly agreed to introduce me to the gathered audience. I thought it appropriate if my friend Thor Wood, head of the theater research department, introduced her as an actress of acclaim. I was sitting in the front row with Lila when Thor began his tribute to Ruth. He indicated that she had made a film debut in Orson Welles's *Citizen* Kane then gone on to be in "thirty-odd films," and star in various TV soaps, most currently playing a leading role in the long-running "All My Children," etc. Thor made her sound like Methuselah with all those years of credit. Ruth, to counteract an image of being ancient, began her comments with "Eric and I went to school together . . . " I have never figured out why she did that, but Lila immediately loudly asked, "What did she say?" To correct Thor's statement about her being in "thirty-odd films," Ruth went on to say that she knew some of the films were odd, but not all of them! Light-hearted moments followed....

With the publication of *The Court Theaters of Europe*, I began giving a series of lectures around New York, New Jersey, and selected cities in the United States at libraries, universities, and museums. Having established a reliable professional network over the years, I was invited to speak at New York University's La Maison Française, Lincoln Center's Bruno Walter Auditorium for students from School for the Performing Arts, the Colony Club, the Montclair Art Museum, the Morristown Museum, and several libraries—around New Jersey, Viscaya in Miami, the University of Denver, the Denver Public Library, and the University of Colorado at Boulder among others.

Noted English theater historian Charles Spencer arranged for me to receive stipends from the Arts Club in London, as well as the Slade School, Croydon College at the University of London for my talks; in Paris, the American College commissioned me to deliver a lecture.

An infusion of alcohol was needed to counteract my painful shyness, when I purposely forced myself to stand up in front of an audience to deliver interesting information on my topic. The early results seemed lame to me, but people were permissive in accepting my modest presentations. Needless to say, I never started a lecture without some libations to support my courage and erase, if possible, my feeling ill at ease. Over the years, my lecture topics expanded and I always used around 90 slides at each presentation to give colorful support to my comments. Slim publications with color reproductions were available to take home as a reminder of the material covered. Happily, my subject matter was always fascinating, and I was proud of the quality of my slides, which helped to make up for early insecurities. My effectiveness as a speaker grew as my success was more fully realized.

While helping to upgrade the theater design collection at the Cooper-Hewitt Museum, I developed a special friendship with its director, Lisa Taylor. She was working with the Smithsonian Institution in Washington D. C. to create the National Museum of Design based on the Cooper-Hewitt Collection. The Carnegie Mansion adjacent to the previous repository for the collection was being refurbished for a grand opening.

It was at this opening when I made a society column notice about waltzing around the Director Lisa Taylor wearing the George Stavropoulos chiffon trousers that he created for me to match the navy blue gown he made for her for this event. She introduced me to everyone who might be helpful on my path. Lisa was particularly interested to meet Lila Tyng, whom she considered a rare, unusual woman. Lisa was supportive of my efforts both as a lecturer and a curator of design exhibitions.

I was commissioned to deliver a lecture on 400 years of the history of costume and scenic invention (including the various court theaters of Europe) at the Cooper-Hewitt Museum on both September 29th and 30th, 1979, and—by popular request—again on January 19th and 20th, 1980. This was the first time that the museum repeated a program; both times it was sold out! By drawing on original designs from the museum collection on exhibit during my talk, together with my slides covering four centuries of design history and my text for the court theaters, a very comprehensive presentation resulted. Towards the end of my talk, I introduced Ruth Warrick, who was glad to comment on her experiences both on stage and film relating to designers. This added a bit of *crème chantilly* to the talk.

At the museum, a new curator for decorative arts was appointed. I met him at one of the museum openings and immediately felt empathy for this charming young man who had a noticeable limp. He was a polio victim. David (wouldn't you know?) had a warm, intense gaze and was full of animated conversation; his knowledge was prodigious and his personality very winsome. We had an immediate rapport, and left the party together.

Philip van Rensselaer once wrote a book about his mother, *Mother Was Always in Love*. I have often thought that maybe I always had the need to be in love. Partially despite his withered leg, or maybe because of it, I had strong feelings for this unusual man named David. We began an intense whirlwind relationship. He adored Lila and enjoyed examining her silver treasures with her—explaining various stamped markings—and took particular interest in the decorative adornments at Lu Shan.

Lisa and Bert sometimes came to visit David and me at either his apartment or mine, after Lila finally closed "480" in favor of a smaller one shared with me. We considered their visit a great honor as they had invitations everywhere but would favor us with an impromptu drop in from time to time. David came to East Hampton with me to visit Walter Herlitschek, who had entertained me over the years at his home there. The enormous, well-tended lawns with old shade trees and the lovely large homes set back from the road always impressed me as being the height of good taste and quiet elegance. It was bicycling there along Long Lane when I felt the sadness of David's affliction, as he pedaled as best he could with only one strong leg. I had not paid enough attention to his handicap when I suggested bike riding. It was the favorite mode of transportation in East Hampton for me during the many visits there over the years. I should have known better, but my long established habit of riding around those lanes overshadowed my discernment. Graciously, David never complained or mentioned his discomfort.

David and I determined that between his keen knowledge and my connections, we had many advantages working in our favor. Jokingly, I was Eva to his Zsa Zsa Gabor. Together we could achieve a sense of security and enjoy an abundant life style, but—early on—I was aware of David's wandering eye and temptation to sample fresh pleasures. Clearly, I needed to watch him, as fidelity did not seem to be his strong trait.

One distressing element was David's dislike for Ysabel, who had returned with obvious signs of ill-health from Colombia, where she felt stifled and very uncomfortable. True, she did not look her best—propped up in bed, low on energy, and without attention to any cosmetic repairs. In fact, she appeared enervated. Bed ridden, suffering internal pain and lacking her usual verve and magic, she distressed him. David had not a small favorable response nor a jot of sympathy. He was glad to escape the atmosphere there and offered no support to my agonizing position. He had not known the vibrant Ysabel; he only saw a wreck of an aging, alcoholic woman.

Ysabel's doctor son, the "dwarf" (6'3"), Alberto had rented a relatively inexpensive apartment in the upper Eighties off of Third Avenue for his mother's use. It was a dull brick modern building in an undistinguished neighborhood. He could claim it as professional in-town office space and take it off his income tax. He worked with a hospital in White Plains, New York, not too distant so that he could monitor his mother's precarious condition.

It had been necessary to perform surgery on Ysabel for compounded medical complaints. During the operation, her heart had stopped and now she was dying. Ysabel told me later that she remembered coming out of her body and looking down at the doctor over her on the table. "He is not fucking me right," she thought! She was revived, but a zipper was put into her chest for immediate future access.

It was a sad apartment with only remnants of her things around, things she felt a particular fondness for—her purple oval bed, the black Coromandel writing desk, and some decorative items from her previous life on Fifth Avenue.

I went most days to tend her needs, sometimes spending the night on the couch in the living room. One day, Ysabel requested I bring her something in which to relieve herself. She was too weak to get up and I could not manage lifting her dead weight to the bathroom and back. As Alberto never brought a bedpan for his mother's comfort, nor provided a nurse, I assumed responsibility as much as possible. I went into the kitchen and returned with a flat frying pan. Ysabel looked horrified! "Not a frypan pan, darling, the silver bowl!" Despite the crenellated edging on the silver bowl that had to irritate her backside, Ysabel preferred it to the very vulgar frying pan—even in her dilapidated, agonized state.

Ysabel had pleaded with her doctor-son to give her an injection to end all her suffering. He did nothing, and made no provisions for someone to help make her days more bearable. It really angered me, attributing it to his love-hate relationship with his mother. One morning, having just arrived at my apartment after a long night tending Ysabel, I wearily answered the ringing phone. It was Alberto. He announced, "Mother just died." I rushed back up to the apartment I left less than an hour before to find a most upset Alberto, and Ysabel dead in her purple oval bed.

Having gone through details relating to Uncle Monkey's death, I urged Alberto to take the Citibank card and remove the modest amount of cash there, giving him the code. The phone rang. It was John Githens and his artist wife, Ingeborg ten Haeff, who were deeply moved by my news. Ingeborg asked me if I would mind tracing Ysabel's hand, as she was doing a series of drawings on hands. She felt Ysabel's hand would be interesting in the collection. I declined, somewhat taken aback, and announced her body was being prepared for removal. The men had arrived with a black plastic body bag and gurney to wheel out Ysabel's remains, leaving me stunned at the efficiency of the body's disposal. Alberto being an officiating doctor helped facilitate matters.

Alberto gave me the small gold pre-Columbian eagle his mother always said was for me, together with some decorative items we decided I would enjoy having as remembrances. He collected her jewelry and items he thought his wife might like, and packed the silver chargers and silver jugs from the kitchen cabinets. He requested I dispose of her wardrobe, chests of drawers, and writing desk. Some of them would go to a local theater group I befriended for use as props, drawers for storage, and costumes. He would have the bed picked up later.

After the shock wore off some time later, I thought about Ysabel's pleas with Alberto to end her suffering. I remembered how he did nothing for days on end, not even supplying a bedpan. Then the thought developed that he planned to give Ysabel an injection, but it took time for him to summon the courage. That is why it seemed remiss of him to ignore her needs. He was preparing for the terrible deed. Finally, the deed was done at last.

He left to go to the bank, and John rushed in to comfort me. I opened a bottle of champagne to celebrate the life (and death) of Ysabel. I was becoming overwhelmed by her sudden death, so John offered to see me back home, taking the remaining unopened bottle with us. After some more bubbly and supportive conversation with John, I tearfully prepared to go out to Lu Shan for a more complete recovery.

At the small bar in the den at Lu Shan, I fixed myself a Scotch and soda and started across the Gothic Hall when Lila emerged from the dining room. She stopped and looked at me, then asked what had happened. When she received the news, Lila put her arms around me in consolation. Her German shepherd dog, Chou Chou, rubbed against my leg and from that moment on became MY dog. She would follow me around, sitting outside the French doors of whatever room I was in. We walked the wiggly path that day together. It was evident to me that Chou Chou responded to my sorrow and wanted to be a friendly comfort. In time, Chou-Chou had kidney failure and died. It was a loss to both Lila and myself as Chou-Chou really was a beloved fixture at Lu Shan.

One wintery night, a friend of Lila's appeared, bearing two very young wire-haired dachshunds. He gave one to Lila as a gift and only charged her for the other one. We were enchanted by the tiny newcomers, who slept in the plate warmer of the Haga stove (with the door carefully left open) at night. The staff were attentive, so that we could make trips without worrying about our new charges.

Liz and Fred join us at Lu Shan.

We pondered over what to name the brother and sister. I suggested Tristan and Isolde, or Siegfried and Seglinda. Lila was not fond of things German, so she resisted the notion. Our good brother and sister waltzing friends, Fred and Liz Fuller, finally gave us the solution. We asked them if they would mind if we called our new puppies after them. They were very delighted and always brought them gifts when they visited. Lila gave me the male, Fred; she kept Liz for herself.

The growing puppies brought much joy to Lu Shan, which was dimmed when they decided to explore what was at the end of the long driveway. Liz got in the way of a passing vehicle; Fred came back whimpering. We knew immediately what had happened. Fred grew into a star attraction at Lu Shan and occupied a very special part of my heart. When I was in residence, he either slept on top of the covers of my bed, or on a pillow on the floor beside the bed. We grew to be greatly dependent on each other and anticipated each other's moves. When I went on trips, he would be thrilled upon my return and leave the comfort of the kitchen help for my attentions.

To honor my birthday and celebrate the publication of *The Court Theaters of Europe*, Lila gave me a costume dinner-dance at Lu Shan. The invitations were from Lee Ping, Empress of China, and all Orientalia. She invited guests to attend as visiting royalty (preferably from the 18th century) to celebrate the birthday of King Gustav III of Sweden. It was a very serious undertaking to determine with appropriate finesse a diplomatic seating chart. Who was to sit on Marie Antoinette's left and right, for example? I took it extremely seriously, as though this fanciful

Portrait of Eric as King Gustav III of Sweden.

dress-up were a real life situation. *Soap Opera Digest* published Ruth Warrick's description of the frolicking royals, complete with color photographs. A friend of mine called me later to exclaim that she nearly fell over at the checkout counter at her supermarket when she came upon the amazing reportage of my birthday celebration.

More than ever, alcohol was a major factor in my daily life. It sustained me under stress, gave me courage in social situations, and boosted my spirits when doubt threatened to overwhelm me. It was my best friend during this whirlwind life of privilege and what others thought to be glamorous. It was hard to ignore the reality of what alcohol had done to my looks. I was bloated, with a swollen belly as though I had swallowed a volleyball. Sometimes, friends did not recognize me when we passed on the street.

Academy Award winner Celeste Holm and Ruth Warrick (Phoebe Tyler from All My Children) join founding president of Apollo Muses aboard the Barge under the Brooklyn Bridge for a concert and presentation of "Apollo's Lyre Award."

Chapter 15

HAVE AT IT SWEETIE, NATURE ABHORS A VACUUM!

The Kaleidoscopic World of Opera was a book developing in my imagination, and I decided it was worth pursuing. Interviews with various singers, conductors, and composers had been done before, but to add to the standard compilation insightful comments from administrative personnel, designers for costumes and scenic inventions, even the box office staff and stagehands, might make for a meaningful blend inherent in the complex creation of a staged opera.

My peripatetic life style brought me to places where opera flourished, and, being the networker I am, I had many contacts at the opera companies to facilitate this research. While Lila engaged in her summertime entertainments at Lu Shan, I headed west to Santa Fe on a special promotional Greyhound bus ticket permitting me unlimited travel for a month for something like $100. I went across the country and back, stopping along the way to visit with friends in Pittsburgh, St. Louis, Santa Fe, Los Angeles, and San Francisco.

With me was a portfolio of twenty erotic male oil pastels the executor of Douglass Semonin's estate asked me to try to sell while on my circuit. I was lent

Porter (as a hooker) sees me off in Santa Fe on my bus trip across America.

a guesthouse in the quiet village of Tesuque, close to the Santa Fe Opera. The main house had a side gallery that I had permission to use for viewing the art. It was a excellent place both to interview potential subjects for inclusion in my book as well as to exhibit the drawings when the right client came to visit.

Singers Evelyn Lear and her husband Thomas Stewart chatted with me about their career; Robert Lynn Batts Tobin discussed various involvements he had had with opera productions and bought one of the Semonin renderings; and Robert Earl Indiana talked with me about encouraging Tobin to buy his entire collection of designs for Gertrude Stein/Virgil Thomson's *Mother of Us All*, currently being performed at the Santa Fe Opera. (I did manage to have a lunch with Tobin at the Compound restaurant on Canyon Road, but did not pursue what the outcome was with Indiana as I was on the road soon afterwards.)

In the autumn, I saw Indiana at the Guggenheim Museum during an opening reception. He apologized for not being in touch with me. I made light of it, totally forgetting we had a verbal agreement of a commission for me should the sale materialize. As is my custom, we did not have a formal contract. I believe people gain integrity by doing the right thing; contracts are only as good as those who sign them. (When working with institutions, it is *de rigueur* to have contracts, and I gave artists whose work I took on consignment a receipt with terms of sale indicated. Otherwise, I like to count on the honesty of others and the value of their word.) A couple of years later, I noticed in Tobin's Park Avenue townhouse a printed catalogue with reproductions from *Mother of Us All*, in the Tobin Collection. Neither of them had informed me of the sale, and the commission is still outstanding, despite attempts on my part to get Indiana to pay what is owed to me. The sale was just under half a million dollars, so my commission was significant.

The final interview in Santa Fe for my projected book on the opera was with the dour founding director of the Santa Fe Opera, John Crosby, who was about to retire. Since our very first encounter in 1968, while I sat on the lawn at the newly constructed opera house by the swimming pool on "the ranch" (an area designated for relaxation with a cafeteria), we did not get along. Crosby had demanded to know what I was doing there. I coolly responded that I had an appointment to talk with designer Hal George, whose designs I was including in the exhibition being mounted in conjunction with the opening of the new opera. Now, years later, our interview was dull and forced, totally unusable.

A young Englishman, Richard Gaddes, was taking over as director. We had met in New York at a gay party given by costume designer John Hall in his West Side apartment. I had expressed my grave reservations about dealing with Crosby, and I later came to have the same feeling toward him when he assumed command. Ned Hall, a noted anthropologist in Santa Fe, once told me that the man at the top sets the tone for those under him. He used the example of generals in the US Army during World War II. Eisenhower's men were different from MacArthur's, and so on. I thought of this in the opera's offices when I passed John Crosby one morning, soon to be followed by Gaddes, and then their top aide, Carolyn Lockwood. Each of them had identical lemon-sucking expressions! In sharp contrast was the staff at the Seattle Opera. Director Speight Jenkins possessed a sunny disposition, as did each member of the staff whom I met while there.

My San Francisco experience was merry. The wig maker called himself "The Confidence Man," because his adept work instilled confidence in the singers by making them look their best. We both greatly enjoyed a "first of the day" tipple, so we arranged to meet at a bar open in the morning in the vicinity of the opera house. After the interview we started back to the opera house. I had hoped to interview Beverly Sills. He thought she was not scheduled to be there that morning, but up ahead I noticed the red mop of hair doubtlessly belonging to Miss Sills.

We greeted each other warmly. I had not seen her since our meeting in London when I requested she send me an autographed photo for inclusion on the wall of my "throne room's Hall of Fame." I suggested putting it between Harry Truman and Eric Bruhn. Weeks later, the photo arrived at Montrose, much to my utter pleasure. It graced the place of honor promised to her. I thanked her for her thoughtfulness while standing on the street in front of the opera house. She asked about how things were going in Santa Fe. When I suggested I include her in my *Kaleidoscopic World of Opera*, Beverly theatrically feigned shock and exclaimed, "I don't want to be in anything pornographic!" We both laughed.

My collection of interviews was pathetic, and I soon realized that though the idea was interesting, there was no hope of my bringing it to fruition. I had used it for validation to travel, while visiting genuine connections in the opera world. My efforts were not strong enough to make a truly interesting book. In retrospect, I felt stymied by the enormity of the project as well as incapacitated by the demands my best friend—alcohol—was making on my system. Though I had never attempted such an ambitious project before, my familiarity with the field of opera and my directorial capacities to blend fragments together into meaningful whole seemed a natural. Yet, I felt daunted and fearful. Alcohol guided me into seeking a safer harbor.

This was the first of two major incidents in my professional life where alcohol interfered with my writing. The second followed a few years later. After the monograph I wrote to accompany my slide lectures on *The Court Theaters of Europe* in 1982, it was suggested I contact Abbeville Press. Nina Abrams, wife of Harry Abrams, a prominent publisher of art books, thought my work could be developed into a larger version. We enjoyed a friendly, social relationship and had a few friends in common: Ysabel, Paul Stiga, and Marina Henderson, who had a design gallery in London. Nina recommended I visit with the two fellows who ran Abbeville Press, just up Park Avenue a couple of blocks north of Lila's "480" apartment. I think she had a family connection there, so a most agreeable meeting was set up.

After viewing the slides, hearing my enthusiastic comments on these court theaters, and perusing my monograph on the subject, both men decided it had the makings of a wonderful coffee table book. They suggested I work on expanding the material. Much to their surprise and disappointment, I turned the idea down. I realized that the amount of added research and rewriting outlined by them would interfere with my daily drinking routine. I had not taken this into consideration before going to the meeting. My hopes had been that they would either buy the rights to my concept and develop it themselves into a larger tome, or assign someone to collaborate with me. This did not transpire. The golden opportunity to have a beautiful and important definitive book published under my name would

Birth of "Designs for a Prima Donna: Dame Joan Sutherland" at Lincoln Center.

have established me as a leading authority in this field. Authors would kill for the chance to be published by a major New York publisher, but I felt unable and unwilling to take on the project. Doubtlessly, this was a major mistake, but I was too hampered to do otherwise. My creative compulsions would have to find other expressions.

A more viable application of my talents soon arose. Thanks to designer José Varona, who mentioned how he and his wife, Mary, spent time with Joan Sutherland and her conductor husband, Richard Bonynge, an idea emerged when he revealed that Joan maintained a personal collection of costumes. I conceived an exhibition tracing twenty-five years of her career, using these costumes as a focal point. Sutherland owned this large collection of costumes so she could perform with greater confidence. They fit correctly, were comfortable, and made her look her best. It was also a clever deduction for tax purposes, I speculated.

The idea of exhibiting the renderings of her costumes, together with the actual costumes, and how she looked in them through photographs, programs, and posters was compelling to me. I knew I had a winner and convinced the Robert Henderson, director of the Library for the Performing Arts at Lincoln Center, to sponsor this dynamic exhibition, with me as the curator. First, I had to get the approval of Sutherland and Bonynge, to whom I wrote a request for a meeting.

Joan Sutherland's secretary invited me to come backstage after a performance of *Don Giovanni* at the Met. Joan would be singing Donna Anna and Bonynge would be conducting. By some quirk of fate, when I took my seat in the opera house, I found my New Jersey neighbor, Catherine Farrelly, sitting next to me. She was intrigued by my upcoming adventure backstage with the great Joan Sutherland.

Usually when I went backstage at the Met after a performance, I would contrive to be at the beginning of the line waiting to speak with the artists. I knew from years of going to the Met how to gain easy access backstage through a door

Gown for La Traviata.

Lakmé costume.

downstage left in the house. It was much faster than going around to the stage door. This time, I purposely placed myself at the end of the line to see Dame Joan. In that way I might be afforded more time with her to discuss the projected exhibition. To my utter amazement, an usher went up and down the line paging me. When I acknowledged his page, he announced that Dame Joan Sutherland would not be seeing anyone else other than Mr. Gustafson that evening! The disappointed mob of well-wishers dispersed, and I—astonished, thrilled, and nervous—was ushered into her dressing room.

Dame Joan sat facing me. She rose with her hand extended in warm greeting. Out of her Donna Anna costume, she seemed comfortable and attentive to my presentation. Richard Bonynge appeared briefly, and he and I made an appointment to meet in the director's office at the library the next Tuesday at 11 a.m. "He's going for a night out with the boys," she said, as the handsome, trim Bonynge departed.

It was then that I blurted out my recollection of her pulling music stands down in Rome. Seemingly oblivious, Dame Joan smoothly led us into a discussion about my coming up to her place in Brooklyn near the Botanical Gardens to make final choices of the costumes she owned for loan to the exhibition. Brooklyn seemed an unlikely place for a prominent conductor and his opera star wife to live, but it was explained to me. An elderly friend of the Bonynges owned a town house, and leased the top two floors to them. As they were not in residence much of the year, it was a convenient home for them when needed. It was a rapid drive from the Met to their door and a quiet place to rest while in residence.

Maestro Bonynge met with me in Henderson's office on Tuesday and the deal was sealed, but not without his having a long, awkward wait for me. I remember my frustration trying to get over from Ysabel's Fifth Avenue apartment to Lincoln Center with the Puerto Rican Day Parade going full tilt. I entered the office panting after jogging most of the way across the park. I was more than an hour late. Bonynge was patiently reading a newspaper. If he was miffed, he did not show it. We proceeded in a pleasant manner, signing a contract of agreement with the library.

When I went to visit Dame Joan at her Brooklyn duplex later that week, her first comment was that she heard I kept her husband waiting for more than an hour. "Well, that's good for him!" she said, with a gentle amusement in her warm, Australian accented voice.

As I noticed that her figure in a day dress was unusual, I could appreciate her wanting to wear only costumes made especially to her needs. Seeing her in her green woolen dress, I could appreciate her large frame and broad hips but demure bust. We sat in comfortable chairs in her unpretentious and comfortable living room. We could have been in Sydney. It was on the third floor of the townhouse, with a pleasant view of the park across the street.

Since I was planning a trip to Italy, we discussed the possibility of meeting up in Rome in the coming months to handle details about the forth-coming exhibition.

Dame Joan was going to sing the title role in *Lucrezia Borgia* at the Rome Opera House and invited me to attend. I felt very gratified by the arrangements and looked forward to these impending events. The contract with the library seemed to cover the pertinent details: insurance, dates of exhibition, and pick-up/return of costumes and designs on loan. The library covered installation costs, but I was to cover the catalogue expenses. A small stipend for me was determined. All seemed rosy and wonderful.

The popular opera commentator on WQXR, George Jellinek, said he would use on his program a taped interview with Sutherland to intersperse with recordings of her voice, if I would provide the tape. I had already arranged to meet Sutherland and Bonynge in Rome. Congruity of projected programs melded nicely. Ruth Warrick was the long-time reigning star of the very popular *All My Children* daytime soap opera on television. Aware of my felicitous trip to Italy with R.C. Gorman and his teenage nephew, showing them the highlights of Rome, Florence, and Venice the previous year, she commissioned me to do the same trip with her, all expenses paid. Ruth's character, Phoebe Tyler, was about to marry Professor Wallingford and go on their honeymoon. This coincided with Ruth's vacation, so she arranged for the scriptwriters to follow our itinerary with their scripted TV honeymoon while we moved about Italy. The characters on the soap opera talked about Phoebe's honeymoon, while Ruth and I vacationed in accordance to their commentary.

Added to our itinerary, at Ruth's request, were a few days on Lake Como at the Villa D'Este. On occasion, we were stopped on the street by visiting Americans.

Joan Sutherland as Donna Anna in Don Giovanni.

They were thrilled to see Phoebe there and wondered if she had left the show. Not at all, she would announce; she was on her honeymoon, locking her arm into mine and smiling tenderly at me!

Joan Sutherland had arranged tickets for Ruth and me at the Rome Opera. Having been told by a good friend traveling with the Bonynges that Ruth Warrick was a very accomplished and distinguished performer, Joan was interested in meeting my actress friend. Joan professed not to have acting ability more than tossing a cape over one shoulder, so she expressed an awe at Ruth's talent. Ruth and Joan hit it off immediately upon meeting, making it easier the next day, when we were to lunch at the old fashioned, sedate Ranieri's restaurant in Rome. After lunch we would be going nearby to a convenient place that the Bonynges had arranged to record the tape for use on WQXR.

Sutherland and Bonynge had a very clever way of leaving the opera house without being mobbed by autograph seekers and photographers. Their friend would take a batch of signed color photos of the opera star and distribute them on the opposite side of the lobby from where the limousine awaited us. While he diverted the crowd, we would enter the vehicle and be ready to depart when he managed to join us in the limo.

With the tape containing the precious interview secured, Ruth and I made our way to Florence. We stayed at my usual Berchielli Hotel along the Arno River and accepted an invitation to lunch at Sir Harold Acton's villa *La Pietra* in nearby Fiesole. The English side of his family had had diplomatic ties with Italy for a couple of centuries, living in this old palatial villa most of that time. Thanks to our mutual acquaintance with Lila and her great friend, Mary Hyde (soon to be the dowager Viscountess Eccles), Sir Harold always invited me to either lunch or tea at his *La Pietra* when I came to Florence. I surmised he enjoyed the company of attractive gay men, knowing something of his membership in the Bloomsbury group and his being the prototype for Sebastian in Evelyn Waugh's *Brideshead Revisited* (later filmed on location at Castle Howard).

After a scrumptious lunch served by his white-gloved retainer, Sir Harold graciously escorted Ruth around the formal gardens of clipped box wood, interspersed with statuary and even an outdoor theater. As all the guests seemed to be going outdoors, I thought it polite to stay behind to keep company with the aged Helen, Queen Mother of Romania, who sat herself down in the enormous marbled entry hall. She commented on how young I was; I think she bestowed the compliment of my being twenty-one, probably based on my youthful gait. Forgetting what David Wallace once instructed me about not contradicting royalty or the Pope, I corrected her. That was a regrettable blunder. She started to bang the marble floor with her cane. "I guess I am just a blind old woman!" she exclaimed, her voice resounding loudly in the large hall in which we were seated.

Sir Harold had a most attractive American young man in his thirties staying at *La Pietra*. Ruth and I invited him back to our hotel for a visit, since he wanted to spend some time in Florence. I took a posed photo of him giving Ruth an embrace on the balcony of her room with the Arno and a bridge across it in the background. It was used in Soap Opera Digest as part of Phoebe's honeymoon in Italy. (A glamorous shot of Ruth and me enjoying a gondola ride along the Grand Canal in Venice was included in that piece, as well. Phoebe's TV husband was on his own vacation elsewhere.) I thought our visitor might enjoy seeing my room and small garden terrace, too. While there, I proudly pointed out the tape with the Sutherland interview, indicating it was worth its weight in gold. By the next day, I realized that the tape was gone. While this mystery was never solved, I did manage to convince Sutherland and Bonynge to do another taping with me when I visited them in San Diego that autumn, before the opening of the exhibition.

Joan Sutherland and Beverly Sills in their only appearance performing together.

For the only time in opera history, Beverly Sills and Joan Sutherland appeared together for a performance of *Der Fledermaus* in San Diego, California. I had learned from previous experience that if I wanted Joan Sutherland to do anything, I should ask Rickie Bonynge to arrange it. Otherwise, she would say NO! This applied to doing a tape to replace the former one. Along with me in San Diego was a limited edition of photographs of Sutherland in three costumes Photoshopped together so that she appeared as three operatic characters on one photo. I wanted her to sign each of these. They would be sold for a modest price, sized to fit in the accordion-folded catalogue. I had twenty posters featuring a blowup of the same photo to be signed as well. All of this was accomplished.

My biggest concern was that I could run into both divas at the same time. Who would I greet first without offending the other? There was no need to worry, as it did not happen. Joan would greet me with a mock punch in the arm; Beverly always had a hug for me. At different times backstage, both inscribed to me the only photo I know of with the two divas together.

It took a year of planning, but at long last *Designs for a Prima Donna: Dame Joan Sutherland* opened at the Library for the Performing Arts at Lincoln Center on October 7th, 1980. I did achieve my original idea for an exhibition documenting twenty-five years of the professional life of one of the most extraordinary opera stars: Dame Joan Sutherland. The largest exhibition put on at the library to date, it used the entire main gallery.

Joan did not like the accordion-folded catalogue I created, but I firmly impressed upon her that I had to do it as inexpensively as possible, since I was paying for it, not the library. As my funds were very limited, I opted for this format. She asked why I chose Lord Harewood to write the introduction. I responded simply because Lord Harewood, Director of the English National Opera Company in London, was considered Mr. Opera in England. He had been on the scene when Joan Sutherland made her earliest appearances there. I was delighted when he agreed to write an introduction to the program for the exhibition. (I gathered after her inquiry that there was little affection between the two, with a snide hint of that in his introduction as well.)

Time was running out before the printing of the catalogue and I had not received Lord Harewood's introduction. I nervously decided to cover my bases by asking the Italian designer and director, Franco Zeffirelli, to write an introduction, as well. It turned out both of them responded, giving me two introductions for inclusion in the exhibition catalogue, together with separate sheets listing every role she performed, with dates and places, and the designers of the costumes on exhibition.

Getting the final touches to the mounting of the exhibition proved more complicated than it should have been. The in-house staff had some resentment about an outside curator coming in, especially for such a major exhibition. Stumbling blocks were put in place, thwarting progress. Once I had a couple of professional costume shop people come in to assist me with the pressing of the costumes. They were willing to work into the night, but the regular staff locked us out. Sometimes, I found mistakes in the labeling, but they went uncorrected despite my supplying the corrections.

Against all odds, the result was spectacular, if one ignored small details such as labeling. Rickie Bonynge confided to me over breakfast in San Diego that he and Joan had heard only raves about the exhibition, even from "the queens from Melbourne who criticize everything." He later wrote me a letter of thanks from their Chalet Monet in Switzerland after the exhibition had closed stating: "We have heard nothing but praise and positive comments about the exhibition from everyone we know who went to it." However, Joan had a fit when I sent her installation shots that indicated the Daughter of the Regiment costume without a crinoline. Her friend, and sometimes costumer, Barbara Matera, had neglected to plump up the skirt with a crinoline, but to take the huge plexiglass walls down would be a costly effort because of union stipulations. I opted to leave the skirt remain as is, especially as very few would notice this detail. Joan fumed . . .

Every day I was present to promote the exhibition and host visitors. The Metropolitan Opera national council members and other VIPs attended, with an invitation resulting for me to give two talks to Asolo Opera members in Sarasota, Florida.

Later, in her autobiography, Joan mentioned the time and effort her intimate friend, Barbara, had expended on this exhibition. She was either misinformed or it was wishful thinking. Barbara spent a minimal amount of time helping me—certainly under an hour, at best. On the other hand, I got very little credit in her book as the exhibition's creator, whose work was slavish in getting it into place, involving—among other things—doing the publicity and promotion, as well as creating the program and its layout.

Our relations had already become very strained as a result of their taking it upon themselves to use my idea of producing a book based on the exhibition but excluding me, without even telling me their intention to run with my idea. As a result of my suffering major burns, I had postponed my creating the book commemorating this exhibition of Joan Sutherland's illustrious career. After a Grolier Club reception, I had asked my Montrose neighbor, Bob Long, who was the chief librarian at the Bronx Botanical Gardens, to come around the corner to nearby "480" for a bowl of pasta and a glass of wine. I took off my dinner clothes and donned a light silk robe.

In a hurry to get water to boil, I used the pressure cooker. Never having used one before, I did not know that the steam had to be released before opening the lid. Fortunately, I had the lid in my right hand, and happily it shielded my face, but the boiling hot steam burned the right side of my body through the flimsy robe. I held a precious unopened bottle of red wine in my left hand, hoping that it would not break as I watched it fall slow motion to the kitchen floor. My dinner assignation was supplanted by a visit to the Lenox Hill emergency ward, where I was flayed (to prevent scarring) by a sympathetic doctor.

It would take weeks of recovery, with singular discomfort. I wrote Rickie Bonynge about this mishap. Though it would delay work on my book about the exhibition, I would make certain that the costumes were returned in good order to their Brooklyn residence at the end of the exhibition. He responded with sympathy, and directed that when I returned Joan's costumes to their flat in Brooklyn, I should not attempt to hang them up as not to aggravate my healing wounds. Leaving them lying in the center of the sitting room would be fine, he instructed.

Unbeknownst to me, Joan and Rickie gathered the elements necessary to recreate my exhibition in book form. They owned the costumes and most of the designs, so the material, together with a text, was only needing organization to be ready for printing. I was astonished when a good friend called to announce that the Bonynges had published my book idea, while I was recuperating from the burns. They neglected even to give me a mention.

Upon discovery of their publishing "my" book, I wrote them a letter congratulating them of the very expensive, printed-in-Japan edition of the *Designs for a Prima Donna*. I noted that it was a compliment to me that they liked my concept so well that they produced it themselves, and even used my title (titles cannot be copyrighted). However, I was very disappointed in their oversight in not crediting me for anything. I requested a copy for the Apollo Muses library, but did not receive either the book or a reply.

My lawyer advised me that, although I had sufficient evidence to prove the book was my idea, it would be very expensive to sue and it would create great negative energy. I decided to get on with life, but mention at appropriate times to those in the performing arts circle my experience with Sutherland and Bonynge. After relating my woeful tale, it was amazing how many people would say, "You think that's bad? Wait 'til you hear what she did to me!" There was even a blog site that collected Sutherland abuses. I ignored joining in with my own blog, but thought karma would take care of it all—and I could always write about it someday . . .

The farm at Lu Shan had been in disuse for years. It was an atmospheric space that I felt would be ideal to exhibit a group showing of New Jersey artists, both in the barns and outside. The barns were in various states of disrepair but very romantic and inviting for visitors to view the works of local talents. I selected work by New Jersey artists and proceeded to organize the presentation. During the exhibition, an art critic asked me if I had ever considered turning this remarkable area into a performing arts center. The idea resonated with me, so I approached Lila with the notion.

"Have at it sweetie, nature abhors a vacuum," she cheerfully responded. Though overwhelmed by the impending fate of becoming an impresario with no track record other than running galleries, I began the arduous tasks in preparing for this immense undertaking.

After determining what to call my enterprise, my first task was to get recognized by the state as a nonprofit organization. I went to the State House in Trenton with preliminary papers to register an official name. My car was parked in a meter ticking away close to the entrance, so I had to register quickly. It turned out the name I first wanted to call the arts organization was not available, so needing a drink and a toilet quickly, I grabbed "Apollo Muses" out of my agonized brain, and never regretted this stroke of good judgment. Apollo was the leader of the nine muses, each of whom represented the various arts. I intended to present programs of mixed disciplines in the arts, so it all seemed very good sense to breathe life into Apollo Muses.

The task of achieving tax-exempt status was more complicated. Thanks to a sympathetic gay lawyer who liked champagne, I managed to get the paperwork completed and approved after some diplomatic maneuvering through legal channels.

Lila agreed to lease me the three barns and farmhouse for $1 per year, which was an enormous help. Everything needed repairs, as well as the barns requiring a major cleaning, before any performances could be held, however. Oscar Murillo, a young Costa Rican man we invited to come to work at Lu Shan while Lila and I spent writing time there, was a constant help organizing the farm buildings. He helped me splash paint abstractions in the style of Jackson Pollock drippings on rolled-out tar paper to be tacked on the machinery barn roof to protect against rainy leaks where the concerts would be held. It was the fastest and cheapest way to make something so inherently ugly both decorative and interesting. The machinery barn was open on the barnyard side, and semi-open on the side facing out over the fields with trees in the distance.

In the large red barn there was a raised area, where a stage was built, complete with proscenium, designed and constructed by a design student located at NYU theater department. Talks, plays, and lecture demonstrations were to be held here. The front portion was for art exhibitions and refreshments.

Thanks to comestible donations from local supermarkets and food purveyors, a simple lunch of cold pasta salad, mixed salad, and cold cuts was to be offered gratis near the tall silo and machinery barn in the barnyard before the concert. This would encourage people to arrive before the concert began, avoiding car door slamming or motor sounds during the performances. It set the tone for the day. Striped blue and white umbrellas at round tables with folding chairs gave a festive touch to the scene. These helped provide visitors with a friendly atmosphere

Luncheon on the terrace at Lu Shan Farm before Apollo Muses events.

Celeste Holm, Toshiko Takaezu, Jerome Hines on the Barge under the Brooklyn Bridge attending an Apollo Muses program.

in which to enjoy nature and each other as well as prepare themselves for the three programs offered that Sunday.

Choosing every Sunday at noon for the season made it easy for visitors to remember both time and day. A break for ice tea and cookies between programs gave everyone a chance to stretch and socialize. I set up a modest gift shop in a small shed near the red barn for those wanting to buy local pottery, artwork, and books by local writers, including myself.

Each Sunday, three disciplines were enjoyed: classical music (either chamber music or soloists with piano or harpsichord), art (discussed by a painter, sculptor, weaver, or potter) and a demonstration of ballet or acting, or a talk relating to the arts. Celebrated artists were in attendance and sometimes appeared as speakers. Ruth Warrick, Celeste Holm, Jerome Hines, Toshiko Takaezu, and many other illustrious, world-renowned talents participated.

However, Apollo Muses programs were primarily to be showcases for young professional artists. My music director, Hugh Keelan, would canvass the New York scene for musicians. I invited winners at the Opera at Florham and the New Jersey Symphony youth auditions to perform. Both performers and subscribers enjoyed the relaxed but stimulating atmosphere. The easy mingling between all made for a warm, enriching experience.

Admission was kept at a minimum, affordable to any pocketbook. I insisted on keeping attendance to forty or under to insure intimacy, avoiding arena type events. A local journalist Michael Redmond asked me if I thought these programs were elitist, for the chosen few. I retorted it was not for the chosen few, but for the few who chose. These *bon mots* made their way into the major press as part of a large coverage about Apollo Muses.

Apollo Muses created an opportunity for people to enjoy a lively communication with the arts in a natural setting without having to travel to New York; the artists, many of whom lived in New Jersey, did not have to travel to venues in the city to perform. Saving time, tolls, parking fees, and restaurant costs made an afternoon at the Lu Shan Farm an attractive and enriching experience for all.

Once or twice a year, Lila would host a gala dinner concert at Lu Shan as a fundraiser for Apollo Muses. Her Louis XV chinoiserie-papered salon was perfect for musicales. It came complete with a carved mahogany 1916 Steinway grand piano. Illuminated by candles and low-intensity electric lights behind the stained glass windows, the Gothic Hall made an impressive dining hall environment for the forty formally attired guests. A curved stairway led to the balcony in one corner, beside the massive stone fireplace with a carved wooden doorway on the other side leading to the actual Venetian dining room. Tapestries and paintings, with French doors to the gardens, completed the impressive impact on guests in the high-beamed expanse of Gothic Hall.

The banquet and concert in this *recherché* grandeur was always eagerly attended, contributing to the coffers of Apollo Muses. Government grants, donations from corporations, foundations, and local businesses infused financial health, as well. Wealthy neighbors gladly sent tax-deductible checks, some with notes expressing their regrets that they could not attend, as horseback riding, bridge playing, or other demanding social commitments interfered with concert or lecture going. I went to the bank pleased with the knowledge that there was more room for others who wanted very much to avail themselves of the Apollo Muses experience. So, everyone was happy! Lila was especially pleased to be a major participant in the midst of these activities, as was her "little brother," who thrived on the complexity of running the arts center.

Though concerts and cultural events had been presented about ten years before at Lu Shan, in 1985 Apollo Muses became officially a not-for-profit organization that could function within the USA. While the barns were being prepared and readied for performances, I began with a few modest afternoons at Lu Shan. Programs were given at museums and libraries, as well. The summer of 1987 was the official opening of Apollo Muses Center of the Arts held at the Lu Shan Farm. That first season, to make a strong initial impact, I planned ten consecutive summer Sundays. It nearly drained me of all energy, but it generated much favorable publicity and developed an enthusiastic following.

I arranged to have each concert recorded for educational TV use and won an award for that effort. I bought a collection of colored jackets to wear, so that I would host each program in a different ensemble. Many of these pastel jackets still hang in my closet, now largely neglected. A nucleus of musicians began to bond; future seasons offered familiar faces who had warmed to each other in performance. I believe musicians who know each other's idiosyncrasies can perform better as a result. English-born Hugh Keelan, the first music director, later went on to

To my good friend and colleague, Eric—
JEROME HINES ...AS... **BORIS GODUNOV**
MET BASSO   Jerry Hines   John 14:6

Opera star and colleague Jerome Hines.

become the conductor of the Scranton Symphony in Pennsylvania. That is how it was supposed to be. Apollo Muses provided the exposure young performers needed to achieve further professional success. Pianist Frank Daykin became a popular attraction and directed the musical programs in the coming years.

My good friend Bruce Whitacre, budding playwright, had written a play with the leading character inspired by my preoccupation with Gustav III of Sweden and the 18th century, using my life at 480 Park Avenue as a backdrop. *Gentile from the Top Percentile* had been produced at a small theater on 42nd Street with me in the front row center wearing my white powdered wig. I knew the actor impersonating me would be wearing one, so I thought I had the privilege being the authentic personage to don it, too. It startled the performer, who had no idea who I was or why I was wearing the powdered wig to the performance.

It seemed appropriate to offer Bruce and his cast the opportunity to perform this play at Lu Shan as part of one of the Sunday programs. This time, I only donned the wig after the play, during the question/answer period with the playwright.

The Masque of Apollo, also written by Bruce, was performed for Apollo Muses audiences. It was comprised of two amusing playlets, one involving the oracle of Delphi with Zeus (audaciously played by me), Apollo, and a golden apple. In the other, I took the role as Louis XIV, in golden slippers with red heels, preciously performing a court dance to the hilarity of the audience. I employed my previous studies in theater arts to direct both of these playlets.

The New Jersey Shakespeare Company came for a lecture demonstration as did the New Jersey Ballet on a few occasions over the years. Eli Wallach's actress wife, Anne Jackson, appeared to read the poetry of Elizabeth Bishop, with glamorous Ruth Warrick and Celeste Holm often in evidence. Performers enjoyed participating in Apollo Muses' programs because of the lovely setting, unusual programming, and the receptivity of the intimate audience. It was a pleasurable way for everyone to spend a lovely Sunday afternoon in the country.

Accolades for Apollo Muses and its founding director from two venerable stars of yesteryear.

To Erie — Blessing
Helen Hayes

Helen Hayes as Queen Victoria.

(Way Down East photo from Vincent Virga collection)

*"Congratulations on all your deserved success.
Ever fondly, Lillian Gish"*

My "Hall of Fame" in the throne room at Montrose.

Chapter 16

GET YOUR ASS OVER TO BETTY FORD

GAILY LIT BOULEVARDS
(A Monologue)

I suppose
The culmination
Was that morning
When I looked into a mirror
And saw a bloated aging queen
With only the slightest resemblance
To my mind's image of myself.

The total of the various experiences
Afforded by a-quart-of-a-day rampages
Flooded my consciousness.
There was a mixture of delicious mad abandon
Tinged with embarrassing, aggressive bad taste:
A magic horror show!

It seemed at that moment—
The only moment possible—
The decision had to be made.
It was time
To hang up those roller skates.

I was thoroughly tired of careening
Down gaily lit boulevards
Only to find myself
At some dead end,
Or in a darkened alley—
Usually with someone
I did not really want to be with!

Gaily lit boulevards can be fun
With all those vibrations,
Alluring inducements promising the unattainable,
Scintillating illusions,
Shimmering aspirations,
Nightmarish loss of control or proportion—
A topsy-turvy world
With little meaning
Outside of the quest for fresh pleasure
And an insatiable thirst.

Broken roller skates make a horrible sound.
Direction is lost and perhaps unimportant.
The lights blur,
Swim before the careening figure.
Few notice or seem to care.
The pulse continues;
Echoes fade
With new voices
Soon to add to the sum memory of
Inconsequentia.

There is no winner in this marathon block party.
Endurance
With grace
Is the badge inconspicuously worn
By the least of the losers.

After writing "Gaily Lit Boulevards," I buried myself in the sheets of my bed in Montrose and did not come out for a day. I felt flayed and exhausted. . . .

During this period, my love affair with alcohol sustained me (or so I thought) in coping with the enormity of the task of coordinating a complicated virgin run of Apollo Muses' initial season on the Lu Shan Farm. Many people had tried to suggest I get help to control my drinking problem. It was to no avail, as I found such comments irritating and foolish. (Lila later told me she did not believe any pressure from her would have been of any use, so she kept quiet.) How could I give up my best friend, alcohol? How could I get through the day without terrible anguish, assuaged only by drink? I believed I needed the flow to keep me on keel, giving me the support and courage to face the pressures of my lifestyle. I contemplated the idea of succumbing to a dramatic death—as so many artists had before me, but my life continued. There had been three out-of-body experiences that scared me. From a corner of the ceiling, I could see me on my bed, with the vodka bottle on the floor underneath and the TV image rolling. Though I had heard it could be wonderful to wander about outside roaming, I wanted only to regain being in my body. This seemed an effective warning that I was dying.

However, I didn't die! I was convinced there must be a reason for this and pondered it long afterwards—with my flare for the dramatic, I wondered if this was this some kind of divine plan involving my participation down the road? I recalled Elizabeth Taylor's admonition to R.C. Gorman while she was visiting

A guest of Elizabeth Taylor in her dressing room after a performance of "The Little Foxes."

her brother in Taos: "Get your ass over to Betty Ford's!" R.C. heard, but I went! In "La Marchesa la Marchetta," which is archived in the Beinecke Library at Yale University in New Haven, Connecticut, I elaborate on R.C.'s and my long association, including meetings with Elizabeth Taylor.

Aside from the filming of *Cleopatra* in Rome, Elizabeth and I had met when R.C., his nephew and I were in New York after our Italian holiday. We were her guests at *Little Foxes*, in which she starred on Broadway. I thanked her then for keeping Richard Burton busy in Rome so that I could use all his tickets, but she smoothly avoided comment. I expected her to roar her big laugh but did not get a response. Another time, we had a surprise meeting in a box at the Met to see Baryshnikov perform, with a dinner dance to follow. Her bodyguard frisked me at the dance, but not, for some strange reason, before, within the box at the opera. Also, with R.C., I conversed with her brother in Taos and almost said something impertinent to his wife when she knocked New Jersey. It certainly was agreeable for Elizabeth to visit Malcolm Forbes, my neighbor, when he presented her with a million dollar check for AIDS research.

William Hurt had just won the Oscar for best actor in *Kiss of the Spider Woman*. Bill and Lila mutually adored each other. He was the stepson of Lila's oldest son, Hank, but neither of them shared a fondness for each other. Bill's mother was Hank's second wife, but like all of Henry's four wives, she died of pancreatic cancer. Last time I saw Bill, he was passed out on the floor under a chandelier at Lu Shan. I called him to congratulate him on winning the award, and to comment on how well he looked. Bill told me I should do what he did: get help! He went to the clinic that The Betty Ford Clinic was modeled on, the Hazelton Rehabilitation Center in Minnesota.

William Hurt visits Lu Shan.

His suggestion, together with the admonition from the empress of the cinema, caused me to pay attention for once. I decided to heed their advice and haul myself over to Betty Ford's clinic at the Eisenhower Memorial Hospital at Rancho Mirage in the Palm Springs area.

Meanwhile, after the first season of ten Sundays at Lu Shan was completed, a commemorative video cassette was created. A splicing of highlights from the various performances with inspiring views of the farmland locale were effectively blended into a charming presentation that I sent to major sponsors at Christmastime, as a reminder of our growing establishment in the community, thanks to their generous support. The film began with my commentary from the Louis XV salon, and it ended with me, dressed as Santa Claus, exuberantly pouring a glass of champagne from an extravagant height with an intoxicated whoop! It is this videocassette, without the Santa Claus antics, that won the TV award for the best cultural achievement in New Jersey.

This film was shown while I was at The Betty Ford Clinic that winter. My counselor used the film to indicate alcoholic behavior run riot. The performance scenes at the farm and of the farm had charm, but my outrageous Santa Claus antic was tasteless. While it was being filmed with me heavily under the influence, I thought it vastly amusing. I only realized after some weeks in recovery, when the film was shown to my bemused fellow inmates, how embarrassing and inappropriate my behavior had been.

My denial had begun to disintegrate into a full acceptance of my need for rehabilitation; though I previously had realized I had become extremely bloated, I now could no longer choose to ignore it or forget my pitiable state any longer. Change through sober, spiritual living was taking hold as a viable option. Finally!

My entrance into The Betty Ford Clinic was not a direct one from New Jersey. I had to fly there from the L.A. airport, which was near Santa Monica, and I permitted myself a stopover to visit with Phyllis Nugent. The night before my flight to Palm Springs, Stephen Garrett, the director of the Getty Museum in Malibu,

invited Phyllis and me to dinner in a toney restaurant in Venice, just south of Santa Monica. I suffered high anxiety about being committed to The Betty Ford Clinic the next day. A few drinks did not quell my tension. Feeling rebellious, upon departing the eatery, I lowered my trousers in front of the window of the restaurant, mooning the diners. Stephen ignored my "last hurrah," while Phyllis giggled nervously. It was my pathetic alcoholic method of dealing with the anger/hostility/futility of my state anticipating the unknown.

An elderly attendant from the clinic was at the airport awaiting me. I could recognize him from his white

Phyllis Babbitt Nugent, my great friend sees me off to The Betty Ford Clinic.

uniform with red and blue insignia. I ducked into the men's room for a few gulps of Stolichnaya from my silver pocket flask. In the BFC buggy, I heard an ongoing testimonial about the wonders of the clinic as we progressed along the desert road, arrayed with flowering bushes, swaying palms, and with lovely mountains rimming the horizon. He informed me how all employees there were alcoholics in recovery, so they knew every trick in the book resorted to by the patients.

I mounted the few steps to the large, plate glass doors leading into the large, attractive reception room of The Betty Ford Clinic. Soon, I was led into an office and seated at a desk where a young, attractive young woman received me. While faced with the boredom of filling out entrance forms, I decided another snort of vodka would be greatly appreciated. I asked the young woman if it were possible to get a sandwich while waiting to be admitted, and could I have that glass behind her head on the shelf? She inquired why I wanted the glass. I showed her the silver flask and said I would be very happy to have a festive drink before I was admitted. Shocked, she snatched the flask out of my hand and announced I was already admitted!

The jungle drums began beating that a live one was in the admittance room. A young man who lived in North Hall came to bring me to the office of my residence for the next twenty-eight days. He told me my counselor was tough but very good at her work. When I met her in the office of North Hall, she asked if my name were Swedish. I assented it was; she said her family were Norwegian and proceeded to recite the tiresome bit about the one Norwegian chasing twenty Swedes through the weeds. I told her I had a good mind to give her a swift kick in the ass. The staff in the office grew very silent; she rose from bending over a file cabinet with a flushed face. "I am surprised you can still blush at your age . . ." I aggressively continued.

This was surprising behavior for me, as I was known to be cheerful and exuberant under the influence, not hostile and angry. My Sunday crowds at the Lu Shan Farm were charmed by my manner, my having infused a goodly supply of eye-openers and get-me-on-my feet libations. This situation was very different. My nervousness and fear of the impending unknown brought up the opposite side of the coin—anger.

Since I did not die, as the out-of-body experiences indicated I was close to doing, I felt there must be a good reason. Over the years, I had tried various ways of cutting down or not drinking at all. These were dismal failures after the first hours or days. I needed help to do what I could not do on my own. Perhaps there was a big lesson for me to learn, and to share with others if and when I could achieve sobriety. If I lost the support, comfort, and tyranny of my best friend, alcohol, how could I survive? This created immense tension and turmoil within me.

After initial paper work was completed, I was shown around the premises of North Hall. A pleasant patio faced a large lawn with trees, bushes, and lovely mountains on the horizon. A sitting room inside was where one could have coffee or tea and chat around a couple of tables. Carpeted hallways on either side of the office led to bedrooms, with a library in the front of the building near the main entrance. The place was comfortable and simple in its appointments.

The next day, my counselor arrived and, before beginning the group session, asked if anyone knew what she had around her neck. I volunteered it was a cheap Norwegian necklace. She wanted us to admire the fine Norwegian filigree work, trying to ignore my insulting comment.

We continued to lock horns. A few days later she told me, during a private evaluation, that I had so much armor on that she could not find a chink in which to start breaking down my barriers, to permit recovery to begin. If I did not cooperate with her, she would discharge me from the clinic, as there was a waiting list of people eager to be helped.

Finally, I changed my attitude and was ready to risk all and reveal myself. This was a puzzling task since I had spent so much time building up secure defenses. How does one just suddenly let go? It did seem odd that, when asked to list my character defects as part of the recovery program, I truly was unaware that I had any! Little by little, the skins of the onion began to peel off and I settled in wholeheartedly to work towards redemption. My group made me feel at home, comfortable, and safe. I quickly adjusted to rehab life, enjoying it along with the wonderful sleep I was beginning to be blessed with, going to bed sober. When I arrived, I looked as if I had swallowed a volleyball. The bulge from my enlarged liver began to diminish noticeably. I was regaining a vitality and exuberance that did not depend on alcohol. In weeks to come, I realized an emotion that I had never, ever experienced before. With careful examination, I realized I felt truly happy! It was exhilarating!

This was deeply soulful, in contrast to the Technicolor fantasies of my past. This was alcohol free, not a pumped up experience magnified by booze. This was an intimation of real happiness, a contentment in the moment!

Everyone was required to share a room; being alone was not an option. Recovery was aided by responsibly getting along with others and sharing in daily life. My roommate was the dreamboat of the entire campus. He was around forty, very handsome and well-built—a Southern gentleman with sensuality pouring out of him. Women enjoyed his intimacies on the sly, and some of the men tried to win his attentions, as well. I was told that no sexual activity was to be indulged in for one year, so I averted any suggestion on his part of hanky-panky. It was difficult and embarrassing once when he approached me stark naked while I was lying on my bed in conversation with him. I ignored his growing closer with his penis approaching my face. I made believe I was not paying attention to him, as I knew I would become yet another of his fawning acolytes; and, I was there for recovery, not sexual intimacies. I congratulated myself on my remarkable self-discipline. I realized how serious I was about getting well.

Instead of bedaucheries, I shared my tapes of Viennese waltzes in our pre-sleep session in the relaxing darkness. I talked of the Waltz Series, Lu Shan, and other glittering aspects of my life in New York/New Jersey, suggesting someday he plan a visit, implying he leave his wife at home. When he was released from the clinic, he gave me his plush white terrycloth bathrobe and a fantasy of "what if?" I harbored the notion that some day in the future we might manage a reunion. Though we spoke of it in later years, we never got to attend a Betty Ford meeting in New York or Washington D.C. together. Our potential meeting was forever cancelled when his wife wrote me news of his death in a car crash near their home.

Almost immediately upon checking into North Hall, my fellow inmates bestowed upon me the honor of being the leader of the Kazoo Marching Band. They had heard somehow that I had something to do with music. In my naiveté, I took my position seriously and rehearsed my group for impromptu performances. With some aluminum foil obtained from the cook in the dining hall, I fashioned a baton from a branch of a tree and wrapped it in a shiny, silvery sheath.

Our band of kazoo players marched from our North Hall to the dining hall daily, playing with serious intent. Blowing through a kazoo was easier for a drunk or drug addict than trying to remember lyrics. When we tried to sing songs, it was limited to the "Star Spangled Banner" or "The Battle Hymn of the Republic." We even had trouble with those. However, kazoos needed no lyrics, just the melody. I was quite pleased with our cheerful efforts. At a Christmas get-together, a woman asked why we didn't have our kazoos on hand for a couple of musical selections. I informed her in the gravest tone that the kazoos were out being tuned at considerable expense, hence no music tonight. She completely believed me!

The highlight of my performing career at the center came at Christmastime, when each of the four houses was requested to perform a fifteen-minute skit promoting the theme of anti-substance abuse. As no one in North Hall had any idea for our skit, I recommended our doing an all-new Nativity Play, rather than boring sit-coms planned in the other houses. No one objected nor was inspired to write the script. Not being controlling, I devised an amusing entertainment, which I then directed and starred in. As I felt it important for laughter to be generated as a strong part of recovery, I cast the characters in a comical way, doing and saying funny things. I decided that I would play the Virgin Mary, but as Mae West would interpret it. Joe (Joseph) would be a puny guy bossed around by Mary. The baby Jesus would be played by a hulky guy in diapers. The Star of Bethlehem would be a pretty bimbo placed high on a pedestal wearing a white peignoir and draped in fairy lights.

Promptly, I called my assistant, Oscar, in New Jersey, to request that he pack the Egyptian robes and Tunisian djellabas I had in my closet, together with the Louis XVI powdered wig. I asked that he hide carefully inside the costumes some fireworks for use on New Year's Eve on the North's patio. It did not seem as though fireworks would be acceptable on the premises, but I took the chance of getting them through. My Santa Claus outfit was requested, as well.

Rumors circulated that my playlet was irreligious, with objectionable material.

I decided to have someone in the Santa Claus outfit announce as a caveat before the play that there might be elements that could offend. This was a warning to leave now if one was so inclined. No one got up, but instead waited with anticipation. (To continue the season's festivities, I wore the Santa Claus outfit the next day in the dining hall while helping to clear up after lunch.)

Our pageant began with the "townspeople" entering and playing "Silent Night, Holy Night" on the kazoos in a procession. Mary had a pale blue chenille bedspread draped as a long shawl over her head and a pink cotton nightgown (the colors I thought appropriate for the Virgin Mary), with the platinum white wig peeping through the shawl. Her arm was over the shoulder of the very large Baby Jesus, and her head was toward the child so that the audience only saw the draped head with wisps of wig, but could not distinguish the face. Mary had her back to the audience while arranging the burly Jesus in the huge box serving as a cradle. His arms and legs were hanging over the sides. Small stuffed animals collected from various rooms were placed around the manger. It wasn't until Joe called attention to the three men arriving from the East on camels that Mary spun around and, with a wiggle, greeted and moaned an "Oh-h...are you the wise guys from the East I've been hearin' all about?" Margaux Hemingway stood on her chair and screamed "Eric, I love you!" in delight, while the audience broke out in laughter at the ludicrous sight.

The audience loved the skit, and even the tough, big ballplayer types came to give me strong hugs of approbation. I realized that in an institutional situation, people relax their prejudices and are willing to accept some guy playing the Virgin Mary as Mae West, and reward him with admiring hugs. This inspired me to push my outrageousness further.

The following day, the aerobics teacher had brought in an LP album of *Swan Lake* especially for me when a group of us gathered to do swimming pool exercises. I had complained about the disco music that we had been subjected to during the previous class. She promised something more classical. While she was in the locker room changing into a bathing suit, I put the record on.

The big bruiser straight guys were lined up knee deep in the pool, linking arms and instructed to do the dance of the cygnets, raising on their toes, then lowering into pliés. This balletic ensemble set the stage for a grand jeté by the swan queen into the pool as the music reached a crescendo . . . the instructor had emerged in time to see this extraordinary and surprising scene. She claimed that she would never be able to see *Swan Lake* again without thoughts of me.

Days of recovery blended into weeks, with me diligently working at clearing away psychic debris resulting from my decades of alcoholic antics. I began each day before dawn with a walk around the lake, thinking about my condition and the prospects of my future life in recovery. I no longer felt I was the center of the world nor believed in my being a genius—special and above ordinary behavior codes. Values and attitudes were changed.

My inspiration for the Christmas skit at The Betty Ford Clinic.

It was very agreeable to be at this desert paradise with supportive colleagues. The same guy who collected me in the admitting room on my first day became a constant companion. On visitors' day, we would walk around the lake on the path with the visitors interspersed. He would proclaim that the desert over there would soon have oil wells pumping, pumping, pumping. His arm swept across the landscape as he loudly announced his plans for development in a pronounced Texas accent. I found his antics and fantasies amusing, and wondered what others thought of his startling statements.

Because intercommunication with inmates in other houses was forbidden, so as to maintain anonymity as well as keep personal recovery private, it became a challenging game for us to try to establish superficial contact with those in another house. There was an amiable woman from Margaux's house who seemed to indicate her desire to be in touch with me. We would write messages and put them in small cereal boxes to be passed surreptitiously while passing each other's table in the dining hall, or on the path along the lake. There was one woman who was in a wheelchair. She became a carrier for small paper bags containing furtive messages as though in a spy thriller. It was an amusing game, never involving exchanges beyond one's first name and a greeting for the day. It was a harmless spice for the day, non-intrusive on anyone's recovery but fun.

Carol, it was established, was my cohort's name. Locating a florist delivery box, I amassed a bunch of half-dead flowers and had it dropped at the desk at her house on campus as a lark. On Christmas morning, I had a wreath of slightly tired flowers twisted together with streamer ribbons collected from various recipients of flowers at the house, and fashioned them around a wire coat hanger that made a sturdy coronet. North Hall had a Christmas poem to be read by a group of us to the rest of the "inmates" collected for this communal breakfast. It was based on the Night before Christmas but ended with the familiar Johnny Carson line: "Here's . . . Johnny" but using "Carol" instead—at that moment, the crown of flowers was plunked upon Carol's head. She was surprised and utterly delighted—so much so, that she refused to take the wreath off until she was commanded to do so by the staff some time later. This kind of harmless fun lightened the days of recovery.

Carol and I continued contact for some years after our Betty Ford days. A year later, after carefully arranging Apollo Muses business, I took time off to make a brief return to the Betty Ford campus. Carol and I met there again during this reunion. She had her silver-plated sugar bowl at home engraved as a mini award for me as a graduate from the center. She presented it to me at the reunion dinner, where Betty Ford was joined by her husband, Jerry, previous president of the United States, and their friends Bob and Dorothy Hope. That week, I gave a talk on recovery at North Hall to the newcomers. Betty Ford herself was losing stamina. I remember giving her a hug and feeling how fragile she seemed. Elizabeth Taylor was there in a wheelchair; she met her next (and last) husband, Larry Fortensky, at this juncture.

My life at the clinic was carefully structured. Between daily self-analysis, group conscience of individual's behavior (where each of us evaluated one another), private sessions with my counselor, lectures and films relating to addiction, and healthy structured living—in dining, exercise, programs, and sleeping times, my progress was evident. My "inmates" commented on my slimming down and improving appearance. I felt stronger, more energetic, and eager to absorb the valuable guidance of those around me.

Also, I was enjoying being there. One of my chores in North Hall was to vacuum the hallways in the mornings. I took vociferous pleasure in singing opera while doing it, making up Italian sounding words when I could not remember the correct ones. My counselor entered through the outside door one particularly cold morning and seemed annoyed at my jubilant singing. I asked her whether I was more Joan Crawford or Rosalind Russell in my Harriet Craig fastidiousness in housekeeping. She petulantly told me she had no idea what I was talking about. Oh well, at least I knew I was striving for developing yet another dimension to my growing Diva roles....

Many of my housemates disliked being at the clinic; I felt just the opposite. I thrived on it and felt very encouraged by the results I was noticing within me. I also had a lot a fun when not engaged in self-improvement. Walking over the manicured lawns, enjoying the flowering bushes and shade of the tall palms, I had lot of time to think— and kibitz, one of my longtime pastimes. One fine morning, I saw one of the two nutritionists coming in my direction. I had just noticed, yet again, the daily waste of ice cubes thrown out at the base of one of the palms. The clinic started each day with fresh ice cubes for some reason. The nutritionist asked me how I felt. I spontaneously had the urge to fool with her, especially as she always had such a serious demeanor. I told her that I had been feeling nauseated and indicated the ice cubes nearby as though I had just thrown them up. She was not amused and walked by without further comment. Behind her was my favorite nutritionist, who laughed at my silly notion of this alcoholic-in-recovery regurgitating ice cubes.

One of my fantasies was enacted during a final day at the clinic. I was excused from stretching exercises and gymnastics for a therapy to improve circulation in my right leg by sitting in the whirlpool outside the gym. At the end of the session, we were to sign out and proceed back to our rooms. I made certain I was the first to sign out so I could start back in front of everyone. I had surreptitiously removed my bathing suit under the white terry cloth robe I was wearing. Walking back to our rooms, I slowly removed the robe near my room, revealing a totally nude body viewed by those behind me. "Oh, Eric," crooned Margaux, as I streaked into my room. It was something I had wanted to do as a playful last gesture at The Betty Ford Clinic.

The day arrived when I was to appear to do my Fifth Step, presenting my Fourth Step moral inventory to God, to myself, and to someone else who the center provided. Though his denominational affiliation was never established, I guessed he was a Protestant from his understated, anonymous code of dress. I expressed the exact nature of my character defects, shortcomings, and the various behaviors that I regretted in my past. He responded to some of my outrageous past with gasps of "Oh, my . . ." but no words of recrimination. After what seemed an eternity, my Fifth Step came to an end. It was suggested I go outside and walk around the lake, thinking about what had transpired. I told him I had planned to do just that.

There was turbulence in the air, as clouds whipped over the mountains on the horizon. I started my perambulation around the lake, when I noticed that not a single other inmate was visible anywhere. There were eighty of us on the campus and usually a few could be seen strolling here or there. Now, no one!

It was a cinematic moment for me when I looked heavenwards and told God I had done everything I was asked to do while here at the clinic. Please acknowledge my efforts. I felt akin to Vivian Leigh as Scarlett declaring to the Heavens that she would never go hungry again. Give me a sign . . . I murmured.

At that exact moment, the sky beyond the clump of trees ahead filled with colored balloons and a loud, whoop of affirmation filled the air! The other inmates had been given slips of paper on which to write their most troublesome resentment. Each slip was to be put into a balloon that would be filled with helium. In unison, the patients would get rid of their resentments by sending them heavenwards with a joyful shout! (I had been excluded from this ritual as I had my Fifth Step to do. I wonder which resentment I would have chosen to put on my slip of paper, had I been there?)

This was a startling affirmation to me. There are no such things as coincidences. My need for validation was fulfilled, along with my colleagues' success in freeing themselves of their worst resentment. This was powerful medicine!

My Mother Ginger in
"The Nutcracker," and my
portrayal of The King in
"The Sleeping Beauty"
were performed for the
New Jersey Ballet in
theaters around the state,
with a special performance
in Bermuda.

Chapter 17

De-Lucing; Decimation Through Death

Just as there was enormous anxiety upon committing myself to The Betty Ford Clinic, there was much trepidation within me upon my release into the real world. After almost a month of nurturing and stabilizing in the safety of that lovely rehabilitation center in Southern California, I was not certain how I would survive on my own on the outside.

I chose to go to my beloved Santa Fe for the early days of recovery before returning to the more complicated world at Lu Shan and New York. Jane Grey and Byron Treaster had an architecturally fascinating modern house on a hill just outside of Tesuque. Painted mauve, it looked like a ship cutting across the arroyos. They were willing to lend it to me in exchange for the small apartment Lila and I had set up in New York after the sale of 480 Park Avenue. It seemed a compatible arrangement for all of us.

With a constancy of intention, I attended recovery group meetings at the Friendship Club. These early days of sobriety needed to be observed with careful attentiveness. I felt vulnerable in my newly found sober living, and I was determined to make every effort to keep from falling off the wagon.

Much as I tried to be a good role model, my artist friend Ann Moul resisted any effort to give up alcohol. R.C. Gorman tried to cut back his drinking and sometimes went on sober bouts with his housekeeper Rose. Neither of them managed for very long, however. I had been warned that few people stay in the program; the recovery rate is dismally low. To avoid pitfalls, I rigorously adopted a regime of prayers of gratitude, now that I had re-admitted a Higher Power other than myself into my life. Further bolsters were a healthy diet with moderate exercise, the study of program literature, and regulated sound sleep. I gathered sober people around me and adjusted my living regime to avoid old habits.

Porter Jean Dunaway and I had an artist friend, Kathy Norton, who often hung out with us. I had met Kathy in Costa Rica, and she even stayed in my accommodation on Manuel Antonio Beach to keep an eye on Lila's well-being, while I visited San José to do some errands for a few days. Kathy knew about my presenting a series of concerts and art events in New Jersey and talked of a great friend in California who was a wonderful pianist. I suggested he come to Santa Fe to perform an afternoon concert at the house I was using in Tesuque. Possibly, he could be featured in a future Apollo Muses event.

Planning this concert gave me an activity. It motivated me into positive action, focusing my free time creatively. With some imaginative efforts using my network of contacts in the area, I summoned an audience that included Ann Luce, who flew in from Boulder. Lila's younger son, Peter, had separated from her in favor of a younger, less challenging woman, much to everyone's disappointment. Resilient Ann flew her plane in with her new beau and assisted in my getting everything ready for this concert.

After my release from Betty Ford, this was my first big challenge, and it helped prepare me for a return to New Jersey, beloved Lila, and my dear wire-haired dachshund, Fred. The concert was well received. I still resisted any temptation to pick up a drink and, with gratitude, continued to count the days of my recovery, now in ever-rising double digits.

When I arrived at Lu Shan, I was about to re-enter "The Night Club," my retreat

My wise friend Fred.

over the three car garage. This was my private quarters, gussied up with the sitting room's wall and ceiling hung in pale blue silk given to me by David IV. My bedroom ceiling was covered with the canvas-backed mural of "The adoration of Venus," which once graced the ballroom at the

Astor Hotel on Times Square before demolition. It was acquired cheaply at auction by a friend of mine who knew I could put it to good use.

The cook, hearing me arrive, let Fred out of the kitchen screen door to greet me. He wagged his tail and started toward me but then began to crawl on his belly. I spoke to him, encouraging him to come to me, but he seemed uncertain. He knew my voice but whose body was I in? I no longer smelled like myself. No alcoholic odors were reeking out of my pores. Who was this impostor with my voice?

Lila was utterly joyful to have me back in residence, as was I. The servants seemed relieved to find me mellowed. I was not as aggressive or critical in my dealings with them. It did not matter too much if the dinner knife was not perfectly aligned with the water goblet, or if the floral bouquet in the center of the table had a few blossoms placed in a casual array. I no longer felt obliged to run the world, giving instruction to all around me. What a relief for everyone, myself included!

We began to plan lunches and dinners for our friends. Some of my friends became welcome additions to Lila's gatherings. Among the attendees was Bruce Whitacre, who began veering away from playwriting and into administrative work with theaters. Actress Ruth Warrick and Jeremyn Davern (from my public relation stints) came to enjoy the sunny days at Lu Shan, and Ginny Dustin, struggling with establishing her cabaret career, drove pianist Frank Daykin out. Unbenownst to me, Frank studied my recovery process with great interest. I became his role model, helping him to find his path to sober living. Other guests included Sylvia van der Stegen, who squeezed in a visit in while visiting with her two young sons

Lila Tyng is honored at the Barge with Ruth Warrick and Jerome Hines attending.

from Paris, and Jasmine Bozin, who appeared with the charming (Count) Albert de Pouzols when they visited the US. Albert had commented that my life was a work of art. He had told me this both in Paris and at his villa in the south of France during my heavy drinking days. This time, in New Jersey, it took on a new significance. My sobriety permitted a clarity to reveal this work of art. Visitors from around the US and Europe dropped in, together with local artists and musicians. Life at Lu Shan was lively, diverting, and pleasurable, due in part to the Apollo Muses attractions.

Some of the friendly neighbors, who had become supporters of Apollo Muses, extended their approval through attendance. Dorothy Dillon Eweson was an early sponsor. Together with her dapper husband Eric, she encouraged our efforts and was to become one of the mainstays in future days of Apollo Muses. After an afternoon concert held in Lu Shan, while the barns were still being renovated, the guests spilled out into the gardens to enjoy refreshments. Once, I overheard a guest ask Dorothy's husband about his occupation. The distinguished, sartorially well-turned-out gentleman replied, "I am a garbage collector." It certainly was a startling response in this elite atmosphere! Eric Eweson was the head of the recycling company that Dorothy had set up to help make the community greener. So, in a sense, Eric was a garbage man!

Another time, I was responsible for startling the guests. Some Far Hill matrons had come for tea at Lila's. Our neighbor, flamboyant Malcolm Forbes, was planning a major fundraiser at his home for AIDS research and was flying some guests in by helicopter. Among them was his favorite personality and chairman of the benefit, Elizabeth Taylor. At the event, he was to bestow a $1 million dollar check to her for this cause.

Aboard the Forbes' yacht with Dorothy.

Recently, Forbes had garnered enormous press attention with his birthday party in Morocco. The king, who had bought the huge Macy-Ladd property in our Far Hills neighborhood—perhaps as a safe place to retreat to in any time of future trouble— participated in the lavish celebration thrown by his friend, Malcolm. Elizabeth Taylor was among the guests flown into Morocco for the birthday festivities.

The hens at tea were cackling on about whether or not Malcolm, who had just divorced his sweet and unassuming wife, Bertie, mother of his children, would marry "that actress." To the grand Far Hills dames, apparently Elizabeth Taylor did not have a name. They denoted their disapproval of her being an actress who was flaunting morals other than theirs, at least in public.

I grew incensed at their haughty, judgmental attitude and announced that if Malcolm did marry Elizabeth, they would have at least three things in common. All heads leaned closer over the table in anticipation of my remarks. I pointed out that they both loved money; oh, yes, they concurred. Also, I went on that they both enjoyed publicity; indeed, they agreed. And, they both like men, although she likes them older. There was a stunned silence with the subject of conversation changed instantly!

Driving around the dirt roads of Far Hills, one could sense why this was an attraction to the very rich who settled here in the 20th century. At this time, New Jersey had no state income tax. Both its proximity to New York City and its being a tax-free zone were irresistible to the wealthy. It was also ideal horse country, which was one reason the roads were unpaved. Dirt roads were kinder to the hooves of the horses. The gentle landscape was ideal for riding and fox hunting. The United States Equestrian Team established itself in the stables of what was previously the Brady Estate. Also, dusty roads discouraged rubberneckers, who did not like getting their cars dirty. Aside from keeping costs down by not paving the roads, the atmosphere was deliciously reminiscent of being in Hampshire or other bucolic parts of civilized England. Surprisingly idyllic, and a very far cry from the Turnpike image of New Jersey, it was a successfully well-kept secret.

The summer Sundays rolled by through the years. Apollo Muses was popular with both the community and interested visitors, who planned long-distance trips to the area to permit attendance at our events. During the icy, snowy winter months, Lila and I would leave Lu Shan for warmer climes. This was a practical move, as the heating bills were enormously reduced when Lu Shan was kept heated to only the minimum, and it was a diverting method to have pleasant weather while working on our manuscripts. Lila was determined to finish the book about her mother; I had the challenge of doing an autobiographical search for a spiritual path through sober living, to be later published as *Cinderella Is a Man; a Picaresque Passage to Serenity.*

We had been to Costa Rica, where we met young, adorable Oscar Murillo, when he worked at the bank where we needed assistance. He was destined to become a great help to us at Lu Shan, assisting the gardener, helping to drive Lila around, and participating in serving at gatherings. In time, we would welcome other young Costa Ricans to help maintain the gardens and apple orchard at Lu Shan, which got a local appellation of "Little Costa Rica." Neighbors began to realize the value of these gentle, hard-working young men, and, through our assistance, they were able to bring more Costa Ricans to the area.

During this period, Lila's milestone birthday party saluting her turning eighty was celebrated at the Grand Ballroom at the Plaza Hotel. Her son, Henry, and his third wife, Nancy, had sent out invitations to a large number of friends and relatives. When Lila saw the invitation, she grew very agitated. I arrived at our New York apartment to find her in a volatile state. She was shocked that Henry had announced to the world it would be her "Four Score" birthday. Lila wanted the world to think she was much younger, as most women might prefer. She felt there was no need to advertise her advanced age.

However, at the lovely dinner dance, Lila addressed the amassed gathering after dinner and read the following:

FOUR SCORE INDEED!
Was that a misprint calling me "four score?"
Or can't my dear son, Henry, keep the score?
He should have said THREE score, not more.
That eighty nonsense, I deplore.
At eighty, dissipations are denied;
One is even WISE, and DIGNIFIED.
I think I'll say I'm fifty.
Oh, it's nifty to be fifty!
Being middle aged,
I'm engaged
In watching future years with insouciance;
For after the Middle Ages, comes the RENAISSANCE!

Sharing this evening with all of you is joy complete.
I think Nancy and Henry are dear and kind and sweet.
Henry, I love the girl who is mated to you
And I am proud to be related to you.
Thank you for this celebration. Together we shall waltz.
I know that you dislike exaggerations and what is false,
And the Bible says: "The truth shall set you free."
Well, I'm free to be four score, ecstatically!

To my utter surprise, Henry then acknowledged his mother's words and asked the orchestra to play a Viennese waltz, requesting that I dance with his mother. There could not have been a better birthday present for Lila. What followed astonished and thrilled me! Alone on the ballroom floor with every eye on us, I waltzed Lila full speed past the first table, while everyone at that table stood and applauded. Spinning past the second table, the same thing happened, and the third, until the ENTIRE ballroom celebrants were on their feet applauding the great lady. Though Lila was eighty, she twirled around the edge of the very large ballroom

*Flicka von Stade performed locally at Princeton,
which many of us gladly attended.*

with youthful ease and grace. It was the finest gift I could bestow upon her, and I know she was deeply thrilled by this unique experience in 3/4 time!

An offer made to Lila in the mid '80s to use a Far Hills acquaintance's vacation home at a gated community on a golf course at Rancho Mirage in the Palm Springs area was accepted, adding to our repertoire of winter escapes. Ironically, it was only across the road from the Eisenhower Memorial Hospital and The Betty Ford Clinic, another respite for me. Later, I joked saying that I worked both sides of the street.

Another drama unfolded for us there at the Spa at Rancho Mirage, where nothing untoward seemed possible. Every day, the watering system turned on with a clicking sound, while the spray danced around on the lawn; golf clubs smacked balls across the manicured greens; the gardeners' clipping of the hedges was barely detected, but nothing else . . . just a constant sun beating down on another perfect day on the desert. Even the palms and flowering bushes seemed motionless in a breezeless atmosphere.

One morning, out on the patio facing the golf green, I greeted our neighbor, who was reading the morning paper. He was a retired CEO from Beneficial Life Insurance, the same company as our host. He anxiously asked me if I noticed that the neighbor on the other side of me had returned. Yes, I responded, Lila and I had noticed the lights in their kitchen the night before. This house had been empty for weeks, but suddenly a bleached blond woman and her dark Italianate companion were unpacking groceries in the kitchen while exchanging affectionate hugs and pats. "Have you spoken to them?" my neighbor inquired. "No, why?" The neighbor showed me the morning paper. It had a story about the woman; she was accused of stabbing her invalid husband in his wheel chair multiple times—in the house next door! She was out on bail, awaiting trial.

Like two kids out to solve a crime from a Nancy Drew story, Lila and I eagerly awaited nightfall, so we could peek into the kitchen windows by standing on a sturdy oak coffee table in the living room. The couple were boringly normal in their interaction, not indicating anything suspicious. What a disappointment. Our vantage point was the only one around for spying into that house, but we came up with nothing.

Lila's youngest son, Peter, separated from dear Ann, was bringing his new trophy, Betsy, for a visit of a couple of days. It coincided with the wedding party being held next door. The accused murderess was marrying her dark, sexy lover, now that her ex was out of the way. Betsy suggested we attend the wedding celebration and bring the bride a new set of cutlery. (Ah, those dreaded knives, again!)

This sojourn in the Rancho Mirage/Palm Springs area introduced Lila to two amazing institutions: the supermarket and the thrift shop. She had her cook or housekeeper tend to shopping, so she had no idea how extraordinary a supermarket could be, especially in Southern California. Lila walked up and down the aisles, resplendent in fruits and vegetables, as though she were in an Arabian souk. The colors and arrangements of the produce stunned her. There was also a very large thrift shop that captured her attention. She could not get over the amount of wonderful garments available for incredibly low prices. It was hard to rein in her urge to buy large amounts of clothing for her granddaughters, staff and friends. Among the many endearing qualities of this unusual woman were her generosity of spirit and childlike enthusiasm.

With the advent of spring, it was time to return to Lu Shan and consult with Gunnar, the gardener, about plantings for the coming summer. I had my programs to organize for the impending Apollo Muses season. Lila and I resumed residence with renewed vigor to catch up on New York happenings as well as enjoy the pleasant life in Somerset County.

Much to my surprise, Lila announced she wanted to do something to give me some future security. We had been sharing a brother-sister life of symbiotic companionship for many years. Sensing her own mortality, she wanted me to have a home of my own. The gardener's cottage on the farm would make a suitable place for me to establish roots. Despite some grumblings from her sons, the house and surrounding acres were formally deeded to me. The house needed renovation and some expansion, making it a challenging and fun project for the both Lila and me. I would relinquish "The Nightclub" to Oscar, who gladly moved from the servants' quarters. Taking it over for his living space gave him more room and privacy. After months of remodeling, The Greenhouse Cottage soon came to life, giving me an added sense of achievement as well as an improved status as a landowner. It was only a pearl hurl to the barns where Apollo Muses continued presenting its culturally enriching programs. Walking or driving up the hill brought me to dear Lila in minutes, so we remained very close. Life certainly took on a most alluring aspect during this period.

It was inevitable that, from time to time, someone would bring up Clare Boothe Luce in conversation. Though maintaining a polite facade, Lila never forgot or forgave Clare for stealing Harry away, and marrying him. Out of loyalty to Lila, I avoided opportunities to meet the infamous Clare. Towards the end of her very stunning life, Clare Boothe Luce left her beautiful Hawaiian home to spend time in New York. I was fascinated by a series of phone calls I received

My most adorable "Big Sister" visits the Greenhouse Cottage.

from various friends during this period. Each time, one of the callers had spent the previous night having dinner with Clare. The conversation was identical. Clare would declare there were two things in her life she regretted never having. This was always an attention-getter as Clare was known to get—one way or another—anything she wanted. Her checkered career was a testament to that fact.

The first thing she never had was a visit to Lu Shan. Lila had promised her mother that she would never invite that husband stealer to Lu Shan, and she didn't. Though they might see each other at some social event often involving family members, the second Mrs. Luce never got the first Mrs. Luce to invite her to the much praised Lu Shan, built by their husband Harry for his two sons and their mother, Lila.

The second thing Clare bemoaned was not having Eric in her life! I never dared approach the notion of being in Clare's company out of deepest regards for Lila, who would have deemed it a betrayal.

I was intrigued by Clare's dwelling upon Lu Shan and me as the great losses in her life, just as I am certain others were when hearing her talk about it. This was the woman everyone thought had everything, but during her final days she obsessed over what she thought she missed out on. It was an odd quirk of fate that I would be included in those last thoughts of hers.

Clare Boothe Luce's death in October of 1987 was early in a succession of deaths to follow. These included those closest to me as friends and family. They spanned the period before Betty Ford's treatment and then some after I achieved a more sober way of living. Despite deaths in spades, I managed to maintain my sobriety and withstand the tempests ahead.

Very menacing storm clouds were gathering on the horizon. Both of Lila's sons had remarried. Both wives were supportive of pushing their husbands to limit Lila's activities as she was overripe with age, and they determined she should adjust to a more sedentary life, preferably horizontal. It was seemly for her to pass on. But—I was obviously motivating her to enjoy a full life with challenges, delaying her having to throw in the sponge and quietly die! Aside from contributing to various Russians who convinced her that supporting their causes was a method of fighting communism, her expenditures were not wildly extravagant. Yet her sons and their wives were determined to conserve as many family assets as possible, making their inheritance more significant. They did not want to live at Lu Shan; instead, they wanted to convert it into cash. Some of her heirs were impatient and yearning to get at the capital after Lila's demise. Only she did not die; we were busily living a full life—however, the plug was about to be pulled!

The two brothers and their wives coordinated a scheme to shut Lila down by assuming control of her accounts through gaining power of attorney. They changed lawyers to one they could direct. They dismissed the household staff friendly to me and fully supportive of Lila's wishes. Overnight the locks were changed. For the first time in twenty-four years, I was locked out and forced to request entry from a hostile employee. Sweet, lovable Oscar was dismissed with no notice. He was replaced by a surly fellow we had known for a few years, but who was known to be crafty and less than sterling. He hooked up with the seemingly wholesome Maria, the cook. They schemed with the heirs to keep me from Lila, and keep Lila out of touch with the rest of the world. Another tough woman was employed to keep an eye on Lila when Maria went home to her family at night.

It was a shock to me, and unacceptable. I stayed away, waiting for Lila to correct the situation. She refused to acknowledge what her sons, her "two jewels," were doing and bemoaned the absence of her "Little Brother." Lila was in complete denial and succumbed to the harsh dictates of her sons. I was not on the premises with her to help her. In her nineties, Lila was frail and confused. I knew if I tried to explain it clearly, she would be heartbroken by her sons' betrayal of her. She retreated within herself, passive-aggressive style.

Visitors were discouraged by Lu Shan's Mrs. Danvers, on leave from *Rebecca's* Manderley. Mail and phone calls were intercepted. "This is war, and I am Hitler," Peter announced to a neighbor in Far Hills, who called him to object to his behavior to his mother and to me. People began to wonder what had happened, and why I was no longer an integral part of life at Lu Shan. It was said by staff members that "Things had begun to disappear," hinting that I was the thief.

My life went into a tailspin. I had to seek professional help to keep my own sanity. It was like something from a gothic novel. Lila withdrew into herself, and despite all efforts to the contrary, she continued to live on for more years, alone and out of touch with everyone who had animated her world. Sometimes friends would stop by with a gift for her, but "Mrs. Danvers" would take the gift with a promise to give it to Lila and then quickly close the door on them.

A few people recommended I marry Lila to free her from the clutches of her family and the servants following their commands. I rejected this incredible notion as being inappropriate. It would have befuddled Lila; made a sham of the sanctity of marriage; and, in the minds of the Far Hills community and the world-at-large, I would be perceived as a fortune hunter. The Luce powerhouse would descend on me. The repercussions frightened me.

Instead, I decided to get away from the awful scene and the Luces by selling my beloved Greenhouse Cottage. My steadfast friend, Dorothy Dillon Eweson, advised me and kindly helped me finalize the purchase of "Thumbelina" in the nearby village of Gladstone. Contiguous to it was a huge cornfield for Fred to ferret out ground hogs. Dorothy lent me the money until the finances from the sale of my house on the farm were straightened out. (Though I had ownership papers in order, the purchaser delayed payments, which held up my closing on the new property.) Dorothy also made it clear to the Far Hills set that she endorsed my integrity in this messy Luce business, giving me sustaining credibility in community. Her companionship and sage advice guided me during the immediate years following my loss of Lila.

Forthright and adorable Ann came to visit Lila, while the Luce brothers were there. Ann was walking a fine line between the Luces and me, fearing losing her alimony by being in friendly, supportive company with their *bête noir*, Eric. She reported that Lila seemed very confused and out of touch. Lila indicated a portrait of Henry Luce (her first husband, who had abandoned her), and with a smile, her eyes twinkling, and her voice warm with love said, "This is a portrait of Eric." Her sons could not have been amused by this confusion of me with their father. In retrospect, it is possible that Lila purposely said it knowing fully the impact it would have on her jailer sons.

During her last days, Lila was committed to the Morristown Memorial Hospital. I did not want to encounter any of the Luces, so I went to see her very early one morning. She was not coherent, rambling on about a burning building and TIME magazine. Her eyes were closed and we had no conversation. Lila seemed to be in a coma-like state. I took her hand and bid her farewell.

I felt frustrated that there seemed to be nothing I could do to make the situation better. The newspapers began to contact me, sensing a story worth pursuing. I thought about the adverse publicity that would be generated against the Luces if I spilled what I knew to a publication like the *National Enquirer*. I also knew that I could put my well-being in jeopardy if I opened my mouth and brought the wrath of the powerful Luces down on me. Big money could buy lots of dangerous things. I did not want to have my knees broken, or to be beaten up or even killed, so I retreated to Santa Fe to hide out, seeking peace of mind. My longtime friend Audrey, who understood the situation fully, suggested I stay with her friends. They kindly took me in and I had the opportunity to find much needed tranquility. Even there, somehow, the Newark *Star Ledger* found me. I declined comment but suggested that a story would some day emerge. I dared nothing further.

After Lila's death in 1999, just five days after she turned 100, I took the liberty of inspecting her will at the County Clerk's office. It was as I suspected. The original will, which I had a copy of, had been changed three times after Lila's lockup. Her scrawled signature was on each, but I knew she could not have been aware of what she was signing in her condition. Each will diminished legacies to her friends and her favorite charities. The final will left everything to the Luce brothers, with the exception of a small bequest to Man'ha Garreau Dombasle in France. Everyone else was deleted.

I do not believe the Luces thought Man'ha would survive Lila, so they left her small bequest in the will. She lived long enough after probate to be eligible. Her death was within the one-year period, so her granddaughter, Arielle Dombasle, as her heir, was eligible to inherit it. I called Arielle in Paris to suggest she have a lawyer look into this.

De-Lucing was the order of the day. If I were to maintain any semblance of positive living, I had to rid myself of the polluting influences of the Luces. I turned myself away from anything that seemed likely to involve me with that family. I even unsubscribed from the Waltz Series and as a Fellow at the Morgan Library, where Henry often attended receptions.

Bless her heart if Dorothy Eweson, a major doyenne of the community, did not make a point of sheltering me from adverse opinions easily generated by my separation from Lu Shan. She asked me to accompany her to many functions where her stamp of approval of me was evident. Dorothy told me she would make sure our friendship never had the terrible repercussions that mine had with Lila. Dorothy was privy to all that was transpiring at Lu Shan and was totally sympathetic to Lila and me. As a pillar of respectability in Far Hills, she became my strongest defender and dearest friend in my time of need.

Years before, Apollo Muses was pleased to welcome Dorothy Dillon Eweson on the executive board as vice president. We were most fortunate to be invited to make use of her home, Corner House, and her father's neo-Georgian Dunwalke, farther along Larger Cross Road, as venues for Apollo Muses events.

Corner House was created in the '50s when Dorothy was married to her second husband, Sidney Spivac. Its ground floor was constructed to hold four rooms of original carved wall panels of Louis XIII (entrance hall), Louis XIV (dining room), Louis XV (sitting room), and Louis XVI (library). She toned down the grandeur of the boiserie by not having the carved walls re-gilded and by hanging art on the wooden panels. Comfortable, unpretentious antique furniture was placed around each room. It was a perfect place for entertaining, whether intimate concerts or

Dorothy and her daughter Christine enlivened Apollo Muses events at Corner House.

receptions. A mansard roof completed the French *manoir*. A grass lawn ran down the incline from the dining room's French windows to the pond below, with a jet fountain in the center. Farmed land and stands of trees blended into the hills in the distance, making a bucolic backdrop.

In contrast to this attractive environment, there was a sprinkling of great sadness. Dear Fred, my wire-haired dachshund, spent 17 years of dedicated friendship with me. His dog collar with a few identification tags would jingle when he followed me to the front of an audience to introduce a performer or impart information. The jingle would follow me on my return to my seat, with some giggles from the amused audience. He was a highly inquisitive and intelligent being who gave me great comfort and companionship in our long relationship. The back seat of my car was Fred's when we went on the road for trips to Florida, or elsewhere. He was prompt to announce when he thought it time to stop for the day by putting his long nose between the front seats to nuzzle my arm. Fred loved visiting motels and sniffing around the surrounding area. When guests arrived at home, he was always available to greet them and receive their kindly attentions. Then, just like that, he was gone . . . that day, Fred had come up to me, breathing heavily. I lifted him up and knew from his breathing that he was in a bad way. I had placed him on a pillow under my work table while I tended to something. I felt like Rodolfo in *La Boheme* at the end of the final act. When I looked at Fred, he had stopped breathing, just like Mimi. I felt Rodolfo's anguished cry: "Mimi!" The curtain descended to a hushed audience . . . I could not speak for some minutes; I was barely able to convey on the telephone call to Oscar an urgent request to come over immediately. He helped me bury Fred under

Toshiko Takaezu, internationally acclaimed potter at an exhibition of her work in East Hampton.

an impressive stone birdbath in the garden at Thumbelina.

This was an extended period of loss. Earlier, in January of '77, my father was put into an institution by my mother, when she was no longer able to manage his care. Both Flo and I wanted to help with expenses of a live-in caregiver. Mother would not hear of it, which made us unhappy and helpless to save him. He died a befuddled, lonely, and broken man. My mother died a few years later in September of '81, a shadow of herself, full of regrets. Both passings were reported to me while I was in Europe by my beloved sister, Flo. I had not seen either of them for some time. My father no longer recognized anyone other than his darling granddaughter, Lori. It seemed futile to visit someone who did not know who I was, so I stayed away after the initial visit. My mother urged me to go but I knew this was an effort to help her justify institutionalizing him. I did not want to do that. I did see my mother in the hospital once, but had great misgivings about her behavior in general. I was conveniently out of the country for both of their deaths, but did visit their gravesite after release from Betty Ford's as a promise to my counselor, who deemed it important that I go there and "tell them what I thought of them."

Interestingly, when I got to their resting place, I felt calmer and very much more forgiving than I would have imagined. For once, they seemed comfortable next to each other. I could see a police station nearby but did not think my mother would have need of it under the circumstances. I left the cemetery feeling serene.

My brother, George, had been named executor of my mother's will. We four offspring each got a cash settlement. Afterwards, Flo, George, and I met at "the Nightclub" at Lu Shan to divvy what was left of my mother's jewelry. Helen was not invited; she had helped herself to things immediately upon my mother's death. This was something my mother had done to her sister when their mother died. Helen adopted that trait from our mother, who had trained her over the years of indoctrination to be her acolyte. We were disappointed in Helen's behavior and none of us had dealings with her for some time as a result. Then, it was only me who did, finally.

George never did make up with Helen before he suddenly died in his sleep in 2001. The eldest sibling, George was always the most removed from his sisters and brother. As a youth, he worked for our father at construction sites. Then, after a stint in the Navy, he went to study engineering at the uptown branch of New York University. He was generally considered to be the most practical and level-headed of all of us, but he presented a superior, remote attitude toward us, as well. Heavy drinking and a huge increase in weight turned him into a zombie during his final years.

Some years before his death, Flo had been taken gravely ill with a rare blood disease. I was delivering two talks in New Orleans on the court theaters and particularly Louis XIV, after whom the French territory had been named 300 years earlier, in conjunction with their Sun King Exhibition in April, 1984. Flo called me to warn me of the seriousness of her illness; there was a possibility of her not surviving. She did not want her sudden death to shock me. I did not want to believe it would happen so quickly, so I continued on to Houston for a quick visit before returning to New York.

Just after arrival in Houston, Gene, Flo's husband, telephoned to announce her death. My host and hostess were disturbed all through the night by my weeping. I was stunned all the way back to New York, and drank in despair on the plane. I had to be taken to the taxi in a wheelchair, weakened and "in my cups." When back in the New York apartment, I began preparing for the trip up along the Hudson River to Croton for the funeral. The expected open casket made the ceremony even more horrible to bear.

It has seemed to me, from previous grievous occasions, that I have been blessed by The Powers that Be with the ability to assuage deepest suffering. Back in my apartment, the phone rang, and it was an attractive young German man whom I had known in Berlin. He was now in the city. He asked to come over, and I could see how I could use this well-timed distraction. I gratefully accepted this unexpected gift.

It might be that I was at a time in life when death becomes more prevalent among friends and relatives. Deaths seemed to be clustering in my life. Publicist Jeremyn Davern was always a very special friend to me. It was always a treat to have "a fowl dinner" at her apartment. She never claimed culinary skills and found doing a chicken dish easiest, but she did not always achieve great success in the cooking of it, hence the play on foul/fowl. However, her conversation was always stimulating. Jeremyn as a very young woman had been an assistant to the colorful Elsa Maxwell, who made her living out of entertaining and introducing people to each other. One could meet the Duke and Duchess of Windsor by paying her a fee, for example. Hence, Jeremyn got to know many people as a result of her exposure with Elsa Maxwell. I met Jeremyn when I did special events with Marianne Strong Associates. Jeremyn was one of her associates and was on hand for the *Lord Jim* premiere, as well as my involvement in other projects.

Over the years, Jeremyn and I had enjoyed many a scotch together with those fowl dinners. Early on, Jeremyn shared a summer accommodation at the Tower

House in Southampton with Barbara Horgan, whom I had the pleasure to meet through her. Barbara worked as George Balanchine's personal aide for many, many years; she was one of his major beneficiaries when he died. Barbara invited me on occasion to the New York City Ballet, and over the years I got to know her parents and see her mother, Dorothy, in Taos, where she summered. At Christmas, I sometimes helped trim the tree at the Horgan Park Avenue apartment.

Jeremyn enjoyed coming to Lu Shan. She liked Lila's conversation and company. It came as a stunning surprise, when she died of some inherited family disease without much warning—a lesson to us all, perhaps. After Jeremyn's death, Barbara mentioned how sad she was that they didn't have the opportunity to grow old together. Barbara and I commented on being last men standing. . . .

Apollo Muses had been operating officially since 1985, but we had been producing events for ten years before that. I was getting weary of writing envelopes for mailings, licking stamps, writing promotions, and titillating the press into coverage for the various programs. Dorothy was a tremendous support in keeping momentum, but after more than twenty years of doing it, I felt depleted both in energy and inspiration.

India had been wooing me away from the care-ridden life of tending a limping Apollo Muses. Between freelance stipends and monies saved from producing Apollo Muses events, I could afford a change. Dispirited, I directed attentions to the wonders of the East. Since Fred had died, I was free to go places where I could not have taken him. With plans for extended travel, I realized it was advantageous to sell Thumbelina in favor of buying a nearby spacious condo. It is easier to close

Dorothy and her brother Douglas Dillon with his wife Suzzie attend an Apollo Muses dinner-concert aboard the Barge.

Toshiko and Dorothy enjoying the company of New Jersey Ballet ballerinas.

up a condo and depart without cares than doing so with a house. An impressive profit was gained, as well as added freedom for travel. Lila would have been pleased. As it turned out, she had taken care of me in a greater manner than the Luces ever cut out of the will!

After a few years, I was made president of the condo association. That brought many entanglements, making my life there too complicated for my taste. A short walk down the road toward the railway station was a delightful carriage house dating back to 1848. As it was smaller and modest in rent, I opted to sell the condo and in favor of the carriage house. This was a wise choice, as I could dedicate more spending money for the exploration of India.

By 2005, I had made several trips to India and had written many travel articles about my adventures. Then, I began to accept speaking engagements to share my enthusiasm for this wondrous Subcontinent. I was on a United States lecture tour talking about India, when my dear friend Dorothy Dillon Eweson died. My life would be diminished without her quiet company at the symphony or opera. She added ballast to my existence.

A couple from Paris asked me about Santa Fe while I was visiting France. They indicated a desire to visit there, offering the Paris apartment in exchange for a place in Santa Fe. I knew of a Santa Fe couple with a very comfortable home who were very willing to do an exchange, especially as they had never been to Paris. The deal was brokered by me. I decided to go to Santa Fe for that period, as well. There was room enough in the house, and I had a car that could get us around.

Home during a Santa Fe winter.

The Bush/Cheney atmosphere around the Republican stronghold of Far Hills was stifling to me. I had quietly put Apollo Muses to sleep after almost twenty-four years of a successful run with a farewell concert at Weill Recital Hall at Carnegie Hall. There was no need to be amidst the ultra conservative atmosphere in central New Jersey. It was so stringent in suppressing criticism that even the controversial saying on a bumper sticker on a car parked at the Gladstone railroad station would invite flat tires and a keyed car to await its owner upon return from the city. I was angered and frustrated at the high-handedness of those running our government, and I felt gagged by the Far Hills narrow-mindedness. It would be a relief to go to Santa Fe.

Almost all my life, I have been an active liberal Democrat. Sometimes I suppressed my feelings in accepting a lunch or dinner at the Southampton Bath & Tennis Club, or its counterpart in East Hampton, where the token black or token Jew was the norm. During the late '60s in Santa Fe, I mingled with the Anglo elite to promote art sales (with some thrill at swimming in that rarified pool of wealth and glamour) while doing a tightrope walk in support of the struggling artists, Hispanics, and Indians. However, time supposedly heals all wounds . . .

Santa Fe lives in a bubble. It took a while for discrimination acts to become effective. The Kennedys, Martin Luther King, LBJ and others instituted much overdue change. Lots had happened since the '60s. What a wonderful change awaited me in the "The City Different" since my days there decades before. What a joy to notice bumper stickers in profusion everywhere, freely supporting or criticizing anything from government to soy milk! The Friendship Club had moved down Cerrillos Road to new headquarters that were much roomier and more comfortable; a gay meeting to deal with alcohol or drug abuse was held at the St. Bede's Episcopal Church off of St. Francis Drive, giving another dimension to my life in recovery.

This vibrant environment was a blessing after the diminishment of my New Jersey existence. Without my great friends Lila, Dorothy and dear Fred, and the challenges of Apollo Muses to absorb my energies, life assumed a drabness I would not endure. Santa Fe revived me. Though the French visitors brought their own problems to our sharing a house together, I was stimulated by my reunion with New Mexico. It was time for a change. "The Land of Enchantment" had won me over, again. I wanted to absorb the vast vistas across the high desert with the Sandia Peak more than fifty miles to the south and the Jemez Mountains in the distance to the west. Nearby, the easterly Sangre de Cristo Mountains snuggled Santa Fe like a protective parent. Nature mingled with the lively tri-cultural activities, blending into a joyous experience.

My life has been enriched by the generosity of friends. When I returned to New Jersey, I knew I must plan to move what I needed to Santa Fe. The rest of the accumulated flotsam and jetsam from more than twenty years of Apollo Muses had to be given away or disposed of in a garage sale or trash collection. There were a series of farewell lunches and dinners. No final good-byes as we all travel and I would make periodic appearances, for sure. Bruce Whitacre assisted me in the garage sale, and Candido Suores gallantly drove me in a van, pulling my car on a dolly across the country to the small guesthouse that I rented on Don Diego, near the center of Santa Fe.

Taking the short cut to Santa Fe at Cline's Corners, I heard Diego Mulligan on his radio show, "The Journey Home." I made note of his studio telephone number for future use. It would be pleasant to do a radio show with him, announcing that I was back in town and available for book-signings and lectures. (Eventually, we did seven shows together.) Our travel route avoided going into hectic Albuquerque and then cutting north. The road had a lovely landscape, rimmed with mountains, and made for a more enjoyable entry—through the high desert of chamisa, Russian sage and piñon—into Santa Fe, the City Different.

Admiring an amusing mural in remote hill town El Rito, above Abiquiú.

Chapter 18

A Sage Who Somehow Strayed

While I was still residing in New Jersey, the Millennium: A.D. 2000 approached quickly. The momentous entering into a new millennium created great speculation, some pertaining to the potential confusion or complications electronics might have in making the transition. Would the bank vaults, ATMs, and timed gates be able to cope with the new year beginning with a "2," or would there be inconvenient mishaps, lockouts, or operational failures? Many people were stashing away cash in case banking problems arose. Would some soothsayers' predictions of doom and destruction prove disastrously correct? We awaited the arrival of year 2000 with mixed emotions ranging from curiosity to trepidation.

My beloved Fred had gone to doggie heaven, so not only was the back seat of my car available for other uses, but I was free during the winter months to travel internationally without responsibilities tying me down. India had long stirred my imagination. It was not clear in my mind just what Hinduism encompassed, nor how it differed from Jainism, Sikh beliefs, the Zoroastrian-inspired Parsi religion, Buddhism, and Islamic ideology—all a part of India's heritage.

The advent of the millennium seemed a propitious occasion for me to investigate India's historic wonders, resulting from having the oldest ongoing culture in the world—ancient Hindu temples, Muslim mosques, a Jewish synagogue from the 1500s, and even vestiges of early Christian settlements that predated those in the

Western world. This was the birthplace of Buddha and the land of gurus, swamis, silks, gems, sandalwood, incense, elephants, and the sacred cow.

I anticipated that I would need enormous energy and an adventuresome intrepidness to tackle on my own the challenges of this undertaking. It was now or never!

I was determined to cope with travel impediments well-established in my mind: dilapidated buses and broken roads clogged with all varieties of carts, cars, trucks, and meandering cows or sometimes camels, goats, and the occasional elephant, or trains that sometimes operated with huge delays belying the promises of time tables. Add to that the constant threat of diseases such as malaria, hepatitis, encephalitis, and cholera, vermin or bug infestations, and the intestinal disorders I had been warned about. It would test my courage and fortitude.

Undergoing a complete regime of shots and medical precautions in preparation for departure, I carefully consulted not less than five different guidebooks on India. The country is one-third the size of the United States (with three times the population). It seems more enormous because the transportation infrastructure is not what an American is used to. Getting around can be a slow process for reasons indicated above, adding to the impression that India is so very vast.

Having an engaging friend who had moved back to her childhood home in India from London, I decided to begin my adventure in Madras. My friend, Katya Douglas, lived in Tiruvannamalai in the general area west of Madras. Also, I liked the idea of Madras, recalling the pleasant textile design. The die was cast: off to Madras, now known as Chennai. What a joy to have had the courage to take the big leap into mysterious, forbidding, exotic India!

Fog enshrouded my taxi waiting in a long queue of lorries and other vehicles on the highway into Chennai. International flights arrive in India before dawn, and traffic on the road is curtailed until a set hour, permitting a free flow into the city. My tension was steadily rising in anticipation of what was about to befall me in this very foreign land. My pre-paid taxi finally began to move as my consternation mounted about what to expect at the Atlantic Hotel, which had been recommended to me by my friend, Anne Mustoe, the intrepid round-the-world bicyclist who had stayed there previously. My mind was tainted by rumors of poor conditions in India. I might have to fend off bugs and vermin in my room. Would I be able to cope with these impending challenges on a daily basis?

Just before arrival at the hotel, I was thrilled to spot my first holy cow. It was slowly ambling along the misty road searching for a scrap to consume. This sight fascinated me, giving me reassurance that India was about to reveal itself to me.

The lobby of the hotel was in half light as the sun had not yet risen, and much of the electricity was turned off. The only arriving visitor, I was led to the registration books at the desk. One ledger was for the hotel and the other for the government controls. While I was writing down my identity, passport number, and visa information, I was amazed at the *puja* (offering) ceremony in progress nearby. Ganesha, the elephant-headed god, was being worshipped by the Hindu staff. Strands of orange marigolds adorned the statue's neck with flickering candles below. Incense, bell ringing, and chants established that I was indeed in India, and it was thrilling.

The lobby was quite attractive but upon exiting the elevator at my floor, it was obvious that no expense was spent on upstairs decoration. The walls were bare and showed the signs of wear from passing traffic over the years. The big moment came when the door to my room was opened and a light switched on. My eyes darted quickly at the bed, under it, and around in the corners but there was no sign of any activity. I entered the bathroom to inspect the facilities and noted again that the place was clean and seemingly free of the dreaded insects and vermin that taunted my imagination. What a relief!

After the staff member departed and wished me a good rest, I investigated the mattress for any telltale signs of bedbugs. Again, I was reassured that so far all the talk about sanitary dangers in India held no validity here. In my lengthy experiences visiting grand friends on both Fifth Avenue and Park Avenue in New York City there was constant evidence of roach infestation and vermin despite costly extermination efforts. Here I was in only an inexpensive three-star hotel in India, not a luxury hotel. However, the comparison was favorable, and I could relax more.

It did not take long to realize with both surprise and appreciation how fastidious was the Hindu sense of personal hygiene. Cleanliness is part of their religion and culture. The paradox, I noticed, is that there is an astonishing disregard for public sanitation, despite the individual practice of personal hygiene. There is an army of civil workers who are supposed to come along and clean up the mess dropped by everyone walking along the streets. (Rubbish bins are not normally available, other than in Goa.) Often, trash accumulates into an unattractive eyesore. In theory, it is a useful way of employing vast numbers of people. Like so many other things in India, the implementation falls short of efficiency.

Museum going is one of my favorite pastimes. What better way to learn something of the history and culture of India than visiting a museum? I am a spoiled American. I was not expecting to find the treasures so poorly tended to in Chennai's National Museum and Art Gallery. The display cases were not kept clean, with traces of mouse droppings inside and around the valuable sculpture. I was soon to learn that money is misappropriated on all levels of governmental activities. It is often surprising that anything functions with such a creaking, eroding infrastructure. However, there is much to impress the visitor, be it the Raj influence of the British building that reshaped colonial India or the many Hindu temples with their flow of colorfully clad worshippers.

In the shaded porticos within the compound of the larger temples, families and friends gather to share food and conversation in between their pujas and prayers. There is a lively interchange here among people who appeared to have so little to be joyful about. Ancient Hindu temples grant succor to the supplicants and usually tolerate foreign visitors, keeping restricted areas off limits. Before entering the temple compound through the gates in one of the high sloping gopurams (towering structures bedecked with myriads of brilliantly polychrome deities), shoes are checked, and cameras stowed away. One can stroll clockwise around smaller shrines and areas for prayer before entering the main sanctuary for observance of a puja. Offerings of coconut, flowers, and fruit are brought for the officiating Brahmin to bless in exchange for receiving a *tika* (usually a red dot smeared on the forehead of the worshipper).

It was reassuring to me to notice that even the poorest Hindu children left their rudimentary dwellings to attend school, their eyes bright, their faces smiling, their hair neatly combed, and clothing spotless. Though barefoot, they exuded a strength and inner contentment that I can only imagine comes from a strong faith-based life. This was a comforting surprise to me. Extreme hardship is the way of life for most Indians. They have become accustomed to it but are supported in their plight by staunch spirituality.

I was to learn that St. Thomas (Doubting Thomas) was believed to have spent his final days here in the Chennai area. Legend has it that he lived in a small cave at Little Mount and walked daily to the beach at Mylapore to preach. It is interesting to note that Christianity came to India before it infiltrated into the West.

The constant presence of spirituality permeates the atmosphere. Loin-clothed *sadhus* (holy men), with their staffs and begging bowls, clustering in front of a temple or ashram; sounds of temple bells mingling with the scent of incense; the calling to prayer of the *mullah* at the mosque—all are parts of the ancient traditions in Southern India, which have been less affected by time and invasion than other portions of the country.

After a few days of walking around Chennai and engaging an auto-rickshaw to see outstanding sights, including a visit to the Kapaleeswarar Temple in the Mylapore sector dating back to the 13th century, it was time to move on. I was eager to visit some of the two hundred temples in the nearby hilltop city of Kanchipuram, noted for its silk factories as well as temples.

The ultimate goal that day was to reach the famous beach community of Mahabalipuram. I thought it would be more adventuresome to go the distance in an auto-rickshaw, which was a mistake. Though seemingly cheaper than a taxi, the three-wheeled vehicle does not permit good viewing from the passenger's back seat. The roof is low and the rolled up canvas (to be let down for wet weather use) hampers visibility, unless one is a child or a midget. Worse, each progression over potholes or ruts jolts the spinal column, creating growing discomfort. Finally, the travel is slower than a taxi. The few rupees saved does not seem worth it when one tallies up the negatives.

Putt-putting south in the auto-rickshaw on Kamaraj Road along Chennai's lengthy Marina Beach, I enjoyed passing the Indo-Saracenic buildings of the government and university on the right. This fanciful combination of Hindu, Muslim, and Victorian Gothic styles reminded me this is a place with roots in all three cultures.

It was about forty-seven lurching miles to Kanchipuram, a most holy city of pilgrimage. I had heard that Ekambareswarar temple is one of the many MUST visit temples there; however, unfortunately, it was closed to visitors. I learned too late that most temples maintain visiting hours, with mid-day closings. Luckily, I did find a couple of temples that permitted me entry. After looking into some silk shops, I continued my putt-putting down to Mamallapuram (as it was called during the Raj) along the Bay of Bengal. Like so many other locales in post-Raj India, this name was changed to Mahabalipuram, to give the town more of an Indian identity. After three hundred years of English tyranny, name changes of streets and cities after Independence in 1947 conferred Indian-ness.

The old fashioned Silver Beach Resort became my resting place for the next week or so. The two storied clapboard hotel had seen better days, but I found it charming. There was an air of Englishness about it, seemingly a carry-over from the Raj. My bedroom was on the second floor, set back from the sea. Flowers had been artfully arranged on my bedspread on the day of check-in, which I found vastly enchanting. The dining room was facing the sea and was screened in to allow breezes but not flying insects. It was very pleasant to enjoy vegetarian dishes lightly seasoned with curry and turmeric, as I do not like highly spiced dishes. Sometimes, I would enjoy a fish caught that day from the Bay of Bengal lapping at the beach in front of me, sautéed with onions and garlic.

Across from its entry was a small boutique run by a young Kashmiri. He showed me many diverse items to tempt any first time to India visitor: shirts of silk or cotton with pajama pants, jewelry, and carved gods in bronze or teak. During the week to follow, I often stopped in to talk with him and sometimes buy a trinket. He encouraged me to return later in the evening for more intimate interchanges.

My curiosity about the Moslem's and Hindu's same-sex practices began to clarify as my time went by in India. I knew that the Empress of India, Queen Victoria, had conferred with lawmakers for the running of India. It was clearly decided that homosexual relations between men was to be unlawful and punishable. When Queen Victoria was asked about creating a provision regarding women, she is reported to have stated: "That is not necessary. Women do not do such a thing!" Lesbians find India a comfortable nesting place, while gay men must show caution and keep activities behind closed doors with curtains pulled. However, the gay rights movement is growing in India, and legislation may bring changes in the near future. My investigations were carefully modulated to this new environment—my caveat was to remember I was not in Provincetown, New York or Santa Fe. Rather, I was a guest in a land with a foreign code of behavior and values, all of which I must learn and respect—or possibly suffer grave consequences.

Silver Beach Resort was perhaps a mile north of the charming town, Mamallapuram, heavily populated with bohemian-styled Westerners. I enjoyed the walk along the beach toward town, carefully avoiding human fecal land mines left behind from the behinds of fishermen below the high tide line. I wondered why they didn't take a tip from cats and bury their shit! Daily ablutions on the seaside were a solution to lack of toilets in their huts. The left hand is used in place of toilet paper; hence, one does not eat with the left hand or pass things to one another with that hand. Splashes of seawater washed off their hands and bottoms. What could be simpler? It did startle me the first few times strolling along the breakers to note the squatting folk serenely absorbed in their task at hand.

Women selling recycled silk saris (now made into scarves) or vending fresh fruit wandered the beach in search of tourist trade. One day, an attractive twenty-ish Hindu man with a sack approached me as I sat on the beach. He engaged me in conversation about where I was from and established that he was a stone-carving artist. Sonny Saravanan proceeded to show me small carvings of deities that he had created. They were strikingly beautiful and reasonable in price. After buying a few, I asked him to show me around his town famous for its ancient wall carvings and the Shore Temple.

The Shore Temple was built by the Pallava king Rajasimha in the early eighth century. The waters of the Bay of Bengal wash the feet of the statue of Vishnu in a cosmic sleep, while the entrance through a courtyard in the back is in a massive wall, atop of which are two reclining bulls and two Shiva towers.

When the tsunami hit this coast in 2005, another temple and ruins were uncovered as the surge of water receded briefly. These stones had not been viewed for many centuries after the seas swallowed them up. I heard talk of these fabled, extraordinary early constructions that lobster fishermen claimed to have seen when diving underwater. A sudden and startling peek into the dim past was briefly noted by astonished onlookers, only to be reclaimed minutes later as the tsunami hit again this beleaguered fishing village.

Sonny became my first real Indian friend. (My dalliances with the Kashmiri shopkeeper were pleasant but superficial.) Daily contact helped our friendship blossom over the coming years. With the help of guidebook descriptions, Sonny explained the wonders of the stone carvings in bas-relief on huge boulders as well as in temples. The largest bas-relief, 96 feet long and 43 feet high, is the Penance of Arjuna. It is also called the Descent of the Ganges. This monumental work is carved on two adjacent boulders and dates from the seventh-century Pallava dynasty.

Sonny walked me around to other smaller temples and caves in the immediate vicinity. This sunny place by the sea offers a good mix of artistry—both contemporary as well as historic—and tourist pleasures such as eateries and shops. Many Western residents resemble remnants of the hippie era, adding to the laid-back feel of the place.

It occurred to me that Sonny was depleting so much energy walking up and down the beach peddling his carvings. Would it not be better to establish a simple workshop cum gallery where sculptures could be viewed and sold? Sonny and other young artists could chisel away in this workshop atmosphere. Tourists like to see artists at work, and then be able to buy some of the resultant objects.

After much consideration, I decided seed money for the creation of a shop and workplace for young stone cutters could be raised through my not-for-profit organization in America, Apollo Muses. This was one of the outcomes of my initial visit here: the formation of the Sathi Gallery for young stone sculptors. Unfortunately, some short years down the road, the tsunami washed the venture away. There have been attempts to resuscitate the workshop and gallery. Time will tell . . .

Being young and adventuresome, Sonny agreed to accompany me on a local bus headed south to the once French city of Pondicherry, now officially called Puducherry and nicknamed Pondy. From the layout of the broad boulevards, the French taste and influence were evident. As in many other cities in India, signs of deterioration were noticeable in this now-polluted city by the sea. The French architectural panache was clearly in need of restoration.

At the end of Goubert Avenue (Beach Road) on the Bay of Bengal is the neat, ideally situated Park Guest House. The facility is meant for members and devotees of the nearby ashram, set up by the former freedom fighter and philosopher Sri Aurobindo and his companion, the Mother, in the late '60s. However, tourists are allowed to stay if they adhere to curfews and institutional rules banning smoking and alcohol consumption. (As a Betty Ford graduate, I qualified.)

While Sonny watched our luggage, I enquired at the desk for the availability of a twin-bedded room. The officious clerk gave me a key to investigate the room upstairs facing the sea. It was very pleasant with a wonderful vista over the sea and gardens below, and at a reasonable price. I eagerly told the young man I would take the room. He asked where the second person was. Upon sizing up Sonny in his poor attire, I was informed that the room was not available. This was my first major wake-up to caste prejudice. Sonny was of a lower order of beings. Despite my strong vocal protestations, this Brahmin haughtily discharged us from the premises!

I was furious and embarrassed for my guide's sake, and resented having lost such a wonderful place to stay. Things happen for a reason or a variety of reasons. We were to discover another lovely place the next day. In the meantime, we settled into a smallish, poorly-ventilated room nearby. Our feelings of frustration, hurt, and anger subsided, as Sonny initiated a very comforting, cozy feeling of exciting intimacy. For the moment, nothing mattered but this pleasured moment...

The next morning, we took an auto-rickshaw several kilometers north to the famous Auroville, a group of villages conceived by the Mother as an experiment in international living. Since the place was inaugurated in 1968 with the notion to reflect the unity of the human spirit, eco-friendly projects are undertaken there.

At the visitor center, I became interested in gaining access to the Matrimandir, an ugly concrete tower containing an amazing crystal used in contemplation. One has to submit a request and return the following day, which I did for both of us. While at the center, I became aware of an ashram named Quiet Beach nearby on the Bay of Bengal. It seemed worthwhile to apply there for accommodations.

Quiet Beach offered modern, airy, and pleasant accommodations that were a joy to indulge in after our experience at the Park Guest House. It was run by an American man from California, who infused the ashram with congeniality. The fusion food (Western-influenced Indian dishes) served on a covered terrace was delicious, and, as a bonus, a modest amount of laundry was done free of charge. The other visitors were an international mix, making for interesting conversation over meals.

While walking on the beach, I attracted many children of local fishermen. School pens were what they asked for, and as I had brought a large number of ballpoint pens for such occasions, I instructed them to meet me at a beached boat almost in front of the walled garden of Quiet Beach the next afternoon at 3 p.m. Sonny noticed from our balcony that some kids began to loiter around the boat early in the afternoon. It dawned on me then that none of the children had wristwatches, and possibly there were no clocks in their homes. So they may have guessed at the 3 o'clock hour. The crowd of youngsters swelled in number by the appointed hour. Sonny tried to have them line up in an orderly fashion, but their enthusiasm seemed unable to be contained. The pens were quickly grasped by the hands of the joyful kids. It was a fun free-for-all, with me feeling like the Pied Piper when I retreated back through the gate in the wall.

The next morning, Sonny and I returned to Auroville for a viewing of the crystal in the Matrimandir. We had our permission paper in hand and proceeded towards the new, ugly tower. A gruff attendant ordered everyone to place their shoes in a specific place, to stand on line in an orderly fashion, and NO TALKING! A Nazi concentration camp came to mind as I slowly progressed toward the cold tower, obeying orders barked by the enforcer in charge.

When we descended from the viewing, I noticed two people standing in the distance under a banyan tree. I had seen them leaving the tower before us, and thought it would be a nice place to sit and meditate. We started over towards them, when the gruff attendant demanded to know where we were going. I indicated the couple under the tree in the distance, and said I wanted to go where the other two people were. "You CAN NOT! That is only for IMPORTANT people!" he barked.

Although I had planned to stay after the viewing to meditate in this special place, my only thoughts now were to escape. A change in directorship of Auroville had greatly altered the complexion of the place. It certainly did not reflect what the Mother or Sri Aurobindo had in mind. In sharing notes with other visitors over the years, we concurred on the off-putting behavior both at Park Guest House and at Auroville.

From Pondicherry, I telephoned my friend who had recently sold her London flat and returned to the family home in Tiruvannamalai, where she had spent her formative years. I announced where I was and that I planned to go to the Sri Ramanashram the next day by bus. Katya Douglas seemed pleased to hear from me but firmly insisted that I come to her home to stay, a more comfortable alternative to the ashram. Osborne House was just down the lane from the main entrance to the ashram, and she suggested it was easy to visit from her home.

It is wise for any visitor to India to quickly adjust to the notion of selective hearing, seeing, and smelling for better enjoyment of the wonders available in the stream of daily activity. Western sensibilities have to be restrained. Because of the paucity of toilet facilities, bus stations have a strong acrid odor resulting from many travelers relieving themselves on the perimeters while waiting to board a bus. Making mental adjustments is a carapace to the assault on the olfactory glands.

The bus station in Pondicherry was little more than a dusty lot with a confusion of buses coming and going. In the morning, Sonny got me on to the correct bus going to Tiruvannamalai. My destination was not far away in miles, but the rickety bus was to make every local stop. This greatly increased travel time but gave me a good glimpse into life in small villages. Groups of young girls in their uniforms were going home from school. They waved, giggled, and smiled sweetly to me, sitting glued to the window. Sometimes, if time permitted, I could pass some of my remaining pens to them. For Indians generally, a Western visitor in out-of-the-way places stimulates curiosity. I was just as curious about them.

Sights and sounds galore picked up on local bus travel greatly enhanced my growing view of Mother India. Marketplaces displaying fruits, vegetables, spices, and flowers; large vessels of aluminum or colored plastic surrounding hand pumps at the communal wells; and the helter-skelter wanderings of cows and other animals were fascinating to behold. By afternoon, I arrived in the center of Tiruvannamalai. There was a mass of chaotic activity around me, but I managed to secure an auto rickshaw. This brief ride delivered me to the gate of Osborne House, which was surrounded by a high wall within which were trees and a large garden. The residence was set back with a couple of smaller brick houses on the right, presumably for resident help.

A series of surprises were about to reveal themselves to me as my experiences in India grew. I had known Katya Douglas in London. She had been a promising film actress and mother of three young girls. Katya was personable, lovely, and amusing. I knew she had an Indian connection from her earlier years, but it was all very vague. Selling the flat on Embankment Gardens that I knew so well, Katya moved back to her family home in Tiruvannamalai, where she had many life-altering experiences. Some of these, I was soon to discover, had to do with the benign influences of the Bhagavan Sri Ramana Maharshi, who was a mixture of Merlin, Father Christmas, a beloved grandfather, and God to the very young girl. "We knew he was discreetly all-powerful and definitely magic—far beyond ordinary mortals. In fact, we knew he was extraordinary but we also took it for granted in the way children do," states Katya in recollection.

Katya's insistence that I stay with her at Osborne House created a lively and comfortable connection to the highly-charged spiritual life in this community. Now that I was pearl-hurling distance from the famous Sri Ramanashram, I discovered that Katya had a famous father. Arthur Osborne created *The Mountain Path*, a magazine published by the ashram, and was a devotee of the Bhagavad Sri Ramana Maharshi. I noted with pleasure that his impressive writings were on sale at the bookstore in the ashram.

Once inside the large iron gates of the Sri Ramanashram, past the various gurus with begging bowls and staffs, I saw peacocks strutting about the spacious grounds. Many monkeys pranced around or were perched on the roofs of the ashram observing the visitors, probably hoping to get a peanut or banana.

My favorite place at the ashram was the audience room where Sri Ramana Maharshi talked with visitors as well as to the peacocks and monkeys. Legend has it that when he heard that the monkeys were going to be rounded up and taken away by some civic organization, the Bhagavan counseled the playful primates to take their long tails and go elsewhere for awhile. When the animal collectors arrived to the ashram, not a monkey was found!

The Bhagavan's black leather chaise longue is still in its original place. In his later life, his legs were so crippled with arthritis that it was necessary for him to semi-recline on the chaise longue. To this day, many people come here to meditate and pray, as well as share mental thoughts with the departed saint.

Meditation was a fairly new practice in my life. I had spent lots of time in quietude ruminating over various things, but only recently attempted to strive for an emptiness to permit an inward flow of energy. I had tried developing meditation since my brief visit to the Sivananda Ashram in the Bahamas, before coming to India. I discovered the complement of meditation to the practice of prayer, believing that prayer was stated intentions "going out" and answers might "come in" through meditation. It was a wonderful addition to my life of burgeoning spirituality.

Here in the Bhagavan's chamber, I sat quietly, clearing myself of all external distraction. After a brief time, the unexpected happened. There seemed to be an elevator going up and down within my chest. I assumed I was falling ill, victim of some overbearing disease. Alarmed that I would be besieged by this mysterious ailment, I rose to return to the comfort of Osborne House. In the courtyard outside, I realized the inner sensation had completely disappeared and I felt perfectly fine. To my astonishment, I was told my experience was one many sought to achieve through deep meditation. My chakras (bodily points of energy) had aligned themselves, responding to my entering a meditative state. I felt the Bhagavan had bestowed upon me a rare gift. I could appreciate Katya's devotion to him since childhood, and her continuing relationship with him. Often, she would kneel by the chaise longue and explain her thoughts and plans, keeping her beloved saintly Ramana up-to-date with her life.

Ramana taught primarily through the sheer impact of his presence. One of his avid supporters and writer about his life, Katya's father, Arthur Osborne, had said, "His real teaching was not the explanation but the silent influence; the alchemy worked in the heart."

Thanks to the seasoned indoctrination to life in Tiruvannamalai and a crash introduction to Hinduism, Katya opened vistas of understanding. She told me there were many charlatans around posing as gurus. She claimed that anyone who struck an uncomfortable pose and held it long enough would attract a following. I was warned there were many spurious gurus who proliferate around this spiritually charged city. People were so desperate to believe in something that they would give blind support to gurus who captured their imagination. Some of these frauds gained substantial wealth hoodwinking their followers.

Whether it be the hugging Amma, Sai Baba, or the many others like them, living gods and saints are a phenomenon in India. (I was to find this out when I participated in a spiritual conference in Orissa a few years later, when I was conferred sainthood!) It is not just the devotions from Westerners, but needful Indians, as well, who are urgently questing a spiritual balm. Indians are prone to worship holy men, in general.

Katya contends that everything one hears about India is true, but so is the opposite. Further, she claims, "This is a country with a big heart in which people live in different centuries on the same street!"

View of the sacred mountain Arunachala from Katya's Tiruvanavnali home.

The ten-day festival Kartikai Deepam was celebrated while I visited Katya. Pilgrims come from all over to climb Arunachala, the mountain that symbolizes Shiva. The ghee (purified butter) that the pilgrims bear as an offering is dropped into a huge cauldron that has been dragged to the top. As the sun sets on the due date, the fire is lit and is kept burning for a week. After dinner when the skies darkened, Katya gathered the household up onto the top terrace to observe the lighting of the ghee that first night, glowing in the distance.

The deities Shiva and his consort, Parvati, fashioned from copper and bronze and adorned with diamond and gold jewelry, are bedecked in numerous floral garlands of jasmine and marigolds. They are purposely created for carrying in procession, because the idols of the gods in their respective sanctums are carved in heavy, immovable stone. The gods are placed on huge wagons or chariots, then wheeled around town and around the hill. It takes the pulling and pushing of hundreds of celebrants to move these chariots around, at a snail's pace, under the admiring gazes of the town folk.

My fortunate stay in Arthur Osborne's house under the warm guidance of his daughter, Katya, launched my further inquiries into the mystique of India. As this pleasant visit ended, it was Madurai that lured me on my southerly passage toward the tip of India. This city of Hindu intensity offers as a major attraction, the vast and impressive Sri Meenakshi Temple.

Madurai is the second largest city in Tamil Nadu, and it old sector is known as Temple City. It was built as the capital of the Pandya dynasty 2,500 years ago.

My companion Raja being bonked by an elephant in Aarathy courtyard.

Supposedly, it name came from the Tamil word for honey, relating to the legend of Shiva shaking nectar out of his locks to purify and bless the new city.

The great Meenakshi Temple is in the center of three concentric squares of streets crammed with shops and stalls. Almost daily there are religious processions leading to and from the temple. A painted temple elephant is led out each evening to offer blessings to worshipers. When a coin is put into its extended trunk, it carefully drops the coin into a receptacle next to the *mahout* (elephant keeper). The trunk is then raised, curled, and lowered gently onto the head of the donor as a blessing.

The *gopura*, with its profusion of gaily-painted stucco gods and demons, is a prominent feature of southern temples. The Meenakshi complex has no less than twelve such towers. The four that are set into the outer walls rise to a height of forty-six meters and can be seen for miles outside the city.

An amusing place to stay within walking distance of Sri Meenakshi Temple is the Aarathy Hotel, near the bus station. Booking a room on an upper floor in the front is mandatory. A stunning view of the Koodal Alagar Perumal Temple across the street can be enjoyed from the room or its balcony. One can almost touch the carved and brightly painted figures on the gopura. An added bonus is the morning and evening visit of the temple elephant, who lumbers into the hotel courtyard for daily meals. Though the hotel accommodations are very simple, the temple view and visiting elephant are big plusses.

In sharp contrast to the pilgrimage city of Madurai is the beach community of Kovalam in neighboring Kerala. I wanted to be there to celebrate the advent of the new century. An overnight sleeper by train from Madurai to Trivandrum (now called Thiruvananthapuram) disgorges the traveler into Kerala's capital city. Former home to the rajas of Travancore, it now boasts a modern international airport and easy access to the lovely beaches at Kovalam, one half hour south by taxi, auto rickshaw, or bus.

One of the surprises upon arrival in Kovalam is the lack of streets. Aside from the main road that enters the beach town and the three arteries running down the sides of the hill to the beautiful Arabian Sea, everything is an interconnecting series of alleys or pathways for

Two small boys guide me through the fishing village near Kovalam.

pedestrians. Porters bear luggage and supplies on their heads through this maze. It is not a place for someone who does not like walking or who is unable to maneuver by foot.

This beach resort at the foot of the hill has three crescent shaped sandy beaches. The most popular is Light House Beach, crowded with shops, restaurants, and variously priced places to stay. At the northerly end of this beach is a stone promontory where I enjoyed sitting in advance of the sunrise each day. I would sit motionless facing the direction the sun would rise and meditate in quiet anticipation. As the sun rose, I could feel its welcome warmth on my face. Eyes still closed, I felt the joyful expectations of the new day dawning. Many people of the East observe the sunrise and sunset as a spiritual means of achieving centeredness and well-being. Ayurveda (Sanskrit: science of life) is a 5,000 year old Indian practice of yoga, massage, and diet that encourages being available for these natural events.

One morning, I became aware of an Indian couple sitting on the rocks near me. From the patterns in her sari and his Nehru-collared *kurta* pajamas, I assumed they were visiting from the north. The Arabian Sea was lapping at the rocks, and a pleasant peacefulness pervaded. As the sun began to rise, the woman began to chant "Om" fluctuating up and down the scale like a bird song; the man chanted a bass line. Their voices were a perfect complement to the sunrise. I was thrilled! When the event of the sun climbing into the sky in full glory was established, I discreetly followed the couple off of the rocks. With words of thanks for their musical prayers, I bade them a good day and returned home, feeling very happy in this enchanting land.

Another addition to my sunrise observances was a flute-playing Himalayan youth. As I sat quietly awaiting the sun, he would softly play on his long wooden flute. It was enthralling. In the ensuing days, a few people who had heard about this happening would arrive and sit on the beach below us to listen and watch for the sunrise. Sometimes, I would then stroll up Cardiac Hill and continue down to the next beach at Samudra where I would do stretches and some simple yoga practices. Then, I enjoyed a quick dip into the surf before taking tea on a raised area shaded by palm trees overlooking the Arabian Sea. Along the road back, I would again pass a small pink mosque with slender minarets bordering the sea, and near it, set back on the other side of the road, could be seen a small attractive complex of colorfully decorated temples dedicated to Ganesha. The quiet co-existence of Hinduism and Muslim faiths symbolized India to me. It was a wondrous way to start another day in this tropical locale.

I almost said "tropical paradise," but I encountered too many unpleasant surprises in Kovalam for that to be accurate. Two shocking events happened on the New Year's Eve of the Millennium. Wanting to avoid the hysteria of the mobs bringing in the Millennium on the beachfront, I went to bed early. Two Hindu Brahmin friends arrived before midnight outside my window to call me and urge me to come to the festivities.

Reluctantly, I got up and dressed to join them. I walked with these two students through the crowds on the beach. The police were very forceful in keeping the local Indians from mingling with the Western merrymakers in the outdoor restaurants. This reeked of prejudice to me. There was a cleared path on the beach. The Indians had to stay near the water's edge, while the Westerners enjoyed the upper area. The cleared path was used only by Westerners to go from place to place. We walked the path, unscathed by the blows from *lathis* dispensed by the police. I presumed my two Brahmin friends were permitted to pass with me in respect for their high caste. I saw many Indians hit by the police for daring to cross the line on their own beach. It seemed grossly unfair and cruel...

Fireworks were shot off. To my surprise, some Indians held the lit fireworks and got burned as a result. I wondered at the childlike quality that would permit an adult to play with fireworks without taking precautions or understanding the risks.

After making a hasty retreat to the quiet security of my room, I heard a ruckus outside as I was trying to go to sleep. I went out and looked over my balcony. In the alley were fighting Indians, viciously attacking each other and spilling blood. It was upsetting to witness. Obviously, they had imbibed much alcohol, and their suppressed anger found release. I do not know if it was a clash of castes or religions, but discontent was rife. Living where the police brutality against their own people was accepted could certainly arouse great resentment and discontent. Not everything in this beach idyll was rosy under the surface.

The Millennium arrived without confounding the electronics servicing vaults, gates, and computers. Seemingly, life was going on with no more gloom or doom than usual, and it was time for me to check into the Sivananda Ashram at Neyyerdam, not very far from Kovalam. I was assigned a room to share with an amiable, slim, blond, and young Englishman named Alan, who worked in Saudi Arabia, but was on vacation. I did pre-dawn meditation and prayers on our terrace under a star lit sky, within earshot of the Ayyappi temple resonating with chanting nearby. It was an intoxicating way to start each day. I had no idea Alan was gay until days later when we skipped attending a session of singing Sanskrit texts with our fellow congregation at the ashram. Spontaneously, we preferred hearing it from his bed. We both reveled in mingling the sacred with the profane, a spice greatly savored in the history of my life.

During those days filled with yoga, karma service (I served out food onto the palm leaves in front of the crossed legged seated fellow participants), chanting, and meditation, I realized that Alan and I were leaving the ashram on the same day and both headed to Kochi. We decided to travel together, taking the longer route by a slow ferry along the colorful backwaters to Alleppee, with a train connection to Kochi. It took several hours and cost the princely sum of about ten cents. John, a playmate I met in Kovalam, suggested meeting me at a hotel outside Alleppey, where we could spend an intimate night together before proceeding into Kochi. Alan congratulated me on the fine male specimen awaiting me in the Hotel Prince's lobby. We all three splashed in the swimming pool, enjoyed an al fresco dinner in the garden, then Alan went to his room and John and I bedded down in ours.

John introduced me to the Bijus Tourist Home on Canon Shed Road in Ernakulam, a commercial suburb of the city of Kochi. Nearby were the ferries to Fort Kochi and Mattancherry, on one of many islands off the coast. Bijus accommodations were to serve me well in the future visits to this area. During the days spent here, I managed to attend a performance of Kathakali. This classical dance-drama of Kerala originated in early the 17th century for temple performances. Strange noises to a Westerner's ear emit from the all-male performers, together with drumbeats and instrumental accompaniment. This is not easily accessible to Western tastes but is fascinating for the intrepid.

In this town, I had my introduction to ayurvedic massage, a 5,000-year-old health inducing practice. As a complement to my massages, my masseur, Antony George, encouraged me to take certain natural medicines as part of my daily routine. One paste in particular was unpleasant tasting, but I submitted as part of the treatment. Long discussions with twenty-year-old Antony about ayurvedic principles were shared over dinner, and some meetings later, I was invited to meet his parents at their home on the outskirts of town.

Antony accompanied me to his family home, as it would be complicated to find on my own. The visit was a surprising adventure into Kerala life. His name indicated he was a Christian. His Western surname George came from his father's first name. For a few generations, the family had practiced Christianity. Upon passing through a garden and going up onto the white-pillared porch, I noticed the enormous mural of Christ on the back wall of the entrance hall. Larger-than-life, Christ welcomed me with open arms. (I was reminded of the impressive male nudes on the entrance hall of Mae West's Santa Monica beach house, which was a very different kind of visual welcome.)

Although it was my first trip to India, I had learned enough protocol to guide me through this initial visit to an Indian abode. I was permitted to shake Antony's father's hand in greeting, but not his mother's hand. I put both hands together in prayer form and slightly bowed to her. I remembered that women are to be respected by avoiding all physical contact. Dinner was prepared, and I was seated at the table facing the kitchen. Antony sat on my right and his father on my left. Elsie, Antony's mother, beamed at me from the kitchen door. Some food was brought in and offered to me, then to Antony. His father did not participate in the meal other than in conversation. He was going to dine later, perhaps with his wife.

This startled me as I was in a Christian household, but it had a flavor of Hindu practice. I learned later that in some strict Brahmin homes the stranger is never invited to take food, or even allowed into the inner sanctum of the house. Above all, the visitor must never enter the kitchen to avoid polluting the food.

I had brought some sweets for dessert. Aside from specific sweets (not at all to my liking as they were cloyingly sweet), cakes made for Western tastes were not eaten in an Indian home. I enjoyed them, myself, however. This was one of many meals I was to partake in at Antony's home over the years to come.

Soon, I was bestowed with the moniker "Grandfather" by the family. In India, this is an affectionate term of respect for an older friend. On future trips, when I was invited to stay in the house, I occupied the room previously used by the grandfather of the house. This made my title doubly suitable.

Though wealthy before the communists came into power in Kerala during the '60s, George now had only the property the house is on and a small piece of land near the water's edge. His mother's large home is contiguous as is that of another relative. All the other houses in the area that once belonged to his family and were lived in by their workers were given to the workers by the government. The income dried up, and George had to take a job in an office managing security guards. That was an enormous comedown in his world. The Christian church and church grounds that were part of George's property went as well. Elsie's family property was inherited by her brother, as is the practice in India. She was left with nothing.

Despite a very sad history, the family is a merry one. George, wearing a *lunghi* tied around his waist, tends his beloved garden every morning very early. Birds of many types wander about near the pond outside Grandfather's window. Often, there is a morning cacophony of barnyard sounds. The breeding of ducks, geese, and chickens help bring in a small income to assist with the household expenses. The George family are brave and dignified people with big hearts.

While Antony was giving ayurvedic massages one afternoon, I decided to make a voyage alone by ferry to Fort Kochi. It is much more pleasant traversing the water than taking the long, commercial roundabout road from Ernakulam. It was refreshing to feel the breeze and sun on my face, hear the water splash against the side of the ferry, and observe the ocean-going cargo vessels in the harbor. The ticket for this adventure costs the equivalent of eight cents!

Having sailed from Portugal, Vasco da Gama arrived in what became Fort Kochi in 1502, seeking spices and converts. He was buried in St. Francis Church until his remains were transferred to Lisbon in 1538. This was the first European church built in India. It became Dutch Reform in 1664, and later Anglican until India achieved independence in 1947. It is now called the Church of India, with Portuguese and Dutch tombstones still in evidence.

A fascinating attraction along the sea in Fort Kochi are the Chinese fishing nets. Chinese traders were thought to have introduced the Chinese fishing nets in the 14th century. Though they can be seen around Kerala, they are identified with Fort Kochi. Heavy stones weigh down the nets, which are suspended in the air and supported by bamboo and wood birdlike structures. These nets can be lowered into the water and then raised when fish may have been trapped within.

There are strong essences of the British Raj lingering everywhere in Fort Kochi. The Parade Ground is an excellent place to imagine life under the British. Large British styled homes under enormous old shade trees abound around this

Antony George in Mattancherry.

open field, used by the Raj for military exercises. Today, youths gather to play cricket, soccer, and just to "hang out."

Mattancherry, a neighboring town, is a short auto-rickshaw ride away. It is an antiquarian's delight, with many shops displaying wondrous treasures from India's colorful past: carved doorways, columns, statuary, furniture, art objects, and carpets. For the average tourist, there are many purveyors of jewelry, shawls, and postcards both old and new. Spice shops abound as this is the Malabar Coast, famous for exotic spices.

A most popular destination for visitors is the oldest synagogue in India, built in 1568. The floor is paved with 1,100 hand-painted blue-and-white Chinese tiles. The first migration of Jews to Kerala is believed to have been in the sixth century BC; a large contingent arrived in the first century AD as a result of Roman persecution in Jerusalem. Later Portuguese and Muslim anti-Semitism flared up, threatening their community. It was not until the less-belligerent Dutch took control of the area that the Jews were able to live without fear. This area in also known as "Jew Town."

A short walk leads to a curious palace-turned-museum. It is fascinating to visit the Dutch palace, built by the Portuguese in the mid-16th century but taken over by the Dutch in 1663. They, in turn, presented it to the rajas of Kochi. Some of India's best mythological murals, including the entire *Ramayana*, decorate the walls, though deterioration over the centuries has taken its toll. As in every palace in India, huge portraits of various rajas decorate the walls of the coronation hall.

Outside, near the foot of the stairway leaving the grounds, a *fakir* playing his pipe is often seated cross-legged. A hooded cobra bobs back and forth in a basket in front of him. A mongoose on a rope stays nearby. Tourists love this scene, and are quick to photograph it. I find it less than authentic India, but so what?

Thanks to my friend John, I met a young rickshaw driver who became my personal driver every time I visited Kochi. Judy, a Christian like Antony, enlivened my visits with his comic singing and amusing antics while driving the traffic-clogged streets of Ernakulam.

After some time, I decided to help Judy buy a used rickshaw, so that he could make more money to aid his ailing mother and infirm sister. We called it "Eric's

"Eric's Joy" with Judy.

Joy," as the banner on top of his windshield proclaimed. It was clear to both of us that Eric's joy pertained to more than having his own auto rickshaw! This investment was to be gradually recycled into helping Antony do further schooling to become a nurse. After some initial repayments, the trickle dried up as meeting family expenses became Judy's priority.

Both Antony and Judy made my visits to Ernakulam far more pleasant and personal. Both of them kindly agreed to take turns escorting me to new places of interest. Judy and I went to Varkala for the beach experience and to Periyar, near Thekkady, for spying on wildlife together. Antony took me to Munnar in search of wild elephants and Parambikulam to trek tigers.

Once upon a time, India was rife with magnificent wildlife of many descriptions. This was before the maharajas and later the English began shooting everything that moved as sport. Before the English decided to deforest much of India in order to make exact cartography studies, wildlife was able to proliferate in the lush woodlands.

Today, there is an effort to save the remaining wildlife in preserves. However, poaching in national parks has continued to be a big problem. In India, regulations are passed and then promptly ignored, doubtless with the aid of *baksheesh*. The remaining wildlife are in danger of extinction.

Finally, the time came to leave India and continue my travel plans. It seemed an exciting program to go to India for the Millenium, plan the next winter in Thailand, the following one in Cambodia, and later on in China. This was not how it was going to happen.

Leaving India after my almost three-month initial stay, I knew that I was caught by the short hairs. The paradox of this multifaceted, mysterious land had me mesmerized. Just when I looked in the palm of one hand to examine a puzzle, and determined that I had the answer, I would look into the palm of the other hand and find that the opposite was true, too! Not only was paradox so evident in India, but the ongoing surprise and thrill of the unexpected in everyday life continued to intrigue me. I incorporated into my ken the notion to expect the unexpected and to take it as a matter of course.

Getting to an age thought of as being very much over the hill in the West, what could thrill a gay man more than visiting a place where old age was revered and beautiful company so readily available? This endearing aspect of India prolonged visits and blended nicely with the natural beauty of the land, peppered with stunning architecture. Another feature appealing to my continual return each year was the affordability of spending a winter there in tropical comfort. After initial explorations around the country, I opted to stay put in certain locales, taking advantage of the economy afforded by renting space rather than hoteling. My usual rental for a house or comfortable apartment ranged around $250 per month, including utilities. This is a fraction of what I would pay for a month in a hotel and much more comfortable. In Kerala, the sound of surf in the distance with musical chants from a nearby temple made the experience unforgettable. I truly had the time to stop and smell the roses. (See Appendix: "Happiness is a House on a Hill in Kovalam.")

After initial adventures into India with Sonny Saravanan (Tamil Nadu), Antony George, Judy, and John Jacobs (Kerala), my comfort and appreciation for Mother India were greatly enhanced. My further explorations into other areas of India were aided by youthful Indian companions and guides: Suhas Kumar Hore in Kolkata (Calcutta); Bismaya Kumar Pati and Dev Panda with his two nephews, Dulu and Kulu, in Orissa; and Ali in Kerala, who came with me for my initial assault on the high Himalayas in Ladakh, when I was a guest of the Indian Government, arranged through the Indian Tourist Office.

This valuable networking enabled me to travel the face of India seventeen times with great facility and pleasure. On occasion, the India Tourist Office would provide a car and driver, and sometimes a fine hotel, as well. Twenty of my travel articles on India would result in print in the *Out & About* magazine section of the seventeen *Recorder* newspapers in New Jersey. Further recompense for my energies expended in sharing my experiences resulted from a series of lectures on travel in India. These slide lectures were given at libraries and schools and at private functions where I was paid to share my informative and lively experiences. I wrote companion pieces to the lectures: *India: Paradox & Treasures*, Volumes One and Two, and *Expect the Unexpected*, eleven adventures of a Westerner sitting in the lap of Mother India, available on Amazon, was produced. A portfolio of color photographs as a limited edition, *Ganesh and Friends*, was a sold-out success.

Then there was Raja. He appeared with his auto-rickshaw near the gate of the attractive Mayfair Hotel on the seaside in Puri, Orissa. I was a guest of the hotel, writing a travel story about Orissa, and I needed the service of an auto-rickshaw to get me around the town. Providence arranged eighteen-year-old Raja to be waiting for me. His rickshaw was older and less commodious than the others, so he was available more often. This worked in my favor. I was delighted to have him as my driver, as his quiet manner charmed me.

After the Mayfair stint, I was going to explore tribal villages in another part of Orissa. When I returned to Puri during the next November for another visit, I would be staying at the Surya, a three-star hotel diagonally across from the Mayfair. Raja would importantly figure into making my life in Puri easier and more pleasurable.

On my way to the tribal villages, my itinerary included a stop-over at Bargarh, where there was an annual week-long festival in progress having to do with young Krishna, culminating in his killing his evil uncle, Kansa. I reluctantly attended, mostly because I had nothing else to do. As had happened before, when a Westerner appears at a local festival, there is a polite acknowledgement of his presence. An announcer usually states the visitor's name and where he is from. Applause follows, then on with the show. In this case, I was requested as a V.V.I.P. (I don't think V.I.P. exists in India) to sit on the stage as part of the court of King Kansa on the throne. The Master of Ceremonies announced my name and country of origin and then told the audience of 10,000 that I would address them. Address them? What could I say? Looking at the evil king on his throne staring at me as I proceeded towards the microphone, inspiration burst forth!

Realizing from all the comments I had heard on the trip bemoaning America's loss of Bill Clinton as leader of the country, I knew that I should play a good will ambassador. I told the masses of people how very glad I was to be here and in India, how much Americans loved India, and pleaded with the audience not to

Raja in fishing village with pink mosque in background.

King Kansa glares at the VVIP guest.

judge Americans by the current man in the White House! I continued on in an anti-Bush speech, occasionally glancing at the stairway leading up to the stage for the appearance of two men in sunglasses and raincoats preparing to cart me of to some forlorn, secret place. The crowd applauded, but I do not know how many understood what I had imparted to them.

Rather than the Secret Service at the foot of the staircase was a distinguished judge, Binod Kumar Pati, with his lovely wife, two pretty daughters, and cute son. They insisted that I come with them to their home for a cup of coffee, which I did. From this brief encounter, an invitation resulted from a distinguished holy man, inviting me to a spiritual conference to be held concurrent to my next scheduled visit to Orissa. The judge and his son, Bismaya, were on the board of the ashram this distinguished man headed. At their suggestion, the swami invited me to the conference. When I answered my acceptance, he then asked me to be a guest speaker, joining a roster of distinguished spiritual leaders of various faiths. With NO credentials, I was too curious to refuse this astonishing offer. It was too mystifying and outlandish to turn down!

That next visit to Orissa (in November of 2005) began with my few days at the ashram. Bismaya and his father met me at the train station in Bargarh, and I proceeded to have lunch with the family at their modest home. Bismaya would then take me to Balangir to meet my host, Swami Sri Saraprajkanda Saraswati. A youthful middle-aged man with an easy smile, "Swami-ji" bid me welcome to the ashram. A huge tent was set up in the middle of the field, with smaller tents around it, where ayurvedic medicines were available and information about the ashram and the program of events for the coming days was distributed. Another tent, with colorful printed cotton throws (or bed covers) affixed against the canvas, created a pleasant dining hall. The adjacent tent was for kitchen duties and food preparation. Nearby was a two-story building that had rooms with attached bathrooms for the guest speakers and visiting swamis or *sadhus*.

My initial talk went surprisingly well. Using my basic awareness of the power of prayer—touching on humility and generosity of spirit, and a few twelve- step program guidelines—I was able to convey a warm and friendly message to the other speakers and the attending throngs. The media focused lots of attention on me, as I was the only Westerner there. I was photographed in the press as well as on television. My white face, contrasting to those of the numerous distinguished speakers, singled me out, making me easily noticeable in the crowds.

The swami invited me have an audience with him one early evening. A beautiful red shawl was presented to me, along with an offer to give another talk to the assembled crowd. I replied in the affirmative, but with growing trepidation. What in the world could I further share with the learned speakers and assembled people? Pondering this situation, I opened the gate to the road in front of the Swami's dwelling. A couple of dozen people were assembled there, trying to get a glimpse of the holy man. Instead, they recognized me from the television, newspapers, and the conference talk. I had a red tika on my forehead and wore a faded pinkish kota/pajama outfit, with a holy red shawl over my shoulders, giving me the illusion of a holy man. As a group, they fell to their knees and began kissing my bare feet! I raised both hands and was about to say: "There has been some mistake—wait!' But my raised gesture became a blessing to the crowd! They were joyful and followed me back to my residence. From the next day until my

Guest speaker at the Spiritual Conference. "Jite Raho!" (Bless You!)

departure, I could see my doorknob turn and people file in for my blessing as they kissed my feet. The novelty wore off, and this Saint was glad to leave the ashram.

What did I speak about on the second go around? Having read Osborne's translation of Sri Ramana Maharshi's *The Nature of I*, I rambled on about "I" within myself, the "I" in all of you, and the "I" in the world. Some of my colleagues on the platform looked puzzled, as the Swami definitely was. as for the large audience, it was not possible to know how much they understood, even though there was an interpreter. Applause resulted, whether out of politeness or not, even if most did not understand much of my talk. It was amusing to be considered a Saint, however.

Shortly afterwards, I received a letter from Binod Kumar Pati, dated April 17, 2008. It moved me; it reflects a spirit of India and I treasure the sentiment:

> We all are deeply concerned about your health and future. We sincerely want that you should come over to India and stay here for the rest of your life. Bismaya, Raja and we all will look after you. Some place at the foot of the Himalayas would be most suitable for your stay. After Bismaya completes his studies we want to shift to the north, preferably, Haridwar or Rishikesh, if of course, things permit. Yours has been like the life of a Hindu sage and your spirit finds solace here. It is believed by Hindus that a Yoga-bharata Rishi, i.e. a sage who, somehow, strayed from the life of high spiritual discipline or Sādhanā, takes birth as an ordinary mortal, but [returns] again to resume his Sādhanā. There is something akin to the same in your life. So, God willing, we should all be together in the Himalayas, in the abode of God, mingling with the Himalayan masters and receiving their blessings. Please take care. Looking forward to a meeting with you in the midst of our family.
> Sincerely,
> Binod Kumar Pati

The Sacred and the Profane were about to have yet another amusing mixing. Back in Puri at the Surya Hotel, I arranged for the V(ery) V(ery) I(mportant) P(erson) press passes to the dance festival to be held at the Puri Beach pavilion. Dev Panda—in his mid-twenties and extremely handsome—was coming from Bhubaneswar, an hour's train ride away, to be my guest overnight. While at the ashram, I had enjoyed talking with him and his two nephews, Dulu and Kulu, who were only a few years younger. Members there just like Bismaya and his father, they helped in the running of the conference and were pleasing company. As I had tickets to both the dance festival in Puri as well as the dance festival at the nearby world-famous Sun Temple at Karnak, I suggested they attend performances with me. Because my hotel room could accommodate only one visitor at a time, the invitation was extended to each of them to come individually. Each young man accepted, titillating my anticipation! It amused me that I could enjoy the intimacy of the entire family, one by one. Probably, discretion would forbid them into revealing to each other any personal aspect of their individual visits.

Raja was commissioned to meet each arrival and departure, which he performed with agreeable competence. It was only after all three guys had left that I discovered Raja refused to accept payment from them for the auto-rickshaw rides, because they were friends of Mr. Eric! Here was a young man, though the highest rank of Brahmin but without much means of support, giving his time and service free of charge! This generosity of spirit from a needy person was astonishing. It amazed me, but warmed my heart even further to young Raja.

Early in the morning, in time to see the sun rising out of the Bay of Bengal, I would walk the short distance to the beach, where I would stretch and then sit in meditation. Raja also got up very early and would join me on the beach. At one point in my meditation, I felt Raja behind me, adjusting my pose. He pressed gently into my spine so that I sat straighter. This small tender gesture reflected a kind thoughtfulness I accepted with gratitude.

One time I forgot something in Raja's auto-rickshaw after returning to the hotel from some local errands. He diligently delivered it to my room. A surge of affection overwhelmed me, and I gave him a strong hug. This led to my pulling his trousers down, and to my surprise discovering an endowment unexpected on such a slight youth. Raja was stunned but bravely endured my forwardness and lust. It was a completely new experience for him, but one that he would enjoy with me over the years to come.

When I arrived in Kovalam after a very long train trip from Orissa, I thought a lot about Raja and missed his warm company. I had just rented a small house with a garden overlooking the not-too-distant Arabian Sea. On impulse, I telephoned Raja in Puri and suggested that I would like to hire him to take care of me and the house for the next couple of months. He agreed and prepared to take the train to Kerala, even though he had scarcely any money beyond the train fare. Bravely, he set off to the unknown and arrived with only a few coins to his name. He must have trusted finding me and have had confidence in my taking care of him.

That was eight years ago. Since then, we have made many trips to various places around India, including one to Nepal. Raja began by keeping my little house on the hill in Kovalam in good order. He marketed and cooked a fusion of Western and Indian food at my suggestion, always improving on my recipes, however. Raja did the laundry and bathed me, too. He practiced massaging my body and gave me good pointers for maintaining my well-being, in general.

This dear young man spoke little English when I met him, but worked at expanding his knowledge of the language. I brought him books to read that were elementary but of interest to a young boy, usually adventure stories. He had never written in script before I began the lessons in writing, reading, reading out loud

for pronunciation, and conversation. The long, awkward silences for lack of an able response of eight years ago are now gone. Replacing the loss of words are conversations in well-pronounced English. He does manage to write in English but needs further practice for fluency. Raja has grown into a handsome, vibrant man. The contrast between when we first met and the Brahmin young man today is enormous.

In these years I have known Raja, he has endured great family loses. Pujas and resolution have helped him strengthen his resolve to overcome tragedy and be a success, not caving in to major setbacks. He and I have become like

Remarkable, wonderful Raja.

family together, which greatly pleases me. We have been symbiotic and caring to

At a palace in Jaisalmir.

Shey monastery in the high Himilayas (Ladakh).

Highest traversable road in the world, going towards the Chinese border from Ladakh.

each other. When he reaches the age of thirty, I am confident his Brahmin tradition will encourage him to take a wife and begin a family.

During these past eight years, Raja and I traveled to the high Himalayas, staying on a houseboat in Kashmir and later at a guarded Moslem enclave above Dal Lake, then twice to Ladakh and the area near the Chinese border. On two occasions, we visited the famous Raj hill town of Shimla. On visits to New Delhi we were often entertained by Bonnie Uppal, an American married to a Sikh who lives there. We visited the Golden Temple at Amritsar in the Punjab as well as Dharamsala and McLeod Ganj, which is home to the Dalai Lama. There were excursions to Jaisalmer and Bikaner to visit the Karni Mata Temple (where pilgrims worship the holy rats), and to the sacred sites along the Ganges at Varanasi, Haridwar, and Rishikesh. We set up residence one winter in Mysore and stayed at three different residences in Goa for three subsequent years, where Raja perfected his fusion menu.

When Raja was not cooking up the selections brought from the market, he was overseeing that my diet had a minimum of chocolate, ice cream, and cookies. He brought me a mug of tea around sunrise and requested I drink some water first. After my brief nap, Raja brought me coffee, again asking that I drink water. This regime was to regulate my bowel movements, so that a comfortable breakfast could follow. He was brought up with cleanliness his byword.

It was a pleasure to introduce Raja to his first airplane flight (to Ladakh); to teach him to swim and float in the sea; to get him to read, write, and speak English; to have him experience boat and quality train travel; to enjoy luxury hotel visits; and to see his country in all its variations of climate, peoples, and topography.

Raja at our Kullu valley retreat.

All this prepared Raja to begin his life with a stronger base. His plans involve operating a restaurant space in Goa: "Raja's Roost, an Art Café." Its specialty is fusion food: Western and Indian dishes. He has gathered a collection of art from tribal lands in Orissa to decorate-for-sale the walls of the restaurant. I have lent him some start up money, and each month Raja scrupulously pays me interest on this money.

Although I shall miss having his warm, protective company in travels in India, it is time for him to assume the mantle of manhood and independence. I find long distance travel very tiring, so I shall hope he will manage to come to see me for a change. I have been to India seventeen times (sometimes twice a year), and shall miss going there, as well as being with Raja. Sometimes, one has to know when to let go, especially if you love the person.

As a guest of the Indian government, I attended the
Sindhu Darshan Festival in Leh, greeted by Ladakh women.

My driver and companion Ali at the antique Maharaja's Palace at Naggar, in the Kullu valley.

Calcutta street scene with goats.

Thubten Norbu Ling Tibetan Buddhist Center in Santa Fe
is a source for practicing mindfulness and compassion.

USHNISHA WITH TIARA:

THE MAKING OF A DIVA

After a peripatetic life resplendent with extraordinary personages in fabulous locales around the world, I wanted to settle into a quieter lifestyle suitable to advanced age. Taking advantage of the powerful, spiritual energies and the thrilling natural beauty of northern New Mexico, Santa Fe seemed an excellent choice. Since relocating there in 2006, the cold winter months were still spent in beloved India with Raja, with the rest of the year in Santa Fe. I had the best of two worlds each year.

These "twilight years" have been imbued with Buddhist teachings mentored by Don Hendricks at the Thubten Norbu Ling Tibetan Buddhist Center in Santa Fe.Absorbing this mindful living has greatly softened some of my rough edges and enormously complimented my twenty-seven years of sobriety.

This did not curtail my sense of the flamboyant. Being available for the unexpected continued as if, dare I say, preordained? Actors over the years would get peeved at me for being asked to appear in some vehicle when I never once auditioned for anything. Directors would ask me to do a role, even when I protested that I was not an actor. This happened in Santa Fe—with significant repercussions.

During an intermission of an HD (high definition) transmission from London of a drama shown at our local Lensic Theater, I was introduced to Clara Soister, one of Santa Fe's major theater directors. This attractive woman interested me,

Mr. Charles, the gayest man in the universe.

especially as I was yearning to expand my acquaintances in town with theatrical backgrounds so that I could share some of my life's experiences.

Clara came to have tea with me the next afternoon. With her she had a script of the play she was about to direct. It was Paul Rudnick's *The New Century*, which had been produced at Lincoln Center's Mitzi Newhouse Theater two years earlier. There was no doubt in Clara's directorial mind that I was perfect to play Mr. Charles, the gayest man in the universe.

Flattered and amused, I agreed to read the script and give my decision. We both snickered when I indicated the role would obviously demand in-depth research; and, being a major role, there would be pressure on me not only to memorize an enormous number of lines, but also to summon the energy required for a demanding leading role.

When I visited the intimate theater and sat in a chair stage center, the few lines I read seemed so comfortable to me that I agreed to rehearse one week with the cast to see how it developed. If it was too overwhelming, I would bow out and not sink the production. The other cast members were very supportive of my efforts and the rehearsals worked well. The cast did many things to help and encourage me to perform this role for the run of the play.

Before my treatment at The Betty Ford Clinic, I could not have attempted playing a leading role on stage. I played a starring role offstage everywhere, with aplomb, but on the stage I froze with fear and insecurity. Getting to know myself over the decades of sobriety and finding an inner peace and centeredness permitted me to come out of hiding. Mr. Charles and I melded into one powerful character, full of dynamic gaiety.

Thank you, Mr. Rudnick, for giving me Mr. Charles, who pulled me out onto center stage. After all the roles I played as a child— imitating Hollywood's princesses-in-distress; growing into puberty with Risë Steven's *Carmen*; living vicariously as the divas at the Met or *en pointe* with the New York City Ballet's prima-ballerinas during college years; wantonly daring entree into the territories reigned over by Mae West, Joan Crawford, Joan Sutherland, and Beverly Sills; and mingling with the other kinds of divas including heads of state, high society, and world-acclaimed personages, it was Mr. Charles who bestowed upon me the highest regal status of having achieved divadom.

With superb androgyny, I can wear the glittering tiara. If I can approach compassion and universal knowledge such as the Buddha has in the mound on his head, his ushnisha, perhaps in time I can imagine my tiara encircling my ushnisha!

(Design courtesy of Porter Dunaway.)

(from the R.C. Gorman collection)

Two playful monkeys!

LA MARCHESA, LA MARCHETTA CHRONICLES
By Eric Gustafson
(Original in the archives at the Beinecke Library at Yale University)

I stood nude for seemingly an eternity while the artist sat behind his easel working on a pastel rendition of my lovely body. Beside him on the floor was a glass of vodka, which he referred to often. For the sake of modesty, I had advised the housekeeper and her assistant not to enter this portion of the house because I would be in the all-together while the artist was working.

At the end of the ordeal, I was astonished, amused and quite annoyed that I had had to hold a pose without clothing when the result was only the profile of my head in colored pastels, with a slash indicating shoulder blades and a pastel rendering of one nipple. I could have been sitting, fully clothed! This was an early indication of the playfully perverse humor of R.C. Gorman, Navajo artist soon to be dubbed "Picasso of America." This portrait has been reproduced a few times, most notably in Gorman's Nudes & Foods, Volume 3, as the introduction to the dessert section. (He inscribed my copy "to my favorite tart.")

The late '60s was a dynamic time to be in Santa Fe. I had been invited to become the director of The Jamison Galleries, across the street from historic La Fonda Hotel. Unlike the other galleries that peddled schlock, we had blue chip Western Art (Remington, Berninghaus, Couse, Blumenshein, Sloan, Henri, among others). There were many fewer galleries then than today, and NONE handled contemporary art. Having left the New York art scene, I realized that many fine artists working in Santa Fe had to rely on New York or West Coast galleries to exhibit their high quality of work. With conviction, I ventured to exhibit these young "unknowns." I was thought to be crazy, but it broke the ice, and today the town is full of galleries showing contemporary work.

At Gorman's suggestion, in 1969, the director of the Navajo Gallery invited me to Taos to view R.C. Gorman's work. (Gorman owned the Navajo Gallery but wanted larger coverage and acknowledgement.) Edmond Gaultney, as Director of Gorman's gallery made a deal with me. He coveted a pre-Columbian necklace that I wore and wanted to trade it for a pastel portrait done of me by the budding "Picasso of America." He would persuade Gorman to execute the portrait as a sweetener to achieving a one-man show at the prestigious Jamison Galleries. Fritz Scholder, the "wunderkind of the Southwest" as I promoted him in advance publicity, was going to show there. They were rivals and Gorman wanted to keep up with the almost-Indian artist. Voilà, my portrait!

Stickers asking "Who Is R.C. Gorman" began appearing everywhere. His gallery parties became the talk of Northern New Mexico. Lots of alcohol poured freely; fistfights, disruptive to the local Hispanic population but exciting to the pot-heads and boozers in late Hippie la-la land, were legend. Artists and other free-living individuals in this community reveled in this updated, back-to-earth spiritually psychedelic world of the noble First American. Anything seemed to go, and R.C. was often in the midst of it all.

In Santa Fe, I very much enjoyed the social scene. The Jamison Gallery openings were very dignified, without brawling Taos style, but alcohol oriented with gentrified guitar playing in the background as fashionably dressed Anglos chatted amiably. The party never ended there, however. Carousing continued either at some off-color bar or in the wonderful home of a like-minded "lotus eater."

R.C. and I cemented a relationship over the many years of the pursuit of fun making, partaking of culinary delights and even traveling to wonderful foreign ports of call. I had moved back East with some trips to Europe shortly after his Santa Fe exhibition. But, I returned on occasion for either another Gorman vernissage, or to celebrate his birthday.

One birthday celebration was held in a restaurant outside Taos. Ann and Peter Luce flew Lila Tyng and myself there in their Cessna. R.C. loved to have "important" people arrive by private plane to visit him, so he made a big fuss over our arrival. He told the head waiter to give me anything I wanted to drink. I said a bottle of champagne but poured into a liter pitcher would be swell. I proceeded to swill this as I circulated through the motley crowd of well-wishers (and hangers-on). There was a group of Hispanic musicians playing. I suggested to them to play a pasa doble. Ann Luce kindly accepted my invitation to dance, but I indicated that we get on top of the long luncheon table. Gamely she joined me and we trounced through luncheon plates and glasses doing our flamboyant toreador passes in perfect timing to the music. The astonished diners and guests were stunned, but no one as amused as our host, who thought it brilliant.

There were several incidents that could be considered highlights of our camaraderie over four decades. Notable among them was the invitation by R.C. to come to Santa Fe to attend a vernissage there. He had heard about the New York newspapers commenting in a social column about my wearing five layers of navy blue chiffon trousers made by the chiffon king, George Stavropoulos. They were the only chiffon trousers made for a man that this major designer ever created. It was George's idea that I should wear something of his to the opening of the Cooper-Hewitt Museum in New York City. The director, Lisa Taylor, was going to wear the same navy blue chiffon as her gown to this glittering event. As Lisa would only entrust me to waltz with her, we would make a remarkable pair each attired by George Stavropoulos. Indeed, to paraphrase the top society columnist: "Eric Gustafson, who has been known to take the rust off Doris Duke but left her her diamonds, waltzed with Lisa Taylor, both resplendent in Stavropoulos navy blue chiffon!"

Gorman had decided that I must wear my chiffon "pants" to his vernissage. I did so with pleasure. Typical Gorman fashion, we had a long, very wet lunch and then changed for the gallery event. That, too, was very wet, to be followed by supper at the fancy Palace Restaurant. Gorman had a table for about six people, and I was seated on his right. A woman with bluish tinted hair from Texas approached the table and politely requested an autograph from this distinguished artist. He gave it with broad good humor. I then imitated the woman and asked for Mr. Gorman's autograph. He told me he would give me one on my ass. So, I stood up and lowered my blue chiffon exposing my left hip. With a wide felt tip marking pen, he drew something and signed it. I thanked him and sat down.

Soon, another bluette appeared at the table requesting Mr. Gorman's autograph. He obliged and joking advised her to see the autograph he just gave me on my bottom. She glanced at me and asked to see it. I quipped that it would cost $2 to view this work of art. She opened her small evening bag and placed $2 on the table in front of me!

Yes, I undid my blue trousers again and allowed my left hip to be inspected. It was not long before more people approached with $2 in hand to see my personalized ass. I found this very mirthful and I thought it was a very amusing way to end an alcoholic evening. It was only later when I took a shower that I realized that I had washed my income producer away…. And I had not even seen it. What a pity I had not thought to have my bottom Xeroxed!

Early in R.C.'s international travel, he was unwilling to tend to foreign travel details. On one occasion, he met me in Rome where I had to help him sort out his enormous hotel bill. There were obvious discrepancies and the over-payments were straightened out thanks to my adroit handling.

A short time later, he asked whether I would consider taking him and his nephew who had never been off the Navajo reservation to Rome, Florence and Venice for a three week holiday, in which time he hoped I would teach his nephew the Renaissance. Money was no object, but he had three demands: He wanted to see the Pope and meet an aristocrat as well as an Italian movie star. Okay, I assured him…

Having had a private audience with Pope John XXIII, I had clues as to how to arrange a group audience. With some phone calls and an appropriate letter, we met Pope Paul at such an audience in the new hall built expressly for this purpose.

To honor his request to meet an aristocrat, I introduced him to my young duchino, with whom I had experienced many dealings, and who lent us his car. R.C. was thrilled to meet the son of an important duke and we enjoyed driving around Rome in his car. Sophia Loren had a large apartment in an area that this car needed to pass to and from, so I pointed out her apartment on several go-arounds.

One night, I invited a very kindly count to join us with his special countess companion, who made for very lively company. In a charming side street near our hotel, we commenced dining on various delicious dishes that really pleased R.C., especially the spaghetti in octopus ink. The nephew had one Coca-Cola while we four consumed our bottles of wine. He then excused himself and walked the short distance back to the hotel to retire for the evening. We continued long afterwards and in a merry haze, walked the couple back to their car in the Piazza del Popolo under a brilliant full moon.

"I really liked that couple," R.C. commented as we continued back to the hotel. At last, trying to get a glimpse into the Navajo mind, I asked what he liked so much about them. "Well, most people after a bottle or two of wine will turn down having more. I really liked them. We had eight bottles of wine without any objections … !"

Florence and Venice sojourns passed quickly with some amusing incidents. Most memorable, perhaps, was our encounter with a certain marchesa who ran a roof-top boite. R.C. and I had been in a gallery exhibiting Erté watercolors. I suggested that R.C. purchase one as the price seemed very fair and he liked it. The woman whose gallery it was seemed particularly personable with a charming aristocratic air. She was indeed a countess, she confessed.

When I inquired where we could go to enjoy the impending sunset, she suggested a nearby building. There was a roof garden there that had been made into a place to partake refreshments. She indicated that the proprietor who claimed to be a marquesa might provide us with champagne to enjoy the very spectacular view.

When we took the elevator to the top floor of the building indicated, there was no answer to our ringing the bell at the entrance. After ringing again, a rustling sound was heard as though someone were hurriedly getting dressed. Moments later, a handsome man still adjusting his clothing greeted us. He suggested we be seated near the windows to enjoy the view. The marquesa would be out shortly. Effusively, she greeted us and was very pleased to sell us exorbitantly priced bubbly. It seemed very likely that we had indeed interrupted a tryst with her handsome waiter, but having an exotic "pelle rosse" (red skin) drinking costly champagne made up for the inconvenience…

From the marquesa's manner, I doubted her aristocratic lineage and opted for a more earthy status. In Italy, a prostitute working in some house of ill-repute might be given a marker from her client after the act. At the end of the evening, she turns in these markers and gets paid accordingly for her work. When I returned to the gallery the next day, our charming countess asked about our visit to the marquesa's boite. When I said that she seemed more a marchetta than a marquesa, the countess laughed gleefully and concurred.

Since that incident, R.C. joking dubbed me "Marquesa, La Marchetta." R.C. loved to give people around him titles. It was his way of "making it" in the Anglo world. His earliest attempts of achieving status in this Anglo world was by owning a gold Mercedes, a large art-filled home and an Olympic size indoor swimming pool, as well as relishing exposure to famous people such as Jackie O, Elizabeth Taylor, and Arnold Schwarzenegger. He adored getting from me autographed to him photographs of Mae West, Joan Sutherland, Grace Bumbry, among others.

Some years ago when Elizabeth Taylor was starring on Broadway in *The Little Foxes*, R.C. and I attended a matinee performance as her guests. Backstage, I finally got to thank her for keeping Richard Burton busy during *Cleopatra*, as Burton had given me his tickets to every event in Rome that were bestowed upon the stars. I had mistakenly admired his devotion to his wife, Sybil and their children waiting on the Appia Antica, to whom he seemed to be returning while I enjoyed his seats at the opera, concert or whatever…I was very surprised to learn about "Burton plucking the brains out of Taylor" upon my return from Greece. No wonder I never saw Taylor at the various cultural events I attended with Burton's tickets.

With R.C., there was always an expansive enthusiasm for the larger than life. As a fellow participant in the birthday party "the Princess" (Ysabel Aya) gave for me, he was thrilled to meet opera diva Grace Bumbry. She had been giving a standing ovation at the Metropolitan Opera the night before. When she arrived at Ysabel's Fifth Avenue apartment, she slipped out of a floor length fur and revealed a gilded gown. RC nervously put his finger to her bare shoulder and asked: Is that your real color? (I nearly swooned as Grace was very touchy about being black.) She looked down at his finger and up to his face and drawled: Yes-s, Is that yours? (Whew, what a relief she took it in stride.) At the dinner table, RC made a big gesture of giving Grace the turquoise ring that he brought to present to me for my birthday. She kindly agreed that we would share it, but forgot that empty promise. I have never seen it again! Years later when visiting in Taos, R.C. dug into a jewelry box and produced another ring which he hoped would make up for the one he had not given to me at that birthday dinner. It is nice when someone makes amends, even if it is years after the fact.

R.C. went a very long way from scratching drawings in the sand on the Navajo reservation as a child to rubbing elbows with the rich and famous. Years of gourmand eating and heavy drinking filled out his physique from the slim struggling artist and young sailor to the successful entrepreneur, whose images of plump Indian women appear ubiquitously on cocktail napkins, writing paper as well as lithographs and other art forms.

Though eager to be accepted in the Anglo world, R.C. Gorman remained connected to his cultural heritage. He spent so much energy in trying to be in both worlds. With his high level of drive and ambition, he made significant marks in both. His generosity of spirit that burst forth at unexpected times can be appreciated in his financial support of institutions dedicated for Navajo education as well as funding for helping his people in various projects.

From my personal exposure to R.C. Gorman in the nearly four decades of adventures and communication with him by phone or mail, I remain amused by our creation of the androgynous, outrageous La Marchesa, La Marchetta.

Appendix 2

HAPPINESS IS A HOUSE ON A HILL IN KOVALAM
(13-I-2006, revised 30-XI-2013)

One day, some 18 years ago during the first year after my "graduation" from The Betty Ford Clinic, I felt a sensation that was new and utterly wonderful. After some evaluation, I was startled to realize that this delightful feeling was a deep sense of happiness!

Though I had many moments of bliss in my madcap alcoholic years of carousing, nothing compared to this profound state of well-being. Perhaps this was a sublime gift among the many rewards for embracing sober living.

Lightning can and has struck the same place twice. Here I am in a most comfortable house overlooking Kovalam Beach in Kerala, South India, literally smelling the roses and enjoying the other diverse and colorful blooms in the surrounding garden. The sound of the rolling surf from the Arabian Sea below mixes with birdcalls from the palm groves and other exotic vegetation. It is a most agreeable environment, so different from my usual beach accommodations occupied during the other six winters here. No gawkers or hawkers of fruit, souvenirs or beach chairs parading past. A comfortable quietude encourages my peaceful delight in being here.

A big factor in this picture is my having invited my auto-rickshaw driver from Puri, Orissa, to come to reside as my companion. He displayed such an easy and dependable manner with an endearing charm during my November visit to Orissa. How could I resist extending an invitation? Raja ("King") is 19 years old, with a quick easy smile and a warm modest personality. (I had predicted that someday my prince would come. Who could know that he would be so young and have an even higher royal standing?) Always kind and thoughtful, he is dedicated to my comfort and safety --- big plusses for a 70-year-old traveling alone in this vast subcontinent.

Anil and Raja complete the ménage.

To complete this live-in menage (as distinct from the several drop-in callers), I have invited a gorgeously sculpted yoga/massage guy, aged 25, to stay with Raja and me. Anil is a tall dancer-manqué with flashing sparkling eyes and teeth whose linguistic skills are minimal, but his usefulness around the house add to the smooth functioning of our white (golden tan)/ beige/ black menage. I have known him for a couple of years and was aware of his need for shelter –– voilà, our cozy set-up!

At this moment of writing, Sanskrit chanting is emitting from the nearby Devi temple, filling the air with beautiful devotional sounds. Today is the big Muslim festival "Eid" so many shops will be closed and activities altered as a significant population in this area is Muslim. Today is the day that goats are sacrificed (in the tradition of Abraham). The meat is distributed in thirds: family, friends and the poor.

Living in a Hindu/Muslim community is highly stimulating, as India is in general. I have enjoyed such kindness and generosity from the Indian locals. There is an easy going atmosphere in Kerala together with a natural beauty, which have been strong attractions to my returning year after year.

However, the serpent in paradise has many guises. Recently, I realized the "bruise" under my right knee was getting more inflamed and the leg was swelling. Raja insisted I stop doing long walks for my pre-dawn prayer/meditation on the rock promontory above the sea in preparation for sunrise observation. He told me to stay off my feet and to plan to see a doctor at the hospital in a nearby town. I am grateful for his caring advice as I would have waited for the swelling to subside. The specialist in this very modern, clean and well-run hospital informed me it was an infection (possibly from an insect bite or cut) steadily progressing deeper into the leg tissue. It was recommended that I be committed to the hospital for intensive rest and an antibiotic treatment. I resisted this notion as I had my two boys to take care of me. Raja firmly made sure I took my strong medicines and kept me with my leg elevated. Along with all his other talents, he made an excellent nurse.

Aside from the superior care I received during my three visits to KIM Hospital, my rickshaw driver (who on his own initiative stayed by my side throughout each treatment even though Raja was there) and many locals extended comforting attentions, indicating heart-warming friendship.

Last year, the year I witnessed from Kovalam the astonishing tsunami, was one of turmoil for me here in other ways. My dear Ali, who was to help me set up a clinic for youths who could not read or write, absconded with a pile of money. He used it to help his father finish building their house. My deep sense of betrayal, together with my threats of police action, marred last season's Kovalam experience. I wondered how Ali and I would relate to each other this year. With a tentative handshake upon my arrival, Ali has extended many services to me as a form of reconciliation. He assisted in my house arrangement and does many errands and good deeds to rekindle our friendship. Hence, accord thrives in this house on a hill in Kovalam, South India.

Post Script: *For those readers who would accuse me of name dropping, please realize this was an early M.O. for a youth from "nowhere" scaling a slippery slope to new identity "somewhere." Be assured, I have only used a fraction of names encountered along my challenging path. Please put those bitter grapes aside for a more salubrious diet of love and compassion.*

Blessings with hugs!
REG

A farewell image of sailing in the Pacific off the California coast, embracing Life with Joy!

Index

A

Abrams, Harry 244
Abrams, Nina 244
Acton, Sir Harold 230, 248
Adams, Diana 20
Agnelli, Gianni 155, 156
Ailey, Alvin 205
Ali in Kerala 312
Allen, Christine 285
Allyson, June 16, 17
Anil 333, 334
Aragno, Anna 154
Armstrong-Jones, Anthony
    (Lord Snowdon) 217
Aronson, Boris 165
Astaire, Fred 22
Athos, Helen 21
Auchincloss, Didi 110
Aumont, Jean-Pierre 31-32
Aya de Salgar, Ysabel 102-105, 109,
    117, 118, 133, 142, 143, 147,
    150-152, 161, 163, 186-188,
    193, 194, 200, 203, 206-208,
    210, 211, 215, 219, 224, 236,
    244, 331
  Alberto (son) 236, 237
  Beatriz (sister) 224
  Cecilia (sister) 224
  Maria, Doña (mother) 106
Aznavour, Charles 72

B

Baker, Josephine 217
Balanchine, George 47, 288
Bandelier, Adolf 181
Bankhead, Eugenia 142
Bankhead, Tallulah 52-54, 56, 67, 142
Banks, Rosemary 43, 44
Barber, Samuel 124

Barker, John 162, 167
Barrault, Jean-Louis 212
Bates, Alan 72
Baum, Timothy 106, 113
Beaseley, Winnebelle 182, 190, 194, 197
Beaumont, Binkie 157
Bécaud, Gilbert 72
Beni, Roloff 94
Bennett, Betsy (Betty) 189
Berenson, Berry 35
Berger, Dr. Henry 112
Bergman, Ingrid 24, 125
Berlin, Bridget 165
Berns, Susan 73, 90
Bernstein, Leonard 55, 57-61, 207
Bexelius, Björn 148, 149
Bexelius, Ilse 148, 149
Bey, Turhan 2
Bianca, Princess of Löwenstein 167
Bing, Rudolf 211
Biolek, Freddie 157
Birsh, Arthur 143
Bishop, Elizabeth 256
Björling, Jussi 28
Bonynge, Richard 90, 245-251
Boothe, Clare 223
    (see Luce, Clare Booth)
Bozin, Jasmine 276
Brando, Marlon 70
Brially, Jean Claude 131
Brownie with Gaylord Hauser 132
Browning, John 125
Bruhn, Eric 114, 115
Brusati, Franco 72, 76
Bumbry, Grace 209-211, 331
Burney, (Lady) Gladys 228
Burton, Richard 87, 90, 262, 331

C

Cadmus, Paul 163

Callas, Maria 105, 210
Campbell, Bob 68
Campbell, Grace 207
Campbell, Joseph 21
Campbell, Patton 122
Capote, Truman 215
Carey, Margot 46
Carlson, Anita 17, 19
Caron, Leslie 16, 69
Carroll, Sandy (Eunice) 99
Carson, Johnny 17
Cavalli, Countess Carla 155, 168
Cavanagh, Barbara 107
Cavanagh, Nannette 106
Channing, Carol 22
Chaplin, Shirley 88
Charlie (at Queens College) 29
Chevalier, Maurice 69
Churchill, Winston (grandson) 73
Clément, René 34
Clift, Montgomery 117
Clooney, Rosemary 13
Coca, Imogene 7
Cole, Clayton 163, 165, 207
Comden, Betty 88
Conti, Mrs. 6
Cooper, Anderson 79
Cooper, Wyatt 55, 56, 79
Corelli, Franco 28
Coward, Noel 71, 106, 147
Crawford, Joan 3, 207, 269, 325
Crosby, John 196, 242, 243
Cross, Milton 9

D

Dalí, Gala 109
Dalí, Salvador 109
Dallesandro, Joe 165
D'Amboise, Jacques 20
Daniel, Clifton 82
Daniel, Margaret Truman 82, 84, 85, 117

Danilova, Alexandra ("Choura") 47
Darcel, Denise 13, 53
Dauphin, Mrs. Claude 69
Davern, Jeremyn 112, 275, 287
David III 207
Davis, Bette 88
Davis, Noel 49, 56-60
Daykin, Frank 256, 275
Dean, Jimmy 25
De Carlo, Yvonne 2
de Kooning, Willem 153
de Kosenko, Maria 40
de Lema, (Countess) Marguerita 206
Delon, Alain 73
deMille, Cecil B. 35
de Montebello, Philippe 101, 112
Deneuve, Catherine 167, 169
Depardieu, Gérard 169
de Pouzols, (Count) Albert 276
Diaz, Justino ("Gus") 154
Dietrich, Marlene 79
Dillon, Douglas and Suzzie 288
DiMaggio, Joe 16
di Montezemolo, Vittorio (Consul General of Italy) 112, 124
Dolin, Anton 47, 48, 122
Dombasle, Arielle 284
Dombasle, Man'ha Garreau 284
Dooley, Virginia 193
Douglas, Katya 168, 301, 303, 304
Duke of Marlborough 153
Dunaway, Porter Jean 242, 274
Durbin, Diana 10
Dustin, Ginny 275
Dutton, Bertha 181, 200

E

Eckstein, Billy 13, 14
Eglevsky, André 20
Elizabeth II, Queen 33
Ellington, Duke 205
Erdman, Jean 21

Eweson, Dorothy Dillon 276, 283-285, 288-290
Eweson, Eric 276

F

Farrow, Mia 35
Ferrero de Ventimiglia, (Marchesa) Marina 155, 168
Feuillatte, Nicolas 156
Flagstad, Kirsten 28
Flores, Lola 207
Flynn, Errol 2
Fogelson, Buddy 197
Fonda, Susan 104
Forbes, Bertie 277
Forbes, Malcolm 276, 277
Ford, Betty 269
Ford, President Gerald 269
Fordyce, Alice 215-218, 221, 230
Francis, Arlene 88

G

Gabor, Zsa Zsa 63, 213
Gaddes, Richard 243
Garbo, Greta 100, 101, 148, 156
Garrett, Stephen 263
Garson, Greer 197
Gasper, Dr. Ray 28, 29
Gasteyer, Carlin 112
Gaultney, Edmond 165, 191, 193, 327
George, Antony 308, 310-312
George family 309
George, Hal 243
Gilmuyden, Karen 101, 126, 213
Gilpin, John 47, 48, 122, 123
Gingold, Hermione 69, 70
Gish, Lillian 257
Githens, John 237
Gorman, R.C. 190-193, 198, 209, 261,

273, 326-331
Greco, José 207
Greenspon, Muriel 154
Grey, Jane 273
Gronich, Silvia 133
Gross, Noel 101, 102
Guggenheim, Peggy 94
Guiga, Shasha 154
Guinness, Desmond 112
Guinness, Lord Iveagh 123
Gustafson, Ebba (mother) 1-6, 8, 10, 12, 15, 50, 286
Gustafson family 5, 42
Gustafson (father) 1, 5, 6-8, 10, 16, 19, 50
Gustafson, Florence Mae (sister) 1, 4, 5, 8, 22, 45, 50, 286, 287
Gustafson, George Edward (brother) 1, 5, 7, 8, 11, 19, 50, 286
Gustafson, Helen (sister) 3, 5, 6, 8, 11, 15, 44, 286

H

Haeff, Ingeborg ten 237
Hagen, Uta 44
Hagerty, Don 74
Halliday, David 55, 71
Hall, John 243
Hamilton, Juan 141
Harewood, Lord 250
Hart, Bill 86, 88, 106
Hartford, Huntington 213
Hart, Kitty Carlisle 216, 217
Hart, Leila Oteifa 85, 86, 88, 106
Hauptmann, Bruno 5
Hauser, Gayelord 132
Hawkins, Catherine 90, 92, 94
Hay, Calla 192, 193
Hayden, Melissa 20
Hayes, Helen 257
Hayworth, Rita 22, 88, 89, 132, 207
Hemingway, Margaux 267, 270

Henderson, Marina 244, 246
Hendricks, Don 323
Hendrix, Jimi 163, 207
Henry (floormate) 50
Henze, Hans Werner 138
Hepburn, David 137
Herman, Jean 5
Hernmark, Agneta 232, 233
Hillerman, Tony 181
Hines, Jerome 254, 275
Hitler 79
Hofmann, Hans 23
Holland, Audrey 63, 65, 284
Holman, Libby 116
Holm, Celeste 240, 254, 256
Hope, Bob and Dorothy 269
Hore, Suhas Kumar 312
Horgan, Barbara 288
Horgan, Dorothy 288
Horne, Lena 88, 206
Horne, Marilyn 212
Horwitz, Elaine 201
Howes, Sally Ann 49
Hubert, Royal 43
Hunter, Robert 67, 205
Hurley, Wilson 198
Hurt, William 262
Hutton, Barbara 107
Hyam, Leslie 100, 111
Hyde, Mary 248

I

Indiana, Robert Earl 242

J

Jack (Flo's husband) 8
Jackson, Anne 256
Jacobs, John (Kerala) 312
Jacobson, Robert 213, 227
Jamison, Margaret 137, 177, 180, 182,
    183, 185, 186, 188, 189, 191,
    198, 199
Jean (Edward Mulhare's friend) 58, 59
Jeanmaire, Zizi 47
Jellicoe, Countess Patsy 122
Jenkins, Paul 184
Jenkins, Speight 243
Johnson, Tilly (grandmother) 15
Jones, Captain Larry 67, 68, 205
Joplin, Janis 163, 207
Jorgensen, Christine (George
    William, Jr.) 16, 17
Josette 168, 169
Judy (rickshaw) 310-312

K

Kahn, Ali 89
Kaye, Nora 20
Keelan, Hugh 254, 255
Keller, Greta 79
Kelly, Gene 16, 22
Kennedy Onassis, Jackie 81, 82, 97,
    100, 101, 331
Kennedy, President John F. 81, 82
Kennedys, The 139
Kent Taylor, Allegra 20, 105, 167, 174,
    126, 213
Khrushchev, Nikita 82
King, Governor Bruce 199
Klaum, Alan 214, 215

L

la Farge, Oliver 181
Laine, Frankie 13
Lake, Veronica 54, 56
Lanza, Prince Angelo 147, 150
Larsen, Ernie (cousin) 15
Lasker, Mary 215, 230
Law, John Phillip 131
Lawrence, D.H. 29
Lear, Evelyn 242
Lee, Ming Cho 143

Lerman, Leo 143
Lichtblau, Lotte 160, 162
Lindstrom, Jenny (Pia) 24
Lockwood, Carolyn 243
Long, Bob 251
Long, Eloise Walker 125, 213, 214
Loren, Sophia 330
Louise, Anita 112
Love, Iris 101
Loveland, Dr. Ruth 103, 132, 133
Love, Robert Lincoln 212
Love, Yveta 110, 212
Luce, Ann 228, 274, 328
Luce, Clare Boothe 223, 280, 281
Luce, Henry III 221, 278, 284
Luce, Henry Robinson 221, 281
Luce, Peter 221, 228, 274, 280, 284,
    328
Lumet, Gail 88
Lummis, Charles 181

M

Magallanes, Nicholas 20
Magnani, Anna 64, 153
Maharshi, Bhagavan Sri Ramana 301,
    302, 303, 316
Mahoney, Leanne 197
Mangano, Silvana 34, 35
Mansfield, Jayne 75
Marina, Marchesa Ferrero de Ven-
    timiglia 155
Marion, Louis 107, 110, 111
Marshall, Natalie 216, 233
Martin, Mary 22, 136
Marum, Ilsa (Illa) 45, 46
Marx, Groucho 55, 56
Matera, Barbara 250
Mayer, Kerstin 231
McDowall, Roddy 90
McFadden, David (David IV) 235,
    236, 274
McNeil, Elsie (Countess Gozzi) 175

Mehta, Zubin 212
Melchior, Lawrence 28
Melville, David Scott (David II) 120,
    126, 128, 129, 131, 137, 188,
    197
Menotti, Gian Carlo 113, 118, 124,
    125, 152, 153, 156
Merman, Ethel 136, 143
Merrick, Gordon 40, 41
Merrill, Gary 88
Metcalf, Betty 116
Michaud, George 198
Micheleit, Nina (Juanita) 68, 69, 204,
    207
Miller, Osborn Maitland (Uncle Mon-
    key) 173, 174, 175, 177, 203,
    204, 231
Mineo, Sal 17, 19
Mitchell, Martha 101
Mongomery (Motley), Elizabeth 112
Monroe, Marilyn 64
Montealegre, Felicia 59, 60
Montresor, Beni 113, 144
Morris, Mary 57
Mostel, Zero 88
Moul, Ann 273
Mulhare, Edward 49, 57
Mulligan, Diego 291
Murillo, Oscar 228, 253, 266, 277,
    280, 282, 285
Mussolini, Benito 175
Mustoe, Anne 294

N

Nancy (from church) 10
Newlin, Jeanne 144
Nilsson, Birgit 22, 28
Nilsson, Christina 213
Nilsson, Christine 10, 11, 113, 148,
    149, 150
Niscemi princesses, Maita and Mimi
    126

Norton, Kathy 274
Nugent, Phyllis Babbitt 263
Nureyev, Rudolf 114, 115

O

Oenslager, Donald 143
O'Hara, Maureen 2
O'Keeffe, Georgia 140, 233
Olivier,Laurence 37
Onassis, Jackie Kennedy 81, 82, 97,
    100, 101, 331
O'Neill, Eugene 23, 29
Osborne, Arthur 302

P

Panda, Dev 312, 316
Panda, Dulu and Kulu 312, 316
Pascal, Jean-Claude 157
Pati, Binod Kumar 314, 316
Pati, Bismaya Kumar 312, 314
Paula (neighbor) 7
Peluso del Giudice, Nino (Titano)
    170, 186, 187, 188
Perkins, Tony 34, 35
Peterson, Olga 4
Petit, Roland 31, 47
Phipps, Noni 153
Pinza, Ezio 22
Pisacani, Lucia 48-50, 56, 60, 63
Ponte, Giò 184
Pope John XXIII 83, 90, 91, 95, 330
Pope Paul 330
Powell, Jane 10
Price, Leontyne 136, 143
Prince Charles 192, 207
Prince, Hal 22, 88
Prince of Hesse, Michael 108
Prince Philip 33
Princess Margaret 217
Prokovsky, André 31, 47
Prokovsky, Mme. 30

Q

Queen Mother of Romania, Helen 83,
    248
Queen Sylvia of Sweden 231

R

Radziwill, Lee 228
Raja 304, 312, 313, 317-319, 333,
    334
Ransohoff, Dickie 134, 151, 152
Ray, Johnny 13
Redgrave, Sir Michael 34, 47
Redmond, Michael 254
Reinhardt, Max 28
Richardson, John 128
Rich, Sheldon 109
Robert (actor/usher) 12
Roberts, David 181
Robinson, Cece 13
Robinson, Francis 143
Romanov, Alexander 126
Roosevelt, Franklin D. 6
Rorimer, James 112
Rosenthal, Jean 136, 160
Rosenwald, "Poor Karen" 85, 87
Rossellini, Roberto 24
Rothko, Marc 184
Rudnick, Paul 324, 325
Russell, Rosalind 269

S

Sai Baba 303
Saltonstall, Nathaniel 25, 67
Sanfelice di Bagnoli, Giorgio 166,
    168-172, 174-176, 186, 187
Saravanan, Sonny 298-301
Schacht, Louise 78
Schippers, Thomas 125
Schippers, Tommy 153
Scholder, Fritz 184, 185, 198
Scholder, Ramona 199

Schwarzenegger, Arnold 331
Scull, Ethel 108, 116
Semonin, Douglass 68, 69, 70, 72
Shannon, Hugh 116, 206
Sheridan, Ann 56
Sills, Beverly 135, 136, 142, 243, 249
Simon, Rita 161-163, 207
Smith, Oliver 136, 143, 162
Soister, Clara 323
Spadone, Terry 25, 26
Spencer, Charles 234
Spencer-Churchill, Lady Sarah 153
Spilman, Jamie 67
Stane, Walter 103, 132
Stanwyck, Barbara 45
Stavropoulos, George 212, 234, 328, 329
Steele, Barbara 94
Steinberg, Emily 9
Stephenson, Sir William 229
Stern, Dr. Frederick 49
Steve (neighbor) 44
Stevenson, William 229
Stevens, Risë 9, 10
Stewart, Thomas 242
Stielle, Josette 167
Stiga, Paul 144, 228, 244
Stoffragen (professor) 16
Sutherland, Dame Joan 87, 90, 136, 245-249, 251, 325, 331
Swanson, Gloria 207

T

Takaezu, Toshiko 254, 286, 289
Tallchief, Maria 20
Taylor, Bert 228, 235
Taylor, Elizabeth 87, 261, 269, 276, 277, 326, 331
Taylor, Lisa 228, 234, 235, 328
Tebaldi, Renata 214
Temple, Shirley 1, 2
Ter-Arutunian, Rouben 137

Theresa, Maria 230
Tobin, Robert Lynn Batts 124, 125, 136, 144, 189, 196, 227, 242
Todd Whitman, Christine 194
Toklas, Alice B. 32, 54
Tom at UCLA 25
Toscanini, Arturo 7
Tourel, Jennie 58, 59
Treaster, Byron 273
Trigg, Louise 195, 199
Truman, Bess Wallace 80-84
Truman, President Harry S 80-85, 229
Turkkan, Zeynep 205
Tyler, Hamilton 181
Tyng, Lila Hotz Luce 218, 220, 221, 224, 225, 234, 237, 238, 241, 252, 255, 261, 274, 275, 278, 281-283, 290
Tyng, Sewell 223
Tysick, Sylvia 47, 71

U

Ulfung, Ragnar 210

V

Valli, Romolo 131
Van Buren Marshall, Nathalie 140, 162, 171
Vanderbilt, Gloria 79
Vandergrift, Mary 110, 111
van der Stegen, (Countess) Sylvia (see Tysick) 275
van Rensselaer, Charlie 107
van Rensselaer, Philip 107, 126, 235
van Rensselaer Strong, Marianne 122
Varona, José 136, 143, 245
Vaughn, Sarah 13
Verrett, Shirley 212
Visconti, Verde 168, 169

von Karajan, Maestro Herbert 152
von Stade, Frederica (Flicka) 194, 279

W

Wagner, Mayor Robert 107
Walkenburg, Janine 121
Wallace, Christine 81, 85, 117
Wallace, David (David I) 80, 81, 83-
    86, 88, 91, 92, 100, 103, 104,
    108, 109, 115, 121, 126, 128,
    147, 167, 248
Wallach, Eli 256
Warhol, Andy 107, 108, 163, 184,
    192, 207
Warrick, Ruth 38-41, 44, 233-235,
    239, 240, 247, 254, 256, 275
Waters, Frank 181
Webster, Nell 112, 121, 123, 129, 137
Weill, Danielle 73, 90
West, Mae 2, 266-268, 325, 331
Whitacre, Bruce 256
White, Miles 136, 142, 143
Williams, Tennessee 103
Winship, Fred 227
Wittop, Freddy 136, 143
Woodlawn, Holly 164, 165
Wood, Thor 144, 233
Wright, Peter 123, 128, 137

Z

Zaheri, Maria 112, 116
Zeffirelli, Franco 250